HIMMLER'S
Secret War

The Covert Peace Negotiations
of Heinrich Himmler

MARTIN ALLEN

CARROL & GRAF PUBLISHERS
NEW YORK

HIMMLER'S SECRET WAR
The Covert Peace Negotiations of Heinrich Himmler

Carroll & Graf Publishers
An Imprint of Avalon Publishing Group Inc.
245 West 17th Street
11th Floor
New York, NY 10011

AVALON
publishing group incorporated

First published in Great Britain in 2005 by Robson Books, The Chrysalis
Building, Bramley Road, London W10 6SP

Library of Congress Cataloging-in-Publication Data is available.

ISBN-10: 0-7867-1708-4
ISBN-13: 978-0-78671-708-8

9 8 7 6 5 4 3 2 1

Printed in the United States of America
Distributed by Publishers Group West

For Jeanie, without whose invaluable assistance and help during difficult times this book would not have been written

CONTENTS

ACKNOWLEDGEMENTS

I would like to thank all those people who have helped with the research and logistical requirements behind the writing of this book. Some took the time and trouble to write to me, whilst others granted an interview; some assisted in translations, additional research, or by voluntarily providing information that it had not occurred to me to ask for.

I would first like to pay a tribute to Herr Gerd Ahlschwede, formerly of the 1st Panzer Division; Mr Steve Alexander; Mr Peter Sinclair Allen; Herr Matthias Coenen; Mr David Cohen; Señor Carlos Alberto Damas; M. Thomas Dunskus; Dr Alfred Grupp of the German Foreign Ministry; Mr Charles Higham; Mr Oliver Hoare; Mr Masahiro Kawai of the IDS, Tokyo; Mr John M. Kelso of the FBI; Mr Colin R. Macmillan; Mr A. Nikonov of the Russian State Archive; Mr Olaf Ollsen; Franz-Dieter Paulsen; Mrs Penny Prior of the British Foreign Office; Mrs Amy Schmidt of the National Archives, Washington DC; Mr T. Sekiguchi; Frau A. Stocker of the Bundesarchiv; Mrs Lucy Takezoa of the National DIET Library, Tokyo; Mr Steven Walton of the Imperial War Museum; Mr Hitomi Watanabe, Second Secretary (Political Division) of the Japanese Embassy; Mrs Linda Wheeler; Herr Viktor Wolf of the Internal Division of the German Foreign Ministry; and Frau Zandeck of the Bundesarchiv.

I would also like to thank those persons, connected either by family relationship to, or exceptional knowledge of the main personalities or events of 1942–45, who extended me their help and assistance: Traudl Junge, Adolf Hitler's secretary; Reinhard Spitzy, Joachim von Ribbentrop's Private Secretary; Herr Emil Klein, former Obergebietsführer and leading man of the Nazi Party; Herr Hans Günther Stark, Rittmeister (Mounted Cavalry) of the Afrika Corp; and Herr Karl Neuer, formerly a member of Heinrich Himmler's personal SS staff.

I am particularly indebted to the following institutions and government bodies for replying to my letters, or who otherwise gave me their time and assistance to aid my research: De Arquivo Historico, Lisbon; the Auswärtiges Amt (the German Foreign Ministry); the Bundesarchiv-Militärarchiv, Freiburg; Companies House, Cardiff; the Federal Bureau of Investigation; the German Embassy in London; the Hoover Institution; the Imperial War Museum; the Japanese Embassy in London; the KGB Archives, Moscow; the National Archives in Kew, London; the National Archives and Records Administration of the United States of America; the National DIET Library of Tokyo; the National Institute for Defence Studies, Tokyo; the Royal British Legion; the University of Kiel; the US Department of Justice; and the Zweites Deutsches Fernsehen.

I would also like to pay tribute to those colleagues and translators who assisted in the logistics of creating this book: Dr Olaf Rose, for his assistance as personal translator during my lecture tours and conferences in Germany, as well as his generous and unstinting assistance during my research and conducting of interviews; Dr Gert Südholt, of Druffel Verlag, who has been of great assistance in my search for testimony from eyewitnesses of Germany's past; Mr F.P. Creagh for his friendship and assistance in matters concerning the security of this book; M. Pierre Vial for his assistance as French translator and Herr Alfred Gottlieb for his very specialised knowledge about the Luftwaffe. I would like to make special mention of Mrs Sabine Wickes for her assistance and hard work in translating the extremely large number of documents necessary to unravel the mystery surrounding Himmler's bid to negotiate peace with the British government 1943–45; I would also like to thank my good friends, Mr David Prysor-Jones and Mr James Crowden, for the many hours of late-night discussion over a bottle of good wine as we pondered the complex situation that was German and British foreign policy during the 1930s and the war years.

Finally, I would like to pay a very special tribute to my wife, Jean. As my business manager and partner in research, she had a very major influence on the writing of this book, and I am indebted to her for her unstinting support through the many worrying and difficult times that lay between the start and finish of this project.

PREFACE

It was a bitingly cold December day in central Munich, where I was just sitting down to lunch in the first-floor restaurant of the old and venerable Künstlerhaus Hotel. Looking out of the large window next to my table, I found myself gazing down upon a tram as it hummed and rattled its way across Lenbachplatz.

I had come to Munich in the winter of 2002 to launch my latest book in Germany; called *Churchills Freidensfalle* (*Churchill's Peace Trap*), it was published in Britain under the title *The Hitler/Hess Deception*. This was the story of how British Intelligence had launched an extremely successful campaign (code name Messrs HHHH) between the autumn of 1940 and the spring of 1941 to deceive Hitler about the British government's stalwart intention to continue the war against Germany, by entering into top secret – but bogus – peace negotiations. Operation Messrs HHHH had the primary objective of persuading Hitler not to launch an attack against the Middle East in the fighting season of 1941, but rather to induce him to believe that certain British politicians were willing to force through a compromise peace with Germany, thereby leaving him free to attack the Soviet Union. The operation succeeded, Hitler attacked Russia – ultimately with disastrous results for Nazi Germany – and the rest, as they say, is history. The press conference, held in the Seidl Room of the Künstlerhaus Hotel, had been a great success and lasted most of the morning. It had, however, been a very tiring exercise, and I was now glad to sit down to lunch in the company of some guests invited by my publisher, Dr Südholt.

It was at this point that I studied my fellow diners and found them to be most interesting. On my right sat an elegant man in his late eighties with hawkish good looks and a commanding manner. This was Hans-Günther Stark, formerly Rittmeister (mounted cavalry) of the Afrika Korps, and holder of the Knight's Cross. He had had a very active war, seeing action in Poland, France, North Africa, and finally Russia, and, as the most senior officer remaining alive, was currently head of the Afrika Korps veterans association. I had spent some time in North Africa myself and have a passion for the desert, so we immediately hit it off, engaging in a lengthy conversation about his wartime career and the beauties of the desert, whilst we finished our starter and awaited the serving of the main course.

It was, however, the man seated opposite me who increasingly took my attention, and whom I found to be the most intriguing. This was an extremely elderly man by the name of Emil Klein, whom, at the age of ninety-nine, one naturally treated with great respect. He was, I am pleased to say, still in full command of his faculties, and he had arrived at the restaurant smartly dressed in a trim overcoat, which he neatly dispatched to a side chair before seating himself down to lunch.

Klein was a man with a chequered past in a way that was more political than had been the career of Herr Stark. Whilst Stark had come from a long line of army officers dating back to the Napoleonic wars, Klein's career had begun when he joined the burgeoning Nazi Party in the early 1920s. Indeed, Klein possessed the rare distinction of being the last surviving participant in the 1923 Munich Putsch, and he had been present on the Odeonplatz when regular troops of the Reichswehr had fired upon Hitler and his band of supporters. In at the very inception of the Party, Klein naturally had known all the leaders of the Nazi Party on close and friendly terms, from Hitler and Göring right on through to Schirach and Himmler. Here was a man who had been an eyewitness to some of the most important events of the twentieth century. He had risen in the 1930s to become an Obergebietsführer (regional leader) of the Hitler Youth under Schirach, and had been appointed Bavarian Minister of Culture and the Interior. In the war, he served with distinction as an army officer, seeing action from Yugoslavia to Russia. It was, however, his knowledge of the early years of the Party that most intrigued me, combined with his memories of the leading men of Nazism.

As the work on my last book – *The Hitler/Hess Deception* – had drawn to a close, I had begun to collate the evidence that there had been a later and most surprising Anglo-German contact. This, communicated to the British government by Victor Mallet, the British Ambassador in Stockholm, had been with Heinrich Himmler.

Here, in the form of Emil Klein, I realised, was an opportunity to ask some searching questions about the younger Himmler – the Himmler of the

1920s and early 1930s – that might give me some clues to his personality. I
began by asking Klein what had been his impression of the man. He considered the question for a few moments before answering.

'Well,' he began, 'you have to remember that I primarily knew Himmler
in the early days, before his meteoric rise after becoming head of the SS.
After that he moved in different circles completely, and became almost
unapproachable.'

I nodded my understanding, and he continued.

'I suppose the Himmler I knew in the early years was a very conscientious man, working hard for the Party in whatever capacity he could get.
He was not at all military minded, but rather saw himself as an up-and-
coming politician.' He paused for a moment to fork in a mouthful of
Kartoffelbrei, which he chewed whilst contemplating how to proceed.

'I knew him best in the years when he was Deputy Regional Propaganda
Leader of Upper Bavaria,' he continued. 'In that capacity he was most
studious and had an almost bohemian air about him that was completely
at odds with the man he later became.' Klein leaned conspiratorially
towards me, and dropped his voice as if he were about to impart some great
confidence. 'You know, this may be hard to believe now, but in the months
immediately after the war, when the full scope of the Holocaust and the
SS's atrocities became known, many of us found it hard to believe it was
the same Himmler who had ordered these acts. It was almost as if he were
two men – the hard-working, studious young man of the early years – and
the sinister, black-uniformed head of the SS, who was unapproachable in
the latter years . . .'

As I stepped out of the Künstlerhaus Hotel an hour and a half later, my
mind was still full of the meeting I had just had with the fascinating Emil
Klein. Here was a man who had lived through the Nazi regime from its very
inception until its last days in 1945, and he had had much to tell me.

The bitter wind, chilled as it swept down from the Alps, stung at my
hands and face, and I instinctively drew my overcoat tighter about me. A
flurry of snow suddenly swirled about the people walking the
Lenbachplatz, heralding the first tentative signs of winter. I stood for a
while watching the people hustle back and forth, yet my thoughts had
regressed more than sixty years, contemplating the intricacies of Himmler's
personality. He had been one of the leading men of Nazi Germany: head of
the Gestapo, head of the SS, head of the Intelligence Service known as the
SD; and yet some of the documents I had recently seen suggested that by
1943 he had been in contact with Britain's Political Warfare Executive.

What had he been up to? And what had been Britain's advantage in having contact with the man commonly regarded as the monster of the SS, the man responsible more than any other for the Holocaust and the deaths of multiple millions? There was a mystery here that needed solving.

I stepped forward across the pavement in the swirling snow and hailed a taxi. It would take me back to my hotel to collect my case, and then I would make for the airport where I could catch the evening flight to London. I was setting out on a journey that would prove to be fraught with difficulty. I had already written several books on Nazi politics of the latter 1930s, and on Hitler's attempts to secure peace at the beginning of the war. Now, however, I was setting out for uncharted territory. I had many contacts in the Nazi political machine, from the daughters of Fritz Todt through to advisors of the German Foreign Ministry, even Ribbentrop's Private Secretary, Reinhard Spitzy, and Hitler's secretary, Traudl Junge. I now even knew someone who had known Himmler in the early years. Yet I had few contacts with the SS, and certainly no one who would have known what Himmler was up to in 1943. The only clue I possessed was a British Political Warfare Executive document that detailed a peace approach by Himmler, via Victor Mallet, the British Ambassador, in Stockholm.

I had little idea as I boarded a taxi that cold December afternoon in Munich that I was setting out on a journey that would take me many months, and many thousands of miles, from the state archives of the United States and Britain to a house in Innsbruck, a mountain chalet near Telfs, a substantial apartment in Stockholm, and lastly back to a large villa on the outskirts of Munich. At the end of my journey, I would possess all the pieces of an elaborate jigsaw puzzle. When finally put together in their right places, they would tell one of the most mysterious and astonishing stories of the Second World War.

PROLOGUE

The winter of 1951–52 would be remembered in northern Italy as one of the harshest in twenty years. The cold had descended upon the country-side early in December; snow fell unabated until it was piled in massive drifts, then patches of blue sky began to appear and the air grew much colder. By the first weeks of 1952, the weather had not improved, the bright sunny days giving way to bitter nights that descended on the land like an icy gauntlet. Then, in the middle of February, the weather broke briefly and it rained icy torrents for a solid week, before the cold gained the upper hand once more and the rain began to turn to sleet and wet snow.

This story begins on an ice-cold Sunday evening in late February, when a French journalist, motoring to Milan, broke down while on a deserted country road between Verbania and Pallanza. Stranded in the middle of nowhere, the journalist, André Brissaud, stood for a short time in the road, his hat held tight to his head against the driving sleet, hoping for a passing car to take him to the nearest town. However, he was out of luck, for it was late and dark, and there was no traffic on the road on such an inhospitable evening.

In the best traditions of the late-night horror film in which the stranded traveller suddenly notices a distant, lonely house and finds salvation, so did Brissaud at this point notice a light burning dimly on a nearby hillside about half a kilometre away. Hoping to find help, he set off and was soon approaching a secluded, substantial villa, half hidden on the hillside by trees thick with hoarfrost.

Brissaud would later recall, 'I went up the central path and rang the bell. An old Italian manservant opened the door, [and] I explained my situation.'[1] The servant agreed to let Brissaud use the telephone, but the Frenchman was still out of luck; the local garage would not be able to help until the following day. During his time on the telephone the manservant had disappeared, but he now returned and informed Brissaud that the owner of the villa had offered him his hospitality for the night.

The servant led Brissaud into the villa's drawing room, where a great fire was burning in the hearth. Here two men sat talking quietly in Italian. Brissaud was introduced to his host, a good-looking middle-aged Milanese, and his companion, who rose but introduced himself merely as 'a Swiss friend'. Brissaud studied the man and found him most curious: 'Not very tall, broad-shouldered. His suit of beige tweed, though well cut, hung loose on him. He had very black hair, sparse, plastered down at the sides, and a penetrating glance.' He was at once struck by the man's face, for it was 'dark yellow, verging on brown'. He noticed particularly his extreme thinness, which stretched his skin tightly across prominent cheekbones above hollow cheeks. Large rings emphasised the brilliance of his eyes. 'Obviously the man was ill, very ill.'

After dinner the three men settled down in the drawing room and the conversation turned to the state of Europe following the Second World War, which had ended only seven years before. Presently the subject of Nazism arose, but on this topic the Swiss seemed to become withdrawn and spoke little. It was, however, a subject that interested Brissaud greatly, and one upon which he was able to discourse at length. Then, at a chance remark he made about the SS, the Swiss suddenly leaned forward intently and demanded, 'For what secret service do you work?'

Brissaud laughed the question off, explaining that he was very interested in Nazism and the SS, and that his work as a journalist had enabled him to pursue his hobby. What he knew about the Nazis he had learnt in this manner. He was able to recall later that 'the Swiss, who listened attentively without taking his eyes off me, then said: "In these circumstances I'm surprised you haven't recognised me. My name is Walter Schellenberg. I was head of the German Secret Service, the SD."'

Brissaud's surprise was absolute. Schellenberg! Himmler's protégé head of Intelligence. Yet how could he have recognised him? He had changed considerably since 1945, and he no longer resembled any of his photographs.

Schellenberg went on to explain to Brissaud that in the last days of the war, at the beginning of May 1945, he had left Himmler in northern Germany to undertake a secret diplomatic mission to Stockholm with the intention of negotiating the surrender of German forces stationed in Norway. However, on 9 May Germany surrendered and on 10 May the Swedes placed him under house arrest. It was at this time, he revealed, that he had begun writing his memoirs, which he hoped might serve to aid his defence if the Allies delayed their demand for his extradition. At the beginning of June he was extradited from Sweden back to the British Zone of Occupation in Germany, whence he was promptly transported to British Intelligence's special prison, the London Cage, in Kensington, London. Here he had been intensively interrogated for weeks by a commission of specialists about secret service matters. Then, towards the end of 1945, he had been taken back to Germany, where he testified in the Nuremberg trials; he was subsequently sentenced in 1949 to six years' confinement. However, he served only two years, owing to ill health, being released in 1951.

'I've got cancer,' he explained to Brissaud without emotion.

In fact, Schellenberg had liver cancer and had only a few more weeks to live. In the meantime he had settled with an old friend from the war years after being expelled from Switzerland (where he had originally settled) as an 'undesirable resident'. Despite the approaching end of his life, Schellenberg still did not confide completely in Brissaud, for he had not lost all his contacts from his time as head of Nazi Germany's secret service. The Milanese he was residing with had been a former high-ranking officer of the Italian Intelligence Service; and a lover from the war years – a former agent who had worked for Schellenberg – had been funding his lifestyle in Switzerland and Italy since his release from prison. This bene-factor was none other than Coco Chanel, the leading light of haute couture, banished from France by the French government on the liberation of Paris for her pro-Nazi activities during the war. On his death Chanel would pay Schellenberg's funeral expenses.

Brissaud stayed on at the villa for a few days, discussing his past with Schellenberg and conducting an extensive interview with the man on his remarkable wartime career. Schellenberg even showed Brissaud a box containing his memoirs, which had recently been returned to him in a state of disarray by the Swiss publishing firm of Albert Scherz.

It is at this point that the mystery begins . . .

Whilst in prison in Germany, Schellenberg finished writing his memoirs, which after several years' work amounted to some seven hundred hand-written pages. After some nefarious negotiation he came to an arrangement with one of the American warders, who smuggled the memoirs out of the prison and dispatched them to the Swiss publisher. To Schellenberg's delight, Albert Scherz agreed to publish and terms were agreed. However, on his release from prison in 1951, he found that the offer to publish had been withdrawn. Furthermore, he had immense difficulty in getting his manuscript (there was no copy) back from Scherz. In the end, and after much trouble, he managed to retrieve his work, but the manuscript was returned in complete disarray, and he was extremely disturbed to discover that the work had been reduced in length to a mere 350 pages. Three hundred and fifty key pages were missing. Schellenberg, his health by now collapsing catastrophically because of liver failure, was unable to sort out the manuscript to discern exactly what had been removed, and shortly after Brissaud's visit to the villa he died.

After his death the mystery surrounding Schellenberg's memoirs was to deepen. Out of a sense of loyalty to his deceased friend, the Milanese Italian with whom he spent his last days had the manuscript re-collated and edited by a German journalist, despite the missing pages. The manuscript was subsequently hawked around Europe's publishing houses, before coming to the attention of the London-based historian Heinrich Fraenkel. Fraenkel took the project on, determined to see the work published, but was surprised within a very short while to receive a visit from a leading British historian who expressed a desire to study the material. Fraenkel handed the manuscript over to the historian, who took it away to 'study'. When it was eventually returned, Fraenkel was horrified to discover that certain passages had again been 'weeded out', literally ripping key episodes of the story away, and removing much of its importance as a personal testament of Germany's head of the Secret Service.

When André Deutsch eventually published a much-condensed version of the memoirs in 1956, under the title *The Labyrinth: The Memoirs of Walter Schellenberg* (later editions were titled simply *The Schellenberg Memoirs*), so much key material had been removed that the book inclined the reader to believe Schellenberg had played a minimal wartime role. It portrayed the former head of German Intelligence as a man who had merely sought to aid an indecisive and troubled Heinrich Himmler, who was beginning to think of his own neck as Germany was heading inexorably towards defeat. Although several key passages of the manuscript had been removed, the same British historian who had weeded the manuscript became one of the most vocal critics of Schellenberg's memoirs upon publication.

Despite the paucity of crucial information left in Walter Schellenberg's memoirs, his importance as head of Amt VI of the RSHA (Reichssicherheitshauptamt – Reich Central Security Office), the secret intelligence service of the SS, should still not be underestimated, and his wartime career had been very substantial indeed. Under interrogation in

Britain in the autumn of 1945, the men questioning Schellenberg wrote the following description of him:

> For a history of Schellenberg much vitriol is required. He was the henchman of Himmler, who made him chief of Amt VI. In terms it was his duty, if the word can be coined, to Himmlerise the German Secret Service. Schellenberg accepted the job and it is true to his character that he disliked the master who fed him. He was a traitor, of course, in the end. He contacted Bernadotte while the Germans were still fighting and aped the role of friend of the Allies. Actually, all he wanted was to save his skin. In office he would be a vile enemy; in captivity he was a cringing cad. In office he would ruthlessly cut down his opponents; in captivity he would as ruthlessly betray his friends.[2]

Critical as this assessment of him was, it was a grave underestimation by British Intelligence of Schellenberg's ability, and a flippant writing off of his importance as former head of Germany's foreign intelligence service. Amongst his other deeds, Schellenberg had kidnapped two British secret agents from Holland in 1939; he had personally overseen the German Intelligence operation involving the Duke and Duchess of Windsor in Portugal in 1940; he had controlled the forging of British currency in vast quantities in an attempt to destroy the British economy; he had, through his own endeavours, taken apart piece by piece the Soviet espionage ring in Germany of the Vietinghoff brothers, causing mayhem in Russian Intelligence; and he had personally arrested Admiral Canaris following the failed 20 July bomb plot to kill Hitler. The 'Benjamin' of the SS chiefs, as Himmler, whose favourite he was, termed him, had been one of the most eminent personalities of the National Socialist regime.[3] Indeed, Schellenberg was so valued by Himmler that, in the winter of 1944, he had been entrusted with Himmler's top-secret peace negotiations to the British via the Swedish diplomat, Count Bernadotte. These negotiations had been conducted solely on Himmler's behalf and had not involved Adolf Hitler. Schellenberg's loyalties lay primarily with his patron, to whom he owed everything, even if that meant going behind the Führer's back and opening secret negotiations with the Allies.

It was this last mission that is the most interesting and which begins to scratch the surface of the symbiotic relationship between Himmler and Schellenberg. Himmler trusted Schellenberg, while Schellenberg relied on

Himmler's patronage; Himmler, for his part, could rely implicitly on his protégé to carry out confidentially some of his most secret missions, which had infinitely more to do with advancing Himmler's interests than with furthering the cause of National Socialism, or indeed Nazi Germany.

This book will investigate the secret missions to seek peace carried out by Schellenberg on the direct orders of Himmler, and there is much to be revealed. By 1943, when Hitler gave up on the possibility of achieving a political and diplomatic solution to the war and came to the conclusion that the only solution now was a military one, Himmler, head of the SS, had realised that Germany could not win the war through force of arms, and that a political solution was essential. Of this he was secretly utterly convinced. He began, covertly, through the medium of his loyal head of foreign intelligence, to contact the British as a first step to negotiating with the Allies to end the war, and if that would not work, then to putting into place the parameters for his own future post-war political career.

The surprising truth is that Himmler, leading member of the Nazi regime and head of the SS, saw himself potentially as a leading post-war politician in the style of the man who would later become Germany's first post-war Chancellor, Konrad Adenauer. We can see clearly with hindsight that there was never the slightest possibility of a man like Himmler being granted any role in government after the war. But it has to be remembered that from his own perspective he had no idea how the war would end, nor indeed could he have foreseen that all the leading Nazis would be subsequently put on trial for war crimes at Nuremberg. The only comparison he could make was with the end of the First World War, when many wartime politicians in Germany had continued their careers under the Weimar Republic. He therefore, as early as 1943, ordered Schellenberg to open a secret line of communication to the British government, with the objective of attempting to assure his own post-war prospects. If he could also in some way hasten the end of the war so as to begin his new career all the more quickly – as head of a powerful SS political faction in Germany – then all the better.

These top-secret negotiations with the British government will be revealed in their entirety, and Himmler's inner-thinking on how he could become a political force in post-war Germany of the latter 1940s and early 1950s will be explored. He was still a comparatively young man in 1945, after all, then aged only forty-five. He could – had he been able to cut a deal with the Allies – have had a career in German politics that might have extended well into the 1960s. However, there was never the least chance of the British government making a deal with a man of Himmler's ilk. They knew too much about him and the Holocaust programme for there ever to have been a possibility of their agreeing terms. After all, the British government had already rejected countless peace approaches from other high-ranking Germans, from leading men of Nazism such as Hitler, Ribbentrop and Goebbels in the early years of the war,[4] to leaders of the German anti-Nazi resistance such as Carl Friedrich Goerdeler,[5] Lord Mayor of Leipzig and civilian leader of the July bomb plot to assassinate Hitler. All were rejected out of hand. The British government was not amenable to negotiating peace with any German whatever his pedigree, be he Nazi or anti-Nazi. This being the case, the question then arises: What was the British government – or, to be more precise, British Intelligence – doing negotiating with Himmler, not only in 1943, but from that year right through until the final German collapse in 1945? In over two years of Himmler/Schellenberg negotiation with the British, there had been much to discuss, from the possibility of a Himmler-led coup in Germany to remove Hitler from power (called 'the Himmler Solution' by British Intelligence), through to more sensitive deals concerning the acquisition by Britain of some of Nazi Germany's most important wartime scientific developments.

To discover the answer to this question, and to reveal why it was that a man like Himmler believed he could negotiate a secret deal with the British, one has to begin by examining Heinrich Himmler's character, for it is only by this means that we will gain an insight into what motivated Germany's most dangerous prince of Nazism.

NOTES

1.   André Brissaud, *Histoire du Service Secret Nazi* (Plon, 1972), p. 15.
2.   *Camp 020: MI5 and the Nazi Spies* (Public Records Office, 2000), p. 81.
3.   Brissaud, op. cit., p. 19.
4.   Doc. No. FO 371/24408, National Archives, Kew, London.
5.   Ibid.

I

RISE OF A POLITICIAN

By the spring of 1943 Nazi Germany had reached its pinnacle of expansion, controlling a vast empire that stretched from the Arctic Circle in the north to the Sahara in the south, from the Atlantic in the west to the Black Sea in the east. Not since the era of ancient Rome had Europe been under such unified political and economic control. At the centre of this Nazi empire sat the Führer, Adolf Hitler, aided by an inner circle of the ruling elite: Hermann Göring, Dr Joseph Goebbels, Joachim von Ribbentrop, and the Reichsführer-SS, Heinrich Himmler.

In the words of Emil Klein, the oldest and most senior surviving member of the Party:

> We felt like we ruled the world. Hitler had promised us so much, and he had delivered on every one of those promises. Yes, the war was still ongoing, but we had absorbed so much territory and the production capacity of so many countries that it could only be a matter of time before we could fight the Allies to a standstill . . . Then, we believed, they would have no choice eventually other than to agree to an armistice.[1]

In one respect Klein was right. Germany *had* absorbed so much territory, turning the production capacity of all the occupied lands to the war effort, that it did indeed appear to many on the Allied side that the country was becoming a superpower. That was extremely worrying, for it meant that the war might drag on indefinitely, sucking the Allies – and this particularly meant Britain – dry of men and resources. Yes, Britain was being supplied by the United States, but she was suffering terribly under the strain of running a 60 per cent command economy – an achievement that was practically unheard of, and one which the country could not sustain for much longer.

In Germany, too the strain of maintaining the war effort was beginning to cause problems, but these were minimised because Germany could call upon the production capacity of the occupied territories. Nevertheless, Hitler ordered a halt to all construction programmes in Germany in an effort to concentrate resources on military production. Thus, within the top leadership of the Nazi Party, the men concerned with the economics of war – and particularly Hitler – were aware that a final push was needed to tip the balance of the war inexorably in the Axis's favour. One last effort might ensure that Germany emerged victorious. It can therefore be seen that in the spring of 1943 the outcome of the war hung precariously in the balance. To many leading people on both sides it seemed, for a few tanta-lising months, that the conflict might swing in either direction.

It is into this situation that one must now insert the personality of Heinrich Himmler, a man who by 1943 had reached the zenith of his power within the Reich. As Reichsführer-SS, Himmler controlled an enor-mous empire. He was head of the Schutzstaffel – the SS – and the Waffen-SS, its paramilitary wing; he controlled the Sicherheitsdienst – the SD – the SS's intelligence service; and he was head of the state police and the Gestapo (Geheime Staatspolizei – the Secret State Police). Indeed, by the summer of 1943 Hitler would also appoint him Minister of the Interior. Yet perhaps what Himmler will be remembered for above all was his control of the concentration camps. He was the man responsible more than any other for the mass murder of millions in the name of racial purity, the pedantic fanatic on the right wing of the Nazi Party whose very name could instil a sense of fear in everyone he met. This fanaticism was voiced by Himmler in 1943 when he declared:

> One principle must be absolute for the SS man: we must be honest, decent, loyal, and comradely to members of our own blood and to no one else. What happens to the Russians, what happens to the Czechs, is a matter of utter indifference to me . . . . Whether the other peoples live in comfort or perish of hunger interests me only in so far as we need them as slaves for our culture; apart from that it does not interest me. Whether or not 10,000 Russian women collapse from exhaustion while digging a tank ditch interests me only in so far as the tank ditch is completed for Germany . . .[2]

In the late spring of 1943 Himmler visited the Luftwaffe rocket centre at Peenemünde that produced the V1 and V2. Here he was met by Walter Dornberger, who headed the centre; he later recorded for posterity his impression of this, the most powerful man in the Reich after Hitler:

> He looked to me like an intelligent elementary schoolteacher, certainly not a man of violence . . . Under a brow of average height, two grey-blue eyes looked at me, behind a glittering pince-nez, with an air of peaceful interrogation. The trimmed moustache below the straight, well-shaped nose traced a dark line on his unhealthy, pale features . . . Only the conspicuous receding chin surprised me . . . With a broadening of his constant set smile, faintly mocking and sometimes contemptuous about the corners of the mouth, two rows of excellent white teeth appeared between thin lips.[3]

A few months later they met again, when Himmler returned to Peenemünde to learn more about the 'wonder-weapons' that were going to turn the tide of the war in Germany's favour. This time Dornberger recorded that:

> Himmler possessed the rare gift of attentive listening . . . His questions showed that he unerringly grasped what the technicians told him out of the wealth of their knowledge. The talk turned to war and the important questions in all our minds. He answered calmly and candidly . . . he emphasised his words by tapping the tips of his fingers together. He was a man of quiet unemotional gestures.[4]

However quiet Himmler's emotional gestures, he was a man of contradictions, from his quietly refined attitude to his peers and a willingness to take on board the knowledge of other people, to his merciless ordering of death for millions with a flick of his pen. This could also be applied to his own secret opinion about how Germany was faring in the war. To the outside world he was the confident Reichsführer-SS, the leading man of the Reich, who might one day succeed Hitler to become the next leader of Nazi Germany (he after all possessed the means to implement his will via the immense power of the SS, even if other leading men of the Nazi Party opposed him). However, to the inner sanctum of a handful of trusted intimates (his private inner circle), Himmler was of a very different opinion. He had come to the conclusion that Germany could not win the war militarily, faced with the combined might of the Allies, so what was now needed was a political solution to the hostilities. Even as he was visiting Peenemünde and conducting morale-boosting tours of his elite Waffen-SS divisions, he was beginning secret moves to open peace nego- tiations with the British government. He was about to betray the trust of Adolf Hitler in order to conclude the war in a manner that would be bene- ficial to his own political interests.

These discrepancies in Himmler's character – from the calm man of intellect to the mass murderer of millions – have led many historians over the past sixty years to attempt to define that character, and many psychia- trists have been called upon to render an expert opinion on him. After much consideration these experts have concluded that Himmler's person- ality was schizoid, this being the easiest way of categorising a man whose being contained so many conflicting 'personalities'. However, such an analysis can take us only a little way towards revealing his inner driving mechanism, the real motivations for his actions. What led the self-assured head of the SS – at the zenith of his powers in 1943 – to come to the conclusion that a political solution to the war was needed, and that he should privately open peace negotiations with the British in complete secrecy from Hitler and the other leading Nazis? Such a strategy cannot be explained in terms of a schizoid personality, or of a man taking unreasoned decisions. A great deal of thought – and inner conflict – went into Himmler's course of action before he initiated it.

We are thus presented with a complex person: a man who wielded immense personal power, but one also for whom the future was a great uncertainty and who tried through his own efforts to ensure that – regard- less of what happened to Germany or the Nazi Party – he would prevail. Such actions hint at an extreme sense of self-preservation, an absolute conviction of his worth as a leading politician. It is not enough to know what Himmler did in attempting to assure himself such a future: we must start the story from the very beginning, so as to reveal both why he took the course of action he did, and how his top-secret negotiations with the British between 1943 and 1945 were the culmination of events that made such a course inevitable. We must turn the clock back to a bright autumn day in 1900, which witnessed the birth of a child destined to make a truly terrible mark on world history.

•••••

Heinrich Himmler's origins very much determined the man he would become, his character being almost fully formed by his mid-teens. From a comparatively young age it was possible to describe him as 'Himmler the uncompromising', 'Himmler the prudish young man', 'Himmler the seeker of an important position in society', 'Himmler the fanatic'. Many people may share such characteristics, but usually such a formation of personality takes place in adulthood. Yet by this time, Himmler's was full and complete. It would stay with him unchanged until his death in his mid-forties, though his pedantic belief in his own mission to further the cause of German racial purity would come much later.

Himmler was born into the bourgeois middle-class world of German society on Friday, 7 October 1900; the son of Professor Gebhard and Anna Himmler (née Heyder), who lived in a comfortable flat on Hildegardstrasse in the centre of Bavaria's capital city, Munich. He was the second of three sons born to Professor Himmler, a teacher of classics at a local *Gymnasium*, an extremely dominant man who would have an enormous influence over young Heinrich's life. Indeed, at the tender age of ten Heinrich was ordered to keep a diary by his father, who wrote the first entry to set the standard and thereafter daily marked the child's diary in order to further Heinrich's education.

Gebhard Himmler was a man obsessed with his position in German society. He had once been tutor to the son of Prince Arnulf of Bavaria, and as soon as his second son had been born, he had written to his former pupil, now Prince Heinrich. Informing him of the baby's precise size and weight, Himmler had asked the prince to become godfather to the child, who was to be named Heinrich in his honour. Not unnaturally, Prince Heinrich was somewhat flattered and agreed to become young Heinrich's godfather. Thus, from his very earliest days, Heinrich Himmler was already having instilled into him that he came not from humble origins, but from an old and distinguished German family that could trace its origins back to the thirteenth century, and that, by association, he had connections to Germany's aristocracy.

Despite Heinrich's bourgeois origins, albeit with hints of pedigree, he had a relatively normal childhood. His father possessed a prodigious intellect and was soon tutoring his young sons in Germany's history and the classics, all of which Heinrich and his siblings absorbed avidly from an early age. Professor Himmler was also an enthusiastic amateur archaeologist and historian, with a deep interest in Germany's ancient past; a time of the Teutons, peasant-warriors, ancient runes and ancient religions. Nightly the Professor would read to his three young sons about their proud and eminent German heritage, and all this Heinrich took on board; it was filed and recorded in the deepest recesses of his brain, but not forgotten. In time it would all be recalled in acute detail, reformed into the mysteries of an ancient Aryan past and made into SS folklore, about which every new recruit was forced to learn.

From a young age Heinrich was able to recite at will the names and dates of Germany's battles, and by the time he entered senior school his knowledge about Germany's history rivalled that of his school teachers.[5] When he went to grammar school, the Royal Wilhelm Gymnasium, he immediately became a 'star' pupil. He was described by his close friend and fellow pupil George Hallgarten as:

> Scarcely of average size . . . downright podgy, with an uncom-
> monly milk-white complexion, fair short hair, and already wearing
> gold-rimmed glasses on his rather sharp nose; not infrequently he
> showed a half-embarrassed half-sardonic smile either to excuse
> his shortsightedness or to stress a certain superiority.[6]

The young Heinrich was the classic 'star' pupil. A touch on the plump side, a lover of cakes and chocolate, as seems to be usual with such young people, he found physical sports a nightmare and was hopeless at them. However, Germany in the era of the *Belle Epoque* was very much a martial country, where every young boy yearned to join the Kaiser's glorious armed forces, and so, too, did the young Heinrich harbour such ambitions. On one occasion, after a particularly torturous session of physical education – an exercise of knee-bends that was almost beyond him – he was asked by his teacher what he wanted to be after school. 'Close to tears, Himmler got out "Naval Officer".'[7] However, such a future was not to be Heinrich's destiny, for although he did not realise it, his weak eyesight automatically excluded him from the Navy. Such an ambition would be academic anyway. By the time he was old enough to join the Navy, the end of the First World War had determined that Germany's Kriegsmarine would be all but erased by the Treaty of Versailles, reduced to a few obsolete battle-wagons fit only for coastal defence.

The First World War burst upon Himmler's consciousness like a blossoming flower, and with the keenness of other youths his age he avidly followed every development. From the war's earliest days he began to note his impressions of the conflict in his diary with all the enthusiasm of a boy

who is surrounded at every turn with patriotic fervour. On 23 August 1914
he recorded:

> Victory of the German Crown Prince north of Metz . . . The
> Germans in Ghent . . . Bavarian troops were very brave in the
> rough battle . . . The whole city is bedecked with flags. The
> French and Belgians scarcely thought they would be chopped up
> so fast.[8]

A month later he noted:

> Now it's going along famously. I'm pleased about these victo-
> ries, the more so because the French and especially the English
> are angry about them and the anger is not exactly insignificant . .
> . An English cavalry brigade has been thrashed (I'm glad!
> Hurrah!).[9]

And so the war progressed, through the remainder of 1914, through 1915
and 1916 and on to 1917. During this time Heinrich kept up both his diary
and his efforts at school, where he continued to receive excellent marks.

In the spring of 1917 Heinrich's elder brother, Gebhard, left school and
joined the 2nd Bavarian Infantry, where he was immediately inducted for
officer training. The teenage Heinrich longed to join up like his elder
brother, but his father intervened and insisted that he remain at school
where he would take his *Abitur*, his final exams that would qualify him for
higher education. The year passed, complete with German victories and
defeats, and with it Heinrich continued his studies at the local
Gymnasium. Yet all this time, in his own mind, he was missing the excitement of the Front; missing the opportunity of becoming an officer like his
elder brother. Then, a few days before Christmas 1917, his prayers were
answered when he suddenly received a letter ordering him to join the 11th
Bavarian Infantry Brigade, based in Regensburg. If Professor Himmler had
any misgivings about his talented son being called up at so late a date in
such a terribly costly war, they were of no avail, and the seventeen-year-old
Heinrich reported to Regensburg on 1 January 1918 as a Fahnenjunker
(officer trainee). His prayers were being answered at last, and he was
following in his elder brother's footsteps.

At Regensburg, Heinrich followed a much-telescoped officer training
course, and here he remained throughout the spring of 1918, receiving his

basic training and performing the physical exercises that he found so hard. There followed several more months of officer training that lasted until October. To Himmler it must have seemed that he would never reach the Front, never achieve distinction in battle, never attain an Iron Cross First Class as his elder brother had done by this time.

However, battle experience was something Heinrich Himmler was not destined to attain, for by the late autumn of 1918 Germany was experiencing severe political problems that were about to render the terrible sacrifices of four years of war utterly futile.

The last months of the First World War saw great political unrest in Germany, with the rise of the Socialists and the Bolsheviks – who were taking their lead from events several hundred miles to the east in Russia. There the Bolsheviks had gained the political upper hand, ousted the Tsar, and now ruled a Soviet Russia. Many left-wing factions had in turn sprung up in Germany, intent on changing the country's political system. They demanded an end to the constitutional past of Kaiser, an end to Germany's aristocracy and the ruling elite, and a change in the political system that would tip the balance of power in the new post-war Germany towards the proletariat.

Just as in Russia, where sailors of the Imperial Navy had mutinied, precipitating the revolution that had toppled the Tsar, so the spark of rebellion reached its flashpoint in the German Navy. In October 1918 the Kaiser's Navy in Kiel likewise mutinied, large numbers of deserters scattering inland to spread the word of revolution amongst Germany's disaffected working classes. Here they fomented social unrest and insurrection, cutting Germany's supplies of materials, food, and power, crippling the country, and causing it to veer dangerously towards the verge of anarchy.

At Regensburg, Himmler wrote to his parents advising them to buy all the coal and food they could, adding, 'Don't let mother go out alone at night. Not without protection . . .'[10] Germany had suddenly been transformed from an ordered, cultured society into one that was dangerous and teetering on the abyss of revolution.

Unable to restore order, and fearing the loss of his life in the same ghastly manner as had befallen his cousin, Tsar Nicholas II, only four months before, Kaiser Wilhelm II's nerve failed. He abdicated and fled the country within a few days, leaving a hastily propped-up Socialist government to cope with the potentially explosive internal situation. Faced with this dilemma, and knowing that the Allied forces were growing steadily stronger, the new German government promptly declared that the war could not be sustained any longer, and sued for peace. Germany had lost the war not only militarily, but also economically and politically.[11]

Following the collapse of Germany's war effort and the armistice, Himmler found himself abruptly demobilised from his Bavarian regiment in the winter of 1918. Destiny, it seemed, had determined that he was not to see active service, nor was he confirmed in his appointment as an officer. All his efforts throughout 1918 had been for nothing, and it was a bitterly disappointed Himmler who now returned to the family home. There he was expected to fall back into the routine of home life, to defer once again to the superiority of his father's position as head of the household, to return to school to finish his education. It must have been especially hard for the young man, who had been given his head and freedom to become an adult for a year, to take such a step backwards. However, step back he did; he returned to the *Gymnasium* to take a special course designed for youngsters who had missed the end of their education as a consequence of being called up for active service.

Despite Himmler's return to education, the social unrest that had descended on Germany after the end of the First World War once again determined that he would be distracted from his studies. In Munich a far-left political faction called the Spartakusbund had managed a Bolshevik-style takeover and declared Bavaria a *Räterepublik* (Soviet republic). By April 1919 there was open fighting on the streets of Munich between men of the Spartakusbund and a right-wing patriotic society called the Thule Society (a nationalist grouping that shared many ideas with the later Nazi Party), who were determined that their beloved Bavaria would not go the same way as Russia. The Spartakusbund then made a fatal error in accepting three Bolshevik emissaries sent from Moscow by Lenin. These three Russian agitators promptly took over the group, and began to consolidate their power-base in Bavaria's *Räterepublik* by instigating a Soviet-style purge.

It was all too much for the newly elected German government. It watched events in Bavaria and blanched, for the Spartakusbund had nailed their colours to the mast by declaring that their ultimate aim was to topple the legitimate German government and set up a Soviet Germany in imitation of that which now ruled in Russia. Prompted by a strong sense of self-preservation, the German government based in Weimar immediately sent in troops to restore order, gladly accepting help from the Freikorps Epp (a right-wing paramilitary organisation affiliated to the Thule Society), and succeeded in toppling the Spartakists. During this time – the spring of 1919 – Heinrich Himmler had not stood idly by, nor had he stayed in education, for he was determined that he, too, should play his part in saving his beloved Bavaria from the Bolshevik agitators. He had therefore joined both the Freikorps and a reserve company of another paramilitary organisation called Oberland, where he was soon appointed aide to the commanding officer. It was as a member of these two organisations in the spring of 1919 that Himmler first came into contact with the far right of German politics, and they had much to say about the evils of Bolshevism, the culpability of certain intellectual Jews in supporting the Spartakusbund. Here Himmler would also learn the Thule Society's opinion that the left wing and the Jews were to blame for undermining Germany's war effort, the myth that they were ultimately responsible, by causing the collapse of the war effort, for Germany's humiliating defeat. These ideas were taken on board by the young Himmler, and he, too, became a believer in the myths surrounding Germany's defeat – the laying of blame at the door of the Jews, the Bolsheviks, and the socialists. It would all go towards building his inner character, and he now began to follow the extreme right.

Following the end of the Spartakus revolution, Himmler once again returned to his studies, concluding his education and gaining his *Abitur*, which would allow him to go on to higher education. It was now the summer of 1919, and he was free to pursue his life as an adult.

Himmler now appeared to make a very strange decision in his pursuit of a career. He was well educated, recognised by many as possessing a prodigious intellect, yet that summer he seemed to take a step backwards, choosing to work in agriculture. His father managed to find him a job on a farm near Ingolstadt. He had to get up at six in the morning to tend to the horses; he then spent a very exhausting full day out in the fields, where he had a lunch of beer and sandwiches about mid-afternoon, before working until the evening, finally collapsing into bed after an evening meal at about 9.00 p.m. Himmler, as we know from his time in school, was not athletic, and he was soon suffering badly under the strain. A move to higher educa- tion would have suited the young man far better, followed by a career in which he was able to work with his brains. Many people have questioned his strange career move; it was not at all in keeping with what we know about his talents.

A clue to why Himmler suddenly found himself working hard on the land came during the Nuremberg trials in 1946, when a former school- friend called Karl Gebhardt was called to give evidence. Gebhardt had become a professor of medicine and during the war had worked in an SS hospital, and what he had to say was most interesting. Under questioning he asserted that Himmler's father had chosen a career in agriculture for his son in order to keep him away from politics after his association with the German right wing through the Freikorps and the Thule Society.[12] Yet again, it seemed, even in early adulthood, the young Himmler had deferred to his domineering father's choice of career.

However, fate now took a hand. The young Himmler was not destined to remain a farm labourer, even if that was a mere step on the road to becoming an agronomist. A bare month after he started, under the strain of the long hours and strenuous work, his health collapsed. He went down with a paratyphus infection and was sent to hospital for three weeks to recover. On his departure from hospital it was decided that he should defer his year of practical agriculture and attend a technical high school to study agronomy. He promptly enrolled in October 1919, and so began his studies once more.

It was whilst Himmler was attending to his higher education that he truly began to become politically aware. Germany in 1919 and 1920 was a country on the verge of political collapse. The far left hated the right, the far right hated the left, and both factions hated the Social Democratic government heading the new German republic that had been born out of the defeat of Germany in 1918. Although the country followed the precarious path of democracy, an awkward step by the government to the left or right might precipitate revolution of the kind headed by the Spartakists and put down only months before.

It was at this time that Himmler's ideology on racial matters began to take definitive form. In the spring of 1920 he read two books that touched on the subject of race. The first was Arthur Dinter's *Die Sünde wieder das Blut* (*The Sin against the Blood*), which Himmler commented was a 'terrifyingly plain' introduction to the Jewish question.[13] The second was *Ultimo*, in which one of the leading characters was a devious Jewish banker; this time Himmler remarked that it 'characterised the Jews very well'.[14] He had, of course, already been very much swayed by the anti-Semitic sentiment propagated by the Thule Society and the Freikorps that blamed the Bolsheviks, Socialists, and Jews for Germany's defeat in the First World War. This ideology had been combined with his beliefs in Aryan/Germanic racial purity and his fascination with a great Germanic past (as instilled into him by his father); and so a right-wing fanatic was born.

Meanwhile the Nazi Party was being born in Munich, and the future leaders of the Third Reich were coming together. By the time Himmler finished his education Hitler had taken over the Party, and those who were to be its key personalities over the next two decades were already in place – Hess, Göring, Rosenberg, Strasser, and, most importantly where Himmler was concerned, a certain army captain who had served on the General Staff in the First World War, one Ernst Röhm.

In August 1922 Himmler graduated from the Munich technical college where he had been studying agronomy, and joined a local fertiliser company by the name of Stickstoff-Land GmbH as a laboratory assistant. For the first time he was truly free from the authority of his father, who had been paying him a small income to keep him in his studies. With this newfound liberty Himmler bought a motorcycle, and made himself indispensable to his right-wing friends by acting as dispatch rider, visiting the outlying communities in Bavaria to spread the word of nationalism.

Even by the time Himmler finished his studies and began work for Stickstoff-Land, he had already laid the groundwork for a career in politics, for in January 1922 he had met Ernst Röhm, the Bavarian Army district staff officer who was also a leader of the paramilitary wing of the Nazi Party, the Reichskriegsflagge. Röhm is best remembered for his leadership of the SA, the Sturmabteilung; however, he did not take over this organisation until 1931, and by then he would be on course to meet his death at the instigation of his studious and conscientious recruit. In the meantime Himmler was pleased to serve Röhm and the Party in the lowly capacity of a minion – one, however, who would soon make his presence felt through his considerable intelligence rather than the rough-necked brawls so characteristic of Nazi activists in the 1920s. He had not yet met Adolf Hitler, but he now moved in the circles of Hitler's backers, and so it would only be a matter of time before they encountered each other. The exact date of their first meeting is not known, but as Himmler was by now a supporter of the Party and working for Röhm, it is believed to have occurred some time during the early summer of 1923.

In August 1923 Himmler finally joined the Nazi Party, a decision that did not sit well with his father. Although a nationalist himself, Professor Himmler saw the Nazis as little better than a bunch of thugs. Instead, he supported the Bavarian People's Party, which espoused a return of the Wittelsbach dynasty to rule Bavaria, and the separation of Catholic Bavaria from the German Weimar Republic in order to form an alliance with Catholic Austria. It was a totally unrealistic agenda, and one that increasingly placed father and son on opposite sides of the political fence.

At the time that Himmler joined Ernst Röhm's paramilitary Reichskriegsflagge (the SA being little better than tavern brawlers and street fighters), it was becoming under Röhm's leadership an altogether more military organisation, recruiting heavily amongst veterans of the First World War. It aimed to be at the forefront of a Nazi revolution that Hitler hoped would sweep him to power. In the summer and early autumn of 1923 Hitler was still biding his time, studying the political developments in Germany in minute detail and looking for the opportune moment to launch a revolution of the kind that had swept Mussolini to power in Italy only a year earlier.

By the autumn of 1923 the German economy was on the verge of collapse, with rocketing inflation that saw a single postage stamp costing 10,000 Marks. The German government teetered precariously as it struggled to manage the fragile economy. As a result Hitler began to think the time was now ripe for a *coup d'état*, a putsch that would see him and his Nazis sweep away the ineffectual government and usurp power. Hitler's second-in-command for the putsch was a powerful force within the Nazi Party, Hermann Göring, who at this time led the SA. Röhm, too, had an important role within the putsch as head of the Reichskriegsflagge. Whilst the SA would provide the clout Hitler needed to control events in Munich, holding Bavarian politicians hostage and providing his security, the Reichskriegsflagge would provide the logistical support required to seize Munich's War Ministry.

Thursday, 8 November 1923 was the date set for Hitler's revolt. Everyone in the movement was primed, armed and ready for their greatest adventure to date. Himmler, too, was ready to act, having been appointed to the position of flag-bearer to Röhm in the Reichskriegsflagge. That evening saw an extraordinary scene, even by German standards of the 1920s, as a political meeting in Munich's Bürgerbräukeller was rudely interrupted by gun-toting, steel-helmeted SA men, led by an oddly fanatical figure in a long black overcoat – Adolf Hitler.

After bursting in, Hitler leaped up on to a chair, fired his pistol into the air, and as a shocked silence descended on the audience, brazenly declared: 'A national revolution in Munich has just broken out.' To which he added untruthfully, 'The whole city is at this moment occupied by our troops. This hall is surrounded by six hundred men.'[15]

Across the city Röhm's men of the Reichskriegsflagge were taking up their position, surrounding the War Ministry with a circle of barbed wire and barricades. Standing in the middle of the barricades, proudly holding up his flag for a press photographer, stood Heinrich Himmler, making his first imprint upon history.

In 1923, however, the thirty-four-year-old Hitler was still a novice at the taking and holding of power, and he quickly lost control of the situation. Within the Bürgerbräukeller a wave of patriotic anthem singing, Nazi saluting, and volatile speeches on the incompetence of the Social Democrats and the evils of Bolshevism took the initiative from him. By the following morning his putsch lay in disarray, and it was at the Bürgerbräukeller that the *Times* correspondent found him still: 'a little man . . . unshaven with disorderly hair, and so hoarse that he could hardly speak'.[16]

During the course of the night Hitler's failure to consolidate his precarious position had been surpassed in naïveté by Hermann Göring who, after eliciting promises from the captured Bavarian ministers – as gentlemen – that they would not act against the revolt, released all his prisoners. However, much to Göring's surprise and Hitler's fury, they now discovered that as soon as the politicians had been released, they had promptly summoned the army to aid them in putting down the coup. Over at the War Ministry, meanwhile, the police had arrived and they swiftly organised their own barricades to surround Röhm's cordon. It was a standoff that Röhm soon realised would doom his position if not relieved by Göring's SA. However, things were by now swiftly building in momentum against the Nazis. On hearing the news that the army had been called out, Hitler quickly organised his little band of revolutionaries into a march on the centre of Munich. The final act of the fiasco was a gun-battle in the Odeonplatz outside the Feldherrnhalle where Hitler and his mob were confronted by the police. It was a battle that would enter Nazi folklore: fourteen Nazis were killed, Göring was injured, and Hitler dislocated his shoulder when he tripped over and his bodyguard fell on top of him.[17]

The putsch was over, and with it any hopes that Hitler, Göring, and Röhm had harboured of seizing power unconstitutionally. There was, however, a difference between Röhm and Hitler. Hitler came to the conclusion that there would now be a long struggle to seize power by legitimate political means, whilst Röhm continued to believe that a revolutionary vanguard – a paramilitary force – could be used to precipitate that change. It was a stance that would bring the pair into devastating conflict a decade later.

In the meantime Mariele Rauschmayer, a close friend of Himmler, wrote to him about the failed putsch:

I should like to thank you and your people for the one beautiful hour in the morning of 9 Nov . . .

She went on in romantic verse, declaring:

Troops of the Reichskriegsflagge in front of the War Ministry. Heinrich Himmler at their head carrying the flag; one could see how secure the flag felt in his hands and how proud he was of it . . .[18]

It is true that Himmler was proud of the role – albeit a small one – he had played. It was his first major commitment to a political cause, one to which he now increasingly gave over his life.

In the aftermath of the failed putsch, Hitler and his closest followers were jailed for short terms, the Nazi Party and the SA were temporarily dissolved, and the Party mouthpiece, its newspaper the *Völkischer Beobachter*, was ordered to cease printing. It seemed to many that Hitler's political revolution had stalled before it had really started. But this was to fail to recognise the remarkable personality of Adolf Hitler. Before the Munich Putsch his was a little-known name except amongst his supporters. Now, following the trial of its leaders, his name was projected directly into the limelight, not only in Germany but on the international stage as well. In the meantime he had to content himself with being out of circulation – jailed in Landsberg Prison for five years, subsequently reduced to six months. He was left to plot his next move.

Whilst his leaders were incarcerated, Himmler continued to be a political activist. He toured the Bavarian countryside north of Munich on his motorcycle, giving speeches to farming communities on the virtues of National Socialism, the evils of Communism and the Jews, the problems of labour and food shortages. His foundations as a politician were being firmly laid in these grassroots beginnings. His diary for 25 February 1924 records that he spoke to a farming community at Rohr for one and a half hours, 'I think quite well.' To hold the attention of a meeting for this length of time suggests that already he was no mean orator.[19]

It was at this time that Himmler met a man destined to become the next decisive personality in his life; this was Gregor Strasser, leader of the Nazi Party and SA in Lower Bavaria. If Röhm had been a man who fulfilled Himmler's military inclinations in the Reichskriegsflagge, it could be said that Strasser instilled into him a proper sense of political awareness, one that was to stay with him throughout the rest of his life. With Hitler's imprisonment in Landsberg, Strasser had been appointed as co-chairman of the Party. In this capacity he was an able organiser, an indefatigable speaker, and a shrewd politician. In the Party's early days he had challenged Hitler for the leadership but lost. However, with Hitler's imprisonment he saw a chance of strengthening his position. He therefore sold his apothecary's shop in Landshut and committed himself fully to the Party; he used some of the money raised from the sale to set up a new Party newspaper, the *Berliner Arbeitur Zeitung*, edited by his brother Otto, and a monthly magazine, *NS-Briefe*, designed to keep Nazi activists informed about developments within the Party. For his *NS-Briefe*, Strasser called upon the talents of another newly discovered protégé, a young Rhinelander named Dr Joseph Goebbels, to act as editor. With the addition of Himmler as a member of his group of confidants, the circle of Nazism was almost complete. All the key personalities of the latter years were now in positions of authority. There was one last facet to Strasser's personality that made his situation within the Nazi Party important. He was a committed socialist, so he actively led its left wing, feeling himself able to act as a counterbalance to the more extreme right-wing elements. In a decade's time, like Röhm, Strasser would feel the full force of Himmler's personality. Only by then it would be too late and it would cost him his life.

In the spring election of 1924 Strasser was elected as a delegate to the Bavarian Landtag (legislature or regional parliament). As soon as he was elected he began to travel around Germany visiting and talking to other right-wing nationalist groups who might be recruited to the Nazi cause. Because he was frequently away from Munich, and even when there found the remainder of his time committed to the Landtag, he decided that he required an assistant to look after his office as Nazi Party leader for Lower Bavaria. He looked about for a short while before his attention was drawn to an able young man who was already travelling extensively about the countryside on his motorcycle drumming up support. This was the twenty-three-year-old Himmler, a supporter living a hand-to-mouth existence whilst giving his time freely to the Party. Instantly everything changed for Himmler; he was put on the Party payroll, and his real life as a professional politician began. However, he did not now begin looking at the world through rose-tinted spectacles; he knew the work was hard and it would take a long time before the seeds planted by the Party would bear fruit. It was a long way from a few meagre seats in the Landtag to gaining the overall control of a nation. Himmler knew that he and other Party members were working for the long term; in a press interview given in August 1924 he stated that 'we few do this hard work undeterred, out of boundless love of the Fatherland . . . a selfless service to a grand idea and a grand cause.'[20]

An insight into Himmler's personality at this time comes directly from Gregor Strasser himself, who talked candidly to his younger brother, Otto, about his new political protégé:

> A remarkable fellow. Comes from a Catholic family, but does not want to know anything about the Church. Looks like a half-starved shrew. But keen I tell you, incredibly keen. He has . . . a motorbike, and he is under way the whole day – from one farm to another – from one village to the next.[21]

It can therefore be seen that Himmler was by now a tireless worker on behalf of Strasser and the Party, his role that of a key parliamentary worker keeping contact with the outlying communities, and converting any he could to the radical new cause that was National Socialism.

With the release of Hitler from Landsberg Prison in the winter of 1924, the Nazi Party was once again launched on the road to power. During his incarceration the German parliament had been dissolved and elections called for 7 December. Not everything went the nationalists' way, however. They had previously held thirty-two seats in the Reichstag, but with only half a million votes they now won a mere fourteen seats, one of which was allocated to Strasser. This was an event of considerable importance in Himmler's career, for with Strasser's move to Berlin to take up his seat in the Reichstag, he became Deputy Gauleiter (district leader) of Lower Bavaria. He was a politician in his own right at last. In fact, not only was he now deputy leader of a political region of the Party – a Gau – but the region he had been put in charge of was one that was sure to bring him to the attention of the Nazi Party leadership, for Lower Bavaria may be considered the crucible of Nazism, 'the kernel of the Hitler party'.[22]

At long last Himmler was near the core of the Nazi Party, in the ideal position to be noticed for his intelligence and ability; he was a devoted follower of Hitler, a capable political activist. It would later be commented: 'the adult Heinrich Himmler separate from the Party and its ideology never existed. Himmler *was* Nazism.'[23] Throughout the remainder of the 1920s he would continue to rise steadily through the Party hierarchy, continue to be noticed by the leaders of Nazism. His course was set, and it would now be only a matter of time before he began to receive into his hands the strings of real power.

In the winter of 1926, whilst he was on holiday, another important event occurred in Himmler's life. Rushing into the shelter of a Berchtesgaden hotel to get out of a winter storm, he careered into a young woman, showering her with melting snow. At twenty-six, he was now not only Deputy Gauleiter of Lower Bavaria, but he had also been made Deputy Propaganda Leader of the Party, complete with a transfer to Party headquarters in Munich. The woman he had run into was the thirty-four-year-old daughter of a West Prussian landowner. Her name was Margarete (Marga for short), and she was a qualified nurse who owned a clinic in Berlin. There was an instant attraction between the two, though she was Himmler's senior by eight years. Very soon they were married; Marga sold her clinic in Berlin, and with the money Himmler and his new wife bought a smallholding at Wasserburgerlandstrasse 109, Waldtrudering, in the countryside north of Munich. Himmler was by this time earning 2,400 Marks a year from Party funds, a small salary by any standards, and the couple quickly came up with a scheme to supplement his meagre income. He would put some of his past expertise in agronomy to use at long last and open a chicken farm; they would gain a valuable second income from the sale of eggs and produce. Thus the demeaning epithet of 'Himmler, the chicken farmer' was born; one promulgated by his rivals within the Party and destined to adhere to his name throughout the coming years. It was, however, only a temporary income-generating measure, and it seems that Himmler himself had little to do with the business, which was run by Marga. Nor was it destined to last beyond a few brief years, for Himmler was about to make his name felt within the Party in a way that would change his and Marga's lives for ever.

By the time he met Marga, Himmler had already broken with Gregor Strasser. Early in 1926 Strasser had attempted to reassert his will over the Nazi Party and tried, unsuccessfully, to usurp power from Hitler. Hitler was now a magnetic and commanding force within the Party, and anyone who harboured ambitions of advancement in the 'cause' already knew which horse to back. Like many, Himmler had switched allegiance without a moment's reluctance. From now on he was Hitler's man through and through. Nor was he the only leading member to switch allegiance at this time; Joseph Goebbels had followed his close acquaintance into the Hitler camp, and in the years ahead he and Himmler would become political allies in their own right.

Within a few months of his marriage to Marga, the hierarchy of the Party at last recognised Himmler as a very capable pair of hands, an efficient organiser, and a devoted follower of Hitler. Accordingly, in September 1927, he was appointed Deputy Reichsführer of the Schutzstaffel – the SS – under Joseph Berchtold. This embryonic organisation had originally been created as an elite new bodyguard for Hitler, the Führer's own Praetorian Guard. Its activities within the Party were strictly designated as those of policing rallies and ensuring that no rabble-rousers were allowed to cause disturbances at organised meetings. Immediately Himmler made his presence felt. He issued his first orders on 17 September, dictating a strict new dress code. No longer would SS men be allowed to dress as they wished whilst on duty; apart from brown shirts, they were henceforth to be uniformly attired in black, in imitation of the old elitist cavalry regiments of the Kaiser's army.

This was not the sole change Himmler made to the SS. He began to turn it into an elitist right-wing organisation within the Party. SS men were not to become involved in intra-Party politicking; they were to distance themselves from the SA, who were increasingly seen as nothing more than rabble-rousers (and on the left wing of the Party at that). They were not allowed to involve themselves in matters that did not concern them; they were to hold themselves ready for the exclusive service of the Führer. The watchword was: 'The SS keeps apart from all quarrels.'[24]

Within a few brief months, under Himmler's leadership – even though he was only serving as Berchtold's deputy – the SS was already becoming an organ for policing the Party. SS men were to report infringements by Party members, they were to take note of the activities of the SA, and they were to instantly report any rival factions within either the Party or the SA. The foundations of a police state were being laid, and Himmler was well on his way to creating a state within a state; an elite body that would one day rival the Nazi Party in authority.

However, in the late 1920s it was still a tiny organisation when compared to the SA. The membership of the SA in the latter 1920s numbered tens of thousands, whilst that of the SS numbered only some 300 men. Yet Himmler had big ambitions for this small body of extremists, and his presence as an important politician within the Nazi Party was about to be felt.

On 6 January 1929 he was at long last appointed Reichsführer, head of the SS. The membership may still have been small, but all the while he had been deputy he had been planning how he could make it the supreme organisation of the Party. It was now time to start recruiting. Within a mere four years he would take its membership to a greatly expanded force of over

50,000 men. By 1931 the numbers were already up to 10,000, and the SS was becoming a force to be reckoned with. It was, however, still relatively insignificant when compared to the SA, which, now under the control of Ernst Röhm, numbered its membership in the hundreds of thousands. Rather than seeing Röhm as a political ally, Himmler perceived his old acquaintance as a rival, although relations between the two men were cordial enough. What Himmler wanted was to take his SS into new territory, to further expand its role. The question was how to do it. Himmler found his answer in June 1931, when a young man who would take the SS into a whole new sphere of influence paid him a visit at his home in Waltrudering.

Ever since the Second World War the name of Reinhard Heydrich has been synonymous with the implementation of the Final Solution. Heydrich was an important personality in Nazi Germany throughout the 1930s and early 1940s until, when serving as Reichsprotector of Bohemia and Moravia, he was assassinated by the Czech resistance in 1942. Himmler would one day make Heydrich the head of Germany's state police and security services, and his importance was such that by the early war years many top men within the Nazi Party regarded the capable if ruthless young man as a possible future leader of Germany.[25] However, the meeting in June 1931 at Waldtrudering was to have immediate consequences for Himmler; it was through his demonic new protégé that the Reichsführer-SS was finally able to consolidate his grip on power.

At this first meeting, arranged through Himmler's old acquaintance in the Party, Baron von Eberstein, the Reichsführer-SS had asked Heydrich how he would go about creating an intelligence department for the SS. He was under the misconception that the twenty-seven-year-old Heydrich had until recently worked for Naval Intelligence, whereas the truth was that he had worked in Naval Communications. However, Heydrich was not daunted. Given a mere twenty minutes to come up with a strategy for the coordination of SS intelligence, he quickly drew up plans; although these were rather sketchy, they greatly exceeded Himmler's knowledge in this sphere. So impressed was Himmler that he immediately entrusted Heydrich with the task of creating the SS's intelligence service.

Himmler was motivated to create his own intelligence network both as a means of bringing intelligence in the Nazi Party to new levels of efficiency and excellence, and so as to consolidate his position within the Party. Both the Party and the SA possessed their own intelligence-gathering departments, crude organisations that kept tabs on the opposition and a lookout for enemy infiltrators. Add to this the intriguing fact that Himmler secretly perceived Röhm's SA itself as a possible future threat to the Party – for this paramilitary organisation with revolutionary tendencies would one day become a rogue elephant that needed taming – and it will be perceived that Himmler was acting to protect both his, and the Party's, interests. Indeed, a member of his SS staff in Munich commented to me,

> We used to call the SA 'Hamburgers': brown on the outside [referring to their brown uniforms], red on the inside [referring to their political tendencies].[26]

Himmler's concern about the growing strength of the SA, and their penchant for attracting the left-wingers of the Party, would increase in intensity in the years ahead until a showdown was inevitable. It was a battle he intended to win, and this meant that he needed his very own efficient intelligence service, one unrivalled in professionalism. To head this new organisation, the Sicherheitsdienst, Himmler chose his new protégé, the very capable Reinhard Heydrich.

On 14 June 1931 Heydrich was inducted into the SS and took the oath of fidelity to the Führer, Adolf Hitler. Within weeks he began to rise through the ranks with dizzying speed, first appointed as Sturmführer (lieutenant) in early August, then, just four months later, as Hauptsturmführer (captain). Twenty days afterwards he was again promoted, this time to Sturmbannführer (major). And all this time, operating out of a two-room flat at 23 Türkenstrasse, Munich, he was actively recruiting men into his new SS intelligence service (men such as the young and newly qualified lawyer Walter Schellenberg), and compiling information on Party members and especially on members of the SA. Himmler was to put this wealth of sensitive information to good use in the years ahead as he assured his place at Hitler's side and consolidated his position as a key politician in the Nazi Party.

It was to be another eighteen months before the Nazi Party gained its first taste of real power, eighteen months of a precarious, seesawing political situation in Germany that seemed alternately about to make or break the Party. Whilst head of the SS, Himmler increasingly found himself playing a political role in easing the Party into power. The SS had by the summer of 1932 reached a membership of 40,000 men, and with its growing size his importance to the Nazi Party had grown proportionately. Now, as well as heading the SS, he possessed a seat in the German parliament, the Reichstag (gained in 1931), and it was a role he relished more and more.

It was at this time that he began to woo German industry and finance, realising that these valuable contacts would be crucial in the years ahead as the Party began to consolidate its grip on the country. By mid-1932 it was becoming increasingly evident to nearly every German that it would be only a matter of time before Hitler and his Nazis, with over 200 seats in the Reichstag, eventually took power. Having arrived at this conclusion, many major industrialists in Germany decided to throw their backing behind the Nazis, as the only 'nationalist', anti-socialist movement capable of saving the country from the worldwide economic depression that had already hit the United States and was showing every sign of biting hard in Germany, too. As a consequence of this fear, large sections of the German nobility and middle classes began to court the Nazi Party, along with a substantial number of top industrialists, who perceived the Nazis as the best hope of maintaining order in Germany and limiting the economic crisis looming on the horizon.

To cement this new initiative, Himmler created the Freundeskreis-RFSS – the Circle of Friends of the Reichsführer-SS. It was an organisation aimed at fostering closer links between German industry and the SS, a group of industrialists who looked favourably upon Himmler as an active liaison between Party and industry. Throughout the 1930s these industrialists would contribute millions of Marks to Party funds. It was to be a relationship highly valued by Himmler, as many leading industrialists joined the ranks of the SS or inducted SS men on to the boards of their companies. Towards the end of the war he would remember his friends in industry, attempting to protect Germany's major industrial players from the inevitable demand for reparations. It was to be the quid pro quo for the assistance German industry and finance had given the Nazis in these early years.

The final months of the Weimar Republic were marked by a great deal of secret negotiation between the Nazi Party and German industry and finance, much of that negotiation being undertaken by Himmler. In the November elections of 1932 the Nazis narrowly missed taking control. Although they had the largest number of seats in the Reichstag, Hitler was passed over for the position of Chancellor (as he had been the previous summer), and it was noted by many that their vote had dropped by two million. The situation was precarious; membership of the Party suddenly showed signs of falling away, and disaffection by Röhm's SA threatened its integrity. What was needed was a political coup to pull Hitler's coals out of the fire. It was at this time that Himmler and his circle of backers provided the vital step that secured Hitler's ascendancy. In the first days of 1933 a secret meeting took place at the home of influential Cologne banker Baron Kurt von Schröder, a member of the Freundeskreis-RFSS and a long-time supporter of the Nazi Party. In the latter 1930s Schröder would become a financial backer of many right-wing European political organisations, such as the Cagoulards in France, in an attempt to bring about a harmonious right-wing Europe. Several meetings between Schröder and Himmler had already taken place during the autumn of 1932, and in January 1933 his role was that of powerbroker between the Nazi Party and the German government as he worked towards placing Hitler in power.

At a secret meeting in Cologne on 4 January 1933 attended by Hitler, Reichsführer-SS Himmler, Nazi Party Deputy Rudolf Hess, and Wilhelm Koppler (a Nazi industrialist who had also been financing Hitler's drive for power), Schröder acted as mediator between the Nazis and Franz von Papen, a high-ranking German politician of long standing who had himself been Chancellor in the autumn of 1932. Papen was empowered to offer Hitler the support of the Rhineland industrialists provided that he, Hitler, agreed to include him in his Cabinet as Vice-Chancellor. In exchange for this agreement, Papen would act as an intermediary to the German President, General von Hindenburg, persuading the eighty-five-year-old statesman that Hitler should be offered the Chancellorship. There was also the matter of the Nazis' approach to government to be negotiated, and in this Hitler was extremely clear about his priorities. He presented a range of policies that would strengthen Germany politically as well as economically, and which would incidentally repay the assistance of the Ruhr industrialists who had helped finance the Party.

The minutes of the discussion between Papen and Hitler reveal agreement in three main areas:

First, Hitler was determined to eradicate Bolshevism from Germany. In answer to Papen's query as to how this was to be done, 'Hitler gave an assurance that communists, social democrats, and Jews would be removed from leading positions in Germany.'[27]

Second was the matter of the revitalisation of German industry following the general downturn in the economy, resulting from the current worldwide Depression. In answer to this, Hitler's plan was twofold and most imaginative. To begin with he had formulated a scheme for the formation of 'employers' associations' – cartels – that would unite industries and strengthen their general position in the German market. In addition, German industry would be stimulated by expanding the economy through government investment; this was to be accomplished by an 'increase [of] the armed forces from 100,000 to 300,000 men, to take in hand the construction of Autobahns, to make credit available to state and local authorities for highway construction, and [to make] government credits available for the aircraft and automobile industries'.[28]

Third, Hitler made it clear to Papen that he was determined to work towards 'the abolition of the Versailles Treaty and the restoration of a militarily strong, economically independent Germany'.[29]

If the Nazi Party had been conceived in the pan-German Thule Society in the early 1920s, this programme reveals that it was finally brought to the altar of power by German industry and high finance, in particular the giant Deutsche Bank, to which Schröder's Cologne Bank was affiliated.[30] And the man who had been instrumental in bringing these two parties together, via his Freundeskreis-RFSS, was Heinrich Himmler, who was now increasingly seen – and particularly by Hitler – as a key player in Nazi politics. Himmler had therefore become, in tandem with his role as Reichsführer-SS, a leading politician of the Nazi Party. The SS had become a tool that he would use time and time again over the coming years to gain political influence over his peers in the Party.

•••••

Tuesday, 30 January 1933 is a date destined to live on in German memory, a date engraved into the German psyche. On that day, less than four weeks after his meeting with Papen at the Cologne home of Kurt von Schröder, Adolf Hitler was finally appointed Chancellor of the German state, and the Nazis' ascendancy was almost complete. The long years of struggle were over for the Nazi Party. They had finally taken power and they had no intention of ever relinquishing that power. The first days of the thousand-year Reich began as the Nazis intended to go on, and within three weeks over 40,000 SA and SS men were sworn in as auxiliary policemen. The seeds of a police state were being planted. However, the Nazis were still in a precarious position. Although they were the largest party, they still did not hold an overall majority in the Reichstag, and so, with the assistance of Himmler's SS intelligence department, the Sicherheitsdienst (SD) run by Reinhard Heydrich, the next stage of the Nazis' premeditated plan for their accession to absolute power was put into effect.

Within a week of the induction of these new recruits into the German police, Heydrich, Himmler's master of Machiavellian plotting, played his hand in the carefully orchestrated game that would see the Nazi Party secure its hold on power.

On the evening of 27 February a red glow could be seen over the rooftops of Berlin. Someone had set the Reichstag on fire. In the immediate aftermath of the event a Dutch Communist named van der Lubbe was conveniently arrested at the scene of the crime. However, the true story of that night's events was somewhat different from that promulgated by the Nazis. Reinhard Heydrich had played a key role in orchestrating an incident that would allow the Nazis to finally move against their most bitter political rivals, the Communists.

Aware that there would be another general election later that spring, on 5 March, Hitler and his minions had no intention of seeing the electorate shy away from giving the Nazi Party an overall majority, one that would make them politically unassailable. It was certain that the Communists would retain at least 100 seats out of the 600 deputies. Hitler controlled some 250 seats. If he could wipe out the critical Communist seats, then he would win his battle for absolute control. Thus he had turned to the SD, ordering them to ensure that the Communists were driven out of German politics for good. The plot had involved Hermann Göring, Prussian Minister of the Interior, and a select band of Heydrich's secret service operatives. They would undertake an act so heinous that the German people would (it was hoped) swing behind the Nazi Party in demanding that these revolutionary Communists be driven from their midst, driven from politics, driven from influence in Germany as a whole. In plotting an act that would allow the Nazis to accomplish this political coup, Heydrich's genius for deception played a masterstroke. His intelligence service, the SD, would attack the very fabric of the German state, something (ironically) symbolic of German democracy and liberty – the parliament itself, the Reichstag.

On the night of 27 February 1933, a select band of SD agents secretly entered the Reichstag through an underground tunnel that connected Göring's official residence to the parliament. Once inside, the incendiarists started a number of fires around the building that ensured it would be devastated. The fires caught quickly and within a short while the building was well and truly ablaze. At the Brandenburg Gate and on both sides of the Spree River a crowd of several thousand Berliners pressed against police barriers. The people looked on in horror as the crackling flames reached high into the night sky.

Hitler arrived at the building at 10.20 p.m. and was met by Rudolf Diels, Chief of Department 1A of the Prussian State Police (the organisation that eventually became the Gestapo) attached to the Ministry of the Interior, and by Hermann Göring.

On meeting Hitler, Göring declared, 'This is a Communist outrage. One of the Communist culprits has been arrested.'[31] Turning to Diels, Göring informed his subordinate, 'This is the beginning of the Communist uprising – they will now let loose the attack. There is no time to lose . . .'

He was cut short by Hitler, who interrupted, shouting, 'Now there will be no mercy! Whoever stands in our way will be cut down . . . Everything connected with the Communists is to be settled.'[32]

Hearing that the police were looking for him, Ernst Torgler, chairman of the Communist bloc in the Reichstag, voluntarily gave himself up. Later that night three Bulgarians – Georgi Dimitrov, Blagoi Popov, and Vassili Tanev – were arrested after a suspicious waiter in a Berlin café informed the police that they had been acting strangely. These men, all Communists, would eventually be put on trial along with van der Lubbe. The proceedings began in September and continued through the autumn until 23 December, with Göring appearing as a key prosecution witness. To the acute embarrassment of the Nazis, Torgler and the three Bulgarians were acquitted. Van der Lubbe was found guilty and executed.

On the morning following the Reichstag fire, Hitler persuaded President Hindenburg to sign a decree 'for the Protection of the People and State'. It was an order that suspended civil liberties and freedom of expression. Across Germany over the next couple of days Communists were arrested and taken into custody. Over the following few weeks some 20,000 Communists were arrested throughout the country and held in prisons and temporary concentration camps. Dr Goebbels, in his capacity as Reichspropagandaleiter der NSDAP (Reich propaganda leader of the Nazi Party), made great capital out of the supposed coup attempt, enabling Hitler to obliterate the Communists in the March elections, and the Nazi Party increased its support by five million votes, raising Hitler's vote to 44 per cent of the votes cast. With the support of a nationalist group in the parliament called the Deutschnationale Volkspartei (the German Nationalist People's Party), headed by Alfred Hugenberg, Hitler had his majority. Within a mere three months Hugenberg's party would be dissolved and its seats taken over by the Nazis.

On 22 March 1933, some seventeen days after Hitler secured his majority in the Reichstag (temporarily set up in the Kroll Opera House),

Himmler opened his first permanent concentration camp a few miles north of Munich, at a disused munitions factory at Dachau. It was the first such establishment in a series that would soon spread menacingly across the country, creating a whole new empire for Himmler and his SS and enabling the Nazi Party to control a nation.

On the following day the Nazis promulgated the 'Law for the Removal of Distress of People and Reich'. Hitler needed a two-thirds majority to make this effective. By the expedient of incarcerating all the Communist deputies of the Reichstag he was able to push it through parliament. For four years this law removed almost all its powers from the German parliament and transferred them to the Cabinet.

Following the success of the Reichstag fire, Himmler's next move was to secure his position as an indispensable source of national security for the Führer. As one part of his strategy to accomplish this, the Reichsführer-SS 'discovered' two secret plots against Hitler's life. The first was supposedly instigated by Count Arco-Valley, who had been arrested for the murder of the Bavarian Prime Minister, Eisner, in 1922. He had subsequently been freed, but Himmler now ordered his preventative arrest. The second, uncovered within weeks, involved three Soviet agents who had allegedly hidden grenades near a roadside statue of Wagner in Berlin passed every morning by Hitler's car. Himmler was not slow to extract the maximum possible publicity for these 'discoveries'. He had, after all, been Deputy Propaganda Leader in the past, and knew how to court the press. He accordingly released the details, complete with a warning that 'Information from Swiss sources leads us to fear French attempts on [the life of] the Chancellor of the Reich and other eminent persons.'[33] He knew he was touching a sensitive chord; during this period Hitler lived in constant fear of being assassinated.

To make his domain complete Himmler now wanted to take over the State Secret Police, the Gestapo – currently the possession of the Prussian Interior Minister, Göring – as well as obtaining control of the entire Reich police. (At that time each German state – Bavaria, Prussia, Thuringia, etc. – possessed its own independent police force.) Well aware of his objectives, Göring was resisting all moves by the Reichsführer-SS to encroach on what he saw as his own territory. And Himmler did not immediately succeed. In response to the threats on his life, Hitler merely asked him to form a special guard of SS for his personal security under the command of SS General Joseph 'Sepp' Dietrich. And so was formed the Führer's personal bodyguard, christened the Leibstandarte-SS Adolf Hitler.

But Himmler was not to be denied his prize of complete control of the police and Gestapo, which he astutely realised could be the key to real power in the Reich. With characteristic tenacity, he soon found himself a political ally in the form of Wilhelm Frick, the Reich Minister of the Interior. Frick wanted to reform the administration of Germany, carrying the centralisation of government to its limit. However, he had come into collision with Göring, who wished to maintain Prussian separatism. Determined not to be defeated by Göring, he made a political alliance with Himmler. In return for Himmler's support for his policy of centralisation, he would support Himmler's campaign for the unification of the separate police forces. One by one the individual states' police – the Länderpolizei – fell under Himmler's control.

In the autumn of 1933 Frick succeeded in convincing Hitler that the total centralisation and unification of the Reich was essential. Eventually Göring bowed to the Führer's decision, and Prussia was incorporated into the rest of the Reich. As a direct result the Gestapo passed into Himmler's control in early April 1934. Thus Himmler had finally achieved one of his key objectives. He was chief of the police and State Secret Police of the Third Reich. His next objective was to make the SS the supreme force in Nazi Germany, and he would not be able to do that until he had emasculated the might of the SA.

•••••

The date was Thursday, 28 June 1934. Hitler had been in power for eighteen months and the Nazis reigned supreme. Throughout the country the order had gone out that the nation's flags were to fly at half mast in remembrance of the humiliating episode of German history in 1919 when the German Chancellor, Erzberger, had signed the Treaty of Versailles, accepting the Allied Diktat imposed on Germany after the First World War. That had been fifteen years before to the day, and the Nazis were not about to miss a propaganda coup of such magnitude.

At Berlin's prestigious new airport, the Tempelhof, it was raining heavily as Hitler and Göring passed the honour guard of SS on their way to the Führer's personal three-engined Junkers 52. Hitler would be away from Berlin for the next few days. First, he was to attend the wedding of the Gauleiter of the Rhineland, Joseph Terboven, in Essen, and then hc had other business to attend to; business that was the most closely kept secret of the Reich, but would captivate the world's press in a mere forty-eight hours. Himmler, the arch-conspirator and consummate politician, was about to settle old scores and finally consolidate his position at Hitler's right hand.

With the accession of the Nazis to power in January 1933, the political clout of Ernst Röhm and the influence of his SA had grown enormously. They were the vanguard of the Party, the army of militant Party workers who infiltrated every aspect of German life in order to enforce the message of National Socialism. They had been the tireless revolutionary activists of the Nazi Party during its rise, and Hitler had relied heavily on them to infect the nation with a fever of political awareness. Now, in the early summer of 1934, the SA numbered in excess of four million, and received three million Marks a month from the state for salaries, uniforms, and arms. It was truly a force to be reckoned with, and woe betide anyone who meddled in its affairs.

Throughout the spring of 1934 Röhm had been pressing Hitler to expand the influence of the SA still further. Now that the Nazis were in power, it had largely lost its raison d'être as a revolutionary organisation. However, Röhm had a remedy. He wanted to give the SA a new purpose, one that would, incidentally, expand his own authority as a Nazi statesman enormously. He proposed that the Reichswehr – Germany's standing army of 100,000 men (as limited under the Treaty of Versailles) – be amalgamated with the paramilitary wing of the SA, which numbered nearly 800,000. Not unnaturally the German Army Chiefs of Staff heard this news with alarm. Were Röhm and his rough-necked band of hard-drinking, noisome revolutionaries – and on the left wing of the Nazi Party at that – going to become the central core of Germany's new army? The Chiefs of Staff, including the Minister of Defence, General von Blomberg (long an enthusiastic Nazi supporter) balked at the notion. They were, however, not alone in being disconcerted by Röhm's demand, and they had a very powerful ally from a surprising quarter who would oppose the idea. Hitler himself was not at all amenable to granting Röhm's wish, and he was becoming increasingly concerned by the growing strength of the SA. He had made his own private arrangements with the heads of the German Army that had helped ease him into power. He had also made it clear both to the Chiefs of Staff and to Blomberg that he intended to break the Treaty of Versailles with respect to the limits placed on the size of the Army, and aimed to restore its status as a first-class European military force. These were plans that involved neither Röhm nor the SA.

Himmler now saw a chink in Röhm's armour. As a leading right-winger, he, too, had become concerned by the inexorable increase in the SA's influence. More than that, he saw it as a revolutionary left-wing force that might one day impose its will upon the Party through sheer weight of numbers and influence. The time had come, he decided, to topple Röhm and the SA, whilst at the same time eradicating the left-wingers of the Party. This would have the double advantage of reinforcing his vision of a right-wing National Socialist Germany, whilst at the same time consolidating his political position at Hitler's side and making the SS the primary organ of the Nazi Party. It was time for the forces of Black to triumph over those of Brown.

However, Ernst Röhm, unaware of the growing intrigue against him, had his own powerful allies. The first of these was left-winger Gregor Strasser. In December 1932 the Strasser–Hitler relationship had irrevocably broken down when Hitler accused Strasser of trying to cheat him of the Chancellorship and seeking to split the Nazi Party. Strasser had countered that, on the contrary, he had sought only to save the Party. In a monumental huff he had resigned his place in its leadership and taken himself off into industry, becoming chairman of the Pharmacology Industry Association.[34] However, Strasser had neither forgotten nor forgiven his bruising encounter with Hitler, and he soon became a central figure in Röhm's search for allies, with whom he hoped to enforce his influence over Hitler.

The second of Röhm's political allies was a little more surprising. He was General Kurt von Schleicher, the last Chancellor of the Weimar Republic, who had ruled Germany in the final weeks before Hitler took over. In wooing Schleicher and Strasser, Ernst Röhm exhibited a great deal more political acumen than history has subsequently credited him with. Röhm was of the mind that the SA should maintain its revolutionary background, and that his organisation should be amalgamated with the Reichswehr to form Germany's new, politically aware, army, which would then number close to a million men. It is not clear whether Schleicher and Strasser supported Röhm's big idea for restoring the fortunes of the SA, but they did look upon an alliance with him as their first step to usurping Hitler's authority by uniting the leftist 'Strasser-wing' of the Nazi Party with the moderate wing of the trade unions. Hitler intended to obliterate the unions, having done a deal with Germany's major industrial concerns through Himmler's Freundeskreis-RFSS. General von Schleicher also harboured a desire to restore a form of democracy to Germany's parliament by relegating Hitler's position as Chancellor to that of a figurehead, and taking the post of Vice-Chancellor on himself in Papen's place (a position that would henceforth hold the real reins of power). For their assistance in this, Strasser would be given the Economics Ministry, and Röhm would become Germany's Minister of Defence.

All Röhm's machinations were, of course, destined to bring him and Hitler into direct collision, for none other than Reinhard Heydrich, through his network of SD informers and intelligence agents, had infiltrated the scheme and informed his superior. For his part Himmler was not about to miss an opportunity like this to emerge victorious as the head of Hitler's sole security service along with his unquestioningly loyal organisation, the SS. Himmler and Heydrich therefore dreamed up a scheme that would both destroy Röhm and break the power of the SA for ever.

Throughout the late spring of 1934 Himmler and Heydrich had been busy plotting, feeding false information to Hitler that Röhm and the SA were preparing for a putsch to oust him and the other leading Nazis, and install a revolutionary government in Berlin. This situation was a cause of considerable concern, indeed anger, to Hitler. He greatly feared that the SA had the numbers to carry out such a scheme; after all, the country was saturated by the SA, which now numbered over four million men, nearly 800,000 of whom were armed paramilitaries. Against them stood Germany's meagre standing army, the Reichswehr, consisting of just 100,000 men. It was a situation that might spell disaster for Hitler's vision of a National Socialist Germany, should Röhm feel confident enough to carry out such a coup.

In concocting the lie that Röhm was preparing for a putsch, Himmler and Heydrich were most convincing, and the Reichsführer-SS was not beyond making his own political alliances to ensure that he successfully brought Röhm and his reactionary left-wingers crashing down. He had therefore made common cause with his former foe in the Party, Hermann Göring, and together the two convinced Hitler that Röhm was indeed planning an imminent coup, destined to take place that summer.

In the first week of June, Hitler and Röhm met for a discussion. It lasted five hours, and again Röhm petitioned for the amalgamation of the Reichswehr and the SA paramilitaries under his leadership. Hitler, by now anxious, gave Röhm the impression that he would make a decision in his favour against 'the gentlemen with uniforms and monocles' and that such a decision would be made in September. Confident that he would get what he wanted, Röhm ordered his SA leaders to take their annual leave in the remainder of June; as for the lower ranks, 'July will be a period of complete

relaxation in which they can recover their strength.'[35] However, he then
unwisely issued a public statement that served only to convince Hitler of
the danger posed by the SA:

> If the enemies of the SA delude themselves with the hope that
> the SA will not report back for duty after their leave . . . they will
> receive a fitting answer at the time and in the form which appears
> necessary. The SA is and will remain Germany's destiny.[36]

Himmler's right-wing clique was still growing, and by now the
Propaganda Minister, Joseph Goebbels, his old friend from the early days
of the Party, had joined Göring in supporting him. The three men started
to draw up a list of left-wingers – called the 'Reichsliste of Unwanted
Persons' – who were to be purged at the same time as the leadership of the
SA. The victory of the Right would not be compromised by old loyalties or
friendship; it would be an ideal opportunity for settling accounts with
enemies as well.

On Monday, 25 June, Hitler ordered the Reichswehr to be secretly
placed on a state of alert. All leave was to be cancelled until further notice
and the troops confined to barracks. In Berlin, Himmler summoned his SS
and SD commanders to a top-secret conference. Here, for the first time,
he briefed his subordinates on the impending danger to the National
Socialist revolution. He informed them about the SA's treachery, and
outlined his comprehensive plans for sabotaging the putsch before it could
take place by launching a preemptive strike to take out the SA leadership,
coupled with the arrest and execution of all those politicians who were in
on Röhm's plot. The clock was ticking inexorably towards a decisive day for
the Party, one that would see Himmler eliminate his biggest rivals.

And so the weekend of 30 June–1 July approached. By now utterly
convinced of the imminence of a Röhm-led putsch, Hitler had left Berlin
for Essen on Thursday, 28 June to attend Terboven's wedding. He was
accompanied by Himmler's partner in deceit, Hermann Göring, who would
ensure that Hitler would have no sudden qualms of conscience about
disposing of his long-time political partner. After the wedding, Hitler paid
a visit to Baron Krupp von Bohlen before going on to the Hotel Kaiserhof,
where he was to spend the night. Here Göring was awaiting him, and in his
hand were numerous messages from Himmler in Berlin. Himmler and
Heydrich had been busy:

the dispatches all stressed the preparation for the SA putsch, some brought details of the armament of such and such assault sections. One of them confirmed that the SA would direct its action against the Reichswehr and gave the list of generals who were to be killed. Another message, the last, gave the date of the putsch; Saturday June 30th, and the time five o'clock in the afternoon. Hitler said nothing but he was pale.[37]

For Hitler it was a time of indecision. What to do? He paced the main reception room of the hotel, which had been turned into his office. A little while later he received a telephone call from Himmler, who informed him that the SA in Cologne had assaulted a foreign diplomat. Hitler was at last angry enough to act. Turning to Göring, he said, 'I've had enough . . . These lunatics must be arrested. Go back to Berlin. Judge the situation and call me before taking action.'

Göring understood that the fruit was ripe, and left content.

That evening Hitler telephoned Röhm at the Hotel Hanselbauer, on the shores of Lake Tegern near Munich, where he was holidaying in the company of other SA leaders. He informed Röhm of his decision to clarify the SA–Reichswehr situation, and ordered him to convene a meeting of SA leaders at the hotel on the following Saturday, 30 June, now just thirty-six hours away. He would arrive at 11.00 a.m. Röhm put the receiver down, almost certainly confident that he had gained the upper hand with Hitler, and that the meeting was to discuss not only the amalgamation of the SA paramilitaries and Reichswehr but also the introduction of leading SA men and members of the left wing of the Party into the government. It was to be a fatal underestimation of Himmler's will to see the right wing of National Socialism prevail against the reactionary forces of the SA, which echoed the words of Papen only the week before: 'Have we experienced an anti-Marxist revolution in order to put through a Marxist programme?'[38]

On the following day, whilst Himmler and his SS leaders in Berlin were making their preparations, Hitler visited a series of work camps in Westphalia, but as the enormous crowds shouted 'Sieg Heil!' and 'Heil Hitler!' the Führer seemed not to notice. He was preoccupied. That afternoon he and his entourage installed themselves in the Hotel Dreesen near Bonn. Here he continued to receive dispatches from Himmler and Göring in Berlin emphasising the growing 'nervousness of the SA, [and] its warlike preparations'. Walter Schellenberg, present with Hitler in Bonn, would later recall that 'Throughout the whole day strange and disquieting rumours reached my SS unit. They pictured a plot, divisions in the Party leadership, imminent catastrophe and radical decisions by the Führer.'[39]

That evening Hitler held a conference at the Hotel Dreesen with a select band of trusted colleagues. One of these was a new arrival direct from Berlin: the third man in Himmler's triumvirate of conspiracy, Dr Joseph Goebbels. Outside, a terrible thunderstorm descended on the countryside. Flashes of lightning zigzagged across the sky, illuminating the scene with a strange and sinister light; the valley resounded with the fury of the storm that poured down cataracts lashed by insane gusts of wind. Schellenberg remembered that 'From time to time the Führer approached the window where I was standing and watched the storm, his eyes lost in a reverie. It was obvious that he was overwhelmed by the weight of the grave and difficult decision to be taken.'[40] Returning to the conference, Hitler's conversation with Goebbels became most animated, ever more so as the Führer's aide brought in a succession of messages from Himmler that detailed the SA's increasing preparations for their putsch. Then, braving the height of the storm, a motorcycle dispatch rider arrived, bringing an urgent message direct from Göring: SA General Karl Ernst had placed his men in Berlin on alert. Wordlessly Hitler handed the message to Goebbels. The conference continued. Little by little, as the hours ticked by, Hitler was worn down by Goebbels's argument that now was the time to act, before it was too late.

Later that night, at 2.00 a.m., Hitler and his entourage boarded two Junkers 52s and departed Bonn for Munich. Earlier that evening Hitler had ordered the loyal head of the Leibstandarte-SS, Sepp Dietrich, to fly on ahead with a detachment of his men. They were to wait until he arrived. Landing at Munich's Oberwiesenfeld airfield at 4.00 a.m., Hitler quickly left his plane and went directly 'in long strides to the waiting cars . . . Far behind because of his awkward limp, Dr Goebbels tried to catch him up.' As he approached his car, Hitler noticed an army lorry waiting, a company of Reichswehr soldiers seated within it. Acutely aware of the critical dangers of the course of action he was determined upon, that a battle between the SA and the Nazi Party – especially if the SA were allowed to launch their putsch – could plunge the country into a terrible civil war, Hitler immediately approached the commander and said quietly, but firmly, 'You will thank General Adam for the military protection he is offering me. But the Reichswehr must remain totally apart from what is happening and will happen. It is not to be involved in it. I insist: it is not to be involved . . .'[41]

Hitler and his entourage then journeyed into central Munich, where he was assured by the Gauleiter, Adolf Wagner, that for the moment at least there were no signs of an uprising in the city. Satisfied that he was still able to take the initiative, Hitler had the two SA leaders in Munich, Generals Schneidhuber and Schmidt, arrested. Leaving orders with Wagner that any SA officers arriving at the railway station were also to be arrested, Hitler and a small entourage of loyal followers set off for the Hotel Hanselbauer, followed by three taxis containing his SS guard. Half an hour later the little convoy arrived at Bad Wiessee, a small village on the shore of Lake Tegern near the hotel. Here, at the last bend in the road before the hotel, a lorry waited, containing the detachment of the Leibstandarte-SS and their commander. Without stopping, the convoy continued and the lorry followed behind. It was time for Hitler's showdown with Ernst Röhm.

Arriving at the Hanselbauer a little after 6.30 a.m., its shutters still closed after the night, Dietrich ordered his SS detachment to surround the building. Hitler went directly to the front door supported by his own SS guard. He gave the signal, and the door was kicked open.

Goebbels was later to record that 'Without encountering resistance, we were able to enter the house and surprise the gang of conspirators still sunk in sleep and put them under immediate arrest. It was the Führer himself who did the arresting.'[42]

After barging into a number of rooms to arrest the occupants, several of whom were found in bed entwined with their chauffeurs or aides, Hitler's sense of offended decorum turned to rage by the time he found Röhm's door.

Hitler drummed his fists against the wood, shouting, 'Open!'

Röhm's drowsy voice was heard from within, asking, 'Who is it?'

'Me. Adolf,' Hitler shouted. 'Open!'

'What, you already?' Röhm exclaimed. 'You're already here? I didn't expect you till noon.'

'Open!' Hitler shouted again.

The door opened and Röhm appeared, massive, naked except for his pyjama trousers. His face was red and swollen from sleep, seamed by the prominent scar that dissected his face from nose to chin; his eyes questioning and surprised.

Full of rage, Hitler shouted a stream of insults at his old comrade, who remained dumb and still only partially awake. Eventually Röhm tried to protest, but Hitler pushed him into the room and slammed the door behind him. Those on the outside never discovered what passed between the two men, but they could hear the pair shouting at each other well enough. Suddenly the door opened and Hitler swept out. In rage he shouted at the men waiting outside, 'This swine is lacking in respect for me. Arrest him at once!'[43]

In the doorway an extremely puzzled Röhm stood scratching his head. He did not understand what was taking place. Two SS men took hold of him. The operation to capture the head of the SA was over, and Hitler and his captives returned to Munich.

In Munich the leaders of the SA had started to arrive at the railway station, only to be arrested by the Gestapo and carted off to Stadelheim prison, where members of the Leibstandarte-SS herded them into cells. Later that morning Rudolf Hess arrived from Berlin and joined Hitler at the Party headquarters, the Brown House.

That very afternoon the bloody suppression of the SA began. At Stadelheim prison its leaders were led out one by one into the courtyard and shot by firing squad. First to die was General Schneidhuber, still completely ignorant of what he had been accused of. Numerous others quickly followed throughout the afternoon. From generals to mere lieutenants, all were purged in a bloodletting that would eradicate the power of the SA for ever. At the Brown House, Hess inquired about Röhm's fate.

'I have reprieved Röhm by reason of past services,' Hitler answered, still unwilling to turn completely against his former friend and political ally.

In Berlin, Himmler and Göring were directing the operation from Göring's palace on Leipzigerplatz. With cold and calculating efficiency they referred to their list, the 'Reichsliste of Unwanted Persons', and dispatched teams of SS and Gestapo across the city to arrest or execute the unfortunates who had fallen foul of them. It was not only the leading men of the SA who were the targets, for Himmler, Göring, and Goebbels had drawn up a comprehensive list of all those they deemed a threat to their vision of National Socialism. Thus, for example, Göring summoned SS Captain Gildisch and simply said to him, 'Find Eric Klausener, President of Catholic Action, and finish him off.'[44] Gildisch departed and Klausener was duly killed.

Throughout the day, whilst liveried footmen brought in refreshments to the men in Göring's office, SS and Gestapo officers delivered little slips of white paper bearing the names of those who had been arrested and taken to the holding centre at Lichterfelde. After briefly studying each one, Göring gave his verdict: 'To be shot . . . to be shot . . . to be shot . . .'

Hans-Bernd Gisevius, an official at the Prussian Interior Ministry, was later to recall the scene in Göring's office as an 'evil atmosphere of hate . . . I breathed an air of tension, civil war and especially blood, a great deal of blood. On all faces, from the sentinels' to that of the lowest orderly, could be read that terrible things were happening.'[45]

It was true: across the city terrible things were happening. Amongst the slaughtered were Councillor von Bose, the chef-de-cabinet of Vice-Chancellor von Papen, and General von Bredow, former head of the Abwehr. Another of Papen's advisors, Edgar Jung, and Colonel von Detten, a flying ace of the First World War, were also murdered. Nor were those of Germany's top politicians who had affiliated themselves to Röhm forgotten by Himmler and Göring. General von Schleicher and his wife were shot in their home, and soon a much bigger prize was apprehended. Himmler's former patron, Gregor Strasser, was seized lunching at home with his wife and twins, whose godfather was none other than Adolf Hitler. He was dragged away by Gestapo officers to their headquarters at 8 Prinz Albrechtstrasse and thrown into a cell. Here he remained for some three hours wondering what was happening. Then he discerned a shadow behind a small sliding window that overlooked an internal corridor. A shot sounded, hitting the wall near his head. Instinctively Strasser threw himself across the room out of the line of fire, but a second shot caught him in the shoulder, throwing him back on to the bed. Two more shots hit him in the stomach and thigh. He lay there bleeding for hours until an SS man eventually entered the cell and finished him off.

Throughout the rest of the day, whilst Hitler was distanced from the centre of control, the bloodbath across Germany continued, as Himmler and Göring eradicated all those who posed a political threat to them or might prove an inconvenience in years to come. Even the SS were not immune from the killings. SS chief Anton, Baron of Hohberg and Buchwald, whom Himmler disliked, died in a hail of bullets, as did Gustav von Kahr, former head of the Bavarian government who had played a conspicuous part in assisting Hitler's 1923 Munich putsch. 'The Night of the Long Knives', as it was soon to become known, seemed to go on without end, and all the while in Berlin Himmler and Göring continued to issue their orders: 'To be shot . . . to be shot . . .'

Having secured Munich from the nonexistent Röhm putsch, Hitler eventually departed for Berlin in the late afternoon. When he arrived at Tempelhof airport an SS guard of honour awaited him, as well as several members of the government, including Göring and Himmler. Hans Gisevius was later to record that 'Hitler got out first. Everything about him was sombre: brown shirt, black tie, leather coat, high regulation boots. His head was bare, his face dead white . . . his eyes blank, looking straight ahead.' He exchanged salutes with his entourage, and whilst the other passengers disembarked from the plane, 'moved painfully, with heavy steps, from one puddle to another. One had the impression he was going to sink in.'

Finally he reached Himmler and Göring. The three men exchanged a few words, then Himmler drew from his pocket a long list. He handed it to Hitler, who began to study it. 'One could see Hitler following the reading with his finger, lingering from time to time over a name. The whispering became more animated. Suddenly he threw his head back with a gesture of such deep emotion, not to say rebellion, that all present noticed it . . . They [Himmler and Göring] had just informed him of Gregor Strasser's "suicide".'[46]

With the Führer back in Berlin, the killing spree lost its intensity, but still the purge of the SA and the Left continued, the majority now being arrested and held in prison to await their fate. That night Himmler, Göring, and Heydrich gathered in Göring's office at the palace on Leipzigerplatz. They had a problem. Hitler had balked at ordering Röhm's execution. He had to be persuaded to turn away from his old comrade-in-arms. Himmler and Göring had come too far in asserting the supremacy of the Right over the Left to leave Röhm alive. If Hitler were to give him a free pardon, he would become a very dangerous if not fatal enemy in the future. The conclusion of the three men, reached late on Saturday night, was simple: Röhm had to die, and the Führer had to be persuaded to issue the order.

On the following morning, Sunday, 1 July, at the Reich Chancellery, Himmler and Göring strove to convince Hitler of Röhm's treachery. The meeting lasted for hours, Himmler taking the lead in insisting that Röhm had to pay the ultimate price for his treacherous plans to usurp power in Germany from the NSDAP (Nationalsozialistische Deutsche Arbeiterpartei) to the SA; had not his intelligence service, the SD, uncovered so much of the plot that it was evidence enough of Röhm's treason? Yet still Hitler prevaricated, citing the past years, the services rendered. What new arguments did Himmler and Göring advance to make Hitler yield, step by step? They remain unknown, but a little before 1.00 p.m. they won.[47] Hitler finally agreed to Röhm's execution.

At 2.30 p.m., in Munich's Stadelheim prison, Röhm was sitting in cell 474, still naked except for his pyjama trousers. The door opened and two SS generals entered. They handed him a pistol loaded with a single bullet, and a copy of the *Völkischer Beobachter*, which announced his disgrace and removal from office. One of the officers told him, 'You have ruined your life, but the Führer has not forgotten his old companion in arms. He is giving you a chance to draw the necessary conclusions. You have ten minutes.'[48]

Ten minutes passed, then fifteen, and still no sound of a shot. Eventually the SS men felt compelled to act. They barged into the cell to find Röhm standing, paper in hand, still not fully comprehending what had happened. The first officer, SS General Lippert, fired two shots, and Röhm fell to the floor, stammering, 'Mein Führer, mein Führer!' SS General Eicke then delivered the *coup de grâce*.

That afternoon, back in Berlin, Hitler was committed to a long-standing engagement – a tea party in the Reich Chancellery garden for foreign diplomats and high dignitaries of the Party. Hans Gisevius would later record that 'I understood at that moment how much the man was on edge that day . . . he was trying to escape from his inner trouble by taking refuge in the pose which from then on became his most efficient weapon.'[49]

In the midst of the party, surrounded by diplomats, elegant women, and Party dignitaries, Himmler did not look in the least troubled. He had carried off the most audacious and successful political coup of his career, and in so doing had ensured his position of authority. Towards the late afternoon an SS officer handed Hitler a message from Munich. It was from Wagner, who informed the Führer that Röhm had refused to commit suicide and had been shot. They were, at this moment, disposing of his body at a local crematorium. 'Hitler turned very pale. He put the message in his pocket and a few minutes later withdrew to his private apartment in the Chancellery.'[50] He had just lost an old and valuable ally to Himmler's machinations.

Later that night Hitler finally stepped in and ordered Himmler to stop the executions. The purge was to end. On Monday morning the Führer appointed SA General Viktor Lutze (an old ally of Himmler, hence he survived) to Röhm's now-vacated post of SA Chief of Staff, and issued an order to the remaining SA demanding of them 'the most perfect discipline, loyalty and fidelity without reserve to the Reich'. Over the summer membership of the SA was reduced by 75 per cent to a little more than a million men, and the paramilitary wing of 800,000 were disarmed and disbanded. No one has ever been able to establish clearly the exact number killed during the purge. Hitler put it at seventy-seven, but it is believed the number may have actually been as high as five hundred.[51]

SS-Obersturmführer Karl Neuer was later to comment to me that 'We members of Himmler's personal staff felt a great sense of satisfaction. For years the SA leadership had looked down on the SS as the junior partners of N[ational] S[ocialism]. Then, with one fell swoop, the Reichsführer changed the SS's fortunes completely. Now we were the elite of the Party, the Führer's bodyguard, the security of the Reich, and Himmler took his rightful place at Hitler's side as one of the leading politicians of Germany.'[52]

Neuer was correct. Himmler's victory was complete: he had used his experience as a politician to make a series of complex alliances with the other leading men of the Reich whom he perceived as supporting his cause – Hermann Göring and Dr Joseph Goebbels – and then, with this alliance in place, he had struck. Over the course of a single weekend he had used the machinery of the SS and SD to shatter the SA and eliminate not only the left wing of the Party, but also his greatest rival, Ernst Röhm. He had secured the position of the SS as a primary organ of the Nazi Party, and a place for himself at Hitler's right hand as a leading politician of the Third Reich. The forces of Black had truly triumphed over those of Brown.

•••••

Throughout the remaining years of the 1930s Himmler's authority as a politician continued to grow, and with him also rose the fortunes of the SS. Within three weeks of the Night of the Long Knives, Hitler rewarded the SS's loyalty to the Party in the face of the (nonexistent) Röhm putsch by raising its stature to independence. It was no longer to be affiliated to the SA, but was to be an independent organ responsible only to Hitler himself. It was now the security wing of the Party, charged not only with the task of protecting the Führer, but also with serving as the elite Nazi organisation that would defend the integrity of a National Socialist Germany against any opposition or insurrection. By the autumn of 1934 Himmler's hand was to be further strengthened when Hitler authorised the formation of the Verfügungstruppe-SS (renamed the Waffen-SS in 1940), to be trained on military lines and destined to become a primary organ of the German Army: a politically aware military force of Nazi elite, loyal to Führer and Fatherland.

Himmler's role as a politician likewise increased; his alliance with Hermann Göring and Joseph Goebbels was of great value to him, and the three men formed a powerful right-wing bloc. Their triumvirate of influence would ensure that policy-making would always take the lead from them, and not generally from the lesser men who had formed their own alliances: men such as Schacht, Hess, and Ribbentrop, who represented a more liberal view. In addition, since Himmler, Göring, and Goebbels were at the apex of power, they were naturally able to sway Hitler to a substantial degree; their influence was considerable and they almost always had the support of the most important man in the Reich, the Führer himself.

As a direct consequence of the SS's role as protectors of the Reich, the weeders-out of undesirables, Himmler's realm of the concentration camps also grew. To begin with, the camps were conceived as places to hold political undesirables (opponents of the Nazi regime such as Communists, Social Democrats, etc.), but very soon the scope of incarceration was expanded greatly to encompass criminals, trade unionists, homosexuals, social undesirables, and Jews (though the mass deportations of Jews to the camps did not start until several years into the war). It became the ultimate tool of a police state for controlling those citizens who were less than enthusiastic about the National Socialist revolution sweeping the nation.

Himmler also continued to gain much influence through his Freundeskreis-RFSS. By the latter 1930s he was recruiting many important Germans to the elite order, and soon blue-blooded aristocrats were eager to become members of the SS: the Grand Duke of Mecklenburg, Prince zu Waldeck und Pyrmont, Prinz Christof and Prinz Wilhelm of Hesse, Count Bassewitz-Behr, Count von der Schulenberg, and Prinz Maximillian von Hohenzollern-Emden. All these men were subservient to their master, the Reichsführer-SS, Heinrich Himmler.

In those last years of peace before the outbreak of the Second World War, Himmler was riding high. He was supported by a loyal clique of important men for whom the Black Order was everything, their leader the high priest of an elite within the world of National Socialism. It was an ethnically German world that was growing not only in importance but also in size, as Nazi Germany progressively swallowed Austria, the Sudetenland, and Czechoslovakia into the Reich. However, it was also a world that was tipping precariously towards conflict, as Hitler time and again took Europe to the brink of war to attain his objectives. Himmler astutely realised that in the times to come it would take a very remarkable man indeed to make sure that National Socialism did not deviate from its objective of creating an ethnically superior Germany. He hoped that man would be himself.

NOTES

1. Interview with Emil Klein, Munich, Germany, 24 November 2003.
2. *International Military Tribunal*, Vol. XXIX, p. 1919-PS – Himmler's speech in Poznan, 4 October 1943.
3. Walter Dornberger, *V2 – Der Schuss ins Weltall* (Bechtle Verlag, 1952), pp. 172–73.
4. Ibid.
5. W. Frischauer, *Himmler: The Evil Genius of the Third Reich* (Odhams, 1953), p. 16.
6. G.W.F. Hallgarten, 'Mein Mitschuler Heinrich Himmler', *Germania Judaica, Bulletin der Koelner Bibliothek zur Geschichte des deutschen Judentum* No. 2, 1960–1, p. 4.
7. Ibid., p. 6.
8. Heinrich Himmler's diary, 23 August 1914, The Hoover Institute, Stanford University.
9. Ibid., 28 September 1914.
10. Himmler letter, 29 November 1918, Roll 98, piece 2. Himmler Documents, Hoover Institution on War, Revolution and Peace, Stanford University, California, USA.
11. Martin Allen, *The Hitler/Hess Deception* (HarperCollins, 2003), p. 4.
12. Professor Gebhardt's evidence, *Doctors' Trial*, Nuremberg, Vol. IX, p. 3958.
13. Heinrich Himmler's booklist, Number 47, Bundesarchiv, Koblenz.
14. Ibid., Number 51, Bundesarchiv, Koblenz.
15. Wolf-Rüdiger Hess, *Rudolf Hess: Briefe 1908–1933* (Langen Muller, 1987), p. 310.
16. *The Times*, 12 December 1923.
17. Allen, op. cit., pp. 65–66.
18. The Himmler Papers, Microfilm Archive, Munich, 13 June 1924: T-175, Roll 99, Frames 2620053 and 2620049.
19. Peter Padfield, *Himmler, Reichsfuhrer-SS* (Cassell, 2001), p. 72.
20. Interview by R. Kistler, 22 August 1924: Roll 98, Folder 1. Himmler Documents, Hoover Institute On War, Revolution and Peace, Stanford University.
21. Otto Strasser, *Mein Kampf: Eine politische Autobiographie* (H. Heine, 1969), p. 15.
22. Knrt Ludecke, *I Knew Hitler* (Jarrold, 1938), p. 259.
23. B.F. Smith, *Heinrich Himmler: A Nazi in the Making, 1900–1926* (Hoover Institute Press, USA, 1971), p. 52.
24. Order No 1, 13 September 1927, Document Centre, Berlin. Cited in S. Aronson, *Reinhard Heydrich und die Fruhgeschichte von Gestapo und SD* (Deutsche Verlag, 1971), p. 48.
25. Louis L. Snyder, *Encyclopedia of the Third Reich* (Wordsworth Editions, 1998), p. 144.
26. Interview with Karl Neuer, Telfs, Austria, 23 December 2003.
27. K. Grossweiler, *Die Röhm Affäre* (Rugenstein, 1983), p. 295.
28. Ibid.
29. Ibid., pp. 205–6.
30. Padfield, op. cit., p. 119.

31. Douglas Reed, *The Burning of the Reichstag* (Covici-Friede, 1978), p. 222.
32. Grossweiler, op. cit., p. 16.
33. André Brissaud, *Histoire du Service Secret Nazi* (Plon, 1972), p. 35.
34. Gregor Strasser, *Mein Kampf* (Heine Verlag, 1969), pp. 212–14.
35. J. Noakes and G. Pridlam (eds), *Documents on Nazism* (Jonathan Cape, 1974), p. 208.
36. Grossweiler, op. cit., p. 451.
37. Brissaud, op. cit., p. 53.
38. Grossweiler, op. cit., p. 439.
39. Brissaud, op. cit., p. 55.
40. Ibid., p. 55.
41. Ibid., p. 60.
42. Ibid., p. 61.
43. Ibid., pp. 62–63.
44. Ibid., p. 64.
45. H.-B. Gisevius, *To the Bitter End* (Houghton Mifflin, 1947), pp. 144–45.
46. Ibid., p. 151; cited Brissaud, op. cit., p. 67.
47. Brissaud, op. cit., p. 68.
48. Evidence of Sepp Dietrich, *Agence France Presse*, 15 May 1957.
49. Gisevius, op. cit., p. 147.
50. Ibid.
51. Brissaud, op. cit., p. 66.
52. Interview with Karl Neuer, Telfs, Austria, 23 December 2003.

2

VENLO, HIMMLER'S FIRST EXPLOIT IN PEACE NEGOTIATIONS

'AGGRESSORS ATTACK GLEIWITZ RADIO', blared the headlines of the Nazi Party mouthpiece, the *Völkischer Beobachter*, on 1 September 1939. The newspaper went on to report that 'A group of Polish soldiers seized the Gleiwitz Radio building last night a little before eight. Only a few of the staff were on duty at that hour. It is obvious that the Polish assailants knew the ground perfectly. They attacked the personnel and broke into the studio, knocking out those they encountered on the way . . .'[1]

Such were the overtures that heralded the start of the Second World War, for as the paper was hitting the streets of Berlin, Munich, Hamburg, and every other major city in Germany, all along the German–Polish frontier massed formations of Hitler's newly restored armies were pouring into Poland in retaliation for the country's unwarranted incursions into German territory. However, it was typical of Hitler's mendacious nature that the Second World War would begin with a lie, for the 'Polish assailants' on the Gleiwitz radio station the night before had in fact been Germans dressed as Poles. The whole event had been a carefully choreographed incident undertaken by men of the SD under Reinhard Heydrich's command, and code-named 'Operation Himmler'.

Operation Himmler was a defining moment in the history of National Socialism. It was both an end and a beginning – an end of the appeasement of the 1930s, and the start of Hitler's wars of conquest. The incident at Gleiwitz was one of the first moves in a complicated game of chess that would see Nazi Germany conquer much of Europe in the initial stages, yet go down to crushing defeat in the end, costing the lives of over fifty million people in the process. However, it would be a crude fallacy to declare that Hitler intended to start an all-encompassing European conflict that would eventually become a world war, or indeed that he truly comprehended that this would be the consequence of his expansionist policy against Poland in

1939. Before we proceed into the war, it is therefore necessary to look briefly at the last months of peace in order to understand how, despite causing this devastating European conflict, certain top Nazis – primarily Hitler himself and Himmler – became convinced that it would be possible to secretly negotiate an end to hostilities with Britain. This was until comparatively recently, with the release of certain documents from the British archives, a quite unsuspected state of affairs.

Throughout the latter 1930s Hitler repeatedly pushed Europe to the brink of war through expansionist policies aimed at uniting all ethnic Germans in Europe into a single powerful entity – a Greater Germany – as described by him in some detail in *Mein Kampf*. The Führer made no secret of his intention to unite the Germanic peoples of Europe, and his top diplomats and foreign affairs advisors, in their conversations with members of the British and French governments, had gone to great lengths to explain this aspect of Nazi foreign policy. British and French politicians were therefore fully aware of Hitler's long-term objective of creating a much-enlarged Germany that would dominate Europe. They did not necessarily like what they heard from men such as Dr Albrecht Haushofer, the Führer's Confidential Advisor on Foreign Affairs (who was well acquainted with such eminent British politicians as Neville Chamberlain, Sir Samuel Hoare, Lord Halifax, and Anthony Eden), but they were pacified to a degree by the knowledge that Hitler was promising unification by legitimate means, through international agreement and plebiscite.

Hitler's first tentative steps towards creating his Greater Germany were largely successful. The *Anschluss* – union – between Germany and Austria took place in March 1938. Political union between Austria and Germany had been a burning issue ever since the 1920s, and so, despite some misgivings on the part of the British and French governments owing to Hitler's use of Austrian Nazis to force the issue, the German Führer had his way; Austria and Germany became one.

Next, as expected by Britain's leading politicians and Foreign Office mandarins, Hitler turned his attention on the Sudeten Germans living under Czech control in Bohemia. The Sudetenland had been Austrian territory until partition by the Treaty of Saint-Germain-en-Laye in 1919, and contained some three million German-speaking people. Czechoslovakia was an artificial creation of the victorious Allies in 1919, carved out of the former Austrian territories of Bohemia, Moravia, and Silesia, and the former Hungarian regions of Slovakia and Ruthenia. Now that Austria was part of the German Reich, so went Hitler's logic, the

Sudetenland, peopled almost exclusively by ethnic Germans, should be united with the Reich. Again, Hitler's diplomats and advisors had been busy ever since the mid-1930s, informing their British and French counterparts that this would ultimately become German policy. Thus British and French politicians were not unduly surprised when, immediately after the Anschluss, the Sudeten Deutsche Party (affiliated to and financed by the Nazi Party) began agitating for union with Germany. However, this was not as simple to achieve as the Austro-German union, for it directly contravened the Treaty of Saint-Germain-en-Laye, and affected the borders of another nation – Czechoslovakia. This time Hitler's desire to absorb fresh territory and another three million ethnic Germans needed a firmer footing in international law. It entailed an international conference, which was held in Munich in September 1938, attended by Chamberlain, Daladier (the French Prime Minister), Hitler, and Mussolini. The Munich Conference went down in history as the crowning moment of appeasement; with a deep-seated fear of conflict, Chamberlain and Daladier gave in to Hitler's demands. As a result the Sudetenland – complete with Czechoslovakia's western border defences and the all-important Skoda armaments factories – passed to the ownership of Nazi Germany. Hitler had once again succeeded in achieving his aims.

It would seem, given Hitler's promise that he had no more territorial ambitions, that peace had been achieved in Europe for the time being. However, even as he was making his guarantees to Chamberlain and Daladier in Munich that September, his diplomats and advisors were already meeting with their British counterparts and imparting the news that Nazi Germany's next step was to see the restoration of Danzig and the Polish Corridor, stripped from Germany in 1919 under the Treaty of Versailles. It may be assumed that at this point British politicians declared, 'Enough is enough, Hitler must be stopped.' This was not what happened. The view taken by the great majority of senior British politicians – though these did not include Winston Churchill and his allies, who were warning against German expansionism – was that if the Germanic peoples of the Polish Corridor and Danzig wanted to seek peaceful union with Nazi Germany, perhaps it should be granted. Such was the tense situation that existed in the early spring of 1939.

It was at this point that Hitler made his big mistake. Many British politicians had become reconciled to the fact that his next move would be to reabsorb the western part of Poland – formerly East Prussia – into the Reich. It would not be a popular move, and certainly Chamberlain had been busy offering support to the Poles ever since Munich. However, if the ethnic Germans of Poland desired unification with the German Reich, and it was legitimately done, there was not much that could stop it. Then, on 15 March 1939, Hitler caused a tremendous shock to Europe's political leaders that revealed him to be a man who could not be trusted. Instead of moving politically to absorb part of western Poland, as the British had been expecting, Germany invaded Czechoslovakia, ousted the legitimate government, and declared the Protectorate of Bohemia and Moravia. It was a slap in the face for both Chamberlain and Daladier, and a direct contravention of all that Hitler had promised just six months before. At long last the democratic leaders of western Europe realised that there could be no deal struck with Hitler or the Nazis.

One of the unspoken rules of foreign affairs and diplomacy is to try by all means to appear consistent in one's objectives, thereby diminishing international fear. However, the Nazis were rank amateurs in the world of international diplomacy, and Hitler could not grasp that concept. As a result Germany's invasion of Czechoslovakia, at the Führer's whim, caused a ripple of fear to sweep across the European political and diplomatic scene. The conclusion: Hitler was a man who could not be trusted, and he was therefore extremely dangerous.

Reinhard Spitzy, Joachim von Ribbentrop's Private Secretary, was to comment to me later: 'That was the big mistake. If Hitler could have resisted Czechoslovakia, then things might well have turned out very differently. The British and French governments would have become reconciled to unification of the Germanic peoples of Danzig and the "Polish Corridor". Instead, it made them determined to box Germany in, even if that meant by force of arms, the very next time Hitler made a move of expansion.'[2]

In Britain, too, many men were of the same opinion: Hitler had made his greatest mistake. Group Captain Frederick Winterbotham, Head of Air Intelligence, a man who had met the German Führer on several occasions, was later to recall: 'Of course we always knew the Nazis couldn't be trusted to keep their hands off their eastern neighbours. We at Air Intelligence had been counselling caution ever since the mid 1930s, but the government was not inclined to listen all the while it was able to strike "deals" with Hitler. Czechoslovakia was a watershed. At last everyone realised the danger, but by then it was almost too late . . . It was at this point that some iron was instilled into Neville Chamberlain, and he became determined to bring matters to a head over Poland . . . Hitler's aggressive expansionism couldn't be allowed to continue . . .'[3]

In Germany, Hitler soon became aware of the change in Britain's attitude to his particular brand of foreign policy. His diplomats began passing
memoranda back to Berlin that stated that the British government would
no longer accept Germany's interference in Polish affairs, nor the unification of Danzig and the Corridor with the Reich. To counter this Hitler
developed a three-pronged approach. First, an all-out diplomatic effort to
persuade Britain and France that he desired peaceful union between the
Reich and the Polish Corridor and Danzig. Second, the opening of negotiations with the Russians to bring about a non-aggression pact, a secret
clause of which was the clearly defined division of a defeated Poland.
Third, to call in Heinrich Himmler and Reinhard Heydrich, and order
them to prepare plans for a ruse that would legitimise the Germans' invasion of Poland in order that they might take what the Nazis wanted by
force. This 'ruse' was given a code name that appealed to Hitler's particularly strange sense of humour. It was called Operation Himmler.

Throughout the last months of peace German efforts on the diplomatic
front were considerable, so keen was Hitler to legitimise his taking of
western Poland, and to stall as long as possible the need for military action.
Indeed, his own advisor on foreign affairs, Dr Albrecht Haushofer, wrote to
his old friend, the British MP Lord Clydesdale, in July 1939, explaining
that Germany had been unfairly stripped of her eastern territories by the
Treaty of Versailles in 1919, and that she now desired a return of this land
and people. He continued:

> I cannot imagine even a short-range settlement without a
> change in the status of Danzig and . . . the corridor . . . (people in
> England mostly do not know that there are some
> 600,000–700,000 Germans scattered through the inner parts of
> Poland!) – but if there is to be a peaceful solution at all, it can only
> come from England and it must appear fair to the German people
> as a whole . . .
> If you want to win a peace without war, you need to be
> regarded as trustees of Justice, not partisans. Therefore . . . if you
> can do anything to promote a general British peace . . . I am sure
> you would do something helpful.[4]

On receipt of this letter Clydesdale (who within a year would become
the Duke of Hamilton) decided to show it discreetly to a few of his top-
ranking political acquaintances. These were the Foreign Secretary Lord

Halifax, the Prime Minister Neville Chamberlain, and his old friend Winston Churchill, who, reading between the lines, was able to discern the direction of Hitler's expansionist policies and commented, 'There's going to be a war very soon.'[5]

Just a few weeks after Haushofer sent this letter to Lord Clydesdale, a meeting took place at the Reich Chancellery between three of the most powerful men in Germany: Hitler, Himmler, and Reinhard Heydrich. At this meeting Heydrich presented his plans for an elaborate deception that would allow German troops to invade Poland legitimately. He proposed that on the night before the invasion, men of the SD would travel to the German–Polish frontier, put on Polish army uniforms, and engage in several simultaneous actions: attacking the German village of Kreuzberg, looting the frontier post at Pilschen, and simulating a violent combat at the frontier post of Hochlinden.

The most provocative incident was to take place at the little border town of Gleiwitz, where there was a radio station. A select band of SD men, disguised as Polish soldiers, would attack and take over the station. They would then interrupt the evening's broadcast by delivering a vitriolic anti-German speech over the airwaves. It would be heard by millions of Germans and would supposedly force a reluctant Germany to retaliate against wanton Polish provocation. With Heydrich's own particular brand of ghoulishness, the realism of the incident would be intensified by the scattering in the centre of the town of a few bodies suitably attired as Polish soldiers: poor unfortunates from the local concentration camp who would be dressed as Poles before being shot. Himmler was delighted with Heydrich's scheme, and the plan received Hitler's approval as well.

Over the next few weeks Germany's political and diplomatic efforts increased exponentially as Hitler sought to legitimise his invasion of Poland, seeking the approval of Britain and France for the unification of Danzig and the Polish Corridor with the Reich. His intention was to obtain what he wanted whilst maintaining peace with the two countries; this despite his certain knowledge that Britain and France had signed treaties of alliance with Poland assuring her of assistance in the event of invasion. However, he simply did not believe that Britain would go to war with Germany over Poland, for Joachim von Ribbentrop, his Foreign Minister, was counselling that Britain could not realistically aid Poland. Bar the fist-waving of a frustrated nation, she would flinch and stand back from the prospect of war. Not all Hitler's advisors agreed that this would be so: certain top men, as Reinhard Spitzy later recalled, were openly stating that 'the English would have no escape possible, because they had given a blank cheque to Poland, and war would become inevitable'.[6]

It was at this point that Hitler took a direct hand in attempting to placate the French and the British.

In the last week of August 1939 he met with the French Ambassador, Robert Coulondre, imploring the French 'not [to] make the mad decision to go to war', insisting that 'Danzig must be returned to Germany, and as for the rest, a vote was planned under international supervision . . .'[7] Coulondre reported back to Paris that Hitler had stated, 'I bear no enmity whatsoever towards France . . . I do not want war with your country; my one desire is to maintain good relations with it. I find indeed the idea that I might have to fight France on account of Poland a very painful one . . .'[8] Hitler then approached the British Ambassador, Sir Neville Henderson. However, instead of being able to mollify Henderson with words steeped in peace, he was coldly informed that Britain fully declared her support for Poland. This was a bitter blow. For the first time Hitler realised that there was a very real prospect of war with Britain over Poland, despite his best efforts to keep that risk to a minimum. The men of Whitehall had heard his placatory words before, over the Sudeten/Czech question, and it was clear that they were not about to be sucked into another deception. In a final effort to placate Britain and France, Hitler offered to receive the Polish envoy to discuss the situation, with the assistance of British and French representatives. However, on the day he made his offer, the Polish government, understandably disturbed at the thought of having its fate decided by the very European nations that had looked after Czechoslovakia's interests less than twelve months before, ordered full mobilisation.

'Hitler went wild with rage. Was he manoeuvring for a diplomatic advantage over Britain and France when agreeing to receive a Polish envoy the next day, Wednesday, August 30, or was it duplicity designed to keep Great Britain out of the conflict? Only Hitler ever knew the exact truth.'[9]

By the following day, August 31, Hitler was decided upon his course of action. Germany's armed forces had been poised on the German–Polish frontier for nearly a month. After his last-minute appeals for support from the British and French, he had found their doors closed upon him. However, he was confident that despite diplomatic protests and a great deal of fist-waving by the British, they would stand back from the brink. After all, even Ribbentrop was advising him that 'despite the English's promises to the Poles, they were too far away to help. They had made empty promises that they would be unable to keep.'[10] At 12.40 p.m. Hitler summoned General Keitel to his office and handed him 'Directive No. 1 for the Conduct of the War'. The invasion of Poland was to begin at 4.45 a.m. the following day, Friday, 1 September. At his office on Prinz Albrechtstrasse, Reinhard Heydrich received a telephone call: Operation Himmler was to proceed that very night.

•••••

On the night of Thursday, 31 August 1939, Operation Himmler was initiated. The preplanned border incidents took place at Kreuzberg, Pilschen, and Hochlinden, where men of the SD took potshots at the locals, stormed the centre of the villages, and vandalised civic buildings. At Gleiwitz the radio station was attacked and taken over. The night staff on duty were beaten up and locked in a cupboard by the SD, who then entered the studio and began shouting pro-Polish slogans across the German airwaves. As Alfred Naujocks, the SD commander, later recalled, while one of his men shouted that 'Germany's leaders are hurrying Europe into war . . . Peaceful Poland is being constantly threatened and bullied by Hitler, who must be crushed at all costs . . . Danzig is Polish . . .' he and his men cheered and fired their guns in the air. By the time they emerged from the building, a detachment of SS had come and gone, leaving a scattering of 'Polish' bodies around the building and town.[11]

At dawn on the following morning, Friday, 1 September, the conquest of Poland began. Operation Himmler had achieved its objectives, and Hitler now had an alibi to support his invasion. 'The Führer [is] calm and slept well,' recorded General Halder. 'Opposed to evacuation [of civilians from the cities] . . . proof that he hopes Great Britain and France will remain at peace.'[12]

Later that same morning Hitler stood before the rich panoply of the Reich's high and mighty gathered at the Kroll Opera House, and delivered one of his most vitriolic speeches against the Poles to date, declaring:

> While recently twenty-one border incidents have been recorded in a single night, there were fourteen last night, *three of them very serious*, so I have decided to speak to the Poles in the language they have used to us for months . . . As from now we answer bomb with bomb . . . I shall conduct this struggle against whomsoever until the safety of the Reich and its rights are secure . . .'[13]

The words alluded to a just cause, the defence of the nation; in reality they comprised Hitler's introduction to the most devastating and all-encompassing war the world had ever seen.

There followed a frantic forty-eight hours of diplomacy in which Britain and France hesitated, and made last-ditch appeals to Hitler to stop his armies and withdraw them back within his own borders. However, Germany's Führer was calling their bluff and they knew it. On 3 September, contrary to Ribbentrop's assurances, Britain and France fulfilled their commitments to Poland, and declared war on Germany. It was a disaster of the first magnitude for Hitler's plans of eastern expansion, for he was now faced with a war in the west that he did not want. On hearing that Britain had finally made a declaration of war, the Führer, seated in his office at the Reich Chancellery, turned to Ribbentrop with a savage look and demanded, 'What now?'[14]

Heinrich Hoffman, the Führer's friend and personal photographer, called in at the Reich Chancellery later that day and found Hitler 'slumped in a chair . . . muttering curses against his Foreign Minister'. He later recorded that:

> I knew, of course, exactly what he meant. Again and again, I had heard Ribbentrop, with a self-confidence out of all proportion to his knowledge and powers of judgement, assure Hitler that Britain . . . would never fight. It was above all the promptings of Ribbentrop at his elbow . . . which eventually brought the Führer and his country to destruction.[15]

In the immediacy of the conflict, Hitler found solace in the fact that Germany's forces quickly overwhelmed the Poles and swept all before them. Against the new method of warfare known as *Blitzkrieg* ('lightning war', a swift and intensive combination of air and ground attack), the Polish Army had little defence. Their forces were below strength and employed antiquated tactics, even throwing cavalry against the well-oiled and deadly machinery of the Panzers. The Poles stood little chance and grew weaker by the day, in comparison with the Germans who daily gained more confidence and ever increasing tracts of territory. A fortnight after the German attack, on 17 September, the Poles' determination to struggle on against the onslaught turned to anguish when Soviet Russia attacked her rear. As the Red Army poured into eastern Poland, Polish resistance began to disintegrate. On 27 September Warsaw fell to the

German Army, and the following day what was left of Poland was parti-
tioned between Germany and Russia. Technically, the country ceased to
exist.

Despite the belligerent posturing, involving a heavy military build-up
on Germany's western frontier with France, there was as yet no sign of
conflict developing between the Anglo-French alliance and Germany.
What was known as the *Sitzkrieg* – the sitting-war – had started. Back at
the Reich Chancellery, the German führer convinced himself and his intimates that 'England and France had obviously declared war merely as a
sham, in order not to lose face before the world.' Having given the Poles
an assurance of protection, he reasoned, they could do little else. Hitler
asserted further that 'there would be no fighting,'[16] and he ordered his
forces in the west not to provoke the Allies, but to remain strictly on the
defensive. 'Of course we are in a state of war with England and France,'
he confided to some dinner guests at this junction, 'but if we on our side
avoid all acts of war [against Britain and France], the whole business will
evaporate. As soon as we sink a ship and they have sizeable casualties, the
war party over there will gain strength.'[17]

On 6 October, the fighting in Poland having ended and there being as
yet no sign of conflict breaking out in the west, Hitler made his first
public appeal for peace, giving an unrepentant yet placatory speech to
the Reichstag. To many in the West, this speech sounded like mere rhetoric, aimed at home consumption. However, unbeknownst to the
Reichsleiters and ministers seated before him at the Kroll Opera House,
Hitler was earnest in his desire for peace, for he had already been making
a concerted effort behind the scenes to negotiate an accord with the
British Government.

On the very day of Poland's defeat, ten days prior to his speech at the
Kroll Opera House, Hitler had held a top-secret meeting at his office in
the Chancellery with Göring and a prominent Swedish businessman
named Birger Dahlerus, a close friend of the British Ambassador in
Oslo, Sir David Ogilvie Forbes. Dahlerus informed Hitler that,
according to Forbes, 'the British government was looking for peace'. The
only question was: How could the British save face? 'If the British actually want peace,' Hitler had replied, 'they can have it within two weeks
– without losing face.'[18] He informed Dahlerus that Britain had to be
reconciled to the fact that 'Poland cannot rise again', but he was
prepared to guarantee the security of Britain and western Europe, in
which he had little interest.

At this point Göring suggested that it might be possible for British and German representatives to meet secretly in Holland, and that if they made progress, 'the Queen [of Holland] could invite both countries to armistice talks', Hitler agreed and ordered Dahlerus to 'go to England the very next day in order to send out feelers in the direction indicated'. 'The British can have peace if they want it,' Hitler told Dahlerus, 'but they will have to hurry.'[19]

This had been Hitler's first tentative step along the path of secret peace negotiations, as he sought to stem the tide of war before it turned against Germany. Now, on 6 October, he stood before the Reichstag, confident that his agent, Birger Dahlerus, was busy in London secretly meeting the Foreign Secretary, Lord Halifax, and putting the Führer's case for a cessation of hostilities. As he told the gathering of Reichsleiters and ministers:

> My chief endeavour has been to rid our relations with France of all trace of ill will and render them tolerable for both nations . . . Germany has no claims against France . . .

He went on to speak about his greater cause for concern:

> I have devoted no less effort to the achievement of Anglo-German understanding, nay, more than that, of an Anglo-German friendship. At no time and in no place have I ever acted contrary to British interests. I believe even today that there can only be real peace in Europe and throughout the world if Germany and England come to an understanding . . .
> One fact is certain. In the course of world history there have never been two victors, but very often only losers. May those peoples and their leaders who are of the same opinion now make their reply. And let those who consider war to be the better solution reject my outstretched hand . . .[20]

Hitler had proffered the hand of peace. Would it be taken up?

Publicly Britain's government, which primarily meant Neville Chamberlain and Lord Halifax, maintained a stony silence for well over a week. After the humiliating political and diplomatic defeats of Munich, Czechoslovakia, and finally Poland, Chamberlain could not afford to be seen to take the road of appeasement again. It would be political suicide. Eventually he issued a statement declaring that if Hitler wanted peace, 'acts – not words alone – must be forthcoming'. He called for 'convincing proof' from the German Führer that he really wanted to end the conflict.

On the following morning, 13 October, Hitler himself issued a statement; it asserted that Chamberlain, in turning down his offer of peace, had deliberately chosen war. Such was the public face of the peace negotiations. But what about the private face? What about the secret visits of Dahlerus to Chamberlain and Halifax, about which only a handful of the British government's leading members were ever informed?

In 1941 the British government issued a report to the British Ambassador in Washington – for confidential communication to President Roosevelt – on *sixteen* peace attempts made by the German government between the summers of 1939 and 1941. The report included the inside story of the Dahlerus negotiations from the British perspective. It revealed that Dahlerus 'was convinced that Göring genuinely regretted the outbreak of the war and short of actual disloyalty to Hitler would like to see a truce negotiated. The unwillingness of the Polish government to treat in earnest about Danzig and The Corridor, coupled, perhaps, with deliberate malice on the part of Ribbentrop, had unleashed the conflict.'[21]

On 12 October 1939, the report revealed, Dahlerus was back in London for another secret meeting with Lord Halifax, at which he communicated the details of Hitler's comprehensive peace offer. This revealed that Hitler was prepared to negotiate the 'Polish situation, non-aggression pacts, disarmament, colonies, economic questions, and frontiers'. Indeed, Dahlerus even stated that 'Hitler had taxed the patience of the German people over the Soviet Union, Czechoslovakia and Poland, and that if Göring, as the chief negotiator, secured peace, Hitler could not risk acting counter to these national undertakings.'[22]

However, by this time both Chamberlain and Halifax were coming under a constant stream of criticism from press, public, and parliament for the years of appeasement that had led Britain down the dangerous road to war. This, combined with an extreme distrust of Hitler, meant that it was very difficult to engage in meaningful peace negotiations. Such distrust, along with Chamberlain's uncomfortable political position, made it almost impossible for either the Prime Minister or the Foreign Secretary to actively pursue Hitler's peace offer to its logical conclusion – be that a form of peace or a temporary halting of the war. As a result the Dahlerus–Göring initiative failed, and the conflict continued unabated.

A consistent theme that would run through these sixteen German peace offers in the first two years of the Second World War was that as one

initiative failed, so another immediately took its place, as leading members
of the Nazi Party sought to achieve peace with Britain. Despite the failure
of the Göring–Dahlerus initiative, it would be a mistake to believe that
Hitler gave up on the notion that he could negotiate his way out of the war
he had started. The hand of the Führer would be seen time and time again
over the next two years, as he sought to achieve peace with Britain.

In the Foreign Office report of 1941, entitled 'The Peaceable Attempts
1939–41' and marked 'For the President's Eyes Only', there would be a
specific omission. The British government did not want the Americans to
know about a separate peace effort that had started as soon as it became
clear that the Dahlerus initiative was failing. This time it would involve the
hand of Heinrich Himmler.

•••••

On 17 October 1939 Walter Schellenberg, now an SS colonel, was
summoned to a meeting with his superior, Himmler's second-in-command,
Reinhard Heydrich. Schellenberg, one of the Nazi Party's most promising
young intellectuals and still only twenty-nine years of age, had risen mete-
orically through the ranks of the SD during the latter years of the 1930s.
Regarded throughout the RSHA (Reichssicherheitshauptamt – Reich
Central Security Office) as Heydrich's factotum, everyone in the upper
echelons of the SS knew that he enjoyed the open approval of Himmler,
who called him 'my Benjamin'. We should, however, remind ourselves of
the observations made by British Intelligence on interrogating him in the
autumn of 1945:

> For a history of Schellenberg much vitriol is required . . . it is
> true to his character that he disliked the master [Himmler] who
> fed him . . . In office he would be a vile enemy; in captivity he was
> a cringing cad. In office he would ruthlessly cut down his oppo-
> nents; in captivity he would ruthlessly betray his friends.[23]

Despite this critical assessment of him, Schellenberg in 1940 was one
of Himmler's most trusted subordinates. As such, he consistently received
'plum' assignments within the SD; he was later to comment, 'I constantly
received my orders directly from Heydrich and Himmler. They entrusted
me with special missions both in the field of counter-espionage and of espionage abroad.'[24]

It can therefore be discerned that Schellenberg was a key player in the SS/SD, one who had the trust of his ultimate superior. During the invasion of Poland he had been seconded to the service of the Reichsführer-SS aboard his special train, *Heinrich*. This had followed Hitler's own train – the *Führerzug* – from which he had commanded operations in Polish territory. Schellenberg's role at that time had been to maintain the closest touch with Heydrich in Berlin, to report to Himmler every morning on SD matters, and to settle all questions relating to intelligence. He had thus been very close to the Reichsführer-SS for several weeks, and his presence had reinforced their relationship. Here is a man, Himmler must have said to himself, who can be trusted with the most sensitive of missions. In the years ahead he would entrust his 'Benjamin' with his most secret endeavours of the entire war; now, however, the capable Schellenberg was just about to receive his first experience in the difficult and unpredictable world of diplomacy and clandestine peace negotiation.

At his meeting with Heydrich at the SD's Prinz Albrechtstrasse headquarters on the morning of 17 October, Schellenberg was introduced to an SS/SD operation that had been proceeding in Holland for the past few months. Heydrich, who had played so significant a role in orchestrating the start of the war through Operation Himmler, would now ironically become instrumental in Himmler's secret bid to negotiate an end to the conflict; for, as he informed Schellenberg, the SS/SD had been in secret contact with the British government since mid-September. This operation, into which Schellenberg was now drawn, has been referred to ever since the Second World War as the Venlo Incident, after it ended in the kidnap of two British agents at the little Dutch frontier post of that name. It would, however, be more appropriate to describe what was to take place under the title – given Himmler's involvement – SS Peace Negotiations.

In 1943 Himmler was again to open a covert line of communication to the British government. A British Foreign Office memorandum on the matter would draw the following comparison with the negotiations of 1939:

> Of course, this is not the first time Himmler or the SS have tried to negotiate an accord with us. However, given the debacle in November 1939, when the Gestapo kidnapped our intermediaries in the mistaken belief that we were complicitous in the attempt on Hitler's life, it is my considered opinion that we should proceed with extreme caution. If Himmler is earnest in his desire

for peace, then the onus should be on him, on this occasion, to
prove his honest intent . . .[25]

Thus it can be seen that within the British Government, the British
Foreign Office *and* British Intelligence the secret negotiations held in
autumn 1939 were considered meaningful peace moves by the
Reichsführer-SS, Heinrich Himmler and the SSD and not merely as a
'sting' to capture British agents in neutral Holland.

On that morning at Prinz Albrechtstrasse, Heydrich informed
Schellenberg that 'for several months one of our agents in the Low
Countries, a deserter from the Czech Intelligence . . . has been in contact
with the British secret service to which he has supplied false information
. . . By transmitting the good political *Spielmaterial* he has patiently,
painfully, won the confidence of the Intelligence Service . . . for the last
month the SD has been in contact with the British Secret Service.'

'Is this agent a Czech?' asked Schellenberg.

'No,' replied Heydrich. 'He is a former German policeman from
Hamburg by the name of Mörz who sometimes calls himself "Fischer".'[26]

Heydrich went on to explain that Mörz (alias Fischer, or Agent F479) –
an early SA member – had been a supporter of Gregor Strasser and had
joined the Schwarze Front. (This was a dissident organisation of National
Socialists who held socialist views.) After the Night of the Long Knives
many Schwarze Front members had fled to the Czech capital, Prague,
where they intended to continue the fight against the right wing who now
controlled the Nazi Party. Mörz himself had escaped to Switzerland before
following his compatriots to Czechoslovakia.

'But how did he come to the SD?' asked Schellenberg.

Heydrich explained that, after the invasion of Czechoslovakia, an SD
agent by the name of Mahr had been sent to Prague to find Mörz. Mahr
located his prey and, in the words of Heydrich, Mörz was presented with
two choices: 'a court and firing-squad' or 'come to work for us'. As the
sinister head of the SD remarked casually, 'He loved life and his wife too
much not to offer his services, which he did.'

Heydrich went on, 'At the beginning of the summer I sent him to the
Netherlands to renew contact with his former Czech employers.'

'Does the old Czech Deuxième Bureau operate in the Netherlands?'

'Yes, in connection with the Intelligence Service.'

'And F479 [Mörz] has renewed contact with his old employers?'

'Not exactly,' confided Heydrich, 'He has made contact with two important agents of the English secret service in the Netherlands, Major Stevens and Captain Best.'[27]

Major Richard Stevens and Captain Sigismund Payne Best were Britain's top intelligence operatives in Holland. Stevens was the British Embassy's Passport Control Officer and Best the head of the Dutch Z Network. The Passport Control Officer and Z Network was an intelligence system developed in the *Belle Epoque* of the 1900s, not only to formalise British intelligence gathering, but primarily to counter the Kaiser's own very effective intelligence service run by Colonel Nicolai. The system had worked well, and soon the new style of intelligence gathering was applied to every country. Every British embassy had a Passport Control Officer who was always an officer of Britain's Secret Intelligence Service, MI6, responsible for coordinating intelligence gathering in his designated country. Under him served the Z Network, responsible for the 'hands-on' gathering of intelligence, espionage, and, when necessary, sabotage. Unfortunately, by the 1930s the system was underfunded and out of date when compared with the highly efficient German intelligence services, the Abwehr and the SD. These received vast investment from a government that fully recognised the importance of top-grade and up-to-date intelligence in protecting their interests. However, the Germans, too, had their problems, for the Abwehr (the senior service and allied to the Wehrmacht) and the SD (the junior service and part of the SS, loyal primarily to the Nazi Party) regarded each other with considerable enmity, so much so that they often expended more effort on watching each other than in dealing with the enemy.

Stevens and Best, Heydrich revealed to Schellenberg, had placed Mörz (alias Fischer) in touch with the Czech Intelligence Service, exiled to London since the German invasion of Czechoslovakia. Mörz had travelled to London at the beginning of September for a meeting with the head of Czech Intelligence, Major Bartik.

Heydrich went on to explain that, through nefarious means, the British and the Czechs had been led to believe that Mörz represented a dissident group within Germany opposed to the Nazi regime. This group might be persuaded to precipitate a coup to overthrow the Nazi Party on the understanding that the Allies would negotiate peace with a new German government.

Within a week of his return to Holland, Mörz introduced Best to an acquaintance of his by the name of Major Solms, who claimed to be in contact with powerful elements in Germany capable of usurping power from the Nazis. This group, according to Solms, were Wehrmacht (German

Army) officers who believed the war to be the utmost folly and Hitler to blame for the disaster that had befallen Europe. He hinted that the head of his organisation was a well-respected Wehrmacht general – he could not name him for the moment because of the need for the utmost secrecy – who had the support of the officer corps. Solms then asked Best for proof that he represented powerful forces within the British establishment who were in a position to negotiate, and requested the names – if Best had any – of anti-Nazi elements in Germany who could be called upon to assist in the removal of the Nazis.

Best reported on his meeting with Major Solms to his Passport Control Officer, Stevens, and within just a few days was surprised to find that 'a very big noise' from London had flown out to Holland to learn more about what was going on. The 'big noise' was Major Haddon Hall, who was acting as an emissary of Colonel Stewart Menzies, second-in-command to Admiral Sinclair, the head of British Intelligence. Major Hall instructed Stevens and Best that they were to maintain their contact with Fischer (Mörz) and Solms, because 'London' was extremely interested in learning all it could about the German dissident organisation that Solms claimed to represent. 'Best thought it wiser . . . not to ask who exactly "London" was, but he needed no crystal ball to reason it out. "London" was no less a person than Neville Chamberlain.'[28] With the war only a few weeks old, Chamberlain was already grasping at straws that might bring about peace without the need for conflict.

However, British Intelligence was just about to fall into Reinhard Heydrich's well-oiled trap. As with so much of the double-dealing and deception in this story, no one was quite who they seemed. Major Solms's real name was Johannes Travaglio. He was an SD officer briefed by Heydrich to participate in the Mörz operation as soon as it became clear that the former Hamburg policeman had made progress in infiltrating the British. Using this ploy, Heydrich hoped to learn the names of anti-Nazi plotters in the Reich, who would then be arrested and interrogated by the Gestapo before a quick appointment with a firing squad. The anti-Nazi group that Solms (alias Travaglio) claimed to represent, of course, did not exist.

Despite the appearance that the Germans had the upper hand, they were subject to doubts about the validity of Best's credentials. Ever since first making the acquaintance of Mörz at the beginning of August, Best had resolutely maintained that he was a member of the British Foreign Office. He had continued in this pretence even at the time of his first meeting with Solms in September. However, the Germans, though, were not about to be deceived by the British, and so they had secretly photographed Best. This photograph had then been circulated in the SD and Abwehr in an attempt to identify him. Within a very few days Heydrich had an answer. An Abwehr officer from Hamburg recalled that just before the outbreak of war he had been sent a photograph by the head of Economic Intelligence. It showed a group of foreign visitors who had been granted access to a major German munitions works in the Ruhr, and one of the group was 'an Englishman who always seemed to be turning up at these affairs'. The Englishman was Sigismund Payne Best. Therefore, reasoned the SD, though Best was not a Foreign Office official, he was Intelligence, and almost certainly an intermediary representing the British government.

In a cleverly thought-out manoeuvre, Mörz communicated to Best that his contacts in the anti-Nazi resistance wanted a firm assurance that they were really dealing with the British government. As a consequence, Best agreed to Mörz's request that a message dictated by him be broadcast by the BBC on one of its German service bulletins. This would confirm his credentials as a representative of the British government. Within a few days the message was broadcast on the BBC's Deutschland-Dienst service. Heydrich, who listened to the broadcast, was thus convinced that the SD had managed to open a line of communication not merely to the British secret service in Holland, but rather to the heart of the government, quite possibly to Neville Chamberlain himself.

Meanwhile, in Britain, Chamberlain believed that he was at last gaining access to dissident forces within Germany who might be able to unseat the Nazis and make peace with the west without a shot being fired in anger. As his Principal Private Secretary, Sir Arthur Rucker, told John Colville, another of the Prime Minister's secretaries:

> Communism is now the great danger, greater even than Nazi Germany. All the independent states of Europe are anti-Russian, but Communism is a plague that does not stop at national boundaries, and with the advance of the Soviet [Union] into Poland the states of Eastern Europe will find their powers of resistance to Communism very much weakened. It is thus vital that we should play our hand very carefully with Russia, and not destroy the possibility of uniting, if necessary, with a new German Government against the common danger.[29]

Thus it can be seen that in Downing Street, Chamberlain and his top aides looked upon the contacts that had been developed with the supposed anti-Nazi dissidents as a means possibly to remove the Nazis from power, and also to end the war. However, Chamberlain, in his deep yearning for peace – for a vindication of his policies of appeasement that would pull the coals of his reputation from the fire of press and public opinion – seemed blind to the dangers of dealing with Germans, especially those who might turn out to be Nazis. A clear indication that he was prepared to negotiate with Germany – and was not too fussy about who its representatives were – can be gleaned from Colville's diary entry of just a fortnight later, when he noted:

> Two Englishmen, called Christie and Conwell-Evans, have been talking to high-placed Germans, of whom one is Prince Max von Hohenlohe [a man known to be Himmler's emissary], in Switzerland about the possibility of getting rid of Hitler and coming to terms with . . . [a] new Government under Göring on the basis of restoring independence to Poland and Bohemia, disarming all round, and agreeing to leave inviolate the unity and boundaries of Germany proper . . . Prince Hohenlohe produced nine points as a possible basis of negotiation . . .
>
> I am afraid the F.O. are rather defeatist about the possibility of procuring peace. The P.M., on the other hand, is in favour of a much more encouraging reply, and is prepared to accept eight out of the nine points, only stipulating that Hitler himself shall play no part in the proposed new order. In return for a change of regime (or at least a modification), restoration of frontiers and disarmament, the P.M. would be prepared to agree economic assistance for Germany, and no demand for reparations . . .[30]

If ever it has been claimed that Chamberlain's policy of appeasement had radically changed since the latter 1930s, Colville's diary entry dispels that notion. Chamberlain was still intent on restoring peace in Europe whatever the cost, even if that meant treating with top Nazis like Hermann Göring. His only stipulation was the removal of Hitler from power. However, he would eventually be willing to concede even that point. As the Mörz/Solms talks began to take on ever more importance – and the likelihood of meaningful peace negotiations became more of a reality – the demand that Hitler be removed from office would shockingly be dropped, leaving the main British conditions for peace sounding empty and hollow.

At the meeting between Heydrich and Schellenberg on 17 October, the head of the SD brought his subordinate up to date on the operation that had seen Mörz and Solms opening discussions with British Intelligence in an effort to obtain the names of dissidents in Germany opposed to the regime. As he revealed, they had discovered that the British were so keen on peace that their approach had not remained restricted to the British secret service operating in Holland, but had been passed right up the chain of command to Britain's leading politicians, and primarily to Neville Chamberlain.

The Stevens/Best–Mörz/Solms operation between August and early October 1939 had undoubtedly begun as an SD 'sting' aimed at obtaining the names of German dissidents. However, Reinhard Heydrich's direct participation post-Dahlerus indicates that a change in priorities had taken place. What had begun as a low-level operation now directly involved the head of the SD, and this indicates the importance with which he now regarded the line of communication to the British government. Heinrich Himmler knew of the Führer's desire for peace in the west, knew that an extremely concerted effort was being mounted to open secret negotiations with the British. When Prince Max von Hohenlohe, Himmler's emissary (as he would be time and time again throughout the war), turned up in Switzerland to communicate terms to Neville Chamberlain and Lord Halifax via Christie and Conwell-Evans, that had been Heinrich Himmler's first attempt to open negotiations with the British leadership, but it had failed. Then, via Heydrich, he was informed that the SD had managed to open a secure line direct to Downing Street, and had been talking to leading Britons for many weeks through Mörz and Solms Travaglio. The only problem was that the British believed they were talking to Wehrmacht officers opposed to the current regime in Germany. However, this, too, could be used to the SD's advantage. The Nazis were shrewd enough to realise that Chamberlain would blanch at the notion of negotiating peace directly with the SS/SD; therefore the ploy of using disaffected Wehrmacht officers to offer peace negotiations with the British would be retained for the moment. The only difference would be that the Wehrmacht officers would in reality be SS/SD.

In his Prinz Albrechtstrasse office Heydrich confided to Schellenberg that 'Mörz returned from London to the Netherlands, then made a short stay in Germany last week. Back in The Hague, he told Stevens and Best that he was the bearer of important news. Captain Schämmel, of the O.K.W. Transport Service, representing a group of high officers of the Wehrmacht . . . wanted to get in touch with the English Government.'

'It's a fantastic story!' exclaimed Schellenberg, stunned by all Heydrich had told him about the Mörz negotiations, and the ploy of using the Wehrmacht.

'No doubt,' continued Heydrich. 'But what's important is that Best and Stevens swallowed the bait. They indicated to F479 [Mörz] their desire to know who the leaders of the opposition were and if they were sufficiently strong to succeed. Captain Schämmel is due to meet them shortly in the Netherlands.'

'But who is this Captain Schämmel?' Schellenberg interrupted. 'Does he work for us?'

Heydrich fixed a cold stare on his interlocutor. 'Captain Schämmel is none other than SS Colonel Walter Schellenberg.'[31]

A glimmer of joy spread across Heydrich's face: Schellenberg's surprise was absolute and complete.

Within a few days of his interview with Heydrich, Schellenberg had set up his own headquarters at a safe-house in Düsseldorf. This house possessed accommodation, offices, a refectory, and intelligence facilities such as its own communications centre and darkroom. From here, remote from Berlin yet near to the centre of intrigue in Holland, whilst also connected directly to Heydrich by a secure line, Schellenberg would participate in one of the SD's most secret and important operations to date. Under the direct orders of Heydrich, Himmler, and, it would later transpire, Hitler, too, Schellenberg would be talking to the British government, and the subject would be peace.

The British would not forget Schellenberg's role during these 1939 negotiations. In 1943, during Himmler's second major attempt to negotiate with the British, one leading Foreign Office mandarin was led to comment:

> That Himmler was earnest in his peace endeavour of autumn 1939 is without a doubt, but we should regard with the utmost suspicion the involvement of his emissary Schellenberg. We all remember the disastrous culmination of those discussions last time, and so we must ensure that on this occasion it is the Germans who make all the initiatives, not us. If there is the slightest hint that Schellenberg or his master are not completely frank with us, it is my opinion that it is best to break off all discussions immediately . . .[32]

It is therefore clear that, at least in the British Foreign Office, there was no doubt that Himmler was involved in the secret Anglo-German contact of autumn 1939, and that the discussions, involving as they did both the British Prime Minister and the Foreign Secretary, were bona fide peace negotiations.

Almost as soon as Schellenberg had set himself up in Düsseldorf, events began to take on a life of their own. Keen not to lose the initiative, he authorised further contact with Stevens and Best. In the first instance he would not be going to Holland himself; instead he decided to raise the stakes a little by drawing the two Britons out to see how far they were willing to go in their determination to facilitate an Anglo-German peace. Accordingly, on 20 October, Stevens and Best accompanied Mörz (who was by this time residing in Holland), Lieutenant Klop (of Dutch Intelligence), and Jan Lemmens (Best's chauffeur) to the eastern town of Zutphen, near the Dutch–German frontier. Here, at 10.00 a.m., they were to meet two German emissaries. After arriving, Stevens and Best settled themselves down in a café and had breakfast while Mörz, Klop, and the driver went on to the little frontier village of Dinxperlo, where they were to collect the two Germans. Eventually, after a two-hour wait, the German emissaries arrived and were driven back to the now-impatient Britons.

Back at the café, Mörz conducted the introductions. The first of the Germans, he said, was Captain von Seidlitz; the other was his subordinate Lieutenant Grosch. In fact, Seidlitz was SS-Sturmbannführer von Salish, and his subordinate, Grosch, was SS-Hauptsturmführer Christiansen. They were both long-serving SD officers trusted by Schellenberg. It was at this point that a problem arose. Stevens and Best had intended to take the two Germans back to The Hague to continue the negotiations, but Seidlitz and Grosch refused, declaring they had to be back in German territory by 8.00 p.m. at the latest. This presented a dilemma for the two Englishmen. After all, they could hardly conduct important peace negotiations in a café; moreover, Zutphen, near the frontier, was in a restricted area, and their presence would soon arouse suspicion. The solution was found by Best, who suggested that they should travel to the home of a friend of his in Arnhem, a mere ten miles away. To this the two Germans agreed, and soon the men were sitting down in an Arnhem villa to what Best called 'a round table conference'.

For the first hour the two Germans were not very forthcoming, leaving most of the conversation to Stevens and Best. The Englishmen were repeatedly forced to give assurances of their credentials to negotiate on behalf of the British government. Eventually Seidlitz (von Salish) opened up a little and began to talk in vague terms about his association with the 'dissident' movement. The main thrust of his conversation, however, was to pursue the question of whether or not the British government would be willing to negotiate a truce – he would not elucidate with whom – and whether Britain was determined to see Germany forced into a humiliating peace. He seemed to be angling towards a British acceptance of the situation in Czechoslovakia and Poland.

At this Stevens, who had already been briefed in London by Colonel Menzies, indicated that the British government would like to see German forces withdrawn from Poland. However, he commented, he could see that this would be difficult, given that the Soviet Union had also invaded Poland and annexed the eastern part of the country. With regard to Czechoslovakia, Britain was inclined to see Germany withdraw from Bohemia and Moravia, but not from the Sudetenland.

Whilst these discussions proceeded, Best had been studying the two Germans, and had come to the conclusion that they were not who they purported to be. They seemed to be far too well briefed on German foreign policy for two middle-ranking Wehrmacht officers; Seidlitz in particular was deftly manoeuvring around Stevens's more probing questions. Slowly but surely Best became convinced that they were engaged in discussions with two Nazis. Indeed, later that day he would radio back to Menzies in London that he had come to the 'conclusion that they were Nazis and probably officers in the SS'. However, he was not unduly perturbed by this discovery, for he concluded that 'It did not seem at all unlikely that Hitler might be trying to pull off a deal with . . . [the British government] at the expense of the left wing of the Party.'[33]

This highly significant assessment confirms that despite Heydrich's best efforts to deceive the British, the two British negotiators were by now strongly suspicious of the Germans' true identity. These were no 'dissident' Wehrmacht officers, but likely to be Nazi officials or even SS. Logic therefore dictates that the British were aware by late October 1939 that a Wehrmacht plot to oust Hitler and sue for peace was unlikely to exist. Hence they must have known that the deception was a German ruse to open negotiations with the British government, and that the Nazi leadership was itself behind the negotiations.

Best's suspicions were soon confirmed when Seidlitz stated that although his superiors were prepared to install a new democratic government in Germany, Hitler would have to remain Chancellor, because he had the support of the German people. Both Stevens and Best emphasised that they were not empowered to grant such a concession, but would refer the matter back to London for clarification. They did, however, tell Seidlitz and Grosch that Chamberlain considered the main enemy of Europe to be the Soviet Union, not Germany, and that the Prime Minister proposed 'a European league of States under the leadership of England . . . with a front against progressive Bolshevism'.[34] This indicates that even in late October 1939, some two months into the war, Chamberlain considered Soviet Russia to be the big danger to Europe, and that an accommodation could be found with Germany – even Nazi Germany – to form an anti-Russian pact.

Shortly after this the meeting broke up. The two Germans departed back to the frontier, while Stevens and Best headed for The Hague. Both parties were satisfied with the way the meeting had progressed: the British because – though they realised that they were dealing with Nazis, quite possibly with Hitler's own emissaries – they felt that meaningful progress had been made; the Germans because they were aware that the British government – meaning Neville Chamberlain – had sanctioned the discussion, which meant there was every chance of these peace negotiations succeeding. In London the Permanent Under-Secretary at the Foreign Office, Sir Alexander Cadogan, noted in his diary that the 'German dissidents . . . were really Hitler's agents', and that he had made his feelings on the subject known to the Foreign Secretary, Lord Halifax. However, Halifax and Chamberlain were still blind to the dangers of dealing with the Nazis; they wanted to proceed with the negotiations, for as Cadogan remarked, 'C[the head of SIS]'s Germans have put a question and I discussed with H[alifax] the answer to give them, and subsequently drafted it.' After that had been done, Cadogan and Halifax 'went over to No 10 with it at 6.30 p.m. [where] Chamberlain approved generally the verbal alterations'.[35]

Back in Düsseldorf, Schellenberg was delighted by all he heard from Major von Salish (alias Seidlitz), and Captain Christiansen (alias Grosch). He duly reported by telephone to Heydrich all that his two subordinates had told him: about the British attitude to peace, about Chamberlain's views on an anti-Bolshevik pan-European league. Heydrich was soon on the telephone to Himmler to report on the excellent progress of the SS peace negotiations.[36]

The next step, now that he had confirmed that the negotiations were bona fide, was for Schellenberg himself to meet the two British intelligence agents. By this means he hoped to take the matter on significantly further than could be accomplished by his two intermediaries. Salish and Christiansen had been operating substantially in the dark, unable to make concessions and not fully aware of the implications of these very delicate negotiations. The only way the process could now be moved forward was for Schellenberg – Himmler's trusted subordinate – to participate, and that would entail his travelling to neutral Holland to meet Stevens and Best.

A week later, on Monday, 30 October, Schellenberg, under the alias of Captain Schämmel of the OKW Transport Service, crossed the border at Dinxperlo into Holland. He was accompanied by an old friend named Professor Max de Crinis, who was to masquerade as a certain Colonel Martini (another Wehrmacht officer).

Schellenberg had spent the past few days coaching de Crinis at his Düsseldorf headquarters on how they were to proceed. Schellenberg would be wearing a monocle to affect a more distinguished air and to 'add a few years to his age'. If he removed his monocle, de Crinis was to stop talking and let Schellenberg take the lead; if he said he felt a headache coming on, then the negotiations were to stop at once. It should not be forgotten that Schellenberg was placing himself at considerable risk by travelling to Holland. As a leading member of the SD he would be a prime 'catch' if he were to be apprehended. Whether this happened or not depended to a large degree on how determined the British were to proceed with the negotiations.

After a tense wait at Dinxperlo, Schellenberg and de Crinis were collected by the Dutch intelligence officer Lieutenant Klop and Best's chauffeur, and taken by car to The Hague, where they were to meet Stevens and Best. Later that afternoon the four men sat down to their negotiations. Within a very short while Schellenberg, still maintaining the pretence of being a Wehrmacht officer, offered the tempting bait that his 'faction' might be prepared to accept conditions limiting Hitler's power in Germany, though he stressed that it was desirable for Hitler to remain head of state. The two Britons did not disagree, and very soon Schellenberg imparted a 'declaration' by his faction, which he requested be sent to London. Accordingly, at 9.25 p.m. Stevens transmitted the following back to London under ciphered transmission:

> MOST SECRET
> Following declaration is sent at the request of German repre-
> sentative. They further promise details of their Party in near
> future. Am arranging to be in daily communication with them, as
> frequent visits present great difficulty . . .

It is important to remember that Schellenberg was masquerading as a
Wehrmacht officer, whilst in reality representing the SS and promoting an
SS peace plan; Stevens, Best, Menzies, Cadogan, Halifax, and
Chamberlain were by now aware that they were most likely dealing with
the SS. So, substituting the word 'SS' for 'Wehrmacht' in the following
document reveals a great deal about the Himmler/Heydrich peace plan:

> Wehrmacht [SS] has the upper hand and although it is
> prepared to defend Germany, will not countenance a war of
> aggression . . . Wehrmacht [SS] feels strong enough to take a
> leading part in formation of a new government but of the Nazi
> leaders would like Göring to be retained in office . . . The object
> of the Government would be the return of Germany to peaceful
> friendly relations with the world and it would be sympathetic to
> a pan-European policy . . . The change of Germany from a war
> to a peace footing is only possible with the full co-operation of
> all civilised countries and therefore the total peace which allays
> all religious, nationalist and ideological differences would be
> guaranteed.
>
> Would H.M. Government be prepared in principle to enter
> into negotiations with the representative of one of the old Royal
> Houses . . . or a person of similar standing?[37]

Some of the suggestions in this 'declaration' are not as improbable as
they at first appear, especially those that refer to the 'formation of a new
government' and the replacement of the country's leaders with the exception of Göring (it must be remembered that he represented the right wing
of the Party and had been a political ally of Himmler since the Night of the
Long Knives). The SS was all-powerful in Nazi Germany, and Himmler
secretly harboured great ambitions for it, planning that it would one day
supplant the Nazi Party as the controlling power. Within a few hours of
Schellenberg's 'declaration' being transmitted to London, a reply was sent
to Stevens to direct his actions. It stated:

> In the event of the German representatives enquiring whether
> you have had a reply to the questions which you said . . . you
> would refer to H.M.G., you should inform them as follows (*not*,
> however, handing them anything in writing):
>
> Whether Hitler remains in any capacity or not (but of course

more particularly if he *does* remain) this country would have to see proof that German policy had changed direction . . . Germany would not only have to right the wrongs in Poland and Czechoslovakia, but she would also have to give pledges that there would be no repetition of acts of aggression . . .

The message concluded:

> It is not for H.M.G. to say how these conditions could be met, but they are bound to say that, in their view, they are essential to the establishment of confidence on which peace could be solidly and durably based . . .
>
> Neither France nor Great Britain, as the Prime Minister said, have any desire to carry on a vindictive war, but they are determined to prevent Germany continuing to make life in Europe unbearable.[38]

On receiving this communication from Stevens on the morning of Tuesday, 31 October, Schellenberg and de Crinis departed from The Hague back to Düsseldorf. Schellenberg immediately flew to Berlin for a meeting with Heydrich to impart what had taken place. After completing his report, he added: 'The British officers declared that His Majesty's Government took great interest in our peace attempt which would contribute powerfully to prevent the spread of war . . . As for engagements and political agreements, they were not for the moment authorised to discuss them . . . They assured us that they were in direct contact with the Foreign Office and Downing Street.'[39] He concluded by telling the head of the SD that the British had invited him to secret peace negotiations in London, and that Stevens had even given him a transmitter (call sign ON4) with which he could maintain contact with the two British intelligence officers in The Hague.

Heydrich's response at this juncture was most interesting, indicating that his orders emanated from the very pinnacle of the Party, and that the 'deception campaign' originally mounted through Mörz the previous summer had indeed been superseded by true peace negotiations in the autumn at the behest of Himmler and Hitler.

'All this seems to me a little too good to be true,' he said to Schellenberg. 'I find it hard to believe that it's not a trap. Be very careful before going to London. Before making a decision I shall have to talk not only with the Reichsführer [Himmler] but more particularly with the Führer. Wait for my orders before proceeding.'[40]

Karl Neuer, a member of Himmler's personal staff at that time, was later to comment: 'I can remember quite clearly the great optimism of the Reichsführer upon hearing the news from General Heydrich concerning Schellenberg's operation in the Netherlands. In the presence of several members of staff he commented to General Wolff: "As I predicted, my dear Wölffchen ['Little Wolf', a nickname], the British do not want this war. We will soon have peace in the west." He then telephoned the Führer. This lasted a long time and resulted in further optimism, which he passed on by telephone back to Heydrich. Of course, we were not to know at the time that this optimism was to be destroyed by the shocking events in Munich, just a week later . . .'[41]

Back in London, on the morning of Wednesday, 1 November, Chamberlain stood before the War Cabinet and revealed to them for the first time details of the secret peace talks he had been conducting with the Germans. Those present were Lord Halifax, Sir John Simon, and Sir Samuel Hoare (representing Chamberlain's pro-appeasement faction), and Chatfield, Hankey, Kingsley Wood, Hore-Belisha, and last but not least, the First Sea Lord, Winston Churchill (the anti-appeasement bloc in the Cabinet). When Churchill heard the details of what had been taking place in Holland, his fury knew no bounds. Not only had Chamberlain and Halifax secretly engaged in a dangerous peace initiative, they had done so behind the back of the Cabinet. In Churchill's opinion the appeasement of Nazi Germany had led to the obliteration of the Czech state, to the invasion of Poland, and to Britain and France facing war just as they had in 1914. Yet apparently Chamberlain had not learnt the lessons of appeasement, and had attempted mediation again. This was bad enough, but Churchill also realised – something that had apparently escaped Chamberlain – that the Prime Minister had unwittingly placed the Anglo-French alliance itself in dire peril. If the Germans were to leak details of the secret negotiations to the French, it would utterly shatter the French government's confidence in Britain's resolve to stand firm in the face of German aggression.

Churchill need not have feared this outcome, for jeopardising the negotiations by putting them to use for some ulterior motive was the last thing on the Germans' minds. Hitler and Himmler were sincere in their desire for peace in the west. Hitler had no desire for war with Britain and France; his overriding priority was to expand German territory eastward at the expense of his eastern neighbours, ultimately including his nemesis, the Soviet Union.

Over the course of the next week Schellenberg maintained regular

contact with Stevens and Best by means of his transmitter, ON4. Via this
medium further details of the peace plan were discussed. These were to be
clarified when he travelled secretly to London for confidential discussions
with Sir Alexander Cadogan and Lord Halifax. Events, however, were
about to take a bizarre and unexpected twist. In Munich, on the night of
Wednesday, 8 November, something happened that would obliterate any
chance of success for Anglo-German peace negotiations.

Every year since the Munich Putsch of 1923, Hitler and 3,000 stalwarts
of the Nazi Party had gathered annually in the Bürgerbräukeller in central
Munich to celebrate the anniversary of the uprising. It was the one event
of the year that Hitler never missed, and he normally stayed late into
the night talking with his old comrades. As usual, he arrived promptly at
8.00 p.m. to a tumultuous welcome amidst much pomp and ceremony,
saluting and cheering. After several minutes of applause, the gathered
devotees settled down to listen to his animated oration on the evils of
Communism, the bravery of the fallen, the glorious futures of the gathered,
the wonders of National Socialism. From experience, the audience knew
that they were in for two hours of pure Führer rhetoric and they revelled
in it, for to be present in the Bürgerbräukeller on 8 November was a great
honour. On this occasion, however, Hitler rushed through his speech and
was finished within the hour. Then, much to the surprise of all those gathered, he shook hands with a few old comrades, put on his hat and coat, and
left. He had been present for just an hour and ten minutes.[42]

Unbeknownst to those gathered at the Bürgerbräukeller, their Führer
had pressing affairs of state to manage now that Germany was at war, and
he wanted to be in Berlin for an important meeting the following morning.
Usually he flew back to Berlin from Munich, but poor weather made such
a flight impossible on this occasion. As a result Hitler had decided to travel
overnight by train, and his private lounge car had been attached to the
Reichsbahn Express, waiting for him at Munich station.

Just twenty minutes after Hitler and his entourage had left, indeed
whilst they were still waiting at the train station to depart, a powerful bomb
shattered the interior of the Bürgerbräukeller, killing a substantial number
of the Party faithful and injuring many more. The bomb had been hidden
in a pillar a mere two metres from where Hitler had stood giving his speech
half an hour before.

On hearing the news of the bombing, 'The Führer's expression froze
into a hard, stubborn mask, and in a peremptory voice harsh with emotion
he exclaimed: "Now I am completely reassured; the fact of having left the

Bürgerbräukeller sooner than usual is the confirmation that Providence wants my destiny to be fulfilled.'"[43]

Conspiracy theories have occasionally surfaced over the years, suggesting that Heydrich, and perhaps even Himmler, had been behind the assassination attempt in order to clear the way for an SS takeover of the country. Once Hitler had been removed from power, a peace agreement could be reached with the west. Nevertheless, however much this would be in keeping with what we know about the purpose of the SS peace talks taking place in Holland, Himmler was still loyal to Hitler at this time, so SS/SD machinations behind the bombing are most unlikely. Himmler had been present at the Bürgerbräukeller with Hitler that evening. Indeed, to a degree the Reichsführer was responsible for saving Hitler's life, for it was on his prompting that the Führer decided not to stay late at the Bürgerbräukeller and fly overnight to Berlin. Himmler's secretary, Doris Mehner, was later to recall: 'The Reichsführer told me on November 8, around three in the afternoon, that the meeting at the Bürgerbräukeller had been moved forward and would be shorter than expected. The Führer would not be returning to Berlin by air, but by train. A private carriage would be attached at eight in the evening to the regular train 71 for Berlin, which left Munich at 9.31. Consequently I was to have Himmler's luggage and that of SS chiefs present transported at the hour stated. The Reichsführer-SS added, "I prefer this solution. By train we are sure to arrive. By plane, with the November fogs . . ."'[44]

On learning of the assassination attempt, both Hitler and Himmler were immediately suspicious of the two British intelligence agents in Holland. They had repeatedly emphasised to Mörz, Seidlitz, Grosch, and finally Schellenberg himself that the British government desired the removal of Hitler from power as a precondition of peace. As it happened, Stevens and Best were due to meet with Schellenberg at the little frontier town of Venlo the following day. Immediately the SD – under Heydrich's direct command – made plans to kidnap the two Britons and spirit them back to Germany, where they could be interrogated and the truth behind the bombing discovered.

The next afternoon, on Thursday, 9 November, Stevens and Best arrived at the Café Backus in Venlo, mere yards from the Dutch customs post guarding the border, to await Schellenberg. He appeared a few minutes later. Almost immediately, however, a gang of six SD officers, led by Alfred Naujocks, dashed across the frontier, shot up the Dutch customs post, grabbed the two startled British Intelligence officers, and made off with them back across the frontier into Germany. The two Britons' surprise was absolute, the Germans' snatch meticulous and well planned. Within hours both Stevens and Best were being intensively interrogated by German Intelligence. Although the Britons could in all honesty deny any knowledge of the assassination attempt on Hitler, they did possess a great deal of sensitive information about the British intelligence network in the Low Countries. Stevens and Best were not hard to break, and as a direct consequence of their interrogation the whole of Britain's secret service network in western Europe was brought crashing down, leaving it with virtually no intelligence-gathering capability.

As it happened, both the British government and its intelligence services were entirely innocent of the assassination attempt. The real culprit was a German carpenter by the name of Georg Elser, an idealistic loner who felt Hitler to be a danger to European peace. He had therefore determined to stop the Führer at all costs, working in secret for many weeks to plant a bomb in the Bürgerbräukeller. Despite his initial success, however, he was a complete novice, and he was apprehended within a few days by the Gestapo on the Austro-Swiss border whilst attempting to flee. Curiously, Heydrich would intercede on Elser's behalf to prevent his execution, and he was held in prison until the very end of the war.

The Venlo Incident, as it became known, would seem to have ensured the failure of the SS/SD peace initiative. All the available documentary evidence after the war indicated that the Anglo-German contact ended with Venlo. However, recent disclosures from Britain's Foreign Office archive have revealed that this was surprisingly not entirely the case, and that despite the difficulties both parties were still keen to negotiate. As mentioned before, this was hitherto unknown to historians.

On 16 November, a week after the abduction of Stevens and Best, Sir Alexander Cadogan drafted a 'Most Secret' report for the Prime Minister. In it he wrote an outline of the negotiations, commenting:

> On October 30th a reply was received . . . [from the Germans] to the effect that the Wehrmacht [SS – Cadogan was aware of Best's submission that he believed the German negotiators to be Nazi/SS] would not countenance a war of aggression and felt strong enough to take a leading part in the formation of a new Government in Germany, but would like to retain Göring . . . in office. Of the Government Herr Hitler would be the constitutional head . . . Without giving any detailed indication of proposals

that might be made by such a new Government, they declared that its object would be the return of Germany to peaceful and friendly relations with the rest of the world and that it would be sympathetic to a pan-European policy [as suggested by Chamberlain].

Cadogan concluded his report with a remarkable piece of news:

> The same Germans have in the last few days contrived to get in touch with us again . . .[45]

This means that, post Venlo, someone on the German side of the negotiations, almost certainly Schellenberg – with the backing of Himmler, otherwise he would not have dared to make the contact – had not entirely given up on the negotiations, and had attempted to keep open the line of communication to the British government.

Later that same day, Thursday, 16 November, the new Passport Control Officer in The Hague (Stevens's replacement), sent a message to Schellenberg's radio, ON4, which revealed that Chamberlain was still prepared to attempt a negotiated end to the conflict. The British attitude to dealing with the Nazis had, however, hardened:

> . . . there must be a restoration of confidence which has been destroyed by [the] existing German regime and which can only be achieved from within by a change both of the regime and of the spirit behind it. We have never contemplated a Europe in which Germany will not play her part as a great and respected nation, but we cannot face renewal of occurrences of past few years and new Government must inspire confidence if discussions are to be possible.
>
> We should like further details of proposals regarding the return of Germany to peaceful relations with the world. Also regarding the change over of Germany to a peace footing with object of achieving a 'total peace'. Daladier [the French Prime Minister] would have to be consulted before discussions.[46]

The following evening, on 17 November, Schellenberg's transmitter was again active, sending a message to the British agent in The Hague that declared:

We thank you for views of His Majesty's Government. Regret not to receive exact formulation [of peace proposal], as in view of fresh circumstances text not known, but necessary in order arrive at final consultations.

Our representative had orders to ascertain which personages nominated by London for conclusion [of] consultations.

How can Daladier be brought in for discussion in consultative form? Still see difficulties in him, especially on account of personage mentioned [Göring] in connection with new Government.[47]

London replied:

Full text of original message would not add anything important to the gist transmitted on November 16th.

Before we could consider any question of discussions, whether by nominated person or in any other way, we must have further information promised about the party and more precise details in regards to proposals.

There would be no need for Daladier to meet personage [Göring]. If proposals appeared sufficiently satisfactory, we would consult with him: we do not anticipate difficulty there.[48]

It is at this point that the communications stop dead. There was no German reply, as far as can be seen from the archive material, so it can only be assumed that at this point the negotiations petered out. The remaining documents are still sealed in the British archives under the seventy-five year rule and will not be available until 2014.

After the Bürgerbräukeller bombing in distant Munich that had almost taken Hitler's life, and which had resulted in the kidnapping of two British agents, it is likely that there was too much distrust of the Germans for the negotiations to have proceeded to any meaningful conclusion. However – and this is very important – as far as Neville Chamberlain and Lord Halifax were concerned, the Anglo-German negotiations, which had lasted six weeks, had been true peace talks. The fact that both the Prime Minister and the Foreign Secretary had personally headed Britain's partic- ipation in these secret negotiations indicates the seriousness with which they were regarded.

It should be remembered that, at the time of the Venlo Incident on

9 November, the war was still only eight weeks old, so a negotiated conclusion to the conflict had still been possible. Yet the very manner of the Venlo snatch of Stevens and Best by the SD finally impressed upon London that the Nazis were beyond the pale. How could Britain engage in meaningful peace talks with the Nazis when they reacted to an internal security scare by kidnapping Britain's peace emissaries?

A few days after the last of these communications between the British and the German authorities, Schellenberg, Heydrich, and Himmler were invited to dine with Hitler at the Reich Chancellery. Before dinner Schellenberg had a private meeting with the Führer to give him a full report on his negotiations with the British, including the likelihood of their complicity in the Bürgerbräukeller bombing. Georg Elser had been arrested by now and was insisting that he alone was responsible. Schellenberg was inclined to believe him.

Over dinner a little later that evening, Hitler turned to Himmler and remarked, 'Schellenberg doesn't think that the two British agents had anything to do with Elser.'

'Yes,' replied the Reichsführer-SS, 'there is no possibility of a link between them and Elser. But it could be that the Intelligence Service made contact with Elser through other channels. They could have used Germans, members of Otto Strasser's [brother of Gregor Strasser] Schwarze Front, for instance, but for the moment we're groping amongst hypotheses . . .'[49]

The meal continued with small talk, whilst Hitler finished his corn-on-the-cob and ate with relish his dessert of *Kaiserschmarren* – a pudding with raisins soaked in sweet sauce. At the end of the meal he suddenly asked Schellenberg, 'What was your general impression during the conversations you had with these Englishmen in Holland – I mean before their kidnapping and questioning?'

'My impression,' said Schellenberg with conviction, 'was that Great Britain will fight this war with all the fury and tenacity of which she has given proof in all wars in which she was thoroughly engaged. Even if we succeeded in occupying England, the government and the leaders would conduct the war from Canada. It will be a life and death struggle between countries of the same stock – and Stalin will look on with interest and amusement.'

For a long while Hitler sat silent, regarding Schellenberg with interest. Finally he said, 'I hope you realise that it is necessary to regard Germany's position as a whole. At the beginning I wanted to collaborate with Great Britain. But she rejected my advances. It is true that there is nothing worse than a family quarrel and, from a racial point of view, the English are in a way our relatives . . . It is extremely regrettable that we are engaged in this struggle to the death whilst our real enemies, to the east, wait tranquilly for Europe to be exhausted. It is for that reason that I don't want to destroy her. But they must be brought to understand, and Churchill first of all, that Germany has also the right to live. And I shall fight England till she gets off her pedestal. The day will come when she will show herself disposed to envisage an accord between us. That is my real aim. Do you understand?'

'Yes, my Führer,' replied Schellenberg, 'I follow your thought. But a war like this is comparable to an avalanche. And who would venture to plot the course of an avalanche?'

'My dear boy,' returned Hitler, 'those are my worries, leave them to me.'[50]

•••••

During the first ten weeks of war Hitler had made two attempts to negotiate peace secretly with the British government. The first approach, which had involved Dahlerus and Göring, had failed, and so, it seemed, had the second, which had involved Himmler and his protégés Heydrich and Schellenberg. The Dahlerus initiative had pandered to Göring's belief that the British would find the Swedish businessman an acceptable intermediary, but it had failed because the British did not trust Hitler. This had led almost immediately to Himmler's participation in the peace initiative, after he found that the SD had managed to establish a line of communication direct to the British government. These SS/SD negotiations had managed to proceed a great deal further than the Dahlerus initiative. They in turn had led to British acquiescence, in theory, in the retention of Hitler as German head of state, and of Göring as a member of the government. By virtue of Sigismund Payne Best's submission to London that he believed the German negotiators to be 'Nazi or SS', it is known that Sir Alexander Cadogan was aware of the situation; if Cadogan knew, then he must have informed his Minister, Lord Halifax, who in turn would have informed Neville Chamberlain. Halifax and Chamberlain had therefore moved to the position of negotiating with Nazis to end the war; it was a highly dangerous strategy that Churchill would have had no truck with, had he been fully informed of what was taking place.

However, it would be a grave mistake to believe that just because these German peace attempts failed, Hitler gave up on the notion that the best solution to the situation in which he found himself was to negotiate peace with the British. Over the months ahead he would repeatedly try through different intermediaries to open peace talks with the British government. Admittedly this became all the harder once Winston Churchill was installed as Prime Minister in May 1940; but war in the west was a disaster for Hitler's long-term plans of eastern conquest. As the British were to discover, he continued to believe that a political and diplomatic solution was required to end the conflict with Britain.

We have seen that Himmler was a man prepared to switch between his roles as Nazi politician and head of the SS. He had now also received his first experience in the complex world of peace negotiations. For the moment, whilst Germany continued to be victorious in every military adventure she embarked upon, he would pursue total German victory and grow comfortably into the role of Reichsführer-SS, head of German state security and the Waffen-SS. However, these victories would not last for ever. When the fortunes of war turned against Germany, Himmler would once again assume the mantle of a politician and attempt to enter into negotiations; only this time the British would have the upper hand.

NOTES

1. *Völkischer Beobachter*, 1 September 1939.
2. Herr R. Spitzy (Ribbentrop's Private Secretary), interview conducted 5 November 2001.
3. F.W. Winterbotham, interview with Peter Allen, 5 January 1981.
4. James Douglas-Hamilton, *The Truth about Rudolf Hess* (Mainstream, 1988), pp. 94–9. For a wider explanation of the politico-diplomatic situation regarding Anglo-German relations at this time see Chapters 1 and 2 of Martin Allen, *The Hitler/Hess Deception* (HarperCollins, 2003).
5. Douglas-Hamilton, ibid.
6. Herr R. Spitzy, interview conducted 5 November 2001.
7. Doc. No. 491, Documents on German Foreign Policy, Series D, Vol. XII (HMSO, 1961).
8. Diplomatic Document No. 242, French Yellow Book, 1938–39.
9. B.H. Liddell Hart, *The Other Side of the Hill* (Cassell, 1948), p. 123.
10. Herr R. Spitzy, interview conducted 5 November 2001.
11. André Brissaud, *Histoire du Service Secret Nazi* (Plon, 1972), p. 232.
12. Liddell Hart, op. cit., p. 200.
13. Doc. No. 106, Documents on German–Polish Relations (HMSO, 1940).
14. A. Bullock, *Hitler, A Study in Tyranny* (Odhams, 1952), p. 505.
15. Heinrich Hoffman, *Hitler Was My Friend* (London, 1955), pp. 115–16.

16. Albert Speer, *Inside the Third Reich* (Weidenfeld & Nicolson, 1970), p. 165.
17. Ibid.
18. Dahlerus Memorandum, pp. 140–5, Documents on German Foreign Policy, Series D, Vol. VIII (HMSO, 1955).
19. Ibid.
20. William Shirer, *The Rise and Fall of the Third Reich* (London, 1964), p. 772.
21. Doc. No. FO 371/26542, National Archives, Kew, London.
22. Ibid.
23. *Camp 020, MI5 and the Nazi Spies* (Public Records Office, 2000), p. 81.
24. Brissaud, op. cit., p. 239.
25. Doc. No. FO 371/30913, National Archives, Kew, London.
26. Brissaud, op. cit., p. 240.
27. Ibid., p. 241.
28. Leo Kessler, *Betrayal at Venlo* (Leo Cooper, 1991), p. 56.
29. John Colville, *The Fringes of Power* (Hodder and Stoughton, 1985), p. 40.
30. Ibid., p. 45.
31. Brissaud, op. cit., p. 241.
32. Doc. No. FO 371/30913, National Archives, Kew, London.
33. S. Payne Best, *The Venlo Incident* (Hutchinson, 1950), p. 123.
34. Ibid.
35. Kessler, op. cit., p. 60.
36. Ibid., p. 65.
37. Doc. No. FO 371/23107, National Archives, Kew, London.
38. Ibid.
39. Brissaud, op. cit., p. 244.
40. Ibid., p. 249.
41. Karl Neuer interview, Telfs, Austria, 23 December 2003.
42. Martin Allen, *Hidden Agenda* (Macmillan, 2000), pp. 142–4.
43. Brissaud, op. cit., p. 287.
44. Anton Hoch, *Das Attentat auf Hitler in Munchen Bürgerbraukeller 1939* (Vierteljahrshefte für Zeutgeschichte, 1969), p. 123.
45. Doc. No. FO 371/23107, National Archives, Kew, London.
46. Ibid.
47. Ibid.
48. Ibid.
49. Brissaud, op. cit., p. 278.
50. Ibid., pp. 279–80.

3
BRITISH INTELLIGENCE SUBVERTS HITLER'S PEACEABLE INTENT

Before exploring the first secret peace initiatives undertaken by Heinrich Himmler, it is first necessary to scrutinise British Intelligence's attitude to negotiating peace with Adolf Hitler, for what was to take place next largely determined how Himmler's future attempts at peace negotiation would be handled.

As we have seen, by the late autumn of 1939 Hitler had made two attempts to negotiate peace with the British government, but both had failed. However, he continued to make pitches for peace over the coming months. Nor were these appeals restricted to the German Führer: the British Foreign Office was inundated with approaches from such men as Joseph Goebbels, Hjalmar Schacht (President of the Reichsbank), Franz von Papen, and Dr Gessler (former German War Minister). These were high-level contacts by German ministers, each keen to enhance his standing in Hitler's eyes as the man who, through endeavour and cunning, had managed to open peace negotiations with the British. All these approaches were handled by the British Foreign Office and passed to Lord Halifax for consideration, but all failed because the British authorities had no intention of negotiating peace with leading Nazis.

There was, however, a different stratum of peaceable intent that attracted a great deal more attention and interest from the Foreign Office and, more particularly, from British Intelligence. Numerous eminent international figures offered themselves as intermediaries, wishing to impart to the British authorities important peace offers from the pinnacle of the German leadership. These eminent persons ranged right across the political, religious, and diplomatic spectrum, from the Pope to General Franco, the German Ambassador in Washington, and the King of Sweden. All these initiatives were mounted between the late autumn of 1939 and the summer of 1940, and all were brought to the attention of the Foreign Secretary, the

Prime Minister, and British Intelligence, for the very good reason that they were all discerned as having the hand of Hitler behind them.

These approaches must be placed in the context of the changing face of the war. Many of them took place during the so-called 'Phoney War' that continued from the late autumn of 1939 until the launching of Hitler's attack in the west in May 1940, and saw the resignation of Chamberlain as Prime Minister, the collapse of France, and the driving of the British Army into the sea at Dunkirk. Yet both Churchill (who took over the Premiership on 10 May 1940) and British Intelligence were intrigued by the timing of the most eminent of these approaches. It was launched at the beginning of August 1940, a mere two months after Dunkirk, when King Gustav V of Sweden sent a letter to King George VI in which he offered to act as a peace intermediary between the British government and Hitler.

Within days Churchill, mindful that much of western Europe had been conquered by Germany in the past three months and that Britain was waiting with bated breath to see if the Germans intended to invade Britain as well, sent a memorandum to Lord Halifax:

> I should reply as follows: In October 1939 His Majesty's Government defined at length their position towards German peace offers in a maturely considered statement made by . . . Mr Chamberlain . . .
>
> Since then, a number of new hideous crimes have been committed by Nazi Germany against the smaller States upon her borders. Norway has been overrun, and is now occupied by a German invading army. Denmark has been seized and pillaged. Belgium and Holland . . . have been conquered and subjugated . . .
>
> These horrible events have darkened the pages of European history with an indelible stain. His Majesty's Government see in them not the slightest cause to recede in any way from their principles and resolves as set forth in October 1939. On the contrary, their intention is to prosecute the war against Germany by every means in their power until Hitlerism is finally broken, and the world relieved from the curse which a wicked man has brought upon it . . .[1]

Such was the public face of Winston Churchill's response to the Hitler-sponsored peace appeals. However, in private and in confidence to his inner circle of close acquaintances, his attitude was most interesting.

On 9 August (a week after King Gustav's offer to mediate between Britain and Hitler had been rejected), one of Churchill's oldest friends, Reginald 'Rex' Leeper, wrote to Hugh Gaitskell, then at the Ministry of Economic Warfare. Leeper was head of Special Operations 1 (SO1), a top-secret branch of Britain's newest weapon in the war against Germany, the Special Operations Executive (SOE). His letter was intended primarily to apologise for failing to send Gaitskell the minutes of a previous meeting; however, he went on to comment:

> You may be interested to know that following Ingrams' B[lack] P[ropaganda] suggestion, I took the idea to the P[rime] M[inister] who felt the German Leadership was now *ripe for exploitation* [author's italics]. I am sure the key to this B.P. lies within Hitler's recent attempts to find an accord. Ingrams and Crossman are going to look into this idea as any below the belt Ops we can initiate at this crucial time can only help.[2]

The knowledge that Hitler was secretly seeking peace was further enhanced for Churchill and Leeper by a most unusual incident that had also occurred in August. It reinforced their belief that Hitler was prepared to go to extraordinary lengths to secure peace with Britain, and that this might, with skill, be turned upon him.

Even as Britain was coming under daily attack by the Luftwaffe – which most British politicians and military Chiefs of Staff believed to be a prelude to invasion – Hitler had dispatched yet another emissary to contact the British authorities. But this one brought a remarkable peace offer. Churchill began to fear seriously that it might split the Cabinet between those who wished to fight on, and those who felt enough had been done in support of Poland and it was now time to negotiate an armistice.

All Adolf Hitler's peace offers thus far had been official and semi-public, made through members of the German diplomatic service or eminent international figures. This time, however, he made his overture to Britain on the strict understanding that it be kept absolutely secret, and that on no account should it fall into the public domain until such time as an agreement had come about. What intrigued the Foreign Office and British Intelligence most was that it was clear that no one else in Germany – politician, diplomat, or foreign affairs advisor – knew about it either.

This latest peace offer had been made in Sweden when the Swedish High Court Justice, Dr Ekeberg, had contacted the British Ambassador in

Stockholm, Victor Mallet. Ekeberg informed Mallet that he had been approached by Hitler's personal legal advisor, Dr Ludwig Weissauer, who wished him to pass on Hitler's peace offer to Churchill and the Foreign Secretary. Mallet immediately dispatched a 'Most Secret' report to London, revealing what he had learnt from Ekeberg:

> Hitler, according to his emissary [Weissauer], feels responsible for the future of the white race. He wishes for sincere friendship with England. He wishes for the restoration of peace, but the ground must be prepared: only after such careful preparation can official discussions begin. Up till then it must be a condition that conversations be quite unofficial and secret . . .

Mallet reported Hitler's five-point peace plan as follows:

> 1 The [British] Empire remains with all colonies and mandates.
> 2 The continental supremacy of Germany will not be called into question.
> 3 All questions concerning the Mediterranean and the French, Belgian and Dutch colonies are open to discussion.
> 4 Poland. There must be 'a Polish State'.
> 5 Czechoslovakia must belong to Germany.

He further expanded upon these terms, revealing Hitler's intentions as Weissauer had conveyed them to Ekeberg:

> that the other European States occupied by Germany [Norway, Denmark, Holland, Belgium, and France] would have their sovereignty restored. It was only owing to the present military situation that Germany now has to continue to occupy them until the peace . . . Weissauer said that Hitler wished to re-establish the sovereignty of all the occupied countries 'auf die dauer' [on a permanent basis]. He has no interest in the internal affairs of these states. Germany's interest is to prevent a fresh war as Europe needs 100 years of peace . . .

Mallet, a career diplomat unused to the shady world of secret peace negotiations, concluded his report with the comment:

I am naturally rather uncomfortable at having become even to this small extent involved in this mysterious proceeding . . . Please forgive my bad typing, but I felt it best to show this to nobody.[3]

This was no insubstantial peace offer by Hitler. In particular, the reference to the reformation of 'a Polish State' was one of the British government's primary preconditions for peace. It also gives a fair indication of what Chamberlain and Lord Halifax had found so tantalising in the autumn of 1939 when dealing with the German Führer through Birger Dahlerus and then Walter Schellenberg. Halifax was still a leading man of the 'pro-peace faction' within the Cabinet, and as such he was immediately struck by the genuine nature of Hitler's offer. However, if he thought it might be a good idea to pursue this peaceable approach, he was to receive a very rude awakening to the realities of the present situation from Sir Robert Vansittart, his Chief Diplomatic Advisor.

Vansittart was another old ally of Churchill, and he, with Rex Leeper (who prior to taking over SO1 had been head of the Political Intelligence Department of the Foreign Office), had kept Churchill informed about the deteriorating European situation in the late 1930s. The two men had then joined Churchill in becoming founding members of the Anti-Nazi League. With such a pedigree, and as a loyal stalwart of the Churchill camp, Vansittart was not about to pander to the Foreign Secretary's belief that this peace approach could be pursued.

Immediately he learnt of Mallet's communication to Lord Halifax, Vansittart wrote a letter to the Foreign Secretary that was intended to educate him swiftly about the true nature of the dangers faced by Britain. Over sixty years on, this letter still makes uncomfortable reading, for it affirms that it was not merely Nazism that presented a danger to British interests, but Germany herself:

> Secretary of State. URGENT.
> I hope that you will instruct Mr. Mallet that he is on no account to meet Dr. Weissauer. The future of civilisation is at stake. It is a question of we or they now, and either the German Reich or this country has got to go under, and not only under, but right under . . . The German Reich and the Reich idea have been a curse of the world for 75 years, and if we do not stop it this time, we never shall, and they will stop us. The enemy is the German Reich and not merely Nazism, and those who have not learned

this lesson have learned nothing whatsoever, and would let us in
for a sixth war even if we survived the fifth [Vansittart was referring not only to the First World War, but also to prior conflicts
such as the Franco-Prussian War of 1870 and the Boer War]. I
would far sooner take my chances of surviving the fifth. All possibility of compromise have now gone, and it has got to be a fight to
the finish, and to a real finish.

I trust that Mr. Mallet will get the most categorical instructions. We have had more than enough of Dahlerus, Goerdeler,*
Weissauer and company.[4]

Despite Vansittart's vehement rejection of any peace offer emanating
from Berlin, and most particularly one that was known to have originated
from Hitler himself, the Weissauer offer was still of major importance.
Lord Halifax, as Foreign Secretary, had considerable influence. Regardless
of Vansittart's objections and Churchill's misgivings, he managed to ensure
that the offer was placed before the heads of the Dominion governments –
Canada, Australia, New Zealand, and South Africa. He did not get things
completely his own way, however, for Churchill inserted both a proviso that
Hitler had to show his good intentions by withdrawing from all the occupied countries before the British government was prepared to negotiate
peace, and his own recommendation that the offer be rejected. The heads
of the Dominion governments concurred with Churchill and the peace
offer was refused.

This last initiative by Hitler, combined with what the Foreign Office
had learnt from the attempt at mediation by King Gustav V, was now
handed over to Rex Leeper's men at SO1. They had very definite plans to
unsettle Hitler's overall war strategy now that he was, in Churchill's words,
'ripe for exploitation'.*[5]

Hitler had demonstrated time and time again over the previous eleven
months of war that he desired peace with Britain. Even after the defeat of
the British Army in France and the flight of Britain's forces from the
beaches of Dunkirk, he was attempting to find avenues to the British
government that would enable him to express this desire. Now, in the
summer of 1940, while the Battle of Britain raged in the skies above
London and the Home Counties, he had once again tried to open a line of
communication to Churchill and Lord Halifax.

* Carl Goerdeler was a prominent anti-Nazi and Lord Mayor of Leipzig. In the autumn of
1939 he had tried to mediate a peace agreement between Britain and Germany, but this too
had been refused.
* Author's italics.

What interested the analysts and theorists under Rex Leeper at SO1, however, was the knowledge that Hitler had kept his last peace approach secret from almost everyone in Berlin. Mallet had reported a declaration by Weissauer that 'only two people in Germany know of his mission'.[6] This was taken to mean that only Hitler's closest confidant, Rudolf Hess, a man expert in foreign affairs, was involved. The analysts at SO1 knew that Hitler trusted Hess implicitly, and that Hess had studied geopolitics and foreign affairs at Munich University under the eminent Professor Karl Haushofer in the years immediately following the First World War. When Hitler's failed Munich Putsch of 1923 had sentenced him and Hess to six months' incarceration at Landsberg prison, Haushofer had visited the two men during their confinement. It was also known that Hess and Haushofer between them had written substantial passages on foreign affairs in Hitler's book *Mein Kampf*; the book had therefore been a collaboration between Hitler's own ideological opinions and Hess's and Haushofer's knowledge of geopolitics and foreign affairs. Hess was the only man, SO1 concluded, sufficiently well versed in foreign affairs and trusted by Hitler to give him confidential advice on how to achieve peace with the British.

What intrigued the men of SO1 most was that Hitler had made a major error. In allowing Weissauer to impart the information that no one in Germany, except himself and one other, knew of the Führer's latest appeal, he had intended to show that he genuinely desired peace and was being open with the British. However, to SO1 it revealed that, not wanting to appear weak or indecisive, he was attempting to negotiate with the British government without the assistance either of his very capable advisors in the Foreign Ministry or any other members of the Nazi regime. He had there-fore relegated himself to the position of a lone individual trying to negotiate peace with the experts in the British Foreign Office and government. The men of SO1 concluded that Hitler, perhaps for the first time, was alone and vulnerable. It was an opportunity they could not afford to miss.

Within a year Rex Leeper's seed of an idea – that Hitler's secret peace approaches could be turned upon him like a weapon – would germinate into one of the most successful and best-kept British Intelligence secrets of the Second World War. However, before looking at this operation, code-named 'Messrs HHHH', it is first necessary to consider the development of SO1 and its relationship to the other organs of British Intelligence, MI6 (the Secret Intelligence Service, or SIS) and its sister organisation, SO2. What was to take place between the summers of 1940 and 1941 would bear directly on British Intelligence's handling of Heinrich Himmler's later attempts to secretly negotiate peace. It would involve the same organisation, the same men, and the same British reasoning. Despite his comment that 'I am . . . rather uncomfortable at having become even to this small extent involved in this mysterious proceeding'[7], it would also involve Victor Mallet, the British Ambassador in Stockholm. Churchill would give him no choice in the matter, and Mallet would find himself under the direct command of one of the most powerful and sinister organs of British Intelligence.

•••••

It is widely acknowledged that British Intelligence's contribution to the war effort between September 1939 and the summer of 1940 was largely ineffectual, and its presence in several key areas virtually non-existent. This was the result both of the British government's chronic underfunding of its intelligence services ever since the end of the First World War, and British Intelligence's inadequate leadership in the latter 1930s.

During the First World War Britain's Secret Intelligence Service had fulfilled a vital role reflected by its substantial budget, which amounted to nearly £250,000 per annum. However, immediately the war ended in 1918 the British government rewarded SIS's contribution to the war effort by slashing its budget to £125,000. This was reduced still further in 1920, on Foreign Office recommendation, to a mere £65,000.[8] Such a ruthless cost-cutting exercise devastated British Intelligence's effectiveness during the inter-war period and resulted in a much diminished organisation. Add to this the fact that the Passport Control Officer and Z Network system, first devised in those far-off, halcyon days of pre-First World War Europe, was by the 1930s thoroughly antiquated and totally inadequate when pitted against the modern German intelligence systems of the Abwehr and the SD, and it becomes clear that British Intelligence was in deep trouble.

The leading men of British Intelligence were well aware of the situation, and by the latter 1930s were desperately trying to find a way to modernise MI6/SIS's intelligence gathering. They realised that its systems were now obsolete and that a complete overhaul of the entire intelligence organisation was necessary if they were to keep up with the Germans. However, such a modernisation would be an expensive undertaking, and money was something they did not possess, for the government persisted in keeping SIS short of proper finance. In the end, through dire necessity, the money was found. But, in a manner more akin to the twenty-first century, SIS was forced to look to the private sector to make up its funding shortfall.

Once the decision to modernise had been taken by SIS, an officer named Major Lawrence Grand was ordered to undertake the creation of a new department that would not only supersede the antiquated Passport Control Officer and Z Network system, but would also have the capability to carry out sabotage. Fortunately, Grand was well connected. Knowing that finance for the project would not be forthcoming from the government, he turned for help to an old acquaintance by the name of Chester Beatty. Beatty was chairman of the Selection Trust Group, which owned substantial mining interests worldwide. He agreed to provide the finance Grand required, but there would be a quid pro quo. He had just acquired a mine in Serbia called Trepca, accessing one of the richest mineral deposits in Europe. Given the fragile political state of affairs in the Balkans, he wanted Grand's assistance to protect it.

In exchange for 'technical assistance' from SIS – which included the presence of Intelligence officers at the mine, and the supply of up-to-date information on the ever-changing political situation in Yugoslavia – Beatty began to make substantial financial contributions to Grand's new project.[9] Grand and the heads of SIS were delighted, for they now had the means to finance the development of their brand-new organisation, the remit of which was officially designated as intelligence gathering and sabotage in enemy territory. Its name was chosen by Grand; he named it Section D – D for destruction. However, all was not as it seemed. Grand was just about to fall from favour.

With the start of the war in September 1939, Britain's Ministry of Economic Warfare (MEW) was ordered to look at all European mining and production, and to assess which were British assets that could be relied upon to maintain supplies during the conflict, and which German assets that could be sabotaged. MEW was headed by the dynamic Labour MP Hugh Dalton, a brilliant economist and a man widely recognised as possessing a prodigious intellect. As a result of his leadership the Ministry was tenacious in pursuing its answers. By the late autumn of 1939 questions were being asked in MEW and the Foreign Office about Chester Beatty's Trepca mine, for no one had been able to work out where its production of zinc and lead – both of which are munitions minerals – was going.

After an investigation by the British Embassy in Belgrade, MEW received a most alarming answer. It was discovered that Trepca had only one significant customer, who took over 70 per cent of the mine's production. This was shipped by rail to the Greek port of Thessalonica, where it was loaded aboard ships bound for Antwerp. Investigation in Belgium revealed that from Antwerp the Trepca ore was carried by rail through eastern Belgium and across the border into the Ruhr – Germany's industrial heartland. The mystery customer turned out to be the German government; virtually all of Trepca's output was effectively supporting the German war effort.[10] The implications for Lawrence Grand and British Intelligence were enormous, for it was revealed that not only had SIS aided Chester Beatty in maintaining control of a munitions mine that was supporting the German war effort, it had unwittingly used German money to finance the creation of Section D.

In the resultant outcry Section D was immediately stripped from SIS, and after some indecision it was eventually attached to Britain's newest weapon in the war against Germany, the Special Operations Executive (SOE). While SIS paid a high price, Grand was not forgotten by the vengeful British authorities. With a complete disregard for his good intentions, he found his loyalty to Britain questioned. Banished to distant India, he was stationed at a lonely radio listening post near the Himalayas for the duration of the war.

Despite its curious and unconventional origins, Section D was to become a key component of SOE, a core around which the entire organisation was eventually to be constructed, and it became closely identified with SOE's role of sabotage in the occupied territories.

One should not forget SIS. It was extremely annoyed at having its newest and most useful tool stripped from it, a situation that would breed enmity so considerable that in the years ahead, a state of war was almost to exist between SIS and SOE. This would pose considerable problems in the future; in one instance a government minister was even required to visit Cairo to investigate the circumstances that were causing the two organisations to pit most of their endeavour (which was costing lives) against each other, rather than against the enemy in the Middle East. This enmity also existed between SIS and SOE in Sweden. The British Ambassador, Victor Mallet, would find himself caught in the middle of the two embittered parties, each distrustful of the other and determined not to let the other side in on its secret operations. As we shall see, that situation was to result in calamitous consequences for the Himmler negotiations.

SOE was a remarkable organisation, destined from its inception to become controversial. Created by the War Cabinet in July 1940, and known ever since as the unit charged by Churchill to 'set Europe ablaze', it was for the first year of its existence really two organisations, each having a very different role.

The major component of SOE, designated Special Operations 2 (SO2), was created by the amalgamation of Section D and the Military Intelligence directorate of the War Office. This latter was the cloak-and-dagger unit charged with sending agents into occupied Europe to foment revolt against the German occupiers and to sabotage anything that aided the German war effort, such as factories, telephone exchanges, railways, and bridges.

The smaller section of SOE, designated Special Operations 1 (SO1), was altogether much more sinister, and so secret that few people ever heard of it, either during the war or after. Having begun its operations out of Electra House on the Embankment in London, it was originally known as Department EH. It was steeped in the art of psychological warfare, involving enemy subversion through covert or 'black' propaganda. Its 'front' activities ranged from acts as simple as the dropping of leaflets over enemy territory, to broadcasting 'free' radio to Germany and the occupied territories. SO1's true raison d'être, however, was 'political warfare', aimed at causing political damage to the enemy by whatever means available. Because of this sensitive and crucial role – a secret war of wits pitted against the Germans for the duration of the war – Churchill immediately recognised SO1's impor-tance as a tool to be used against the Nazi leadership. He therefore ordered not only that his close acquaintance Rex Leeper should be placed in charge, but that the entire operation be relocated to Woburn Abbey, the country seat of the Duke of Bedford, safe from the London Blitz deep in the Bedfordshire countryside.

However, despite being Prime Minister, Churchill did not always get his own way, and even in the act of creating SOE he was to be frustrated by cross-party politics. Churchill was head of a coalition government, and so, after considerable pressure from Clement Attlee, the Deputy Prime Minister and leader of the Labour Party, he was forced to make Hugh Dalton the Minister for SOE. Churchill did not like the capable Dalton, who was still also the Minister of Economic Warfare, and he had his own ideas about who should head SOE. He wanted Lord Swinton, a long-time colleague and fellow-thinker who had supported him during his 'wilder-ness years' and over the call for rearmament in the 1930s. And though Churchill lost the first round in the battle for the control of SOE, he was just as tenacious as Dalton, and considerably more cunning. Within a year of obtaining his brand-new Ministry, Dalton would fall from power with shocking speed.

In the meantime, however, there were almost immediately indications that things were not going to be comfortable for Dalton at SOE. Even as he attained his glittering new ministerial post in the summer of 1940, he found that he had in effect become step-parent to terrible twins. One of these he wanted and understood; the other he never really came to grips with, and in the end it would prove to be his undoing. SO2's remit for sabotage and resistance in occupied Europe was a form of warfare that Dalton believed himself well able to orchestrate; it complemented very nicely his Ministry of Economic Warfare. However, he had scant experience of the dark-side organisation, SO1, and he found this unit troublesome. SO1 was led by Churchill loyalists, men with whom Dalton had little in common. He found it difficult to comprehend how far they were capable of going in their efforts to undermine the enemy.

•••••

SO1's very first operation, mounted at the end of August 1940, gave an almost immediate indication of its potential as a formidable weapon. Rex Leeper and his band of carefully selected men, with a pedigree in deep deceit and subterfuge that dated back to the First World War, were highly enthusiastic about their new organisation, and determined to mount an ambitious act of political warfare as their opening gambit.

Leonard St Clair Ingrams's 'Black Propaganda' suggestion of early August 1940, which Leeper had reported to Gaitskell, was now combined with SO1's knowledge of the Weissauer peace initiative, and a very original 'sting' was dreamed up to unseat Hitler's strategic plans for the conduct of the war. An outline of the scheme conceived by Leeper, Ingrams (a leading member of SO1), and Richard Crossman (head of the German Section) was clearly laid out in the minutes of an SO1 meeting held at Woburn Abbey:

> We should . . . encourage the Germans to attack Russia by misleading Hitler and by hinting that the large sections both in Britain and the United States who preferred to see the overthrow of the Russian rather than the German regime might be prepared to force through a compromise peace between Britain and Germany and combine to destroy the common enemy, Communism.

The minute went on:

> At the invitation of the Minister [Hugh Dalton], Mr Anthony
> Eden put forward a number of questions arising out of what he
> had already heard, after which the Committee was adjourned.[11]

Also present at that meeting, as well as Hugh Dalton and Anthony
Eden, were Sir Robert Vansittart, Hugh Gaitskell, Robert Bruce Lockhart,
and twenty-five other leading men of SO1, the Foreign Office, and the
Ministry of Economic Warfare. Their purpose was to discuss the mounting
of a secret operation against Hitler to trick him into making a fatal strategic
error. Hitler had made so many secret peace initiatives during the first year
of the war that these men were confident that they could depend on one
more. Only this time, unbeknownst to the Führer, he would be played like
a fish on a long line.

Leeper was now to learn of a fortuitous set of circumstances that might
be used to entrap Hitler, tempting bait that he knew the Nazis would find
hard to resist. SO1 already knew that Hitler had been aided in his
Weissauer initiative by Rudolf Hess; they also knew that both Professor
Karl Haushofer and, more particularly, his son Albrecht (Hitler's
Confidential Advisor on Foreign Affairs) were very close to Hess. The
Finance Director of SO1 was a man by the name of Walter Roberts, a City
of London banker seconded to the organisation for the duration of the war.
Roberts informed Leeper that his aunt, Violet Roberts, together with her
late husband, Herbert (a Cambridge don), had been very close friends of
the Haushofers ever since the 1890s. Karl Haushofer and his wife, Martha,
had visited them in Cambridge during Haushofer's lecture tour of Britain
in 1894. Given that the Roberts and the Haushofers had been close friends
for over forty years, might not this situation present an ideal opportunity to
start the ball rolling in the operation to entrap Hitler?[12]

Leeper evidently thought so. Within a very few days, at the end of
August 1940, Violet Roberts was approached by SO1 and asked to help her
country. Under the guidance of SO1 she wrote a personal letter to Karl
Haushofer, bemoaning the disaster of war, expressing her hopes for an early
end to the conflict, and offering her services to Haushofer if he wished to
contact any leading Britons in order to work towards peace. She gave her
reply address as PO Box 500, Lisbon, Portugal. This seemed a welcome
opportunity to Haushofer and Hess; as luck would have it, the letter
arrived at exactly the same moment that Hess was consulting Haushofer

on how the next peace approach to the British could best be made. However, Hitler, Hess, and the Haushofers were just about to fall into SO1's trap. Violet Roberts's reply address, widely known as a postal address of Thomas Cook in Lisbon, was throughout the Second World War operated by British Intelligence.

A few days after Karl Haushofer had spoken with Hess, he wrote to Albrecht in Vienna, summoning him back to Germany for an important meeting. The three met on 8 September, and Hess was keen to hear any guidance that the well-connected Albrecht might be able to give him. Albrecht had several people in mind (close acquaintances he had made in the 1920s and 1930s whilst on extended visits to Britain), two of whom emerged as the most likely choices. The first was Sir Samuel Hoare; as British Ambassador to Spain he had the advantage of being in a neutral country, which made communications and access an easy matter. He had been a prominent member of Chamberlain's pro-appeasement faction in the latter 1930s, and so the Germans believed he would actively pursue any possible peace initiative. The second was 'the closest of my [Albrecht's] English friends: the young Duke of Hamilton, who has access at all times to all important persons in London, even to Churchill and the King'.[13]

Back in Britain the plan to entrap Hitler was given a code name. Hitler, Hess, and the two Haushofers all had one thing in common – the letter 'H' that started their surnames – and so, it is presumed (no explanation is given in the relevant documents), the scheme was named after them: 'Messrs HHHH'.

It soon became apparent to SO1 that the bait proffered in the name of Violet Roberts had been nibbled, for they received through the PO Box 500 address in Portugal a letter addressed to the Duke of Hamilton from Albrecht Haushofer. Bearing the date 23 September 1940, it stated:

> My Dear Douglo,
> Even if this letter has only a slight chance of reaching you – there is a chance and I want to make use of it.
> First of all to give you a sign of unaltered and unalterable personal attachment. I do hope you have been spared in all this ordeal, and I hope the same is true of your brothers . . .
> Now there is one thing more. If you remember some of my last communications before the war started you will realise that there is a certain significance in the fact that I am, at present, able to ask you whether there is the slightest chance of our meeting and

having a talk somewhere on the outskirts of Europe, perhaps in
Portugal. There are some things I could tell you, that might make
it worth while for you to try a short trip to Lisbon – if you could
make your authorities understand so much that they would give
you leave. As to myself – I could reach Lisbon . . . within a few
days after receiving news from you. If there is an answer to this
letter, please address it to . . .[14]

It has never been officially admitted whether there was a reply to
Haushofer's letter, and too many wartime documents have been destroyed
or withheld, both in Britain and Germany, for it to be possible to explore
this question satisfactorily. However, a rather surprising source confirms
that communications did take place and reveals a great deal about what
was really going on.

On 24 October 1942 Lavrenti Beria, head of Soviet Russia's security
service, the NKVD (the People's Commissariat of Internal Affairs, fore-
runner of the KGB), wrote a report for Stalin on what he had discovered
that British Intelligence was up to in 1940–41, prior to the German attack
on Russia. In this he asserted that not only had Albrecht Haushofer written
to the Duke of Hamilton, but Rudolf Hess had done so as well. Suspecting
collusion between the British and the Germans, Beria had launched an
investigation as a result of Hess's notorious flight to Scotland in May 1941
(of which more later). In the following months he managed to obtain a very
useful source of intelligence: Frantisek Moravetz, the Chief of Czech
Military Intelligence in Britain. Moravetz had informed the NKVD resident in London that 'All Hess's letters to Hamilton did not reach him but
were intercepted by British Intelligence where the answers to Hess in the
name of Hamilton were manufactured.'[15]

This report was not entirely accurate: Moravetz had somehow managed
to transpose Hess's name with that of Haushofer as the writer of the
letters. It may be that he was trying to impart that the originator of the
communications behind Haushofer had been Hess, or that he himself had
misunderstood. Nevertheless, despite this discrepancy, it is perhaps significant that the head of the Czech Bureau in London – the British government's liaison to the Czech government in exile – was Robert Bruce
Lockhart. A close friend of both Churchill and Rex Leeper, Lockhart
worked for Special Operations 1 out at Woburn Abbey. He had also, incidentally, been a close friend of Frantisek Moravetz since the early 1930s,
when he had been a banker in Czechoslovakia. Lockhart therefore had

inside knowledge about Operation Messrs HHHH, and was almost certainly the source of Frantisek Moravetz's information, although it is doubtful whether Lockhart ever told his friend about the true nature of SO1's operation.

At the same time as SO1 received Albrecht Haushofer's letter to the Duke of Hamilton, the next phase of the operation swung into action when Sir Samuel Hoare, the British Ambassador in Madrid, proffered another tantalising morsel of bait to the Germans. He met with the Spanish Minister of the Interior, Ramón Serrano Suñer, Franco's brother-in-law and a well-known German sympathiser, and told him that 'England had lost the war and was only making her situation worse by resisting further.'[16] On hearing this, Suñer promptly reported on his meeting with Hoare to the German Ambassador, Eberhard von Stohrer, who in turn transmitted a memorandum of the conversation back to Berlin.

Any such report was bound to be eagerly lapped up by the Nazi leadership. It was just the sort of intelligence that might indicate a weakening of the resolve of certain high-ranking British politicians to drag the war on to a bitter and protracted end. And, little over a week later, the Nazis were further heartened to receive a similar report from Hoyningen-Huene, their ambassador in Lisbon. As he claimed, a member of the British Embassy in Lisbon had informed a Portuguese diplomat that 'the organisation of London [is] completely destroyed by the air raids, looting, sabotage, and social tension'. However, the most important news Hoyningen-Huene imparted was that 'Anxious capitalists fear internal disorders. Growth of opposition against [the] Cabinet is plain. Churchill . . . [and] Halifax are blamed for sacrificing England to destruction instead of seeking a compromise with Germany, for which it is still not too late.'[17]

From the Nazi leadership's point of view it began to appear that, with a sufficiently generous offer, political opposition in Britain to a compromise peace might collapse, and some diplomatic progress might at last be made.

In itself, Haushofer's letter to the Duke of Hamilton had been necessarily mundane, for he had feared it coming to the attention of the British authorities. If that had happened (and it is important to remember that Hess and Haushofer were making an attempt to circumvent the Churchill government), then the avenue of the Duke of Hamilton might have been closed to them. However, Haushofer's guarded use of language in asserting that 'there is a certain significance in the fact that I am, at present, able to ask you whether there is the . . . chance of our meeting . . . somewhere on the outskirts of Europe . . .' indicated to the men at SO1 that their labours to contact the Nazi hierarchy were beginning to bear fruit. He would not have been granted permission to travel to a neutral country without the permission of Hitler or Hess. Yet, beyond this letter – and it is certain that SO1 used the Haushofers as a medium to contact Hitler and Hess – there was no sign, so far, that anything would come of their endeavours. It remained to be seen whether the Germans would take the bait dangled by Hoare in Madrid and the member of the diplomatic mission in Lisbon. In fact, SO1 did not have long to wait.

Before embarking on an account of the mysterious events that were now to take place, it is important to make clear Sir Samuel Hoare's political pedigree as a loyal Briton. It has often been asserted since the Second World War that Churchill banished Hoare from London to Madrid because he had opposed him during the run-up to war, having been, with Neville Chamberlain and Lord Halifax, one of the leading men of appeasement during the 1930s. To a degree this was true – Hoare had done all in his power to placate the Nazis and avoid conflict – but now that war was raging he had become a stalwart supporter of the British cause, determined like Churchill to see Nazi Germany defeated at all costs. Hoare had therefore been sent to Spain with a very special mission given to him personally by Churchill. He had been appointed Ambassador Extraordinary with Plenipotentiary Powers, and his purpose was to make sure that Spain remained neutral. This was extremely important: if Spain were to join the Axis, Britain would inevitably lose Gibraltar. Without Gibraltar, Britain would lose access to the Mediterranean, and without the Mediterranean, she might lose North Africa and Egypt. Thus a neutral Spain was crucial if a chain reaction of disaster was not to take place that would turn the war still further in Germany's favour. As it turned out, Generalissimo Franco was not keen to plunge his country into war, but his attitude was certainly influenced by the leading Spanish generals – or at least by the many millions of pounds sterling used by Hoare and his naval attaché, Gareth Hillgarth (another close acquaintance of Churchill), to bribe as many of those generals as they could to advise Franco to stay out of the conflict. The ploy succeeded, and Spain remained neutral.

In the events that follow, one might be forgiven for gaining the impression that Hoare was a member of the anti-Churchill camp. That, however, was exactly what SO1 wanted the Nazi leadership to think. And it was important, for Hitler and Hess were just about to make a most ambitious bid not only to negotiate peace with Britain, but also to oust Churchill from the Premiership.

During the second week of November 1940 Hoare received a message inviting him to a confidential meeting with the Papal Nuncio in Madrid. It is not clear where this meeting – which occurred on Thursday, 14 November – took place. Possibly it was held at the home of Colonel Juan Beigbeder y Atienza, leader of the Falange in Madrid. He had a prior track record for acting as intermediary between Britain and Germany, and his home had often been used for such covert meetings; indeed, Albrecht Haushofer had secretly met with Hoare in Beigbeder's home in July 1940. Alternatively, the meeting may have taken place at Hoare's private residence at Calle de los Hermanos Becquer No. 3, which curiously was next door to the home of Stohrer, the German Ambassador.

This was extremely unusual, and it is known that Hoare had picked this house specifically, knowing full well who lived next door. Helmut Blummenstrauss, a member of the German Legation in Madrid during the war, has asserted to me that Hoare and Stohrer, and later Count von Molkte, secretly met on several occasions during the war. He understood that at these meetings – which always took place in Hoare's house – Stohrer imparted further German peace appeals.[18]

Also present at the meeting with the Papal Nuncio was Captain Hillgarth, who took copious notes and subsequently typed up the report for dispatch to London. Hillgarth was a significant figure: he was SOE's top man in Spain, and Hoare's 'fixer'. He was also trusted implicitly by Churchill; he always stayed with the Prime Minister at Chequers when he visited Britain, and he was destined to become one of the key players in the Messrs HHHH operation.

Upon sitting down to discussions with the Papal Nuncio, it soon became apparent to both Hoare and Hillgarth that this was not just another mediocre appeal for peace by a well-meaning intermediary. Rather, they were sitting before an emissary direct from Hitler, Hess, and Haushofer, who brought an extremely comprehensive peace offer specifically for Sir Samuel Hoare's ears only. Hillgarth was to report:

> At this meeting he [the Papal Nuncio] informed Sir Samuel that he had been requested to communicate the following peace offer on the behalf of the German Government representative the Ambassador met last July at the home of Beigbeder (APA [Aussenpolitischesamt – foreign policy office] representative Haushofer), when the last round of peace offers were made.

The Nuncio informed the Ambassador of the German Government's sincere wish to end the hostilities, and that he had been asked to hand the following details for transmission to a party who would be willing to act upon them . . .

1 A confidential meeting as soon as possible in Switzerland between the representatives who are prepared to negotiate . .

2 Norway, Denmark, Holland, Belgium, and France would be independent free states, able to choose their constitution and government; but opposition to Germany must be excluded and assurances of non-retaliation given. Germany would withdraw her military forces, would not claim military concessions in these countries, and is prepared to negotiate a form of reparation for damage inflicted during conquest.

3 All aggressive weapons to be destroyed and then armed forces reduced to correspond with the economic and strategic requirements of each country.

4 Germany requests the return of her former colonies but would advance no other territorial claims. South-West Africa might not be claimed. Germany might consider the payment of an indemnity for improvements effected in the colonies since 1918, and the purchase of property from present owners who might desire to leave.

5 The political independence and national identity of 'a Polish state' to be restored, but the territory occupied by the Soviet Union is to be excluded from discussions. Czechoslovakia would not be prevented from developing her national character, but is to remain under the protection of the Reich.

6 Greater European economic solidarity should be pursued, and the solution of important economic questions solved by negotiation and national European agreement.

Finally Hillgarth noted, in his report back to London, that:

The Nuncio added to these details that the APA representative [Haushofer] had informed him that Hitler's desire for peace was based on the principle that he wished there to be 'no victor or vanquished' stigma applied to any of the negotiating parties, and that any agreement reached would have to be validated by a plebiscite in all countries affected by an agreement.[19]

The nature of the concessions the German Führer was prepared to make in order to attain peace with Britain must have astounded the men at the head of SO1. This was not even a deal worked out through a process of hard negotiation. It was Hitler's opening gambit, in which the expert hand of Albrecht Haushofer could be discerned; an offer so generous and pragmatic that it would be very tempting to anyone who genuinely wanted peace.

Regardless of its generous nature, from Churchill's and SO1's point of view there could be nothing more dangerous. Everyone had become used to Hitler's penchant for wielding a big stick, employing the threat of dire consequences if he did not get what he wanted. However, his offer of such remarkable concessions was an extremely threatening development. Should the terms become public, it had the potential to render British resolve to stand firm against German aggression to a shuddering halt.

What had begun as a subtle trawl to entrap the German leadership by bogus peace negotiations – the intention of which was to gain the psychological upper hand over Hitler and trick him into invading Russia – had suddenly become a deadly game indeed. It had been one thing to attempt to exploit Hitler's desire for peace through political warfare, but the last thing anyone had expected was for him to come back with a peace offer so generous that it left most of Britain's war aims sounding utterly hollow. What would happen if the governments-in-exile of Norway, Denmark, Holland, Belgium, and France were to discover that Hitler was offering to withdraw his forces from their countries without a fight, and what was more had even suggested he was prepared to pay reparations to those countries for the damage inflicted during their conquest? And there was an even graver issue at stake here. Under no circumstances could the Americans ever be allowed to discover that Hitler was offering peace. Should they do so, they might well cut back on Britain's war aid, and perhaps even exert pressure on the British government to accept Hitler's terms. It would certainly end Churchill's hope of dragging the USA into the war on Britain's side, a hope on which he was dependent if Britain was ultimately to defeat Germany. This was most definitely a peace offer that could not – must not – ever reach the public domain; the consequences were too terrible to contemplate.

There was, however, an element of Hitler's peace offer that intrigued the men of SO1, once they had carefully analysed Hillgarth's report of the meeting between the Papal Nuncio and Hoare. It was plain that this latest approach was not pitched to the British government. Hitler, it seemed, perhaps on the advice of Haushofer, had now given up on the notion that he could negotiate peace with Churchill or his government. Churchill had made it clear time and time again that he considered Hitler and Nazism to be evil incarnate and that he was determined to see Nazi Germany destroyed. He had rejected out of hand all Hitler's prior attempts to negotiate peace. The Papal Nuncio had therefore been very specific in stating to Hoare that Hitler's latest overtures were directed towards 'a party who would be prepared to act on them'. SO1 took this to mean that Hitler was aiming his latest pitch at a faction within the British government who were prepared to negotiate a peace deal with Germany, and oust Churchill and his pro-war supporters. The reason the Papal Nuncio had been sent specifically to Hoare was that Hitler, Hess, and Haushofer perceived him to be a member of the anti-Churchill clique within the government. They had seen only the outward signs: that Hoare, a former leading government minister, had been demoted by Churchill and banished to Spain. They had not understood Hoare's true purpose for being in Madrid.

Churchill, Leeper, and his top men at SO1 were nevertheless determined to take a great risk and continue to play out the game they had embarked upon. If the danger that anyone might find out about Hitler's generous peace offer could be minimised, there was much to be gained – if only Britain could trick the German Führer into attacking the Soviet Union.

By the autumn of 1940 Churchill was not only extremely concerned that British forces were being defeated by Germany in every military campaign they fought, but also that Nazi Germany was receiving considerable economic succour from the Soviet Union – machine parts, munitions, oil, petrol, and food, all of which aided the German war effort. If it had merely been the case that Russia presented a lurking, but neutral, menace in the east, then intentionally to turn Germany on the Soviet Union would have been a highly immoral act, advantageous to Britain only in that Russia would become a pit into which Hitler would be forced to pour ever greater quantities of valuable military resources. However, Russia was not merely sitting on the sidelines of the conflict. She was providing significant aid to Germany, and this legitimised viewing her as a target.

Indeed, at this very time, in the autumn of 1940, Karl Schnurre, head of Division W6 of the German Economic Policy Department, wrote a report that declared:

> The supplies from the Russians have heretofore been a very substantial prop to the German war economy. Since the new

economic treaties went into effect [earlier this year], Russia has
supplied over 300 million Reichmarks' worth of raw materials . . ."[20]

The resources provided by Russia therefore gave Germany an advantage over Britain that Churchill, Hugh Dalton (in his dual role as
Minister for SOE and of Economic Warfare), and SO1 determined must
be neutralised at all costs. SO1's decision to delude Hitler by bogus
peace talks, to 'encourage the Germans to attack Russia by misleading
Hitler . . . that large sections in Britain . . .[who] preferred to see the
overthrow of the Russian rather than the German regime might be
prepared to force through a compromise peace between Britain and
Germany',[21] was undoubtedly made with this in mind. It would not only
give Britain a much-needed second front, sucking the German war
machine dry of men and *matériel*, it would cut off a valuable source of
war supplies to Germany as well.

A final, and very significant, factor also came into the equation as SO1
determined to turn Hitler on Russia. MI14, the military assessment branch
of Military Intelligence, was convinced that in the fighting season of 1941
(i.e. the late spring and summer) Germany would continue its campaign
through North Africa, heading for Egypt, and that German forces would
leapfrog from the Balkans to Anatolia.[22] The head of Intelligence at MI14
advised Churchill that this was likely to take place in 1941 as the prelude
to a German invasion of Syria and Iraq. The latter was crucial to Britain's
war effort, for she was Britain's primary source of oil. If Germany invaded
Iraq and cut off the oil, Britain would lose the war.

Add all these factors together – the succour Russia was giving
Germany's war effort; Britain's need for a second front; the very real British
fear that Germany was going to attack Iraq in 1941 – and it became clear
to Churchill and SO1 that Messrs HHHH must be pursued if Britain was
to win the war.

•••••

Within a month of the Papal Nuncio's visit to Hoare, the next phase of
the Messrs HHHH operation swung into action, and Hoare's role in the
affair became a little more clearly defined. It is evident that there had
been further Anglo-German contact in the intervening period, for on
17 December Captain Hillgarth sent a ciphered telegram to London:

> Further to my meeting with Gen. Vigon this morning I can
> confirm that a safe arrangement for the carriage of my Minister
> [Hoare] over dangerous territory has been concluded. Gen. Vigon
> was most helpful and confirmed that both the arrangements for
> the 20th and return on the 21st have been cleared with the rele-
> vant parties . . .[23]

General Juan Vigon was chief of the Spanish Supreme General Staff
and head of the Spanish Air Force. Despite being an important member
of the Franco government, he saw himself as a moderate, and had
already attempted on several occasions to broker an Anglo-German
peace. These efforts had been gently rebuffed by the British, but they
now turned to Vigon for his assistance in aiding Hoare's secret mission.
It had been arranged for the Spanish Air Force to fly Hoare and
Hillgarth over 'dangerous territory' – occupied France – to Switzerland
for a very special meeting on 21 December. Vigon, of course, was
unaware of the British subterfuge, but almost certainly believed that he
was facilitating Anglo-German peace negotiations. Hillgarth's telegram
of December 1940 does not, it is true, state that Hoare's destination
was Switzerland. However, nowhere else in Europe could Hoare have
flown over 'dangerous territory' to a neutral land: only Portugal,
Sweden, Switzerland, and Spain were neutral in a continent swamped
by war.

The matter of who it was that Hoare flew to Switzerland to meet that
December weekend in 1940 is a little more complicated, but the extraordinary answer reveals much about how seriously Hitler, Hess, and
Haushofer were now taking the negotiations. Of primary significance is the
date when Hoare was in Switzerland; this, combined with what was discovered after the war, provided the answer. It is known that Hillgarth arranged
a flight for Hoare on Friday, 20 December, and a return flight on the
following day, Saturday, 21 December, but on the German side there
surfaced clear evidence of another flight. The astonishing fact is that
Rudolf Hess did not board his plane only on Saturday, 10 May 1941, and
fly to Scotland. Evidence has surfaced that he made a series of flights
between the autumn of 1940 and the late spring of 1941 – only no one
knew his destination.

Helmut Kaden, the chief test pilot at Messerschmitt and the man
personally responsible for Hess's private Messerschmitt 110E (registration
VJ-OQ), recalled after the war that Hess apparently made three attempts

to fly to Britain. According to Kaden, he made his first attempt on Saturday, 21 December 1940:

> when he took off in clear weather but returned after just three hours, to make apologies to staff. He had dropped his signal pistol . . . [he claimed, which] had lodged underneath his seat . . . and jammed the rudder controls. It was freed by the jolt when the Messerschmitt landed, and recovered by Hess before we reached the plane. But it prevented him continuing on that occasion.[24]

Taken at face value, this statement appears to indicate that by December 1940 Hess was already prepared to fly to Britain. However, for several reasons this cannot be true. To begin with, we know that the negotiations involving Hoare had only just begun, so there was no reason to fly to Britain to visit a party with whom the Germans had only just made contact. The second reason why Kaden must be incorrect is that information was an extremely dangerous commodity in Nazi Germany. After Hess's flight to Scotland in May 1941 everyone with whom he had contact was rounded up by the security service and questioned. Moreover, these were extremely sensitive peace negotiations, kept secret even from Göring and Reichsaussenminister (Foreign Minister) Joachim von Ribbentrop. Haushofer had advised Hitler and Hess that previous attempts to negotiate peace had failed because they had been semi-public. Nor did Hitler, in secretly offering to withdraw German forces from western Europe, want to appear weak before his fellow Nazis. It thus becomes clear that he could not afford to let anyone in on the secret. No one knew.

Hess would therefore certainly not have told Kaden or any other personnel at Messerschmitt about the real purpose of his flights. They were mere subordinates, and Hess, the Deputy-Führer of the German Reich, would not have felt in the slightest inclined to inform them about his destination or his purpose for flying. Thus Kaden's opinion that Hess's objective on 21 December 1940 was Britain must have been an assumption based on his subsequent knowledge of Hess's destination on 10 May 1941. However, his testimony is valuable, for it gives us two key details. It tells us the date of Hess's flight, and reveals how long he was away from the Messerschmitt aerodrome at Augsburg, just a few miles from Munich.

Hess's Me-110E was an extremely powerful all-weather capability fighter-bomber. With its twin Daimler Benz DB-610N engines, it was a high-quality aircraft capable of a top speed of over 360 miles per hour.

Let us assume that Hess flew his plane at its upper cruising speed of 310 miles per hour. Augsburg is 150 miles from Zurich, a flying time of a mere thirty minutes at 310 miles per hour. With the return journey, that gives a total flying time of one hour. According to Kaden, Hess was away from Augsburg for 'just over three hours'. This means that he could have been in Switzerland for nearly two hours, during which time he could have met with Hoare, who had gone to considerable effort to be in Switzerland the same day. With regard to the possible location of their meeting, it was recently discovered that Rudolf Hess had two aunts who lived in Switzerland. The first was Emma Rothacker, who possessed a substantial and secluded villa on the outskirts of Zurich at Herzog Strasse 17; the second, Helene Hess, lived in the countryside east of the city near the airport. It is therefore entirely possible that the meeting took place at one or other of these two houses. If it did not, it is known that Albrecht Haushofer had a number of close acquaintances who lived in Switzerland, so it is also possible that he was able to facilitate a confidential meeting place.

The details of what was discussed at this meeting will probably never be known, though it may be surmised that the terms of the peace offer brought by the Papal Nuncio were paramount. It is also likely that Hoare and Hess discussed how such a peace deal could be implemented. As would become apparent over the next few months, Hess and Hitler did not believe they were negotiating with the British government, but rather with a powerful peace faction headed by Lord Halifax and Hoare himself, who were poised to usurp power constitutionally from Winston Churchill.

With Neville Chamberlain's resignation in May 1940, Halifax had almost become Britain's Prime Minister instead of Churchill. However, his credibility as a war leader had been severely damaged by his support for Chamberlain's policy of appeasement in the latter 1930s. He had been charged by the press with being one of the 'guilty men', and the mud had stuck. From that time – May 1940 – until December 1940, he was increasingly a man under siege, constantly sniped at by the press as one of those responsible for Britain's present predicament.

Halifax had continued in his role as Foreign Secretary, but it was a difficult position; like Hoare before him, he was about to be demoted. His subsequent career also had many similarities with that of Hoare: both were loyal Britons determined to see the Nazi menace defeated, and Halifax would, like Hoare, be given a vital role by Churchill. In December 1940 he was made Ambassador to the United States, charged with making sure that

Britain maintained good Anglo-American relations in order to secure as much war aid as possible out of the USA. Although to many (especially the Germans) it appeared that Churchill and Halifax were enemies, the Prime Minister was a shrewd politician and played a very clever hand indeed. He knew that Halifax could be trusted in an important diplomatic position, and the post of Ambassador to the United States was probably one of the most vital of the entire war.

However, Hitler and Hess deduced that this new development offered them much hope. It matched exactly what they perceived to be the political situation in London, that it was possible for a 'peace party' to usurp power from Churchill and his pro-war clique, as they had come to understand it through the advice of Albrecht Haushofer. As they interpreted events, Halifax, a man receptive to peace, had been banished to Washington by a Prime Minister fearful of a political rival. This undoubtedly reassured Hitler, Hess, and Haushofer that Halifax would be a man amenable to a compromise peace.

Within a few days of Hoare's trip to Switzerland on 20 December 1940, Hitler took a crucial decision in the direction of the war. He ordered that preparations be made 'to crush the Soviet Union in a quick campaign . . . even before the conclusion of the war against England'. This was the infamous Directive No. 21, his order to prepare for Operation Barbarossa. Unbeknownst to the men of SO1 at Woburn Abbey, their objective of making Hitler feel confident that he could attain peace with Britain, thereby freeing Germany to attack Russia, was already beginning to take effect. The preparations, he stated, 'requiring more time to get under way are to be started now – if this has not yet been done – and are to be completed by May 15, 1941'.[25] That was a mere five months away, and as time went on Hitler would become more and more eager for a peace deal with the British. It was the sort of deep yearning that would play directly into SO1's hands.

•••••

In the first weeks of 1941 SO1's operation to trick Hitler and Hess was given full rein. Despite Hitler's top-secret directive to his army Chiefs of Staff to prepare for the invasion of Russia, Britain's military assessment organisation, MI14, was still advising Churchill that the Germans intended to invade the Middle East in that year's fighting season. In January the Prime Minister's office sent a memorandum to MI14 asking specifically if there was any sign of Germany turning upon the Soviet Union. MI14 replied that, on the contrary, relations between Germany and Russia were amicable, that Russia was continuing to aid the German war effort, and that it seemed unlikely in the short-to-medium term that Germany would attack Russia.[26] It was all very frustrating, for Hoare and Hillgarth were now fully engrossed in secret negotiations with Hitler, Hess, and Haushofer; indeed, Hoare had recently been back to Switzerland for another meeting with the German leadership. This time, however, his presence had been drawn to the notice of the Ambassador to Berne, David Kelly. Alarmed at the news that the Ambassador to Madrid had mysteriously been in Switzerland, Kelly sent to London at 8.10 p.m. on 18 January the following 'Most Secret' ciphered telegram:

> Information has come to my attention that the Ambassador to Spain Sir Samuel Hoare was in Berne today. How can this be? Please advise. I need not inform you of the delicate situation here particularly with respect to the Swedish courier Blonde [sic] whom I do not wish to compromise.[27]

What occurred next reveals that in Britain, as in Germany, there were men in the know, and men out of the circuit of information. Kelly was most definitely out, for he was tersely notified:

> The Foreign Secretary acknowledges receipt of your information.
> To confirm or deny the presence of the Ambassador to Spain might compromise his future work. You may be assured that if matters relate to Anglo Swiss relations you will be informed.
> Please refrain from enquiry if such an instance comes to your attention again.[28]

Despite the almost instantaneous rejection of Kelly's involvement – and his telegram undoubtedly set alarm bells ringing in Whitehall, Woburn Abbey, and Downing Street – this communication is important. It reveals that Hoare was once again in Switzerland, this time on Saturday, 18 January 1941; that date is significant, for there is clear evidence that Hess, too, made another flight on the same day.

On the morning of 18 January, Germany's Deputy-Führer set out on a second mysterious journey. This time, whilst he was waiting for his plane to be prepared, he handed two sealed envelopes to his adjutant, Lieutenant Pintsch. One envelope was addressed to Hitler, the other to Pintsch himself. Hess was very specific in instructing Pintsch that if he did not return in four hours he was to open his letter and personally take the other to Hitler.[29] Helmut Kaden assumed that this was another of Hess's attempts to fly to Britain; he testified after the war that it was Hess's second unsuccessful attempt to fly to Scotland, commenting that 'Hess . . . [again] returned after about three and a half hours. On this occasion, he reported that there was something wrong with the Anflugnavigation system, a form of radio compass which had been installed in the machine . . .'[30]

Regardless of Kaden's evidence, Pintsch on this occasion was able to reveal Hess's true intentions. He was flying somewhere specific in his plane and estimated that he would be no more than four hours. His destination could not have been in Germany; if that were the case, why fly? He could merely have driven there. His destination could only be a foreign country – Switzerland – and it was no coincidence that Hoare was present again, on yet another Saturday. Only this time Hoare was unlucky enough to be spotted by someone who reported his presence to Ambassador David Kelly.

It was at this point that SO1 began encountering problems in its operation, specifically from two unexpected quarters.

In distant Washington, Lord Halifax, who had only been in the United States a few weeks, was attending a reception when he suddenly found himself approached by an intermediary who announced that he was acting on behalf of the German Ambassador. The man further revealed that he was aware of the Hoare–Hess negotiations, and made it clear that he was making an approach direct to Halifax, circumventing the proper line of negotiation. This development was potentially extremely dangerous, for it indicated once again the unpredictability of the Nazi leadership. They just did not seem to be able to play by the rules – albeit that those rules were dictated by London – and negotiate strictly through Hoare. Instead, they were now attempting to open a direct line of communication to Halifax, the man they *thought* they were ultimately dealing with. Halifax recoiled in horror at the idea of these leading Nazis attempting to contact him directly, especially when his name alone was being bandied about as a possible peace leader of Britain, and Hitler and Hess were in reality negotiating only with SO1 at Woburn Abbey. Everyone concerned immediately realised that if the Americans were to discover the nature of the secret negotiations, and mistakenly believed they were genuine, this would cause irrevocable damage to the Anglo-American relationship. America might well revert to its isolationist position, cut back on war aid, and insist that the British government treat in earnest with Hitler to end the war. Sir Alexander Cadogan, the Permanent Under-Secretary at the Foreign Office, was instructed to transmit a 'Most Secret' telegram to Halifax immediately:

> Further to your telegram to the Foreign Secretary . . . regarding the approach by an emissary of [German Ambassador] Dieckhoff concerning the H matter, I have been instructed to pass on the following guidance.
>
> All matters regarding H must be managed under the strictest diplomatic protocols, as we instructed Sam [Hoare] to inform the emissary last November. As we all agreed, the emissary was ordered not to contact you directly, so as to confuse their assessment of the situation, and to prevent your compromise should there be a mistake. We do not believe the opposition would intentionally leak as it will end their whole operation, and we certainly would not as we are not supposed to know – but mistakes do happen.
>
> Both Winston and Anthony [Eden] agree that if any further approach is made, feign anger and walk away. For our part we have informed Sam to tell the emissary that any further attempts to influence you will result in an immediate end to negotiations.

Cadogan concluded his telegram:

> I need hardly emphasise how dangerous a failure during the coming sensitive stage could be. Please destroy this telegram after digesting the content.[31]

Cadogan's telegram is very revealing. Primarily it refers to the 'H matter', confirms Hoare's involvement in negotiations since the previous November when he had met the Papal Nuncio, and mentions that he had instructed the Germans that on no account was Halifax to be contacted directly. Of great importance is the information that 'We [i.e. Churchill and Eden] do not believe the opposition [the Germans] would intentionally leak as it will end their whole operation, and we certainly would not as we are not supposed to know.' This is a crucial statement. It is the smoking gun; it reveals that all the subterfuge – the pretence of negotiations proceeding with a nonexistent peace faction within Britain – was being conducted with the full knowledge of Churchill, through the political warfare organisation operating out of Woburn Abbey.

This would be pivotal in the years ahead when the successor to SO1 engaged Heinrich Himmler in secret negotiations, for it was a pedigree that this sinister organisation carried with it. By then, however, it was being led by a man considerably more dangerous than the mild-mannered Hugh Dalton.

The second of SO1's problems during February 1941 arose from a most unexpected quarter, and served to confirm Churchill's worst fears about the appointment of Hugh Dalton to the ministerial post as head of SOE.

After a meeting of the SO1 executive on Saturday, 25 February, a mere week after Halifax's difficulty in Washington, Dalton became so alarmed by what he discovered to be the true objectives of the operation to trick Hitler that he panicked and wrote a letter to the Foreign Secretary, Anthony Eden. In this letter he declared:

> I have been in deep contemplation ever since the matter we discussed yesterday with the P.M., and feel I must put my concerns to you before we take any further action.
> Leeper's assessment on Saturday was pretty close to the mark, and his conclusion that despite being unable . . . to win in Europe, we could win a world war has, of course, been bandied about for the last month or two.

In voicing his fears as to SO1's objectives, Dalton reveals that a secret strategy session had taken place behind the closed doors of Woburn Abbey. His letter also makes it clear that those present had reached a significant conclusion: Britain alone could not win a European conflict. If, however, she could expand the conflict into a world war, then she would be able to suck in enough allies – and this primarily meant Russia and the United States – to cause the ultimate defeat of Nazi Germany. Dalton went on:

> . . . what Winston now proposes is a truly terrible thing, and I am not sure my conscience will allow me to participate.
> I have always maintained that in this war body-line bowling of the Hun is justified, and the Messrs HHHH Operation . . . was intended to fulfil that function, but I do not believe we can be morally justified to use it to cause the suggested end result . . .[32]

Dalton was not a weak man, nor was he opposed to the use of subterfuge to defeat Germany, and the way he recoiled from the devastating course of action being pursued by SO1 surely took his colleagues by surprise. He must have suddenly been struck by what the terrible consequences of a German invasion of Russia might be – and it should be remembered that over twenty million people were to die in that theatre of the war.

Dalton concluded his letter to Eden by using an old political ploy to bring an adversary on side by asking for his counsel and advice, stating, 'I would appreciate your opinion.' But if he believed that the moderate Eden would support him against Churchill and the strong-willed men of SO1, he was to be bitterly disappointed. Furthermore, he made two fatal errors. First, he overestimated his importance as Minister of SOE and Economic Warfare. Second, at the same time as writing to Eden, he wrote to Churchill, voicing his doubts. This was a dreadful mistake, for the Prime Minister immediately perceived Dalton's comments as a weakening of resolve. He would have no truck with men he could not rely on.

Within a day of receiving Dalton's letter, Churchill ordered his stalwart supporter, Sir Robert Vansittart, to write to Rex Leeper:

> Dear Rex,
>
> I thought I should send you this short note concerning the H[ugh] D[alton] matter. I have rarely seen Winston so annoyed as when he received HD's letter yesterday. It has thrown the whole matter in turmoil, but I believe we can keep HD on side long enough to conclude the matter at hand.
>
> I would appreciate first hand news of any problems with HD, as I believe BB had been given the go ahead to reduce him once the operation has reached its conclusion.[33]

'BB' was Churchill's loyal aide and friend Brendan Bracken, described by some as his 'faithful chela', a man whose political career rose and fell with that of his mentor. Bracken had been a supporter of Churchill during his 'wilderness years' in the 1930s; when Churchill attained the Premiership in May 1940 he had not forgotten his friend, and had brought him into the government. By early 1941 Bracken had become the Prime Minister's Political Private Secretary. Once Dalton had been 'reduced', Churchill would further reward Bracken within just a few months, by making him Minister of Information. SO1's successor, the

Political Warfare Executive (PWE), would eventually be attached to the Ministry of Information, and hence it came under the direct control of the ruthless Bracken.

After the war Dalton would call Bracken a 'most malevolent influence upon Churchill', and a 'force of evil'.[34] It was no coincidence that with Bracken's assumption of control of SO1/PWE in the summer of 1941, the organisation became considerably more sinister and secretive. With Churchill's implicit blessing, it was to be almost a law unto itself.

Despite Dalton's extreme discomfort with the objectives of the Messrs HHHH operation, the plan was pursued throughout the spring of 1941. It is known that Hoare held several more meetings with Albrecht Haushofer in Madrid, and on Saturday, 19 April, Hess was once again prepared to fly to his secret destination. On this occasion, however, something went wrong. He sat in his aircraft on the Augsburg runway waiting for a telephone call before proceeding. When it came, he cancelled his flight, saying, 'That's it, it's off for today!'[35] Hoare was not in Switzerland waiting; instead, he had hurriedly left Madrid for a secret meeting with the Governor of Gibraltar, General Mason-MacFarlane, who had just returned from seeing Churchill in London. However, Hess was not a man to be put off. There was after all a great deal at stake for him and Hitler, and the decision whether or not to invade Russia would ultimately determine who would win the war. Within seventy-two hours, on Tuesday, 22 April, an urgent memo was drafted by the Foreign Office in London querying the astonishing news that Rudolf Hess had turned up in Madrid.[36]

It has not been possible to establish absolutely whether a meeting between Hess and Hoare took place in Madrid. Many of the Madrid Embassy files from this period – April 1941 – are still classed as 'Unavailable', all significantly closed until 2017: the same date as the Hess dossiers in the British archives at Kew. However, we can be sure that Hess was in Madrid at this time. It has been claimed that he was in Spain to deliver a message from Hitler to Franco, but there is no record in the Spanish archives of such a communication being delivered during this period, and Hitler was most unlikely to employ his Deputy-Führer as a mere messenger-boy. It is therefore possible that Hess visited Madrid for a different purpose. It is known that he had been frustrated in his attempt to meet Hoare in Switzerland the previous weekend, so it is almost certain that this was his reason for visiting Madrid within just a few days. The most likely venue was again the home of Beigbeder, which as we have seen is recognised to have been the location of all the Hoare–Haushofer meetings.

Despite the difficulty in ascertaining the true purpose of such a meeting, a firm clue as to what would have been discussed is given by a letter Hoare wrote to Sir Alexander Cadogan just a few weeks previously. The subject of this communication threw SO1's carefully stage-managed operation into complete turmoil:

> . . . I have now had a further meeting with Haushofer at the home of Beigbeder. I understand he is here at his superior's insistence . . .

Hoare explained all was not well, and went on:

> . . . it was evident during our meeting that he and his kin are now becoming most agitated by the lack of progress.
>
> During the course of our conversation H[aushofer] asked why Edward [Halifax] had not yet made any move etc. I explained the complexities of the situation, which would make any action a long process. H[aushofer] understood completely, but responded that his superior has insisted on a meeting with a close representative of the man of influence on neutral territory. After I pointed out that this was out of the question, H[aushofer] informed me that it has already been arranged for their Head of AO [the Auslandsorganisation, a foreign policy department of the Nazi Party] to journey anywhere for a confidential meeting, if it would resolve the impasse.

He concluded his letter with the comment:

> . . . their demands are unrealistic if not dangerous, but I am also convinced we shall have to facilitate some sort of meeting if the matter is not to fail.[37]

This letter gives a clear indication of Hitler's demands by April 1941. The Germans were becoming extremely frustrated by what they perceived as the slow progress of Halifax in making his move – any move – against Churchill. During his meeting with Haushofer, Hoare had explained that it was an extremely delicate and complex situation, and that Halifax was having to proceed very carefully. Haushofer had understood this, but related that his 'superior' – Hitler – had 'insisted' on a meeting between their 'head of AO' (the Auslandsorganisation) and someone Hoare cryptically referred to as 'a close representative of the man of influence'.

The head of the Auslandsorganisation was a man named Ernst Bohle, a close acquaintance of Hess and Haushofer, who had until 1937 been a British citizen. Since moving to his ancestral home in Germany in the early 1930s, his rise within the Nazi Party had been meteoric, and by 1941 he was a very important man indeed. In the late 1930s he had also, incidentally, been sent to Britain on a diplomatic mission to strengthen Anglo-German relations. He then met many leading men in British politics, including not only Hoare and Halifax, but also Churchill humself.

The identity of the 'close representative of the man of influence' is a little harder to ascertain. But, within a week of the Foreign Office report concerning Hess's visit to Madrid, a British diplomat by the name of William Strang became involved in the Messrs HHHH operation. And in addition to revealing the extreme importance attached by SO1, Eden, and Churchill to the German demand for a high-level meeting, what he did next also reveals this man's identity to us.

Strang was a high-flyer in the Foreign Office; an old acquaintance of both Leeper and Hoare, whom he had known for nearly twenty years, he was also one of the key Foreign Office men in the know about the Messrs HHHH operation. He was therefore brought in to conduct a highly delicate matter concerning a member of the Royal Family. He met this person on Friday, 25 April 1941, asking him to help out in the operation to deceive Hitler. On the following Monday, 28 April, Strang wrote to his old friend Alexander Cadogan to report: 'Further to our discussion concerning the H matter last week . . . I attended a meeting with HRH the Duke of Kent last Friday. After I explained a little of the situation he seemed most willing to assist in this most delicate affair.'[38] However, Strang commented, the Duke of Kent – younger brother of King George VI – was a perceptive man who understood the extremely sensitive nature of what was being asked of him; he was unwilling to help without assurance from an official senior to Strang that he really was aiding the British government, and not becoming entangled in some dubious scheme of British Intelligence. That fate had befallen his eldest brother, the Duke of Windsor, and look what had happened to him – banished to the far side of the Atlantic for the duration of the war.*

* In the autumn of 1939 the Duke of Windsor was asked by General Ironside to conduct morale-boosting tours of the French defences; his true mission was actually to spy on the defences and report back on all he saw to the British High Command. Once he had completed his task, he was discarded by the British authorities, and his flirtation with the Nazis in Spain and Portugal in the summer of 1940 resulted in his banishment to the Bahamas for the duration of the war. For further information, see Martin Allen, *Hidden Agenda* (Macmillan, 2000).

The Duke of Kent was therefore insistent on assurances before he helped Strang and SO1; it was reported that 'before placing himself at our disposal he [Kent] has requested that either you or the Foreign Secretary clarify one or two details of his task. Also, he wishes his acquaintance, [the Duke of] Buccleuch, to be present, as he [Buccleuch] has met the visiting gentleman concerned [Bohle], whilst he has not.'[39] In fact, Buccleuch's relationship with Bohle was closer than passing acquaintance, because he had stayed at Buccleuch's Scottish country home, Drumlanrig Castle, which happened to be just a few miles south of the Duke of Hamilton's seat, Dungavel House.

Prince George, Duke of Kent, was no novice in the world of diplomacy and foreign affairs. The most politically astute of King George V's sons, he had undertaken fact-finding trips to Nazi Germany in the 1930s, and diplomatic missions for the British government. Most notably, he had been part of a British delegation to Portugal in June 1940. Officially he was there to attend celebrations of the country's 300th anniversary, but secretly he was present to undertake negotiations with its head of government, Antonio Salazar, the purpose of which was to keep the Portuguese out of a war that was engulfing the whole of Europe.[40] The mission had succeeded: Portugal remained neutral, and the British Foreign Office recognised Kent as a useful politico-diplomatic mediator.

However, of much interest to SO1, and the reason why Kent was now being deployed in the operation to deceive Hitler, was that it was known that the Germans believed Kent to be sympathetic to their cause. In the mid-1930s he had secretly met Alfred Rosenberg, a prominent Nazi and friend of Adolf Hitler. During this meeting the German was given to understand that Kent was acting on behalf of his father, King George V, who wanted to learn all he could about the radical new political force sweeping Germany. The Nazis had taken Kent's interest to mean he was a supporter of National Socialism like his elder brother, Edward, who became King on the death of George V. After his abdication in December 1936, Edward, as the Duke of Windsor, had maintained his sympathy for the German cause. The leading Nazis therefore misunderstood the Duke of Kent's role, believing him, too, to be a friendly ear in Britain.

Kent's involvement at this juncture reveals who the Germans perceived 'the man of influence' himself to be. Haushofer was not only extremely knowledgeable about 'England and the English', he was also an expert on the British constitution. He was thus well aware that it was not enough for Hitler and Hess merely to have seduced Hoare and Halifax with words

of peace. If the Hoare/Halifax 'peace faction' was to have a credible opportunity for assuming power in Britain, Winston Churchill would first have
to lose a vote of confidence in the House of Commons. Halifax would
then have to be invited to form a new government by none other than King
George VI. This long drawn-out and complicated process was the only
way to place Halifax in position both as Prime Minister and as a man then
able to agree to peace with Germany. It was thus not only necessary for
Hitler to agree peace terms with Halifax; the British King would also have
to be brought on side to ask Halifax to form a new administration. In their
latest round of talks with Hoare, the Germans had therefore sought an
assurance that he and Halifax had the support of King George VI – 'the
man of influence'. This could only be achieved by a meeting with his
'close representative', his younger brother, the Duke of Kent.

The efforts of William Strang and SO1 to secure the Duke of Kent's
participation in their secret operation were swiftly concluded in the last
days of April, for SO1 was by now working against the clock. So were the
Germans, for Hitler was far advanced in his plans to invade Russia that
summer, having convinced himself that an Anglo-German peace would be
agreed within just a few weeks. He therefore wanted the meeting to take
place as soon as possible, so that he could gain an accurate picture of the
true state of the negotiations whilst obtaining some idea of how soon he
could achieve peace with Britain. SO1 did not have long to prepare for the
Kent–Bohle meeting; however, they did insist to the Germans that under
no circumstances would it be possible for the Duke of Kent to leave British
soil. This was undoubtedly an attempt to stall for time, but by now Hitler
and Hess had no intention of being put off. Sir Samuel Hoare had therefore been informed that this was not a problem: the German emissary
would fly to a secret meeting on British soil. Arrangements were quickly
made for the meeting to take place on the night of Saturday, 10 May 1941.
The location would be the home of 'the closest' of Albrecht Haushofer's
'English friends': Dungavel House on the west coast of Scotland, the
country seat of the Duke of Hamilton, which possessed an up-to-date
airstrip and hangar facilities.

Whilst SO1 and the British Foreign Office were doing all they could to
facilitate a meeting that would satisfy German demands, in distant Spain a
subtle spilling of information was undertaken to keep the Germans firmly
hooked upon SO1's barb. What was said is known because the Italian
Ambassador in Madrid, Francesco Lequio, sent a ciphered dispatch back
to Rome reporting a recent statement by Hoare to a German emissary. The

British government was not secure, Hoare had claimed, and Churchill could 'no longer rely on a majority [in the House of Commons]'. More intriguingly, Lequio reported, Hoare had declared that sooner or later he expected to be 'called back to London to take over the government with the precise task of concluding a compromise peace'.[41]

Taken at face value, this would appear to be a damning indictment of Sir Samuel Hoare's loyalty. However, given what is known about his unswerving belief in the British cause, and his work for Operation Messrs HHHH, it is clear that this was merely more bait to be dangled for the Germans; bait that would convince them of Hoare's sincerity as a man plotting to oust Churchill and make peace. This, it was hoped, would induce the Germans to fall utterly for SO1's scheme. As events were to turn out, the British did not have long to wait.

SO1 had spent months convincing Hitler, Hess, and Haushofer that a faction within the British government was preparing to oust Churchill and make peace. This was just the sort of situation the Germans had suspected might exist, one that could be brought to fruition with a little prompting. The negotiations had proceeded through the autumn and winter of 1940, and into the spring of 1941. However, the Germans wanted to see some buds of encouragement on their carefully nurtured bush of peace. They had therefore demanded a meeting with 'a close representative of the man of influence', who could assure them that the Halifax/Hoare faction had the support of the King. Reluctantly the British had agreed to this, but the meeting was to take place in total secrecy on British soil. The British were expecting the head of the Auslandsorganisation, Ernst Bohle. They had been led to believe this during Sir Samuel Hoare's most recent meeting with Albrecht Haushofer at the home of Beigbeder in Madrid; indeed, it is known that Haushofer himself believed that Bohle was to be the emissary. The British had therefore made the Duke of Kent aware of whom he was destined to meet; and, as luck would have it, the Duke of Kent had asked for his close friend, the Duke of Buccleuch, to attend the meeting since he knew that Buccleuch had met Ernst Bohle in the 1930s.

As far as the British were concerned, everything was beginning to mesh together nicely. The secret meeting would take place on the weekend of 10–11 May 1941. Bohle would be convinced by the Duke of Kent that Halifax had the support of the King; the German official would then depart fully convinced of the Britons' sincerity, and a very British political coup d'état would soon take place, ousting Churchill from the Premiership. This would convince Hitler that a change of government in Britain was imminent, allowing him to attack Russia with impunity in the belief that Germany would soon have peace in the west.

If everything took place as the men at SO1 envisaged, Britain would soon have the much-needed second front: a pit into which Hitler would be forced to pour ever greater quantities of men and *matériel* if the Russian bear was not to begin swallowing Hitler's Germany whole. However, SO1 was about to have its carefully nurtured plans thrown into complete disarray.

•••••

On the night of Saturday, 10 May 1941, three groups of Britons were gathered in three very special places.

At SO1 headquarters, Woburn Abbey, several prominent men were waiting to be kept informed hour by hour about the secret meeting soon to take place in Scotland. Present that night were the Foreign Secretary, Anthony Eden, and his close associates from the Foreign Office, Vansittart, Cadogan, and Strang. Also present were the originators of SO1's Messrs HHHH operation, Leonard St Clair Ingrams and Richard Crossman, Robert Bruce Lockhart and Rex Leeper, together with their superior, SO1's Minister, Hugh Dalton, who had in recent weeks been under a steady onslaught from Brendan Bracken. He was hanging on to his position as head of SOE, but only just, and he knew that every man present at Woburn Abbey that night was waiting to see him brought down at the hands of his nemesis.

Fifty miles to the northwest of London there was another gathering of important men. Just outside Oxford was a substantial country house called Ditchley Park. In 1940 the owner of the estate had loaned the property to Churchill for the duration of the war as an alternative country retreat to Chequers, which it was feared might be targeted by the Luftwaffe. However, Ditchley Park was not merely a comfortable country house. As soon as it had been handed over, the property was quickly transformed into an efficient command centre, complete with communications rooms kitted out with numerous secure telephone lines, deciphering equipment, teletypes, and a transmitter powerful enough to communicate with the farthest corners of the globe. Thus Churchill, whilst ensconced at Ditchley Park, was as fully in command of the war as if he had been in the Cabinet War Rooms deep beneath Whitehall. Present with him that weekend were his old friend Sir Archibald Sinclair, the Secretary of State for Air, and his loyal supporter Brendan Bracken. Curiously, Churchill would also have another house guest that weekend – President Roosevelt's special envoy, Harry Hopkins.

Whilst these men, whether at Woburn Abbey or with Churchill at Ditchley Park, watched the clock and prepared themselves for this most sensitive phase of the Messrs HHHH operation, upon which would hinge the direction of the war, far to the north in western Scotland several others were also gathered. For them, however, considerably more was at stake. They were about to meet the German emissary, Ernst Bohle, and their slightest error could result in the Germans realising that the peace negotiations were entirely spurious. Any such conclusion on the Germans' part would have catastrophic results, for with it would come the understanding that Britain would never make peace – and that would mean war without end until either Britain or Germany collapsed. Present at Dungavel House that evening were the Dukes of Kent and Buccleuch, a Balt identified almost certainly as Baron 'Bill' de Ropp (a member of British Intelligence who had accompanied the Duke of Kent during his meetings with Alfred Rosenberg in the mid-1930s), and a representative of SO1 named Voigt. A man from the Foreign Office may also have been present to advise Kent, but this is unclear.

All these men in Woburn Abbey, Ditchley Park, and Dungavel House were awaiting Bohle, the head of the Auslandsorganisation. But SO1's plans were about to go devastatingly awry in a manner that the men in Woburn Abbey had no way of envisaging. That night's events would soon grab the world's headlines as one of the strangest incidents of the entire war.

Later that evening a lone German plane flew in from the North Sea, passing over the coast of northern England before almost immediately crossing into the Scottish lowlands. Travelling at breakneck speed, it took up a heading across Scotland and into the vicinity of Glasgow. In the plot room of RAF Turnhouse, near Edinburgh, the Duke of Hamilton (a wing commander serving in Fighter Command) watched as a WAAF teller began to move the plot of the aircraft designated '42J'. Two Spitfires on patrol out over the Farne Islands were ordered to engage the mysterious aircraft, and a third was scrambled from RAF Acklington to assist them. However, none of the Spitfires could make contact, and the plane continued on its way unmolested. By now it had dipped below radar cover and was estimated to be thundering its way across the Scottish countryside at a speed in excess of 350 miles per hour. As it approached the west coast of Scotland a mere half-hour later, two Czech pilots, Vaclav 'Felix' Bauman and Leopold Srom, were scrambled from RAF Aldergrove and ordered to intercept the German aircraft now heading towards the Firth of Clyde. On reaching the Clyde in record time, the two Czechs spotted their target. However, just as they were about to attack, an urgent message came through on their radios ordering them to 'Stop action and return.' Believing there had been a mistake, Bauman responded that he was within range of a 'kill', but he was cut short and told, 'Sorry, Felix, old boy. It is not possible. You must return. Now.'[42]

By now the German plane was a mere nine minutes' flying time from Dungavel House. It was 10.40 p.m. and almost dark. At this point events began to take on a life of their own, and SO1's ability to stage-manage the situation began to fail – for the very good reason that the Germans had thrown a spanner into the works by sending someone other than the expected Ernst Bohle. At 10.45 p.m. the aircraft flew over Dungavel House, but by now something strange was beginning to unfold.

In 2000 a former WAAF, using the pseudonym of 'Mrs Abbot' as she wished to remain anonymous, revealed that on the night of 10 May 1941 she and a friend had been leaving the kitchen of Dungavel House when they were surprised to see that the airstrip's landing lights had been turned on.[43] So unusual was this occurrence, contravening the strictly enforced blackout regulations, that they hoped the lighting-up had not resulted from 'some infernal electrical fault that would attract Jerry raiders and get us killed'.

Moments later the two women were relieved to see the lights blink out, plunging the airstrip into darkness. But to their surprise they immediately heard an aircraft coming in low over the countryside. They 'half expected the lights to go back on again. But they remained off.' Some ten minutes later, they 'heard an aircraft – presumably the same one – pass over again'. It did not – indeed could not – land in complete darkness, and flew away uncertainly to the north.

The true identity of the German in the plane was about to become known. Determined not to kill himself trying to land his plane in the dark, the pilot decided to parachute to safety, believing himself to be in close proximity to his destination. However, he was wrong, and he landed several miles away at a smallholding near a farmworker's cottage. He was helped from the ground by the farmer and taken indoors. Meanwhile, several Royal Signals personnel from Eaglesham House, a mere mile away, rushed to assist in his apprehension. To begin with, the German insisted that his name was Alfred Horne, and asked repeatedly to be taken to Dungavel House. But he was out of luck. It was clear to all that he was German, and enemy visitors were not given the right to dictate where they would like to go. Shortly afterwards men of the Home Guard arrived and he was taken away to Glasgow for interrogation. Once the prisoner was in the Home Guard's hands it was soon established who he was. Everyone's shock was absolute, particularly those at Dungavel House and Woburn Abbey; they had been kept abreast of the situation by the Duke of Hamilton, who rushed overnight from RAF Turnhouse to Glasgow to confirm the man's identity.[44] The mysterious visitor was in fact the Deputy-Führer of the German Reich, Hitler's closest confidant, Rudolf Hess.

Since the end of the Second World War, much has been published about Hess's flight to Scotland on 10 May 1941. Every aspect of that flight, from each twist of his plane to the countermeasures taken by Britain's defences, has been examined time and time again in an effort to discern any fragments of truth that would reveal the true purpose of his mission. However, the technical details are unimportant when compared with what has been discovered about the Messrs HHHH operation, about the expected arrival on British soil of a German emissary in the midst of a desperate war. When the truth is known – that certain high-ranking Britons, engaged in secret peace negotiations, were expecting a plane, albeit one carrying a different emissary – the whole situation then begins to make a great deal more sense.

From the moment that Hess bailed out from his plane, the whole of SO1's carefully choreographed operation took off at a tangent. Everything that occurred after 11.09 p.m. on Saturday, 10 May 1941 – the moment Hess landed straight in the public domain – has to be viewed in light of the fact that it was all completely unplanned.

'RUDOLF HESS IN GLASGOW – OFFICIAL' declared the *Daily Record* within just a few days. It went on to state that 'Herr Hess, Hitler's right-hand man, has run away from Germany and is in Glasgow . . .'[45]

From the moment Hess's arrival in Britain became public knowledge, the British government embarked on a damage-limitation exercise aimed not only at preventing the Messrs HHHH operation from collapsing before Hitler took the fatal decision to launch his attack on Russia, but also at hiding the fact that top men of the British government, Foreign Office, and Intelligence Service had participated in a plot to deceive Hitler by feigning to enter into peace negotiations. If the fact that Hitler had offered pragmatic and realistic peace terms were ever to become public knowledge, it would inevitably cause a crisis in the Anglo-American relationship. The Americans would be entitled to ask why, if Hitler was offering such generous peace terms, was such an earnest endeavour not properly pursued? Inevitably the governments-in-exile of France, Belgium, Norway, Denmark, and Holland would have looked askance at the British government, and rightly demanded to know why they, too, had not been consulted.

The days following Hess's arrival in Scotland were hazardous for Churchill, Eden, the Foreign Office, and SO1, and their situation was not eased by a further incident the very next day.

Early on the morning of Sunday, 11 May, the Duke of Kent, with the Duke of Buccleuch as a passenger, was driving away from Dungavel House when he suffered a moment's distraction. Within just a few hours, Ingrams at Woburn Abbey sent a message to Voigt at Dungavel House 'concerning the accident . . . on the Douglas to Lanark road between a car driven by HRH the Duke of Kent, and a coal lorry'.[46] Voigt promptly dispatched to Rex Leeper a message headed 'Most Secret', in which he reported, 'I can confirm that neither the Duke, nor his passenger, Buccleuch, were injured, and in view of Lanark's close proximity to the event of last weekend, steps have been taken to ensure the accident remains unreported by the press . . .'[47]

•••••

And so SO1 concluded its first grand scheme of deception and political warfare. Hitler felt the loss of Hess deeply, and SO1 documents reveal that despite continued contact between Haushofer and Hoare, he was also suspicious of the British. However, he still believed that it would be only a matter of time before Lord Halifax made his move to oust Churchill from the Premiership and negotiate an armistice with Germany.[48] Despite its final bizarre twist, SO1's campaign was a complete success: Hitler continued to be deceived, for the moment, about the true state of British politicians' resolution to maintain the war until Nazism was defeated. Within just a few weeks, by now fully committed to an invasion of Russia, he would launch Operation Barbarossa. He had moved a vast preponderance of his armed forces to the east, the construction of railway spurs to specially built airfields in Poland had been completed, and all his top commanders were awaiting the order to launch their attack. Add to this the knowledge that Russian intelligence had been watching the German build-up with increasing concern, and it becomes clear that SO1 had successfully manoeuvred Hitler into a position whereby he had no choice other than to launch a strike against the Soviet Union.

'When I awoke on the morning of Sunday, the 22nd [of June],' Churchill would later recall, 'the news was brought to me of Hitler's invasion of Russia. This changed [my] conviction into certainty.'[49] It was the event that Churchill had long hoped for. Ever since the debacle of Dunkirk, and throughout the Battle of Britain, he had known that Britain alone could not defeat Germany. The head of SO1, Rex Leeper, had commented during one of its Saturday meetings at Woburn Abbey that it was becoming increasingly clear that Britain was unable to win in Europe on her own.[50] Yet this did not mean that Germany was invincible; it meant that the British had to resort to their wits, encouraging the Germans to commit the fatal mistake that would give Britain a much-needed ally. It was the first round in a war of wits that SO1 resoundingly won, and Hitler undoubtedly lost.

In accomplishing this feat, SO1's abilities in political warfare were proven beyond a shadow of a doubt. It convinced Churchill that this very capable tool (soon to be renamed the Political Warfare Executive, or PWE) should now become even more effective. Under the leadership of his stalwart centurion, Brendan Bracken, PWE would be pitched in a battle for the control of political warfare against the remainder of British Intelligence. It was to be a battle that Bracken – with the support of Churchill – would win. SO1/PWE was thus to be considered a state within a state, responsible to no one; with the start of the top-secret Himmler negotiations in 1943 that would ultimately lead it down a very dangerous path indeed.

In the years ahead PWE would undertake further missions of great importance in unsettling the Nazi leadership. Its operations were to range from relatively minor work, such as advising the British government on the most psychologically damaging ways of conducting the bombing campaign in Germany – 'If the raids are bluntly declared to be reprisals . . . they may easily be regarded as a typical example of "British hypocrisy". The raids [on major German cities] should be preceded by a solemn warning delivered by the Prime Minister . . . Such a warning would itself cause considerable apprehension . . . in Germany'[51] – through to the engagement of leading members of the Nazi leadership in highly secret talks whose object was to cause political damage to Germany.

Other leading men of the Nazi regime, unaware that their Führer had already attempted to negotiate peace with the British and failed, would now decide to play a hand in the game. The most important of these men would be the Reichsführer-SS, Heinrich Himmler. When the PWE found itself in touch with Himmler and the top men of the SS, it would adopt a very grand objective indeed for its next deception campaign. What Hitler, Hess, and Haushofer had plotted to do to Churchill in 1941, Churchill and Bracken would scheme to do to Hitler in 1943 and 1944. It would be a most audacious operation, the consequences of which might be of enormous benefit to the Allied cause. The Political Warfare Executive was therefore ordered to manipulate Heinrich Himmler's secret intent to secure peace with the Allies so as to precipitate a coup attempt against Hitler that would leave the Nazis struggling to keep control of a country plunged into political chaos.

NOTES

1. Doc. No. FO 371/24408, National Archives, Kew, London.
2. Doc. No. FO 837/593, National Archives, Kew, London.
3. Doc. No. FO 371/24408, National Archives, Kew, London.
4. Doc. No. FO 371/24408, National Archives, Kew, London.
5. Doc. No. FO 837/593, National Archives, Kew, London.
6. Doc. No. FO 371/24408, National Archives, Kew, London.
7. Ibid.
8. F.H. Hinsley et al., *British Intelligence in the Second World War* (HMSO, 1979), Vol. I, p. 49.
9. Nigel West, *Secret War: The Story of SOE* (Hodder & Stoughton, 1992), p. 12.
10. Ibid., p. 14.
11. Doc. No. FO 898/009, National Archives, Kew, London.
12. Allen, *The Hitler/Hess Deception* (HarperCollins, 2003), pp. 96–97, 109.
13. Doc. No. RG226 T542, Roll 59, National Archives, Washington, DC.
14. Doc. No. C109 D002194, Foreign and Commonwealth Office Library, London.
15. File No. NKVD 20566/24.10.42, KGB Archive, Moscow.
16. Doc. No. 104 Ser. D, Vol. XI, Documents on German Foreign Policy (HMSO).
17. Doc. No. C3084 D613511, Foreign and Commonwealth Office Library, London.
18. Herr H. Blummenstrauss interview, conducted 19 September 2003.
19. Doc. No. FO 371/26991, National Archives, Kew, London.
20. Doc. No. F5/0458-0462, Auswärtiges Amt, Bonn.
21. Doc. No. FO 898/009, National Archives, Kew, London.
22. Doc. No. WO 190/893, National Archives, Kew, London.
23. Doc. No. FO 371/26199, National Archives, Kew, London.
24. Roy Convers-Nesbit, *Failed to Return* (Patrick Stephens Ltd, 1988), p. 63.
25. Doc. No. 532 Ser. D, Vol. XI, Documents on German Foreign Policy (HMSO).
26. Doc. No. WO 190/893, National Archives, Kew, London.
27. Doc. No. FO 371/26542, National Archives, Kew, London.
28. Ibid.
29. James Leasor, *Rudolf Hess: The Uninvited Envoy* (London, 1962), pp. 73–81.

30. Convers-Nesbit, op. cit., p. 63.
31. Doc. No. FO 371/26145, National Archives, Kew, London.
32. Doc. No. CAB 127/206, National Archives, Kew, London.
33. Doc. No. FO 898/14, National Archives, Kew, London.
34. Wolf-Rüdiger Hess, *My Father Rudolf Hess* (W.H. Allen, 1986), pp. 185–86, cited in Allen, op. cit., p. 152.
35. Nesbit, op. cit., p. 63.
36. Doc. No. FO 371/26945, National Archives, Kew, London.
37. Doc. No. FO 794/19, National Archives, Kew, London.
38. Doc. No. FO 898/14, National Archives, Kew, London.
39. Ibid.
40. Audrey Whiting, *The Kents* (London, 1985), p. 97.
41. Documenti Diplomatici Italiani, 1939–43, Ser. 9, Vol. I, Lequio to Miny, 14 March 1941.
42. Andrew Rosthorn, *Sunday Telegraph*, 21 February 1999.
43. L. Picknett, C. Prince, S. Prior & R. Brydon, *Double Standards* (Little Brown, 2001), p. 269.
44. Allen, op. cit., pp. 234–42.
45. *Daily Record*, 18 May 1941.
46. Doc. No. FO 898/14, National Archives, Kew, London.
47. Ibid.
48. Allen, op. cit., pp. 245–74. For further information on SO1's Operation Messrs HHHH, see Allen, op. cit., passim.
49. Winston Churchill, *The Second World War* (Cassell), Vol. III, pp. 300–1.
50. Doc. No. FO 837/593, National Archives, Kew, London.
51. Doc. No. FO 898/193, National Archives, Kew, London.

4

HIMMLER FALLS INTO THE HANDS OF THE POLITICAL WARFARE EXECUTIVE

In April 1976 Britain's main code-breaking and intelligence-gathering organisation, called the Government Communications Headquarters (GCHQ), released a small selection of what are known as the Venona decrypts. These documents, which were still regarded as top secret until the mid-1970s, revealed that throughout the war years Britain had been intercepting and deciphering signals dispatched back to Moscow by Russian agents. This ability to decipher what the Russians believed to be their unbreakable code had continued into the 1950s and 1960s, and had a direct bearing on the Cold War; hence the information that British code-breakers had cracked a large number of the Russians' codes during the Second World War was necessarily kept secret well beyond the time when the content of these signals was of major significance to anyone other than historians. However, the release of certain of the Venona decrypts takes the story of Germany's covert attempts to negotiate peace in a new direction. It also marks out a whole new territory for the Political Warfare Executive, one that it hoped would enable it once again to defeat the German leadership in the secret war of wits.

On 13 April 1942 a Russian agent identified as Aleksander A. Pavlov, the Tass correspondent in Stockholm, sent a coded message to his controller in Moscow, a certain Captain Mikhail Aleksandrovich Vorontsov, reporting on a most important piece of intelligence that had come his way. It was something that might have significant consequences for Russia's war against Germany:

> The banker Baron Waldemar von Oppenheim arrived in Stockholm on 8 April . . . He had with him 20 kilograms of diplomatic mail for two addresses: the German Legation in Stockholm and . . . the Swedish Ministry of Foreign Affairs . . . [Agent] PER

. . . reported that he had two meetings with the Swedish banker [Marcus] WALLENBERG, whom he asked to get in touch with English financiers on the question of concluding an Anglo-German peace based on a return to the position up to 1939 and on the question of launching a joint attack on the USSR with the aim of destroying it totally. WALLENBERG . . . recommended applying directly to the British Legation . . . Oppenheim on 12 April flew by special plane to Berlin.[1]

A supplemental page to the GCHQ submission reported that, under the heading 'Baron Oppenheim visits Stockholm to discuss peace proposals with Wallenberg':

> It was later stated that his [Oppenheim's] purpose was to make unofficial contact with the British Commercial Attaché on behalf of the German Government and through the agency of Swedish business connections; and rumoured that he was to present Hitler's peace offer to the British.[2]

It had been nearly a year since Hitler had last attempted to open a line of peace negotiations with Britain. On that occasion he had engaged in deep subterfuge by attempting to negotiate a separate peace with Lord Halifax, with the aim of ousting Winston Churchill from his position as Prime Minister.

However, a lot had changed between the Halifax negotiations and the spring of 1942. Hitler, still believing that peace with Britain might be achieved, had launched Barbarossa, the invasion of the Soviet Union. But the stunning successes of the summer campaign, the rapid gaining of vast tracts of Russian territory when German forces had been hard pressed to keep up with the disorganised retreat of the Red Army, had given way to the harsh realities of the clinging miasma of mud in the Russian autumn, followed by the terrible privations of unspeakable cold during the Russian winter. Worse yet, despite their summer success, German forces had failed to take Moscow or the other major Russian cities, leaving the German Army to fend for itself in the winter countryside where the snow and bitter winds swept in from both the Urals and the Arctic Circle; and the winter of 1941 had been exceptionally harsh.

That winter had also seen Churchill's hopes realised when the Japanese attacked Pearl Harbor on 7 December, and the United States entered the war. SO1's secret policy meeting of February 1941 had thus seen all its objectives met: it looked as if Rex Leeper's 'conclusion that despite being unable . . . to win in Europe, we could win a world war'[3] might be realised. Britain had successfully hung on against the German onslaught until the conflict expanded into a world war, and now it appeared possible that the tide would, one day, begin to turn against Germany.

For all his faults, including perhaps a touch of deep megalomania, Hitler was a clear-sighted politician. He was Führer of the German Reich, receiving into his hands all reports on the war – be they on military, economic, political, or foreign policy – and he fully understood their implications. In the face of overwhelming Allied force, Germany's military situation might become unsustainable. Despite the propaganda that he and Dr Goebbels daily poured forth to the German people, Germany was far from winning the war. Perhaps, and most worrying of all, she might find herself in a position where she would lose.

Hitler had thus, by the spring of 1942, come to the conclusion that if at all possible, now was the time to offer to make peace with the Allies. It was clearly better to enter such negotiations from a position of strength, before Germany's military situation deteriorated and he found himself trying to negotiate from a position of weakness. He realised that once such a position was reached, the Allies would smell blood; they would not be content to negotiate, but would rather pursue the conflict until Germany went down to crushing defeat or accepted a humiliating surrender.

And so it was that, in April 1942, Hitler dispatched Baron von Oppenheim to Stockholm charged with the task of opening a line of negotiation to the British government. His choice of place of contact with the British, as well as the neutral intermediary, was well thought out, and would become of increasing importance in the years ahead – not only for Hitler, as he made his futile attempts to cut a deal with the British, but also for the next major player in the world of covert peace negotiations, Heinrich Himmler.

Stockholm in 1942 was an island of peace in a sea of woe and conflict. Sweden had shrewdly managed to maintain her neutrality during the previous three years – no mean feat considering that she found herself uncomfortably close to some of the regions of heaviest conflict during the war. To her northeast lay Finland, which had been in conflict with Russia since November 1939; to the west lay Norway, invaded by Germany in April 1940; to her south lay the German Reich, at war with the Allies, and since the summer of 1941 fighting brutally and bitterly against the Russians.

Sweden, on the coast of the Baltic – an extremely dangerous place during the Second World War – was the only Scandinavian country not at war. She was also, incidentally, one of the few venues in Europe (the others being Spain and Switzerland) where Germans and Britons could meet in secret to discuss the progress of the conflict. Sweden – and Stockholm in particular – was thus a very important place during the war years.

Hitler's choice of intermediary with the British was interesting. Forty-three-year-old Marcus Wallenberg was a leading Swedish businessman and banker. The head of the Enskilda Bank, he was also Chairman of Sweden's Delegation for War Trade, and responsible for negotiating the country's wartime trading arrangements with the Allied powers. In that capacity he travelled frequently to Britain and the United States, and had met most of the leading politicians in both countries. Indeed, just seven months earlier, Victor Mallet, British Ambassador to Sweden, had written to Anthony Eden:

> My dear Secretary of State,
>   My friend Marcus Wallenberg leaves for England by the same aircraft as this letter and I know he very much hopes that you will have the time to receive him . . . He is of course first and foremost a patriotic Swede, but he has never attempted to conceal his strong pro-British feelings . . . My personal relations with him and his family are those of the closest friendship.[4]

Despite this glowing testimonial, and Mallet's undoubted belief that he was a staunch supporter of the British cause, there were other elements to Wallenberg's character, elements that made him ideal to the Germans as an intermediary with the British. It is little known that Wallenberg and the Enskilda Bank were instrumental during the war years in concealing German industrial and commercial assets in Allied countries. The Americans in particular were extremely sensitive about German-owned companies trading in the United States, one such being Bosch, which was still German-owned, though the Enskilda Bank hid the fact from the Americans by serving as the holding company for Bosch Germany's American shares.

This fact on its own would act as a magnet to Heinrich Himmler. Through the Freundeskreis-RFSS (the friendship circle of the Reichsführer-SS), not only was he in close contact with Bosch, but there were high-ranking members of the SS on its board. Himmler always had in his grasp every aspect of the SS's role in Germany – whether state security, army, or business interests – and so he was undoubtedly aware of Wallenberg's assistance to Bosch, and many other major German companies, in trying to maintain the commercial status quo despite the ravages of war.

Wallenberg was thus a respected international figure. He partnered King Gustav of Sweden at tennis, and was on close and friendly terms with Victor Mallet, the British Ambassador. Such a respected person, known to assist both sides during the war and located in neutral Sweden, was bound to attract the attention of those in Germany who wanted to contact the British with a view to making peace. The first of these men was Hitler, who attempted to use him to contact the British authorities in April 1942. However, the Germans, be they as eminent as Hitler, or as lowly as a lone diplomat in a neutral country (and there were many during the war years who attempted on their own initiative to open a line of negotiation), unknowingly had an impossible task to convince the British of their earnest desire for peace. The stark truth is that the British government had no intention of negotiating a peace deal with any German, Nazi or not.

Sir Robert Vansittart's letter to Lord Halifax in the summer of 1940 (see p. 85) has already given us a clue as to why the British held to this attitude:

> It is a question of we or they now, and either the German Reich or this country has got to go under, and not only under but right under . . . The German Reich and the Reich idea have been a curse of the world for 75 years, and if we do not stop it this time, we never shall . . . The enemy is the German Reich and not merely Nazism . . . All possibility of compromise has now gone by, and it has got to be a fight to the finish, and to a real finish . . .[5]

Thus the British authorities were resolved from the early days of the war either to reject any peace approaches out of hand, or to turn them on the Germans in acts of political warfare. In the summer of 1940, whilst the government was still shocked and dismayed by the rout of the British Army in France that necessitated the evacuation of Dunkirk, Hitler's peace offer through Weissauer had been rejected without a moment's hesitation. It is therefore not surprising that by April 1942, with the Russians inflicting heavy losses on Germany and the United States drawn into the conflict, Hitler's latest attempt to negotiate peace was also destined to be rejected.

The British authorities guessed that the Germans might continue to make offers of peace. They had, after all, begun to do so in the very first days of the war, and were to continue until the last days of the conflict. Yet what occurred next piqued British interest; it was not that the government intended actually to talk peace with any German, but rather that a prime opportunity presented itself for the Political Warfare Executive to use German peaceable intent so as to damage Germany politically. The men at PWE were looking out for a fresh chance to strike another damaging blow against the enemy. As events turned out, PWE hoped that the damage would be critical, and would shorten the war by many months.

•••••

On 7 May 1942 Britain's Ambassador Extraordinary in Madrid, Sir Samuel Hoare, dispatched a ciphered telegram to the Foreign Secretary, Anthony Eden, in London. In his message Hoare revealed that 'Max Hohenlohe has arrived here with his wife . . . He wishes to see me urgently before May 25th when he returns to Germany . . . He implies he has a matter of utmost interest to tell me. Do you wish me to see him or not?'[6]

At 11.55 p.m. on the night of 11 May, Eden sent back to Hoare a message marked 'Secret'. It stated:

> I should much prefer that neither you nor any member of your staff should meet Hohenlohe. With the recent outbreak of [German] peace feelers and rumours in . . . Sweden . . . it is exceptionally important to give the enemy no opportunity for misconstruction. If news of such a meeting became public . . . the damage would far exceed the value of anything the Prince [Hohenlohe] could possibly say.[7]

Intriguingly, Hoare appears to have taken no notice of Eden's instructions, for on 12 May he dispatched a 'Most Secret' ciphered telegram to Sir Alexander Cadogan, informing him of a meeting he had authorised between his military attaché and Hohenlohe. It is interesting that Hoare used the same Spanish intermediary – Colonel Beigbeder – for facilitating Anglo-German contact as he had throughout the Hitler–Hess–Haushofer negotiations the previous year:

> Brigadier Torr met briefly with Prince Hohenlohe at the home of Beigbeder yesterday evening. Hohenlohe declared he had a most important and discreet peace offer to make. He revealed

that he has been sent here by Himmler, who wants to know whether we would be willing to treat with him as an alternate leader of Germany. Hohenlohe stated Himmler has the support of Germany's leading industrialists, who want rid of Hitler as he has led Germany into a very damaging war of which there is no end in sight.

Hoare ended his message by asking:

Do you wish any message to be passed to Hohenlohe before he departs back to Germany on 25 May?[8]

It is not possible to determine from the archive records whether a message was sent back to Hohenlohe to pass on to Himmler. A great many documents from this file are withheld until 2020, and are thus still secret. However, Himmler's involvement in peace feelers at this point was a very interesting development, and it undoubtedly caught the attention of both the Foreign Office and PWE. We know this because the Hoare telegram is clearly marked as having been passed on to Robert Bruce Lockhart; having been a key figure in SO1, he was now a leading member of the PWE. The mention of Germany's industrialists was also noteworthy, signifying as it did that Himmler was still in close contact with German industrial and commercial interests.

This situation would become all the more significant within twelve months. In 1943 Himmler, remarkably, backed an attempt by Skoda to negotiate an immunity from British bombing of its factories in exchange for guarantees that this enormous industrial concern would cut back on its war production. Intriguingly, the approach was made through the British Embassy in Stockholm; at a secret meeting the intermediary, a Mr Linder (the Swedish Manager of Omnipol), 'spoke of a . . . secret agreement concluded between M.E.W. [Britain's Ministry of Economic Warfare] and I.G. Farben [one of Germany's largest industrial concerns] and said that Skoda wished to make a similar agreement, and wanted to know on what terms Skoda could avoid being bombed . . .'[9] Hidden deep within the file headed MOST SECRET, and released only in the late 1990s, is a note that declares, 'It is learnt from a secret source in Denmark that Himmler has been in the background, because it has now been disclosed that he is attempting through various channels, to establish direct contact with England.'[10]

It can thus be seen that Himmler was both very keen on opening direct lines of communication to the British authorities, and in using his contacts in German industry – developed since the mid-1930s through his Freundeskreis-RFSS – to present himself as a moderate and clear-thinking man who wished to restrict the extent of the conflict, leading perhaps to peace.

These were Himmler's first ventures in the world of peaceable intent. He was still somewhat of a novice in this realm, as is evident from his use of Prince Hohenlohe in May 1942 to make a very low-key pitch to the British government through the Madrid Embassy. However, the Reichsführer-SS, as we have seen from his past, was an intelligent man and a quick learner, and so it was not long before his peace overtures began to take on a comprehensive and serious tone. It was a situation that would present a very interesting and seductive opportunity to the Political Warfare Executive.

•••••

In order to understand how important the Political Warfare Executive was to become in Britain's covert war of wits against Nazi Germany, it is now necessary to look at its development. With the conclusion of Operation Messrs HHHH in May 1941, Churchill had let Brendan Bracken off his leash to bring down Hugh Dalton, the Minister for both the Special Operations Executive and Economic Warfare. SOE (primarily meaning SO2) and SO1 were to become key weapons in the war against Germany, and Churchill was determined that both these organs of intelligence should be run by men in whom he had confidence; supporters during his 'wilderness years' in the 1930s, who possessed a clear understanding that in this war there could be no room for taking a moral stance.

As a consequence, as soon as the Messrs HHHH operation was over, Dalton, too, was finished. 'Reduced' under terrible psychological and political pressure from Bracken, he lost both his Ministry of Economic Warfare and the Special Operations Executive. He would spend the remaining years of the war with a minor role at the Board of Trade, a position where his sense of moral values would not obstruct Churchill's determination to defeat Nazi Germany by any means necessary. Churchill appointed Lord Selborne (a staunch Tory and loyal friend for twenty years) to the Ministry of Economic Warfare, and made him the key politician responsible for SOE.[11]

With the removal of Dalton from his position at the helm of SOE, Churchill decided to remove SO1 from its orbit. SOE would henceforth consist solely of SO2, charged with the responsibility of conducting cloak-and-dagger operations against Nazi Germany in occupied Europe. SO1, which in the summer of 1940 had become the home of Britain's experts in deep subterfuge and psychological combat, would be made an organisation of warfare in its own right. To enhance its strength, in the summer of 1941 Churchill made Brendan Bracken Minister of Information, and to his new ministry he attached SO1, henceforth to be known under its new and more precise title of the Political Warfare Executive.

PWE, as it became known, would continue with its primary task of broadcasting propaganda into Germany and the occupied countries, but hidden behind this 'front' was a select band of experts in the arts of deception, subterfuge, and political warfare; their object was to launch select operations against the German leadership in order to cause as much political damage as possible. The raison d'être of this group was to unbalance the precarious ant-heap that was Nazi Germany, where political alliances were a matter of expediency to be abandoned if an opportunity presented itself for self-advancement. This, PWE knew, was the Nazis' weak point; they did not have a long political pedigree, and as a result they were susceptible to British schemes of political warfare.

At the time of its move from SOE to the Ministry of Information (MoI), Sefton Delmar, one of SO1/PWE's leading experts, defined the organisation's primary objectives: 'We want to spread disturbing and disruptive news among the Germans which will induce them to distrust their government and disobey it . . . Our politics are a stunt. We pretend we have an active following to whom we send news and instructions.' A key objective of PWE, he explained, was to make the majority of the German people believe that the British were in communication with a secret band of loyal Germans who 'once thought Hitler pretty good, fought alongside him . . . but are now appalled at the corruption, godlessness, profiteering, place-hunting, selfishness, clique rivalries, party-above-the-law system, which the [Nazi] Party has instituted'. He concluded by stating another core objective: to make the German people believe that 'The Wehrmacht soldiers, the best element in the Volk, are being bumped off . . . while the SS party police are being given cushy jobs at home to make Germany safe for the Party.'[12] Friction would thus arise between the politicians and the honest majority of German citizens; the latter would feel that they were being duped by the Nazis, who would be made to look like exploitative and self-seeking manipulators.

Such were the public – 'front' – activities of the PWE. However, its covert activities, plied between the summers of 1941 and 1945, were more controversial. They would be kept top secret for the next sixty years, and even now, in the twenty-first century, are most difficult to uncover.

To run this organisation – skilled in the art of propaganda broadcasts to Germany for the purpose of subversion, and capable of mounting secret operations of political sabotage – Brendan Bracken organised an executive committee of five top political warfare experts. This 'Committee of Five' comprised Robert Bruce Lockhart (who acted as liaison to the Foreign Office); Brigadier Brooks (responsible for operations); Ivone Kirkpatrick (a leading member of the Foreign Office, who had in-depth knowledge of Nazi Germany, having been First Secretary at the British Embassy in Berlin in the 1930s, where he met all the leading Nazis); Rex Leeper (who as head of SO1 had mounted the Messrs HHHH operation, had been in charge of the Political Intelligence Division in the 1930s, and was a specialist in the art of deception and political warfare); and Major Desmond Morton (who was close to Churchill as his personal assistant, with special duties regarding the Enigma decrypts – reading Nazi Germany's most secret messages throughout the war).[13]

This was the pedigree of PWE's leaders, and they recruited heavily from men known to have skill in political warfare and the mounting of intelligence operations against Nazi Germany. After Operation Messrs HHHH, for the next twelve months or so the organisation reverted to its primary role of sending deceptive propaganda to Nazi Germany and the occupied territories, as detailed by Sefton Delmar. Whilst mounting this campaign, which itself played a significant role in the war effort, the top men of PWE kept a keen lookout for the next opportunity to launch a secret offensive of political warfare.

In order for the Nazis to be rendered vulnerable to exploitation, a rather special set of circumstances needed to come together. It invariably required that the Nazi leaders should be engaged upon a course of action they wanted to keep from their colleagues. Such opportunities were few and far between, but they always seemed to involve the yearning among leading Nazis to engage in secret peace negotiations. Hitler had already been stung once, and was suitably chastened by the experience; all his future approaches would be semi-official and very cautious. Of the other Nazi leaders, Göring would have been a possible target, but he did not possess the political influence in Germany to make such an effort worth while. Goebbels had attempted to contact the British authorities in 1940, but so believed his own propaganda about Germany's eventual victory that he had made no such attempt since. Ribbentrop was naïve and not very effective as a Foreign Minister; he might well want to negotiate peace with Britain to improve his standing in Hitler's eyes, but neither British Intelligence, the Foreign Office, nor PWE rated him highly enough to mount an operation against him. The only Nazi considered worthy of a deception campaign was the man who had in his grasp the security strings of the Nazi state, the only man with his own army, a man who considered himself possessed of the intellect necessary to negotiate peace secretly with the Allies. This was Heinrich Himmler, and to PWE he presented a very tempting target – if only circumstances were to present themselves that might leave him open to attack. As events turned out, there would not be long to wait.

•••••

In the autumn of 1942 the British Foreign Office commissioned a report entitled the 'Summary of Principal Peace Feelers', the purpose of which was to document in outline all the German peace approaches of the previous twelve months. It proved very interesting, for it demonstrated that many factions in Germany had been earnestly seeking a compromise peace with Britain. The report, which in the words of Foreign Office mandarin Frank Roberts 'contains too much political dynamite', was to become a blueprint for future activities against the German leadership. This was confirmed by another Foreign Office official, Mr Harrison, who commented in the accompanying civil servant minutes: 'I should say that 80 per cent of this document was composed by Mr Crossman [head of the German Section of PWE] with an eye to political warfare against Germany.' Harrison went on:

> When we went through the latest plan for political warfare to Germany about a month ago, we accepted (though with consider-able reluctance on my part) the thesis of a Himmler . . . group, but we accepted it for the purposes of political warfare only, and only for [distribution to] the limited number of persons concerned therewith.[14]

Thus it is clear that by the autumn of 1942 the Foreign Office and the Political Warfare Executive were toying with the idea of finding a method to cause chaos in Germany by turning the different political factions within the country upon each other. Amongst the twelve different peace approaches detailed in the report, two stood out as very significant. One was Himmler's approach to Hoare in Madrid:

> On the 11th May, 1942, [the] military attaché [Brigadier Torr] met Prince Max [von Hohenlohe], who declared that –
> (a) Himmler and the SS were now the great power in Germany and that Himmler could be used to destroy Hitler and Göring.
> (b) The German industrialists who were bent on getting rid of Hitler were prepared to use Himmler for this purpose.[15]

However, it would be a mistake to believe that Hitler was not still trying to play a hand in negotiating peace with the Allies. In fact, he had recently raised the stakes considerably by making overtures to the USA. This caused considerable alarm in Whitehall and Downing Street, for the British wanted at all costs to keep German peace approaches from the Americans. Hitler's first overture to the Americans had been made during November 1941, when the German Chargé d'Affaires in Washington was ordered to make enquiries in the USA to discover the 'reaction on public opinion in the United States and Great Britain if Hitler, after the defeat of Russia, appealed for a negotiated peace . . . [with] Germany agreeing to an American guarantee of the British Empire'. Nothing had come of that approach, and so Hitler tried again in the summer of 1942, sending a personal emissary to a prominent American citizen residing in Switzerland who had connections to the US diplomatic service. This man, Mr Wight, was astonished to receive into his hands information that:

> Hitler was willing to discuss terms on the basis of conditions before August 1939, but with the following reservations:–
> (i) Austria to remain part of the Reich.
> (ii) Sudetenland to remain incorporated in the Reich, but the independence of Czechoslovakia to be restored.
> (iii) Poland to regain her independence, but the question of access to the sea to be subject of discussion.
> (iv) The question of Alsace-Lorraine to be the subject of discussion between the Powers.
> (v) Gibraltar and Suez to be placed under some sort of international regime.[16]

Nothing could have been quite so dangerous to the British government's resolve to continue the war against Germany. The last thing the men in the Foreign Office, Whitehall, and Downing Street wanted to hear was that Hitler, or indeed any Nazi, was entertaining the notion of making a peace approach through the USA. Brethren the Americans might be, but Winston Churchill and his supporters in government could not be sure that they might not seize the opportunity actually to accept one of these approaches and take it on as a means for concluding the war, making a deal that left the Nazis in power. Therefore, though Hitler's most recent offer had not been taken up by the American government (after a confidential word from the British authorities warning of the danger of such approaches), the British Foreign Office, Whitehall, and PWE determined that they would do all in their power to induce the Germans to aim any future peace approach at the British authorities, and to keep all knowledge of such overtures from the Americans.

Another peace approach was detailed by Crossman in his report. Although not countenanced as an option per se, it held out much hope to the PWE of causing political damage to Germany in the years ahead if nurtured properly. Early in May 1942 Monsieur Visser't Hooft, General Secretary of the World Council of Churches in Geneva, arrived in Britain and held a meeting with Ivone Kirkpatrick, a leading member of the Foreign Office and one of the Committee of Five at PWE. Visser't Hooft revealed to Kirkpatrick that he had been approached by 'a group of Germans' who represented an anti-Nazi and anti-Hitler clique in Germany called the 'Kreisau Circle'. This group had secret support from all sections of German society: the Church, Foreign Ministry, civil service, army, and trade unions. What intrigued the British was the fact that this group claimed to be planning a coup d'état in Germany to remove Hitler and the Nazis from power, and intended then to open peace negotiations with the Allies. The group's plan was still in its infancy, but, as we shall see, in the months ahead it would find itself supported by the PWE and SOE. After all, a coup in Germany was exactly what PWE wanted to precipitate, so as to cause maximum damage to the German command structure, leaving it open not to a negotiated peace, but rather to comprehensive defeat at Allied hands.

This strategy was made explicit in a paper written in the summer of 1942 by Mr Harrison, and submitted to William Strang, Alexander Cadogan, and the Foreign Secretary, Anthony Eden. It specifically expressed the notion of causing political disruption in Germany, perhaps leading to a coup and chaos that would give the Allies an edge over the Nazis. Harrison began his paper by stating:

> I have tried to foresee developments in Germany next autumn, and have suggested how we might profit from them. The matter is primarily one which concerns P.W.E. I am pretty sure . . . they will be only too glad to undertake more active steps to stir up discontent in Germany. The decision whether or not they should be allowed to is a political one.[17]

He went on:

> Indications have not been lacking that there may be launched from Germany next autumn one of the most serious peace offensives of the war. It is not too early to be considering this possibility and measures for dealing with and profiteering from it.

The paper made it clear that two possible situations might be foreseen; first:

> A smashing German success on the Eastern Front, as a result of which the German position is made immensely strong both militarily and economically. Even though it would almost certainly mean the indefinite prolongation of the war, such a development could, I think, be counted on automatically to consolidate the German home front behind the Nazis.
> In such circumstances Hitler might be expected to put forward . . . in the name of a united Europe, a comparatively unpalatable offer of peace . . . Such an offer would no doubt be rejected out of hand.[18]

Harrison next detailed the second possible scenario:

> A German reverse in the East . . . resulting at best in a military deadlock and the prospect of another winter in Russia and a serious two-front war in 1943.
> In such circumstances it is not unreasonable to expect that German morale would sink very low . . . If the Russian armies

were still intact, the prospect of another winter with food and living conditions even worse than last year and allied bombing even heavier would be likely to engender serious unrest and even anti-Nazi movements.

As outcomes of these two scenarios, Harrison predicted three potential developments, two of which might with skill and cunning be turned to British advantage. The first possibility he could envisage was as follows:

> Hitler and the Party still firmly in the saddle might make a peace offer roughly on the lines of an evacuation of western Europe by German troops . . . with special arrangements to cover Poland, Czechoslovakia and Austria.
>
> Any such offer by Hitler to ourselves would no doubt be met on the lines . . . that we will not negotiate or have any truck with Hitler.[19]

This first scenario offered no advantage to PWE since, unlike the Messrs HHHH operation of 1941, there would be little opportunity of turning Hitler's peace approach upon him. The Führer was not likely to fall into the same trap a second time.

However, two further possibilities were put forward by Harrison, and these occasioned much hope that PWE might be able to 'stir up discontent in Germany'. He noted first that:

> There might, either separately or concurrently, be peace feelers from alleged anti-Nazi circles . . . and the like, enquiring what terms we would be prepared to offer if Hitler and Co. were overthrown.
>
> The answer would presumably be that we were not interested in such approaches and that we had reached the stage where only actions counted. Let them act first and then we might be prepared to talk.[20]

This emphasised that the British authorities were not keen to negotiate with any party in Germany, even if it should mount a scheme to topple Hitler. The last potential future situation put forward by Harrison makes this even clearer:

It is conceivable . . . that, if conditions became very bad, military and administrative circles might actually combine to overthrow Hitler and sue for peace.

It is at this point that Harrison's paper becomes particularly interesting from a PWE perspective, confirming as it does the line of thinking behind the proposed use of peace approaches to cause political damage to Germany:

I take it as axiomatic that this is the target at which we should aim, since whether or not we are prepared to negotiate with such a group, its emergence could not but cause confusion in Germany and seriously weaken German resistance . . .[21]

The true British stance with regard to negotiating with any peace faction in Germany was made even more explicit in Harrison's final statement:

While it is arguable that we do not wish to negotiate peace, even entirely on our own terms, with *any* group in Germany until Germany has been smashed, it is undeniable, I think, that the emergence of such a group, whether or not it was successful in overthrowing the regime, would enormously contribute to an Allied victory . . .

However, there was a drawback to this strategy, and Harrison was quick to note it, remarking that even if such a political coup could be induced in Germany:

We are . . . faced with the dilemma that the only circles [of sufficient power and standing] in Germany which can be used as active instruments for overthrowing the Nazis are themselves tainted and suspect . . .

Harrison concluded his report:

There are of course risks in such a course [of action], but the reward might be great.[22]

Having read Harrison's report, Anthony Eden commented, 'Bruce Lockhart should see this paper . . . for its very able exposition of the German scene.'[23]

Robert Bruce Lockhart, over at PWE headquarters, did indeed read the report; his thoughts on how the German peace initiatives could be used to cause political damage to Germany were mulled over and passed to Richard Crossman, head of the German Section. However, the scheme that would be developed must have made the men of the Foreign Office blanch, both at its audacity and at the extreme risk PWE was prepared to take. The top men at PWE decided that it was not sufficient to support some hotchpotch group of anti-Nazis in Germany. If real progress was to be made, they should aim their sights high and attempt to use one of Germany's leading and most feared men and his organisation. It was a scheme fraught with danger.

•••••

In Germany, during the summer of 1942, Heinrich Himmler began to think seriously about how to proceed in the realm of secret peace negotiation. His initial efforts had come to naught, but he was not a man to give up easily on such a notion. When the war started he had been one of the most enthusiastic followers of his Führer, and as news of the successes in Poland, Norway, the Low Countries, and France had come rolling in, he had become more and more convinced that Germany was destined to be the leader of a right-wing Europe. Then had come the great adventure, the fulfilment of Hitler's dream of creating an empire in the east out of Russian territory as far as the Ural Mountains; an empire encompassing the Ukraine, which was to become the breadbasket of the Reich, and the Caucasus, which possessed enough oil and natural resources to power the thousand-year Reich long into the future.

However, Hitler's dreamed-of empire in the east was fast becoming a nightmare for Germany. The stunning successes of the first months of Barbarossa had quickly fallen away during the autumn rains that turned thousands of square miles of front line into a quagmire. Germany's elite armies had become so bogged down that it was almost impossible to conduct offensive operations against the Russians. Then had come the Russian winter of 1941, far harsher than anyone had anticipated, and hard on men and machines alike. However, despite the terrible climatic conditions, the Russians had continued to launch counterattacks, and managed some reversals in Germany's fortunes on the eastern front. At the end of that terrible winter the deep snow had melted, and back had come the endless realm of Russian mud. If anyone in the German High Command

A teenage Himmler (standing behind his father) pictured with his family in 1917.

Himmler, the up-and-coming politician, pictured here in the mid-1920s, at a time when he was the Deputy Propaganda Leader of the Nazi Party. USHMM, courtesy of James Blevins

Himmler, Reichsführer-SS, at target practice. USHMM, courtesy of James Blevins

Hitler, Martin Mutschmann (NSDAP Leader of Saxony), Ernst Rohm (Leader of the SA) and Himmler review a parade in 1933.

Himmler, Reichsführer-SS, pictured here in the mid-1930s at a time of unparalleled personal success. USHMM, courtesy of James Blevins

Vidkun Quisling, Hitler's puppet Prime Minister of Norway, meets with Himmler in 1943, at a time when Himmler was secretly talking to the British. Chrysalis Image Library

Himmler and his sinister protégé, Reinhard Heydrich, pictured here on 12 March 1938, the day of Anschluss between Nazi Germany and Austria. akg-images/Ullstein Bild

Himmler, wearing his ceremonial dagger, watches troop movements in the early years of the war. USHMM, courtesy of James Blevins

Himmler, pictured here with Ernst Kaltenbrunner (Head of the RSHA) on the far right. USHMM, courtesy of Archiv der KZ-Gedenkstaette Mauthausen

Karl-Heinz Kramer, Himmler's man in Stockholm. Kramer would be the man British Ambassador Victor Mallet would negotiate through to Himmler. Martin Allen

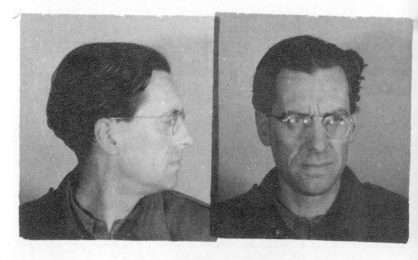

Walter Schellenberg, head of Amt VI of the SS Intelligence Service, the Sicherheitsdienst or SD, pictured here in British custody at the end of the war. Between 1943–45 he played a pivotal role in the Himmler negotiations.

Bettmann/Corbis

Winston Churchill welcomes President Roosevelt's envoy, Harry Hopkins, to London in 1941. In the background stands the ruthless head of the Political Warfare Executive, Brendan Bracken.

Bettmann/Corbis

Sir Robert Bruce-Lockhart, leading man of the Political Intelligence Department and a member of the Committee of Five of the Political Warfare Executive. In 1945 Lockhart would sanction the decision to 'eliminate' Himmler as soon as he fell into British hands.

Hitler congratulates Himmler, the loyal head of the SS, on his 43rd birthday, little suspecting that the Reichsführer was already in secret negotiations with the British to ensure himself of a post-war political career. akg-images

Colonel Claus von Stauffenberg, the driving force behind the conspiracy to kill Hitler on 20 July 1944. akg-images

Knights of the SS at the height of power. Himmler flanked by his loyal lieutenants, Karl Wolff (left) and head of the intelligence service, Reinhard Heydrich (right).

20 July 1944: An hour before the assassination attempt.
Colonel Claus von Stauffenberg (far left), Puttkamer,
Bodenschatz and Keitel (far right) greet Hitler before the
building where the bombing took place. Photo12.com_Oasis

Hitler's trousers, blown to tatters by Colonel Stauffenberg's bomb on 20 July 1944. akg-images/Ullstein Bild

A shaken Hitler visits the injured a few hours after the 20 July bomb attempt on his life. Topfoto

Above left: Hitler and Himmler deep in conversation during a winter walk near the Berghof in 1944. Ullstein bild-Frentz

Above right: Count Folke Bernadotte, Vice President of the Swedish Red Cross. Himmler would make his last bid for peace through Bernadotte in 1945.
USHMM, courtesy of the National Archives

Below: Heinrich Himmler, dead on the morning of 24 May 1945, whilst in British custody. Bettmann/Corbis

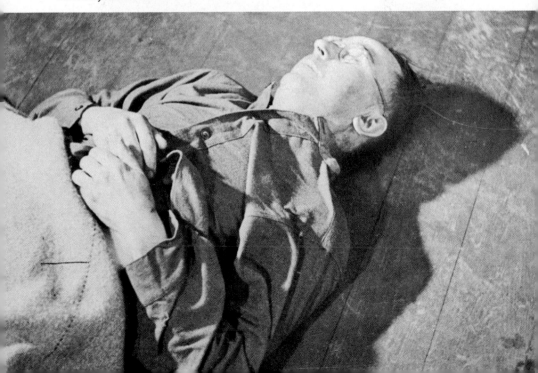

had harboured the notion that the Russian offensive would be a quick campaign, they had been thoroughly disillusioned of that idea. Russia might well prove to be the Germans' undoing. Germany could not maintain a two-front war, committed to defence in the west against Britain and the Americans whilst struggling to maintain the upper hand against the Russians in the east.

Himmler could see as clearly as Hitler that in the long run Germany's military position was untenable. He knew of the Führer's desire to negotiate an accord with the Allies in the west, leaving Nazi Germany free to pursue her crusade in the east to drive the Bolshevik hordes back beyond the Urals. He was also aware that Hitler had ventured on several occasions to open peace negotiations with the British, though it is certain that no one in Germany apart from Albrecht Haushofer knew of the Führer's gambit to negotiate a deal with Lord Halifax prior to the launch of the Russian invasion in June 1941. Many prominent Nazis, however, perceived a severe problem in Germany when it came to attempting to open negotiations, and that problem had a name: Joachim von Ribbentrop.

The triumvirate responsible for the Night of the Long Knives – Göring, Goebbels, and Himmler – were particularly well aware that Foreign Minister Ribbentrop had made a devastating error of judgement in the run-up to war. His earnest counsel that Britain would not go to war for Poland had left Germany fighting a war in the west that the Führer had never wanted. Hitler, too, knew that Ribbentrop had been wrong, but he was reluctant to turn on his Foreign Minister and dismiss him. Ribbentrop had, after all, brought Hitler his foreign policy successes of the 1930s, achieving the Anglo-German Naval Agreement and the *Anschluss* with Austria, and had managed matters very well when pressuring the British, French, and Italians into supporting Hitler's claim to German sovereignty over the Sudetenland. However, since the summer of 1939 he had been substantially sidelined by the other leading Nazis, who perceived him as ineffective, arrogant, and ill-informed about the true political state of Europe. Count Ciano, the Italian Foreign Minister, quoted an acid comment made by Prince Otto von Bismarck that Ribbentrop 'is such an imbecile that he is a freak of nature'.[24]

Since the late spring of 1940 Hitler had completely excluded Ribbentrop from his efforts to open secret negotiations with Britain, and it is known for certain that he was absolutely not informed about the Hitler–Hess–Haushofer attempt at peace mediation with Lord Halifax in 1941. Nor was he involved in Hitler's subsequent attempts to open a line of negotiation with the British. Despite his previous mistakes, this may seem strange: Ribbentrop was Hitler's Foreign Minister, and should therefore have played a key role in any such negotiations. But Hitler had been explicitly advised by Albrecht Haushofer that Ribbentrop was a liability, and that the Allies would have no truck with any peace overture involving him. Hitler in any case knew Ribbentrop's shortcomings, knew he was not a man to be involved in sensitive attempts to open negotiations with the Allies; after all, the British government, too, blamed Ribbentrop for his poor advice to Hitler during the run-up to war in 1939.

Many of the leading men in Nazi Germany therefore knew that if peace was ever to be achieved with the western Allies, Ribbentrop must not be part of the negotiating process. There was too much at stake for his arrogance and lack of judgement to be allowed to play a part. Himmler, ever the astute politician, was very much aware of this situation. In the summer of 1942 he met discreetly with Albrecht Haushofer at the Munich home of his lawyer, Carl Langbehn.

Following the collapse of the Hitler/Hess negotiations with Lord Halifax and the loss of Rudolf Hess to the British in May 1941, Haushofer had been quick to align himself with several powerful new patrons. The first of these was Martin Bormann, Hess's replacement at Hitler's side, for whom he wrote several in-depth reports on both foreign affairs and the possibility of negotiating peace with the Allies at a future date.[25] The second was the Reichsführer-SS Heinrich Himmler, who knew that Haushofer was one of Germany's leading experts on foreign affairs. Indeed, he had met him many times in the 1930s when, often in the company of Hess, Haushofer had been present at high-echelon gatherings in Berlin to advise Hitler on foreign policy. Himmler, now keen to obtain some expert advice, therefore asked Langbehn to arrange a confidential meeting. This took place on the evening of 12 August 1942 at Langbehn's home,[26] and there Haushofer tendered his advice to the Reichsführer-SS on the problems faced by Germany in opening negotiations with the Allies. One of his key observations was that if any leading politician in Germany – i.e. one of the top Nazis – 'did desire to negotiate with Britain, the very fact that the German Foreign Minister was Ribbentrop would make it difficult for any negotiations to get off the ground'.[27]

Haushofer confirmed to Himmler that Ribbentrop was anathema to the British, stating that 'the Ribbentrop situation' would 'get in the way of any negotiations'. If anyone in Germany managed to open a line of communication, Ribbentrop would eventually have to take part – as

Foreign Minister – and that would be 'fatal' to the success of such negotiations.[28]

It is known from many sources that the resourceful Himmler, in the words of Walter Dornberger, 'possessed the rare gift of attentive listening'.[29] He would therefore have carefully absorbed all that Haushofer said: Ribbentrop should not – indeed, could not – be allowed to participate in any future peace negotiations, at whatever stage, if they were to succeed. Moreover, if he were eradicated from the politico-diplomatic scene it could only help in the long run. Such a conclusion was to result in the most concerted effort to date to remove Ribbentrop from Hitler's orbit.

In pursuing this goal Himmler had a capable ally in the form of Walter Schellenberg, who had begun to play an increasingly important role in the Reichsführer's life since the assassination of his head of Intelligence, Reinhard Heydrich, in Prague that June.

A mere ten days after Himmler's meeting with Albrecht Haushofer in Munich, the Reichsführer-SS was in Zhitomir in the Ukraine for a conference with his Waffen-SS commanders. Whilst he was here he had a secret meeting with Schellenberg, who had travelled all the way from Berlin specifically to see his chief. By the summer of 1942, like many in the upper echelons of the German command, Schellenberg had come to the conclusion that there was no longer any hope of Germany winning the war. There was only one alternative, and that was to negotiate a deal with the western Allies. This view, combined with what Himmler had learnt from Haushofer in Munich, served to emphasise to the two men the fact that Ribbentrop was the 'main obstacle to peace'.[30] Himmler was prepared to go further, and said to Schellenberg that there could be 'no alternative solution . . . as long as that idiot Ribbentrop advises the Führer'. Agreeing with his chief, Schellenberg promised to work towards securing Ribbentrop's downfall by Christmas.[31]

Little did Himmler know it at the time, but Schellenberg already had information that might bring Ribbentrop tumbling down. Through his Intelligence Service he had managed to obtain a secret medical report on the Foreign Minister that revealed that he had a chronic kidney condition, concluding that the illness might be impairing his mental powers.[32] To a man like Schellenberg, this constituted a flaw in Ribbentrop's substantial armour, having as he did the support and confidence of Hitler. The only question remaining was how best to manipulate the situation and present the evidence of Ribbentrop's failings. He had an idea how this could be done, for he had already learnt through the Intelligence Service of a man in Berlin who was also plotting Ribbentrop's downfall.

•••••

In mid-September 1942 Germany's military position took yet another step towards disaster. Summer had again turned to autumn, and still the Russians had not been defeated. In Hitler's eyes another key opportunity – that year's fighting season – had been lost. In the spring of 1942 the commander of Army Group South, Field Marshal List, had been ordered to use his substantial and well-trained forces to sweep through the Crimea towards the Caucasus, and proceed a further 350 miles to take the Russian port city of Batum far to the east near the frontier with Turkey, thereby denying the Soviet Black Sea fleet its last base. He was then to move inland towards the Caspian Sea to take the Caucasus oilfields. This was an enormous undertaking, and though List's forces took the Crimea, they failed in the last two key objectives. The summer campaign had stalled in the Crimea, and Germany failed to wrest control of the precious oilfields from the Russians. As a result by 24 September Hitler was incandescent with frustration and fury.

At the Führer's forward field headquarters, 'Werewolf', at Vinnitsa deep in the Ukraine, he wielded an axe and began to sack his top commanders. The first to fall was Field Marshal List, but Hitler did not stop there. He also fired two of his best Panzer Corps commanders, Wietersheim of the 14th Panzer Corps and Schwedler of the 4th Panzer Corps, for not achieving their objectives in the north that summer. After these two generals had been sacked, Hitler next turned upon his Chief of General Staff of the Army High Command (OKW), Colonel General Franz Halder. He was replaced by Colonel General Kurt Zeitzler, a logistics specialist who was known by all to be a pliable yes-man. Had Hitler thought logically about the situation, he would probably not have dismissed these commanders; it was not their fault that the Russians were putting up stiffer resistance than anyone had expected. But he was not being logical. These were the first frantic acts of a desperately worried man who knew that the tide was turning inexorably against Germany, and Hitler was desperate. He was aware that if Russia could not be defeated within the next twelve months, the war would be lost, and that would result in Germany's utter destruction.

Back in Berlin at the very same time that Hitler was firing his top commanders on the eastern front, Walter Schellenberg met for a quiet tête-à-tête with a man he believed might be able to assist him in unseating Ribbentrop from his perch at the apex of German foreign policy. This man was the forty-seven-year-old head of Section D III, Abteilung Deutschland (the German Section) of the Foreign Ministry, a certain Martin Franz Julius Luther. A keen Nazi and a member of the SA, Luther had been the sole member of the Foreign Ministry invited by Reinhard Heydrich to the Wannsee Conference the previous January, at which the preparations to exterminate all Europe's Jews had been orchestrated.

Luther had come to Schellenberg's attention through Walter Kieser, his assistant at the Foreign Ministry, who was also a ranking SS officer. Kieser and Schellenberg had been to university together, where they had studied law, and it is undoubtedly through their continuing friendship that Schellenberg came to hear of Luther's newfound loathing for the arrogant Ribbentrop and his wife. Always a man with an eye to the main chance, Schellenberg thus found himself with an ideal medium, if Luther could be persuaded, to oust Ribbentrop from his position close to Hitler.

Martin Luther, an influential figure in the German Foreign Ministry, had a most curious history. Like many of the leading Nazis, he did not have a background in politics, the civil service, or indeed foreign affairs. A successful Berlin businessman who had owned a furniture-removal firm and a house-decorating company, he had first come into contact with the Ribbentrops in the late 1920s when hired by Ribbentrop's wife, Annelies, to renovate their home in the affluent Berlin suburb of Dahlem. Annelies took an immediate liking to the useful and energetic Martin Luther, who was an enthusiastic Nazi even then. Over the subsequent years he began to play an ever more important role in the Ribbentrop household. To celebrate the 1936 Berlin Olympics, the Ribbentrops hired him to transform the grounds of their Berlin mansion for a summer gala dinner. His work was meticulous, and the relationship was thus further strengthened. When Ribbentrop was appointed German Ambassador to Britain, he and Annelies took the capable Luther with them to run their London household, and he became more and more part of their inner circle. Hitler appointed Ribbentrop Foreign Minister in 1938, and he in turn immediately inducted his protégé into the Auswärtiges Amt (Foreign Ministry) as a reliable confidant, a man whom he could his trust in his efforts to reform the old-fashioned ministry and reeducate it in Nazi methods. Unsurprisingly, many of the stalwarts of the Auswärtiges Amt disliked intensely the Nazi upstart foisted upon them by Ribbentrop, and Luther in turn rode roughshod over the old Ministry mandarins as he began to Nazify the institution.

Within months Ribbentrop would promote his super-protégé with dizzying speed. Luther was appointed head of his own department, the Abteilung Deutschland, which dealt with home affairs as well as interdepartmental liaison with the other organisations set up by the Nazis such as the Auslandsorganisation controlled by Ernst Bohle, the Aussenpolitisches Amt under Alfred Rosenberg, and the SD, which had until his death in June 1942 been headed by Reinhard Heydrich.

By late 1942, however, relations between the Ribbentrops and Luther had soured.

To begin with, for all his other faults, and enthusiastic Nazi that he was, Joachim von Ribbentrop was not a monster in the ilk of his fellow Nazis. Yes, he was domineering and liked to throw his weight about; yes, he liked to ride around Berlin in an enormous Mercedes limousine flanked by a guard of sinister SS men in full regalia. Yet there was a subtle facet to Ribbentrop's character that set him apart from the likes of the rabid anti-Semite Julius Streicher, Joseph Goebbels (who daily poured forth propaganda against the Jews from his cup of hate), or indeed Heinrich Himmler, who was determined to cleanse the Reich of the Jews and *Untermenschen* (subhumans) and make it a land of Aryan supremacy. Ribbentrop was from a more cultured and wealthy background than his contemporaries; he had been a millionaire resident of Dahlem in the 1920s, and his lifestyle had also encompassed several Jewish acquaintances before he determined to throw in his lot with the Nazis as a means of carving out a political career for himself. (Those acquaintances were dropped as soon as he became a Nazi.)

During the Wannsee Conference of January 1942, at which Luther had been the Foreign Ministry's representative, the Nazis had secretly adopted a policy of exterminating all the Jews of Europe. This decision did not sit easily with Ribbentrop. Although in the autumn of 1942 he did send a communication ordering the deaths of 8,000 Serbian Jews, it is known that even in this instance Luther was taking the lead and possibly forced his minister's hand. Ribbentrop was most uncomfortable with Luther's wholehearted support for Heydrich's scheme to eradicate the Jews. Indeed, until the very end of the war, he stoutly refused to believe that Hitler – whom he idolised – was the motivating force behind the policy. In 1946, when finally presented with the undeniable evidence of what had taken place, a shocked Ribbentrop remarked to Dr Gustav Gilbert, the prison psychiatrist at Nuremberg:

My God! Did Hoess [commandant of Auschwitz] say [the exterminations began] in 1941? . . . There is no doubt that Hitler ordered it? I thought that perhaps Himmler, late in the war, under some pretext . . . But '41 he said? My God! . . . But we never dreamed it would end like this. We only thought they [the Jews] had too much influence – that we could solve the problem by a quota system or that we would transport them to the East or Madagascar [the Madagascar scheme, in which the Jews of Europe were to be resettled in a land of their own off the coast of Africa, was one favoured by Ribbentrop] . . .[33]

And it was over this matter that a major difference of opinion arose between Ribbentrop and Luther. Ribbentrop was arrogant and ineffectual, but deep down he was no mass murderer. Luther, on the other hand, had been totally won over by Heydrich's arguments, and he wanted to accelerate the process, sweeping up all Europe's Jews for transport to the east and extermination. He comprehended the whole horrible scheme, imparted to him by Heydrich at Wannsee; Ribbentrop, though undoubtedly aware of the policy that was now to be adopted by the German Reich, failed to grasp its full implications. By the time he understood what was to take place, Luther had become a monster of his own creation, and it was too late. Luther had the backing of the highest men in the land – including both Hitler and Himmler – for this most terrible mission; thus fortified, his prestige and power were beginning to eclipse Ribbentrop's. It was a situation that was bound to come to a head.

The second reason for Ribbentrop's breach with Luther had nothing to do with high foreign or political policy, and infinitely more to do with the personal enmity of Annelies von Ribbentrop. Ever since the 1930s, Luther had (strangely, when his growing importance in the Foreign Ministry is considered) been responsible for the maintenance of the Ribbentrops' many homes, a duty whose fulfilment entailed pandering to Annelies's every wish. A separate branch had even been set up within the Abteilung Deutschland specifically to manage the upkeep of the Foreign Minister's six official residences all over Germany, from a castle at Fuschl in the Alps to a magnificent and newly built palace in the centre of Berlin, at 73 Wilhelmstrasse. In the summer of 1942 Annelies had decided to revamp the decor of her husband's Wilhelmstrasse palace. She called in Luther and begun issuing him with orders, much in the manner she had always done. However, on this occasion Luther took deep exception, especially when Annelies insisted on changing all the tapestries *four times* before she was satisfied.[34] He objected to being treated as a mere flunky by his boss's wife and retaliated by imposing a limit, through his department at the Abteilung Deutschland, on the amount of money Annelies was allowed to spend on the Ribbentrops' homes. On hearing of this, Annelies was deeply offended. Had not she and her husband taken the ungrateful Luther into their hearts and home when he had been a mere decorator and furniture remover? She immediately took her complaints to her husband who, under pressure from his domineering wife, and deeply concerned at Luther's growing power in the Foreign Ministry, at last felt prompted to act.

Ribbentrop had begun to hear rumours that Luther and men serving under him in the Abteilung Deutschland were expropriating Foreign Ministry funds for their own purposes, so he ordered Kurt Prüfer (a bitter enemy of Luther since 1938) to undertake an investigation into allegations of corruption in Luther's department. However, he had to move carefully, for Luther knew all the skeletons in the Foreign Minister's cupboard, having in the past been ordered to undertake ruthless intrigues against Ribbentrop's rivals and eradicate all opposition to his methods in the Foreign Ministry. He was also the primary man at the Ministry responsible for undertaking 'the dirty work of the Final Solution'.[35]

For his part, Luther believed Ribbentrop to be an incompetent Foreign Minister and had his own ideas on how German foreign policy might progress under his own leadership. Furthermore, he did not consider that Ribbentrop was doing all he should to carry out the annihilation of Europe's Jews. Now Luther was to discover that he had a corruption inquiry hanging over his head (it was due to report back in February 1943) that could destroy his career. It became clear to Luther that in the interest of self-preservation he should act to destroy Ribbentrop before he was himself destroyed. The hand that had fed was about to be bitten.

At Luther's secret meeting with Walter Schellenberg in a hotel room in the centre of Berlin in early October 1942, the two men initially regarded each other with extreme caution. Luther, who did not know Schellenberg, was wary of this mysterious approach from a leading man of the SD who professed to be an emissary from Himmler. It was not unknown in Nazi Germany for the SS/SD to set up 'honey-traps' in order to expose treason that could land a man in a concentration camp or before an execution squad. Nor did Schellenberg know Luther. Being a longstanding member of the SA, Luther might not look kindly on the SS and might still feel beholden to Ribbentrop; enough, perhaps, to expose the plot to unseat the Reich's Foreign Minister from his place at Hitler's side.

However, over the course of the meeting Schellenberg managed to impart to Luther the Reichsführer's deep concern at Ribbentrop's inept leadership of foreign policy, emphasising that it was in everyone's interest at this time for Germany to have a competent man at the helm of the Foreign Ministry. An extremely cautious Luther had tentatively asked whether Schellenberg might consider him suitable material for the leadership of the Auswärtiges Amt. Certainly, Schellenberg assured Luther. Had he not already been trusted by Heydrich and shown his commitment to the very difficult mission ahead, that of eradicating the Jewish problem from Europe? This in direct contrast to Ribbentrop, who had been disliked intensely by Heydrich, and was even now showing deep reluctance to participate in the SS's mission to solve the Jewish problem by enacting the Final Solution.[36]

The two men left their secret discussion each satisfied with what had been agreed. At a time when he was subject to a corruption inquiry ordered by Ribbentrop, Luther had suddenly found himself engaged, with the backing of Heinrich Himmler, the most powerful man in the Reich after Hitler, to work towards the political demise of the Foreign Minister. Was it good fortune that had come his way, a lifeline that might yet see him rise to become Nazi Germany's Reichsaussenminister? Only time would tell, but of one thing he could be sure: that there would be a price to pay for Himmler's support. It must have been evident to him as he left the meeting that he would henceforth be Himmler's man, body and soul. Luther must have felt confident that October afternoon, for surely Himmler, head of the Reich's state security and the all-powerful SS, was stronger by far than Joachim von Ribbentrop. However, he was destined to have a shock, and the Reichsführer-SS would be revealed as a man prone to indecision and doubt.

Towards the end of 1942, whilst still trying to maintain a front of loyalty and cordial relations with Ribbentrop, Luther, aided by his assistants Walter Büttner and Walter Kieser, submitted a blueprint to the Foreign Minister for possible peace terms with the western Allies. The document proposed a future European federation; the restoration of sovereignty to all the occupied countries, including Poland and Czechoslovakia; and economic aid and leadership by Germany. Ribbentrop, who had not expected such a helpful document from Luther at a time when relations between them were on the point of irrevocable collapse, studied the peace plan with interest. Keen to enhance his standing in Hitler's eyes, he eagerly took the proposals to the Führer, carefully omitting the fact that others in his Foreign Ministry had devised the document, and presenting it as his big idea for bringing peace to Europe.

Hitler took one look at the document and angrily tore it to bits before Ribbentrop's eyes, declaring that when the time came for peace, he would have no need of such a plan. He then furiously castigated Ribbentrop for wasting his time with such useless proposals. Ribbentrop left the meeting much chastened and utterly convinced that the evil Luther had intentionally set him up. The incident did much to harden his resolve to be rid of his protégé as soon as possible; if only Prüfer would hurry up with his inquiry, giving him the ammunition to destroy Luther once and for all.

Back in the Abteilung Deutschland, Kieser and Büttner held Ribbentrop responsible for Hitler's rejection of Luther's plan. It had been no set-up, but on the contrary an earnest attempt to advance a possible way out of a disastrous war. They were sure that if Luther, as Foreign Minister, had presented the plan, Hitler might have listened. They were not to know, of course, that by the winter of 1942 the Führer had given up on a political and diplomatic solution to the war. Only a very few of his intimates, such as Himmler, were aware of this.

And so 1942 drew to a close, and with it the last of Germany's military successes; there were to be a few more days of hope, but in the main there would be only bad news from now on. In the first days of 1943 Schellenberg covertly arranged a meeting between Himmler and Luther, hoping that the Reichsführer would see in Luther a newfound ally, a man loyal to the SS who would aid him in his secret search for peace. The meeting took place as if by chance (for everyone had to be very careful not to reveal the slightest hint of conspiracy) at a reception hosted by Dino Alfieri, the Italian Ambassador to Berlin. It lasted a mere ten minutes, and its real purpose could not be discussed for fear of being overheard, but Luther left confident that he had made a good impression on his new patron, and that he could not possibly fail with the backing of such a powerful man. But the Reichsführer, in contrast, was unsure of his new ally. Himmler had not liked Luther's obsequiousness in the slightest, and had been highly irritated by his overfamiliarity.[37]

Over the past two months, since his meeting with Schellenberg, Luther had been busy in his spare time plotting the downfall of Ribbentrop. He had been given a copy of the medical report, acquired by Schellenberg, that suggested that Ribbentrop's renal condition had made him mentally unbalanced. However, such a document was not enough to topple the Foreign Minister. It was known by all that Hitler looked favourably upon Ribbentrop, not because he was an effective originator of foreign policy – that was a role the Führer took on himself – but because he simply did as he was told. What was needed, both Schellenberg and Martin Luther had concluded, was powerful evidence that would reveal Ribbentrop's incompetence before both Hitler and his eminent fellow Nazis, making his position untenable. This, it was hoped, would give Hitler no choice but to remove Ribbentrop from office and appoint a new Foreign Minister. Therefore, in the last weeks of 1942 and at the beginning of 1943, Martin Luther had been busy compiling a comprehensive and devastatingly frank detailed dossier on all Ribbentrop's mistakes, bizarre decisions, and megalomaniac arrogance – any unfortunate incident that revealed his unsuitability to remain Foreign Minister. This evidence took some time to compile, but it was agreed with Schellenberg that it would be ready by the second week of February, when they would strike what they hoped would be a mortal blow against Ribbentrop. It would be a race against the clock, for at about the same time Prüfer was expected to submit his report on Luther's corruption. In fact, despite Luther's best efforts at obstruction, he lost the race, and Prüfer submitted his report to Ribbentrop on the afternoon of Thursday, 6 February 1943.[38] Yet Luther's luck appeared to be with him, for Ribbentrop was extremely busy on that day, and decided not to bother reading the report until after the weekend.

However, things were about to go badly wrong for Luther from an unexpected quarter. He planned that copies of his report would be sent to all the leading members of the Nazi government (Goebbels, Göring, Ley, etc.) on Monday, 10 February. This, he hoped, would precipitate Ribbentrop's downfall within a very short time; all these men would turn to Hitler and say, in effect, 'Ribbentrop is a liability and cannot remain at the helm of German foreign policy.' Now, despite all the plotting and deception orchestrated by Schellenberg, his own mentor, Himmler, suddenly took a most extraordinary decision. It is not known exactly why he suddenly changed his mind; it may be that by his own convoluted methods he came to the conclusion that he did not need to topple Ribbentrop, because he was going to circumvent both Hitler and Ribbentrop in carrying out secret negotiations with the western Allies. Alternatively, he may have decided that a very much damaged Ribbentrop would be beholden to him as his saviour, and that he could gain considerable influence in this way. Whatever the thought-process behind the decision, on Saturday, 8 February, he sent a copy of Luther's report to the Foreign Minister himself.

Ribbentrop was apoplectic with fury when he read the contents of the report. It did not even grant him the dignity of stating that his ideas on foreign policy were at odds with Germany's best interests. Its core argument was that he was mad, and it proceeded to relate a whole string of incidents to prove that claim. Ribbentrop immediately ran to the Führer, denouncing Luther and demanding that his treacherous subordinate be executed forthwith for treason. Hitler's response was strange. He confirmed his confidence in Ribbentrop, but refused to have Luther executed. Instead, Luther was sent to Sachsenhausen concentration camp, where he was treated as a privileged inmate until the end of the war. At the Führer's insistence, the whole event was to be suppressed and kept from the public domain: should the content of Luther's report become known, it might damage Germany's international standing. News of the putsch attempt against Ribbentrop did, however, eventually reach diplomatic circles, and many an ambassador and diplomat dined out on the story with much hilarity for months afterwards. Thus Ribbentrop was irretrievably damaged, in spite of Hitler's efforts to protect him. He became increasingly suspicious of his subordinates at the Foreign Ministry, seeing plots around him at every turn, and placing his trust in no one in case another such event was to occur again.

We do not know what Schellenberg's reaction was when Himmler suddenly decided to turn against the plot to oust Ribbentrop. It would surely have left him puzzled, though perhaps it did not; maybe Himmler confided his decision to Schellenberg at the last moment. Any account in his memoirs of Himmler's reasoning, and of whether he himself knew what was about to happen, may have been expunged by British Intelligence early in the 1950s; or perhaps he decided to take the secret to his grave. Either way, events in the war at the beginning of 1943 soon made the Luther incident pale into insignificance, revealing to any Nazi who had not yet realised that Germany could lose the war that things were now going badly wrong.

•••••

On 31 January 1943 General Friedrich von Paulus surrendered the remnants of a whole army at Stalingrad, and on 2 February the Russians succeeded in mopping up all further resistance. It was Germany's biggest defeat of the war in the east thus far, and caused mourning all over the country. Hitler was beside himself with rage, for he had ordered no surrender, insisting that Paulus and his troops should fight to the last man in the defence of a totally destroyed city. As Churchill was later to comment, 'This crushing disaster to the German army ended Hitler's prodigious effort to conquer Russia by force of arms.'[39] To many people in the upper echelons of the German High Command, and indeed in the Nazi government, it was becoming clear that Germany was going to lose the war. It might take a year or two yet, but eventual and complete defeat was the prospect that now beckoned. Himmler was thus all the more determined to open secret negotiations with Britain, and 1943 would see his most earnest attempt yet to come to some agreement with the western Allies.

However, the parameters of such a very serious matter as the opening of secret peace negotiations had now changed. In mid-January Churchill, under the code name of 'Mr P', had flown to Casablanca for a conference with 'Admiral Q' – President Roosevelt. The purpose of the conference, now that the Allies had largely succeeded in wresting northwest Africa from Axis control during the last two months of 1942, had been to discuss the next phase of the war. As Churchill was to communicate to London on 20 January:

> Admiral 'Q' [the President] and I called a plenary conference this afternoon, at which the Combined Chiefs of Staff reported progress. It was a most satisfactory meeting. After five days' discussions and a good deal of apparent disagreement the Combined Chiefs of Staff are now, I think, unanimous in essentials about the conduct of the war in 1943.[40]

The 'essentials' agreed were basically that, first, the European arena of conflict would take precedence over the Pacific; i.e. the Germans were to be defeated before the Allies turned their attention upon the Japanese. Second, the Allies would endeavour to open a second front against the Axis in Europe with an invasion of Continental Europe in 1943 (this was projected to take place through the Continent's soft underbelly, the south and Italy, hopefully precipitating a decision by the Italians to abandon their German partners). Finally it was agreed that there should be no negotiated truce with the Germans until they had been utterly defeated. In Churchill's words, this was 'a declaration of the firm intention of the United States and the British Empire to continue the war relentlessly until we had brought about the "unconditional surrender" of Germany and Japan'.[41]

Despite this assertion that there would be no peace discussions until
Nazi Germany irrevocably accepted total defeat, certain men in Britain, at
PWE, were about to enter into their most comprehensive discussions yet
with one of the leading men of the Reich.

In Germany news of the 'unconditional surrender' policy adopted by
the Allies was greeted with pragmatic resolve to continue the war undeterred. In any case, the Nazi leadership had no choice. As Hitler told his
Party leaders in early February, 'he felt liberated as a result from any
attempts to persuade him to look for a negotiated peace settlement'.[42] For
Hitler, the Casablanca Conference resolution altered nothing. It served
only to confirm that his obdurate stance – victory or defeat – had been
vindicated. Any hope of a compromise peace was now ruled out. 'For
Hitler, closing off escape routes had distinct advantages. Fear of destruction was a strong motivator.'[43] This 'motivation', Hitler hoped, might prove
decisive in instilling in his commanders, fighting men, and the nation,
the fact that Germany's bridges had been burnt behind her, that there
was no choice now but for victory. However, to one man, Hitler's stance
served only to confirm the correctness of his own secret decision to negotiate with the British, so as to establish the parameters of the post-war
German political scene. He now determined that 1943 would be the
decisive year.

•••••

At the beginning of 1943, in fact at almost exactly the same time as the
Casablanca Conference was taking place, Sir Samuel Hoare in Madrid
sent a submission to the Foreign Office in London revealing that Prince
Hohenlohe had once again been attempting to open a line of negotiation
with the British government. However, as the civil servant minutes accompanying the report made clear, the Foreign Office, at least, had little incli-
nation to talk to the head of the SS:

> Hohenlohe is in Spain as Himmler's agent with the object of
> entering into peace negotiations with H[is] M[ajesty's] G[overn-
> ment]. Wirth [a confidant of Himmler's, SS-Obersturmführer,
> and head of the Stuttgart police] in Switzerland is independent of
> Himmler. Both he and Hohenlohe are definitely hostile to Hitler
> who is becoming the scapegoat of German discontent.[44]

However, Mr Harrison – writer of the FO report that had landed on the desk of Robert Bruce Lockhart at PWE in the summer of 1942 – commented:

> Himmler is probably the most hated man in Europe . . . I simply cannot see him either as a rival to Hitler or as trying to negotiate peace with us. Himmler has agents of his own abroad who report to him directly and Hohenlohe is in fact his agent in Spain.[45]

Despite this acid comment on Himmler's popularity – and it was in all probability most accurate – the men of PWE were not singing the same tune as the Foreign Office. The FO wanted nothing to do with any German if it involved negotiation: there was a strict directive from Churchill and Anthony Eden not to provide the German government with any succour by giving it reason to believe that Britain would be amenable to a negotiated truce. On the other hand, though the Political Warfare Executive had no intention of *real* negotiation, it's raison d'être was to cause political instability in Germany, one strategy being to open a line of false negotiation with a leading Nazi in the hope of precipitating a leadership coup. If that man were Heinrich Himmler, head of the Gestapo, monster of the SS, then so be it.

PWE did not have long to wait before the Germans made their next move. However, they were cautious as to how they proceeded, for Himmler was very much afraid that his endeavours might become public knowledge. At his Zhitomir discussion with Schellenberg in the summer of 1942, he had made it clear that such a leak must be prevented at all costs. It might cause irremediable damage to Germany's negotiating position on the world stage, for public knowledge of a peace appeal by him or any other leading Nazi would make Germany appear weak and uncertain of victory. As it happened, the British had no intention of leaking details of these confidential negotiations, for the very good reason that they hoped by such talks to precipitate the political demise of Hitler and bring about a sudden end to the war.

In the spring of 1943, with this very idea in mind, the head of MI5, Sir Stewart Menzies, proposed that stringent conditions must be applied to the Germans – and this necessarily meant the Himmler approaches – if they wanted a conclusion to hostilities. First, if a political coup were to take place, Hitler must be placed under house arrest out of the orbit of political influence, possibly in his Alpine residence at Berchtesgaden. Then a de facto government should be set up in Germany, comprising a 'Council of Twelve' under Himmler's control. Only after this had been achieved should the British agree to negotiate an armistice.

However, little did Menzies know it, but the Political Warfare Executive was already talking to representatives of Himmler by March 1943. Under interrogation by the British authorities in the autumn of 1945, Schellenberg attested that, though Himmler was at first unwilling to contact the British himself, his lawyer, Carl Langbehn (having been in receipt of politico-diplomatic counselling by Albrecht Haushofer), was sent to Stockholm. There, with the assistance of Marcus Wallenberg, he made his first tentative contact with the British Ambassador, Victor Mallet. The exact details of what was discussed have never been revealed, though Mallet communicated to Lockhart in London that:

> I was invited to Marcus Wallenberg's home last evening where, to my surprise, he presented a visiting German named Karl [sic] Langbehn, who he revealed was Himmler's agent. Langbehn wanted to know under what circumstances H.M.G. would treat with Himmler as an alternate leader of Germany, and repeatedly referred to the 'Himmler Solution.'
>
> I am not sure whether anything is to be gained from this contact, which I find rather distasteful.
>
> Langbehn revealed he will return in a fortnight should we wish to take the discussions further.[46]

Following his meeting with Mallet in Stockholm, Langbehn made a very interesting second journey to further Himmler's hopes of negotiating an armistice. He travelled back to Germany and then on to Switzerland, where he met with a man named Gero von Schulz Gävernitz. A naturalised American of German parentage, Gävernitz was very close to the head of the OSS (Office of Strategic Studies) station in Berne, Allen Dulles. (A key figure in American Intelligence, Dulles would one day become head of the CIA, the successor organisation to the OSS.) An active and potent opponent of the Nazi regime, throughout the war years Gävernitz assisted Dulles in making, and maintaining, contact with movements in Germany that might be in a position to topple Hitler and make peace with the Allies.[47] In the years ahead, this line of communication would become of great significance to Himmler. This time, though, Langbehn's meeting with Gävernitz did not go as well as the Germans had hoped, but they were made aware that the Americans' interest had been piqued; what was needed was a meeting with Dulles on a more intimate level. This, the Germans hoped, might yield a better result. Accordingly, within just ten days of the meeting between Langbehn and Gävernitz, Prince Max Hohenlohe turned up in Switzerland and asked Dulles to meet him. The venue was originally to be a remote mountain ski resort near the village of Les Diablerets; however, Dulles was suffering from a bad case of gout and was in no condition to go clambering around on a mountain. It was therefore finally agreed that they would hold their discussions in a parked car near the border with Liechtenstein.

As luck would have it, Hohenlohe and Dulles were not strangers, Dulles having met Hohenlohe when he was a junior attaché at the US Embassy in Vienna in 1916. After the First World War, Hohenlohe had been a frequent visitor to Dulles's home on Long Island. Now, during this latest meeting, Prince Max von Hohenlohe revealed that he had come as an emissary of the SS, having received his instruction 'directly from Himmler'. He tentatively asked whether, if Himmler and a select band of men in the SS toppled Hitler, the Allied governments would be prepared to negotiate with Himmler to end the war. Himmler's peace plan entailed maintaining the frontiers of Germany as they had been before autumn 1939; Hohenlohe asked whether the Americans would accept the status quo in Europe, and also whether they would be prepared to make a separate peace, shutting out the Russians from any part of the discussions.[48]

The exact details of what passed between Dulles and Hohenlohe in that car have never been made clear, for the relevant documents on the conversation are still embargoed in the archive at CIA headquarters, Langley.[49] However, certain details surfaced after the war, when the Russians captured Hohenlohe's own report on the discussion. According to this, Dulles saw the situation as follows:

> He was fed up with listening all the time to outdated politicians, émigrés and prejudiced Jews. In his view, a peace had to be made in Europe in the preservation of which all concerned would have a real interest. There must not again be a division into victor and vanquished, that is, contented and discontented; never again must nations like Germany be driven by want and injustice to desperate experiments and heroism. The German state must continue to exist as a factor of order and progress; there could be no question of its partition or the separation of Austria.[50]

Despite Dulles's promising response to Hohenlohe, it appears that the men at the pinnacle of power in Washington, DC, did not share his enthusiasm, in the spring of 1943, for cutting a deal with the head of the SS, and Himmler's peace appeal once again fell on deaf ears. As a direct result of this rejection, he determined from now on to talk, via Schellenberg, exclusively to the British.

Back in Stockholm, Victor Mallet found himself in receipt of a very strange letter from Ivone Kirkpatrick (who, it will be recalled, was a member of the Committee of Five at PWE). The letter instructed Mallet to return with absolute secrecy to the home of Wallenberg when invited, for a second meeting with Langbehn, to 'draw the German out, to see how far the dissent in the Nazi regime runs'. It concluded that under no circumstances was he to make his actions 'known to any other member of the Legation, and prepare your report back in person'.[51] It may be assumed that Victor Mallet felt very uncomfortable in his new role as intermediary to the Germans, for it is known from his previous correspondence with London that he saw his position in Sweden as an extremely sensitive one. A career diplomat, he had never before engaged in the sort of shady operation that the Political Warfare Executive was now asking him to undertake.

Intriguingly, in the Intelligence report on Schellenberg's debriefing at the end of the war, there is no mention of the meetings between Langbehn and Mallet in Sweden, though it is known that Langbehn was operating under orders from Schellenberg and Himmler. Why Schellenberg decided to keep this secret is not known, but it may be that he later realised the extreme sensitivity surrounding Britain's covert wartime negotiations with the infamous head of the SS. Either way, what occurred next revealed the high hopes invested by Himmler and Schellenberg in the negotiations secretly taking place in Stockholm. When Mallet was next summoned to the home of Marcus Wallenberg for a secret talk with a German emissary, he would find himself confronted with a man a great deal more important than Himmler's lawyer.

NOTES

1. Doc. No. HW 15/50, National Archives, Kew, London.
2. Ibid.
3. Doc. No. FO 898/306, National Archives, Kew, London.
4. Doc. No. FO 954/23B, National Archives, Kew, London.
5. Doc. No. FO 371/24408, National Archives, Kew, London.
6. Ibid.

7. Ibid.
8. Ibid.
9. Doc. No. FO 188/460, National Archives, Kew, London.
10. Ibid.
11. David Garnett, *The Secret History of PWE* (St Ermin's Press, 2002), p. 123.
12. Ibid., p. 43.
13. Ibid., p. 77.
14. Doc. No. FO 371/30913, National Archives, Kew, London.
15. Ibid.
16. Ibid.
17. Ibid.
18. Ibid.
19. Ibid.
20. Ibid.
21. Ibid.
22. Ibid.
23. Ibid.
24. Malcolm Muggeridge (ed.), *Ciano's Diary 1939–1943* (Heinemann, 1947), p. 342.
25. Doc. No. RG226 T253, Roll 59, National Archives, Washington, DC.
26. Ibid.
27. Ibid.
28. Ibid.
29. Walter Dornberger, *V2 – Der Schuss ins Weltall* (Bechtle Verlag, 1952), p. 172.
30. Walter Schellenberg, *The Schellenberg Memoirs* (André Deutsch, 1956), p. 344.
31. Ibid., pp. 352–53.
32. Ibid., p. 284.
33. G.M. Gilbert, *Nuremberg Diary* (New York, 1948), p. 170.
34. Schellenberg, op. cit., pp 365–66.
35. Michael Bloch, *Ribbentrop* (Abacus, 2003), p. 398.
36. From a conversation between Peter Allen and Hans Berger (former member of Schellenberg's staff at Amt VI of the SD), November 1958.
37. Bloch, op. cit., p. 400.
38. Donald M. McKale, *Kurt Prüfer* (Kent, Ohio, 1987), pp. 172–73.
39. Winston S. Churchill, *The Second World War* (Cassell, 1954), Vol. IV, p. 570.
40. Ibid., p. 547.
41. Ibid., p. 548.
42. Nicolaus von Below, Als Hitlers Adjutant (Mainz, 1980), p. 330.
43. Ian Kershaw, *Hitler, 1889–1936: Hubris (1st volume); Hitler, 1936–1945: Nemesis (2nd volume)* (Penguin, 2000), p. 577.
44. Doc. No. FO 371/34447, National Archives, Kew, London.
45. Ibid.
46. Doc. No. FO 800/868, National Archives, Kew, London.
47. Leonard Mosley, *Dulles* (Dial Press/James Wade, 1978), pp. 138, 171.
48. Ibid., p. 145.
49. Ibid.
50. Ibid., p. 146.
51. Doc. No. FO 371/30913, National Archives, Kew, London.

5
PWE SPRINGS ITS TRAP

In the spring of 1943, two events took place in Germany that were to have an inevitable impact upon the Schellenberg–Himmler attempts to open a secret line of peace negotiation with the British. These events would demonstrate that no matter how high one might be in the ranks of Nazi officialdom, in the turbulent and backstabbing world of Nazi, SS, and SD intrigue one had to be extremely careful not to fall foul of the Party, nor indeed of those men whose only means of advancement was to orchestrate the downfall of their superior.

In January 1943 Himmler had finally decided to appoint a successor to Reinhard Heydrich, who had been assassinated by the Czech resistance the previous summer. It might have been expected that he would appoint Walter Schellenberg to this most important post in the German security service; but no, for his own Machiavellian reasons he chose a forty-year-old Austrian named Ernst Kaltenbrunner. Like many men in the upper echelons of the SS, Kaltenbrunner had trained as a lawyer, and he was a man of all-consuming ambition. Tall, with a thick neck, piercing eyes, and a deep scar dissecting his long face, he had become a member of the RSHA, the Reichssicherheitshauptamt (Germany's SS-run security service), in the late 1930s. His career within the RSHA had not been one of unparalleled success, but nevertheless he had risen steadily through the ranks, becoming close to Heydrich by the 1940s, and in early 1943 Himmler appointed him to the supreme post in Reich security.

The first event to pose some inconvenience to Schellenberg's and Himmler's efforts to negotiate with the west occurred not long after this appointment was made. In April 1943 Kaltenbrunner asked to see Schellenberg, and the meeting was not a cordial one. Kaltenbrunner, jealous of the Schellenberg–Himmler relationship, informed Schellenberg that he was dissatisfied with his work at Amt VI (the political secret service for foreign countries) and not at all happy with Schellenberg's 'direct contact with Himmler over his head'. Furthermore, he accused Schellenberg of 'the attempted gratification of his own personal ambitions and unwarranted interference with the work of . . . Kaltenbrunner's [own] protégés'. He added that he 'had reported adversely on Schellenberg to Himmler, and that it would be in the interest of both parties if Schellenberg and he were to go their separate ways'.[1]

In spite of his determined attempt to remove Schellenberg from Himmler's orbit of influence, Kaltenbrunner was on shaky ground, and he knew it. Refusing to resign, Schellenberg remained head of Amt VI, while Kaltenbrunner was too aware of his close relationship with Himmler to risk sacking him. However, 'although Kaltenbrunner did not dare directly to dismiss Schellenberg, he now made every effort to make his position untenable'.[2]

Regardless of the difficult position he now found himself in, Schellenberg knew he still had the support of his ultimate superior. And the Reichsführer, for his part, needed Schellenberg: he could not afford to risk being revealed as a traitor for his secret peace negotiations in the west, aimed at achieving the overthrow of Hitler and enabling the so-called 'Himmler Solution'. No one, especially a man like Ernst Kaltenbrunner, could be allowed to discover the truth behind the work Schellenberg was secretly undertaking on Himmler's behalf, for its revelation to Hitler, in whatever form, would lead inevitably to Himmler's political ruin.

Kaltenbrunner's first intervention was but a slight inconvenience to Himmler and Schellenberg. A second occurrence, however, was to prove somewhat more threatening. It came about through a bizarre twist of fate. In May 1943 a coded British signal was intercepted by the Germans and passed to the chief of the Gestapo, Heinrich Müller, an ally of Kaltenbrunner. He managed to get it decoded, and was astounded to discover that it referred to a secret line of contact between the British authorities and a certain Munich lawyer named Carl Langbehn. Now, Müller and Kaltenbrunner must have known exactly who Langbehn was – that he was the Reichsführer-SS's neighbour in Munich and his lawyer – for the Gestapo possessed detailed records on every important German in the Reich; but did they refer the matter to Himmler? No, they did not. Deeming the British message clear proof of high treason, 'Gestapo' Müller (as he was known) took the information directly to Hitler, who furiously declared Langbehn a traitor and ordered the unfortunate lawyer to be slung in Berlin's Moabit Prison, charged with being a British agent. Normally this offence carried a mandatory death sentence at the hands of the Volksgericht (the dreaded 'People's Court', set up to carry out the quick punishment of men and women accused of treason). Himmler refused to be drawn into the affair, perhaps for fear of what Langbehn might say under interrogation. However, in a deft manoeuvre to stave off indefinitely any action that might interfere with his plans, or indeed reveal them to any other leading Nazi, he interceded on Langbehn's behalf. He insisted that the man receive excellent treatment, and that all proceedings against him be deferred until he himself had conducted his own private inquiry.

It was evident that Langbehn could no longer be considered a player in the affair. Even assuming that Himmler managed to win his release (which was unlikely, considering the evidence against him), he would be too closely watched by Müller's men of the Gestapo to play any further part in the proceedings. It was at this point, therefore, that Schellenberg took over responsibility for establishing communications with the British.

His next step was intriguing. Acutely aware of the necessity for such a line of communication to be as reliable as possible and to make use of the best available intermediary, he first determined to see if he could find a neutral other than Marcus Wallenberg. He knew Wallenberg was responsible for Swedish trade with the Allies; suspecting he might be too close to the British, Schellenberg began to search for someone better suited to Himmler's particular needs.

With this in mind, he invited two Swedes, a certain Brandin and Møller, directors of the Swedish Match Company, to Berlin to meet with Himmler.[3] As it happened, the meeting did not go as Schellenberg hoped; the two Swedes exuded little confidence that they would be able to assist the Reichsführer-SS in his search for peace, though they asserted that they would make their best endeavours. It became clear to Himmler's right-hand man that he would have to rely on the efforts of Marcus Wallenberg. After all, Wallenberg had enabled Langbehn to meet with the British Ambassador, Victor Mallet, and his Enskilda Bank was assisting German commercial and SS interests. Schellenberg was of a wary nature and inclined to trust no one, even Himmler – for he knew that the Reichsführer would drop him like a stone if news of his secret talks with the British became public knowledge – but in the case of Wallenberg he had no choice. The Swede was the ideal intermediary to talk to the British Ambassador in Stockholm, and so the die seemed cast.

At the beginning of June 1943, within just a few weeks of Brandin's and Møller's meeting with Himmler, Schellenberg left Berlin bound for

Stockholm. Travelling to Sweden under the guise of official business for the Reich, he carried with him a briefcase containing an inscribed porcelain plaque, which he was to present to Brandin in recognition of his 'services to the Third Reich'.[4] However, whilst in Stockholm, Schellenberg undertook another, much more secret mission; one that involved a meeting with Victor Mallet at Wallenberg's home on Saturday, 7 June.

The groundwork for this meeting had been laid by SS Colonel Carl Rasche, a director of the Dresdner Bank and a long-time acquaintance not only of Wallenberg, but also of the OSS station chief in Berne, Allen Dulles, with whom he had had commercial dealings since the 1920s. Rasche was known to be pushing what Swedish Intelligence was openly calling 'the SS solution': peace in the west and Himmler to take over as Führer. However, Schellenberg had necessarily to be extremely careful, for if news of his undertaking in neutral Sweden should leak to the international press or become public knowledge, it would almost certainly cost him and Himmler their heads. No matter how much power Himmler wielded as Reichsführer-SS, it could be snatched away by Hitler in the twinkling of an eye if the Führer heard of a plot against him before its instigators were ready to act.

On Sunday, 8 June, Victor Mallet dispatched a short missive to Robert Bruce Lockhart in London. Bearing in mind that he was under strict orders to involve no one else in the mysterious proceedings, he had typed it himself:

> SECRET
> Dear Bruce,
> Further to my last letter, I have again been approached by Marcus Wallenberg to meet a German emissary at his home. This meeting took place last night, and the discussion was most interesting.
> Marcus's German was quite forthright and introduced himself as the right-hand of Himmler in all matters of foreign affairs, and was empowered on Himmler's behalf to enter into negotiations with us to conclude a peace in the West on the understanding that HMG would recognise the legitimacy of Himmler as the new leader of Germany.
> Of course, I stated that this undertaking was beyond my authority to grant, but that I would refer back to London for guidance. I am informed that the German will return in four weeks for

another meeting, by which time he expressed the hope that HMG would be willing to concede that continuing the war was a disaster for Europe, and that support of Himmler is the best means to restore peace to the continent.[5]

Within just a few days of Mallet's letter arriving in London – and it is almost certain that in the meantime he was quick to show it to Ivone Kirkpatrick, his counterpart in the Committee of Five at PWE – Lockhart wrote a brief but vital memorandum to Leonard St Clair Ingrams at PWE:

> We must endeavour at all costs to keep any knowledge about the Himmler peace approach from the Americans. They may well reject an appeal from Himmler, but we cannot presume that our cousins will take this course. I therefore feel it prudent to instruct Mr Mallet to proceed cautiously with these negotiations, and if in so doing we can precipitate political instability in Germany, then we could consider it a job well done.

Lockhart concluded:

> Perhaps you could give some thought to the matter of how we can turn this peace appeal to our advantage.[6]

Ingrams was no novice in the world of deceit and subterfuge; considered by many as a master in the secret war of wits being played against the Germans, he had been one of the key men who had conceived the ploy of tricking Hitler into attacking Russia through Operation Messrs HHHH. His involvement in what was now taking place in Stockholm can have had only the most sinister of connotations, and it was ultimately to have major repercussions.

•••••

The British were now confident of gaining the upper hand in utilising the German desire for peace to accomplish a long-term strategy of destabilising Hitler's Germany. However, the men at the Foreign Office and PWE failed to recognise that the German emissary (it is unclear whether they realised they were dealing with Schellenberg at this point) was not – regardless of his instructions from Himmler – a man to place all his eggs in one basket. Even while Victor Mallet was laboriously typing out his letter to Robert Bruce Lockhart, and Lockhart was instructing Ingrams, Walter Schellenberg was already plotting his next move in this complex game of psycho-political chess. He had not entirely given up on the idea that it might be possible to negotiate a peace deal with the Americans. By 1943, having become the senior partners in the western alliance, they would be capable of forcing through such a deal even if Churchill was reluctant. After all, Churchill had thrown Britain's lot in with the USA, had accepted American war aid, and was even now undertaking military operations in concert with US forces. But there had been a subtle change in the relationship since the success of Operation Torch in taking northwest Africa, and the Casablanca Conference that followed. Churchill had long hoped for a partnership of equals to vanquish the forces of evil represented by Nazi Germany, but the Americans now saw themselves as taking the lead; despite Churchill's late recognition of this fact, the British were impotent in the face of overwhelming American economic and military might. Hence the subterfuge and trickery employed, in particular by PWE, to keep the Americans out of the covert talks with Himmler. However, the British were about to be undermined. Schellenberg, as head of Amt VI, was acutely aware of the Anglo-American political situation, and was determined to see if he could establish contact with the Americans, effectively pulling the rug out from under Churchill's feet.

To accomplish this ploy he adopted a dual approach. First, he involved an old acquaintance with whom he had prior dealings through his role as head of Amt VI. This was a man named Ernst Rieth, the German Consul General in Tangier, 'a man of considerable position who had large interests in oil and many connections with England and even more with America'.[7] The two met in Berlin on Schellenberg's return from Stockholm, and their discussion was most interesting. Rieth put forward the view that Germany should withdraw from the war and that in order to attain this end, negotiations should be undertaken as soon as possible, particularly with the USA, which might find some form of compromise peace to be in her interest.[8]

Schellenberg agreed that Rieth should 'explore the potential possibilities of such a compromise', but at the same time he adjured him to proceed with 'extreme caution'[9] because of Hitler's recent order banning any diplomatic approach to the Allies to seek a compromise peace. Rieth's position was doubly complicated by the fact that his ultimate superior at the Foreign Ministry, Joachim von Ribbentrop, had wholeheartedly supported Hitler's stance and ordered that all diplomatic contact with the Allies be dropped forthwith. Thus Rieth's conversations with the Americans would, prima facie, be dangerous: his post was directly subordinate to Ribbentrop, who was likely to hear of any such activity through his own very effective intelligence network in the Foreign Ministry.

Regardless of all this subterfuge and endeavour, it quickly became apparent that Rieth was in no position to open secret negotiations in Tangier with the USA; the particular American he talked to was not interested in any kind of behind-the-scenes deal to save the Nazis. Schellenberg had to resign himself to the fact that Rieth's tree of hope was quite barren.

Schellenberg's second attempt to open a line of communication to the Americans was extremely ambitious and, for a while at least, looked like bearing fruit. Once again in Sweden, he was introduced to an American named Abraham Stevens Hewitt. The contact was made via Felix Kersten, Himmler's masseur, who had been given permission to move to the safety of neutral Sweden. There he had expanded his practice, and Hewitt was one of his clients.

An agent of the OSS, Hewitt was Roosevelt's own special envoy to Sweden. After the war's end, in 1946, British Intelligence would take an interest in him, commenting that he 'had been sent by Roosevelt as his European observer to Stockholm and it was believed that he had been charged with a special study of the German situation. It is also said that he had formerly been married to a Vanderbilt, was now married to a Haghesson and had influence with Mrs Roosevelt.'[10] This information would also have been known to Schellenberg through his Amt VI network, and it presented a most interesting opportunity to talk to a high-ranking American who was believed to have the ear of the President.

Within a few days of the introduction (and Himmler was adamant with him that Kersten was not to be further involved, for he feared losing the services of his wonder-working masseur), Schellenberg 'went to visit Hewitt at the latter's hotel in Stockholm and opened discussions quite frankly on the general [war] situation'.[11] After a lengthy and in-depth discussion on the possibilities of disengaging Germany's western forces from fighting the Allies (the Russians were purposely to be excluded), Hewitt's suggestion 'briefly summarised, consisted of the transfer of as many Wehrmacht troops as possible to the East in order to stem the Russians, and at the same time the conclusion of a compromise peace with the Western Powers'.[12]

The prospect of peace on terms that both he and, more importantly, Himmler, wanted, must have seemed tantalisingly close to Schellenberg.

Here at last was a high-ranking American close to President Roosevelt, and he was suggesting peace in the west, whilst at the same time allowing Germany to drive back the Russian hordes in the east.

There was, however, a problem. Hewitt readily admitted to Schellenberg that he personally had 'no authority to make [peace] proposals, but he suggested he would return by air to the U.S.A. for instructions, and if his plan met with approval'[13] he would endeavour to meet again with Schellenberg in Lisbon, Portugal.

In fact, Schellenberg and Hewitt met again three days later at the home of Helmut Finke, one of Schellenberg's agents in Sweden. At this meeting it was agreed that if Hewitt's peace plan was acceptable to Roosevelt and had the support of the US authorities, he would insert an advert into the *Svenska Dagbladet* and the *Stockholm Tidningen* for eight consecutive days announcing:

For sale, valuable goldfish aquarium for 1,524 Kr[ona].

In the end, it took Hewitt longer than he had expected to get back to Washington, owing to the fact that he could not reveal to anyone the true purpose of his urgent request to see the President. Schellenberg heard indirectly from Kersten that Hewitt's departure from Stockholm had been continually delayed 'and that further, after he had succeeded in returning to America he had fallen into disfavour on account of his proposal'.[14] He ordered that every edition of *Svenska Dagbladet* and the *Stockholm Tidningen* be scanned by Amt VI for many weeks, but the expected advert from Hewitt never appeared, and he was forced to concede that his best hope of assuring peace with the Americans (who would force the British to fall into line) had come to nothing.

There now seemed no alternative to conducting his negotiations via Wallenberg and Victor Mallet in Stockholm. It is to be wondered whether Schellenberg, having come to this conclusion, was uneasy at dealing with the British. After all, a torrent of hatred for Nazism, Germany, and the leading men of the Reich cascaded each day from their broadcasts and parliamentary statements. How could any realistic peace negotiations take place with a nation so devoutly resolved to see the destruction of Nazi Germany? If any such doubts existed in Schellenberg's mind, he somehow slaked his worries, and resolved now to throw in his lot with the Wallenberg–Mallet peace talks. Little did he realise it, but the only people he would in fact be talking to were Brendan Bracken's masters of

deception at PWE, and they had very clear objectives about what they
wanted out of the negotiations.

•••••

It was at this time that, largely thanks to the rivalry between the various
branches of the British intelligence services, an extraordinary situation
arose in the British Embassy in Stockholm. Victor Mallet was soon to find
himself suspected of espionage by the very Intelligence officers who had
been appointed to look after British interests. Long after the war ended,
Peter Tennant, the Embassy's press attaché (and also attached to it as an
undercover SOE officer), was to recall that 'The atmosphere [in the
Embassy] was petty, childish and demeaning', and confessed that he had
been partly to blame.[15]

The incident had its origins in the spring of 1943 when Tennant noticed
that Mallet was holding regular, and strictly private, meetings with Marcus
Wallenberg. This in itself was not a matter of concern, but as the SOE
representative in Stockholm – and therefore responsible for Embassy security – Tennant was keen to discover what Mallet was up to. His attention
was firmly grabbed almost immediately when he discovered that Mallet
was meeting with a certain Dr Karl Goerdeler at Wallenberg's home. As has
previously been mentioned, Goerdeler was Mayor of Leipzig and a leading
member of the anti-Nazi faction in Germany; he had connections to the
Molkte group, whose long-term aim was to topple the Nazis from power in
a coup. He was also connected to Adam von Trott of the Kreisau Circle,
which, as we shall see, had the same objective. Mallet had therefore been
meeting with Goerdeler under the guidance of PWE, with the objective of
giving succour to any anti-Nazi organisation that might be able to precipitate political turmoil in Nazi Germany. But he now found himself
suspected of conducting secret – and possibly unpatriotic – negotiations
with leading Germans.

Tennant's suspicions were confirmed within just a few weeks of beginning his observations, when he noticed a more sinister German visiting
Wallenberg's home at the same time as Mallet. As the SOE representative
in Stockholm, he was well versed in spotting Germans in neutral territory,
for he received regular submissions of photographs and files on leading
Nazis to assist him in his work of undertaking surveillance of Nazis operating in Sweden. In Mallet's letter to Robert Bruce Lockhart of 8 June
1943, he had referred to an unidentified German who was Wallenberg's

friend, but whom he knew to be the agent of Himmler. He did not, however, know the man's true identity or he would have informed Lockhart. Tennant was not so hampered, and on observing the visiting German was immediately alarmed when he recognised him to be the head of Amt VI of the RSHA, SS-Brigadeführer Walter Schellenberg.

According to Tennant's evidence after the war, he also spotted Mallet meeting with someone identified as a German lawyer named Dr Schmidt. This was almost certainly an alias: the man was probably Himmler's lawyer, Carl Langbehn. In a state of confusion and panic about what was unfurling in front of his eyes, Tennant submitted a top-secret report to his superiors in London on the mysterious conduct of his ambassador; he was apparently having meetings with a number of leading Germans, one of whom he knew for certain was a top man of the SS.

In fact, the inter-organisation rivalry between PWE and the British Intelligence services, SIS and SOE, had already become detrimental to the effectiveness of British operations in Sweden. Under Brendan Bracken's leadership PWE was a law unto itself; and he very jealously protected all its operations from the other organs of British Intelligence. Many complications were to occur in the months and years ahead as PWE, SIS, and SOE strove to proceed with their own secret operations, trying not to step on each other's toes. This was exactly the situation that had now arisen in Stockholm.

Tennant's report went unacknowledged, and six weeks passed before Mallet's manner suddenly became frosty and untrusting. Tennant realised that Mallet had somehow been informed about what he had done. He was puzzled. Here was clear proof that his own ambassador was covertly meeting with leading Nazis, perhaps treasonously so; yet not only had London ignored his report, but Mallet had discovered what he had done, and still no orders emanated from London to direct his actions. What if Mallet was, for some mysterious reason, compromising British interests in the sensitive neutral state, or even worse passing information to the Nazis? It was a situation that caused Tennant many sleepless nights. Despite the lack of orders, 'Tennant, with some relish, [now] made Mallet a prime intelligence target, while Mallet struggled to maintain his dignity and make life as unpleasant as possible for Tennant.'[16] Finding himself in a very difficult position – as a lowly intelligence officer spying on his own ambassador – he received some support from the naval attaché, Henry Denham, who shared his concerns, but Denham was powerless to offer real help.

Nevertheless, assistance was soon on its way in the form of the newly appointed SIS officer to Stockholm. Peter Falk was a former Rugby schoolmaster who had been inducted into MI6 at the start of the war. He had impressed his superiors at SIS after his attendance at the Churchill–Roosevelt conference in Reykjavik in 1941, and since that time his promotion had been swift. After a stint at MI6 headquarters in London in 1942, he had now finally been assigned overseas to one of the most sensitive of posts. Here he could expect to come into daily contact with German nationals – especially members of the intelligence services – who spent a great deal of time watching each other and attempting to glean each other's secrets. Within just a few days of his arrival in Stockholm, Falk sat and listened to Tennant's concerns about the mysterious behaviour of their ambassador. He was immediately sympathetic to Tennant's problem, and equally suspicious of Mallet's conduct. He therefore contacted London and enquired whether there was an operation underway that involved Mallet; London – i.e. SIS – responded, as it previously had to Tennant, that it was unaware of any reason why Mallet should be covertly meeting Nazis at the home of Marcus Wallenberg. It is evident that PWE, under the guidance of the all-powerful Brendan Bracken, deemed its operation involving Mallet top secret, something in which it had no desire to involve SOE or SIS, in whatever form. This would complicate matters enormously. The two top intelligence men in Stockholm – Tennant and Falk – now committed valuable time to watching Victor Mallet and attempting to discover what he was up to.

Prior to his departure for Stockholm, Falk had been briefed in London that his prime target in Sweden was a German SD agent named Karl-Heinz Krämer, who was operating out of the German Embassy. He was instructed to 'combat Krämer's activities, a role which was to take precedence over everything else'.[17]

On his arrival in Stockholm in the summer of 1943, Falk found to his satisfaction that SIS already had an agent known as 'P' working in the German Embassy. 'P' soon produced for Falk a plethora of information, including the fact that Krämer had arrived in Sweden the year before with his wife and daughter in tow, and had for some time lived in style at the Grand Hotel. He had then taken on a substantial and stylish house in a very smart suburb of Stockholm called Stora Essingen; however, he also kept on his apartment at the Grand Hotel (at the German state's expense) for entertaining.

Falk's task of observing Krämer was a difficult one. Krämer enjoyed extraordinary privileges. He did not seem to be tied to the activities of his fellow Intelligence officers at the Embassy and, strangely, was openly calling himself 'Himmler's special representative in Sweden'. He even had unique access to the German air attaché's special message scrambler – GLYST – with which he was able to contact Berlin. Falk soon discovered that in addition to these privileges, Major Golcher, the Abwehr station chief in the Embassy, had been ordered by Berlin to allow Krämer to see all the intelligence information that the Embassy staff accumulated before it was dispatched back to Germany. It was all very strange, and made Falk acutely aware that his was an important target who would need watching carefully. He soon concluded that he would have to acquire an agent close to Krämer in order to discover what he was really up to in Stockholm.

Like everyone in this world, Krämer had a weak point, one that Falk was quick to discover and would exploit brilliantly. This was done not through agent 'P' at the German Embassy, but by someone quite literally rather closer to home. When Krämer came to Sweden, his wife had quickly hired a German maid to pander to all her needs. Herr and Frau Krämer were alike in many respects; owing to their imperious and snobbish manner, they both seemed readily to antagonise everyone with whom they came into contact. This was particularly true of Frau Krämer, whose relationship with her maid soon deteriorated to one of purest animosity. Indeed, the maid so hated the Krämers that in a moment of anger she even confessed to an Austrian lady friend that she felt like murdering Frau Krämer; but she needed the job and money, times were hard, so she was stuck with the family.

It is on such twists of fate that worlds can sometimes turn. The Austrian woman was married to a Swedish assistant at the British Embassy, and Falk was soon to learn of the Krämers' fractious home life. He had a quiet word with the woman, who heartily hated the Nazis – this was why she had moved to Sweden in 1938 – and she was quickly hired as agent 'Frau E'. Working carefully with 'Frau E', Falk made an approach to the Krämers' maid, who was soon recruited as 'Frau H12' and put on the SIS payroll as agent 36704.

To Falk's satisfaction, 'Frau H12' turned out to be an intelligent and resourceful woman, keen to provide her new masters in London with all the information she could about Krämer's activities in Sweden. She revealed to Falk and 'Frau E' that in Krämer's study at home in Stora Essingen, there was a desk containing a drawer that was kept permanently locked. Falk was keen to gain access to the information in that desk, and 'Frau H12' was able to tell him that the only opportunity was at 6.45 p.m. when Krämer took his daily bath. His bath always lasted exactly half an hour. The key to the desk was clipped to his trousers, and this was the only time he let it out of his sight.

Within just a few days 'Frau H12' managed to take an impression of Krämer's key in a pat of butter; from this someone at the British Embassy was able to make an exact duplicate. It worked; and, via 'Frau H12', Falk found himself in receipt of a constant stream of photographs of the contents of Krämer's desk. He was thus provided with an amazing haul of documents that proved that someone at the highest level was passing information to the Germans about British government and Allied decisions.

Falk was stunned by the plethora of detailed information Krämer had managed to obtain on the Allies; it even included rough drafts and secret memoranda on the private discussions between Churchill and Roosevelt at the Quebec Conference of 1943. Such a leak of information to the Nazis on Allied thinking and war strategy was bad enough, but Falk realised that other photographed documents provided by 'Frau H12' revealed that there was a high-level British leak, too. Amongst the papers obtained was a memorandum from spring 1943 regarding American proposals for the post-war trusteeship of 'dependent peoples'; in other words, the Americans were already drawing up their road-map for the control of post-war Europe. Falk realised that he was witness to the ongoing work of an agent with access to some of the Allies' most closely guarded secrets. As if this were not shocking enough, copies of British Cabinet documents and War Office minutes nestled in Krämer's drawer alongside Foreign Office letters from the office of the Permanent Under-Secretary of State, William Strang (who, it should be remembered, had been so influential during Operation Messrs HHHH, and was now, by all accounts, involved in the Stockholm affair).[18]

Within a very short while Falk was flown back to Britain for a meeting with Anthony Blunt, the SIS man who had been put in charge of the Krämer situation. Falk and Blunt met at the Reform Club in London where they discussed the matter, and it soon became apparent to Falk that Blunt – and by implication SIS – doubted the authenticity of the papers gleaned from Krämer's desk. However, Falk was persistent and tenacious, and little by little he convinced Blunt not only that the papers were genuine, but that they revealed a British leak at the highest possible level. Someone in Stockholm was meeting with Krämer – a man known to call himself publicly 'Himmler's representative in Sweden' – and was involved in passing or trading top-grade British intelligence.

'Falk's lucky discovery was Anthony Blunt's – i.e. SIS's – first glimpse of what might possibly be on offer . . . [to] Walter Schellenberg and Heinrich Himmler. Secret negotiations were still going on between Schellenberg and

Mallet; now Blunt had a cogent reason to take these negotiations more seriously.'[19] It was plain that someone high up in the British Establishment was talking to the Nazis, which meant – by virtue of Krämer's position in the SD – Schellenberg and Himmler. Only two questions now puzzled the men of SIS. Who would be so brazen as to disclose minutes of Cabinet meetings and Foreign Office documents to the Germans at such a sensitive stage of the war? And, what was more, what was the true purpose behind such damaging disclosures?

A strong hint about what was taking place is revealed by a PWE minute from Leonard St Clair Ingrams to Robert Bruce Lockhart:

> As the process of the Mallet negotiations proceed, we must endeavour to keep Himmler's man in Stockholm firmly on the hook. We have come too far now to let this very tasty fish just swim away. If we are to accomplish our desire of political turmoil in Germany, then I feel sure that a few more tantalising pieces of bait may see our objectives achieved. Further to our discussion yesterday, I will ask Crossman [German Section of PWE] if B[rendan] B[racken] will sanction the release of some further sensitive information to keep our fish well and truly hooked.'[20]

This document gives the clearest indication yet of what was really taking place in Stockholm. Mallet – operating under PWE control and probably authorised to do so not only by Ivone Kirkpatrick at the Foreign Office, but also possibly by Churchill – was now very deeply involved in the PWE scheme indeed. He had in the early summer of 1943 been meeting top Germans, from Langbehn to Schellenberg, at the home of Marcus Wallenberg. Schellenberg for his part had dispatched an agent – Krämer – to Stockholm to maintain the contact, and to undertake meaningful discussions and trades of information with the British Ambassador as a means of establishing good faith. Unfortunately, PWE had kept its complex operation secret from everyone else in British Intelligence. SOE and SIS had inadvertently stumbled on PWE's operation and misunderstood the implications of what was taking place. Of course, there was no high-echelon British spy passing secrets to the Germans in reality; rather, Mallet was trading Allied secrets with the SS/SD in an unwholesome business designed to make Himmler feel confident enough to move against Hitler and cause political turmoil in Nazi Germany.

It was now that a rather flamboyant British figure entered the proceedings. His name was Ewan Butler, and though he officially emerged from SOE, he had in fact been seconded to PWE to assist Mallet in his negotiations with Schellenberg and Himmler. A fluent German speaker, for some years before the war Butler had lived in Germany where he had struck up a close friendship with Reinhard Heydrich. In fact, they became so close that on Butler's birthday in 1938 the two men, drunk at the time, entered into a childish ceremony in which they became 'blood brothers'. As he had been so close to Heydrich – indeed, was permitted the privilege of addressing him with the intimate 'Du' – Butler had naturally met many prominent Nazis in the pre-war years, including Schellenberg and even Himmler. He was therefore a natural choice to help Mallet in his sensitive and secret negotiations, a British counterpart to Krämer. There was, however, a drawback to his employment, one that would have made Mallet blanch had he known before Butler was flown out to Stockholm. Working as a journalist in the pre-war years, Butler had become a confirmed alcoholic, and he periodically went on day-long benders that reduced him to a dishevelled and drunken heap. If this was not bad enough, before dispatching him to Sweden as Mallet's assistant, SOE first had to extricate him from the Virginia Water Mental Hospital on the outskirts of London, where he was being treated for manic depression. It was not an auspicious start to a sensitive and potentially dangerous operation. However, given Butler's credentials as a fluent speaker of German who knew the right people in the country, PWE undoubtedly felt it could not do without his services.

Within days of his arrival in Stockholm, Butler managed to alienate most of the British Embassy staff, particularly Tennant and Falk. He resolutely refused to involve them in his strictly secret mission, and they were extremely puzzled by the extraordinary treatment Mallet bestowed on him. Whilst most of the Intelligence agents at the Embassy were operating out of huts in the grounds, Butler was given a spacious first-floor office. His living accommodation, too, raised more than a few eyebrows. Whereas most of the staff were allotted barely manageable flats in and around crowded Stockholm, he was provided with a magnificent apartment in the centre of the city that boasted marble floors and great crystal chandeliers. Like his German counterpart Krämer, he was soon subject to much jealous comment.

By the autumn of 1943 the Mallet–SD/Himmler negotiations were still going on. Mallet had now been given an assistant to help him in his sensitive task – if he could be kept away from the bottle – and Mallet was in desperate need of that assistance. He was not an Intelligence operative versed in the art of deep deception and lying to the enemy; he was a late middle-aged career diplomat, almost out of his depth and forced to participate in an operation that he found, in his own words, 'distasteful'. He was to find that his assistant would make his task more troublesome still.

•••••

Back in Germany, Himmler's determination to strike a deal with the western Allies was becoming of ever greater importance. During the summer of 1943 it became clearer by the day that for Germany the war was fast unravelling. In May the combined might of the British and Americans had finally wiped out all German resistance in North Africa, which was now in Allied hands. At the beginning of July the battle of Kursk had taken place, in which the Soviet Fifth Army was victorious and Germany lost 70,000 men. The Germans were steadily being driven out of Russia on a thousand-mile front. The end of July had also seen the resignation of Mussolini and the succession of Marshal Badaglio. Throughout the summer German intelligence had picked up hints that the Italians were preparing to negotiate a truce with the Allies, leaving Germany exposed to an Allied invasion from the south. German intelligence had not been wrong, and on 8 September Italy surrendered unconditionally; the Pact of Steel was at an end, and Germany was left without her primary ally.

Although the summer of 1943 was a bad season for Nazi Germany, still Himmler prevaricated. He wanted the elusive peace with the western Allies that would allow Germany to move on; to end the disastrous war she could only lose; to see the SS rise to the fore as the new power in post-war Germany with himself at the helm. Yet still he could not bring himself to betray the Führer he and his men had sworn their souls to defend. Was not the SS motto 'My Honour is Loyalty'? However, if Himmler thought himself no mean politician, he had not reckoned with the British. They were masters in the art of negotiation, seemingly undeterred in the slightest by how long the process took to complete. If they did not get what they wanted, they were entirely capable of taking themselves off and refusing to talk again until the opposing party had either conceded defeat, or agreed to some new set of terms.

Himmler had a problem. From the outset of the Stockholm negotiations the British had made it clear that they would only agree to peace in the west with the removal of Hitler from power, either under house arrest at Berchtesgaden, or preferably dead. This was a condition he found it incredibly hard to agree to. Himmler had been loyal to Hitler since the early 1920s, twenty years ago, and with the Führer's rise to power, so had he risen also. Did not Hitler refer to him as 'der treue Heinrich' (my loyal Heinrich)? How could he, the head of Hitler's personal army, now turn traitor, seize power, and make peace with the British and Americans? Yet this was exactly what the British were demanding; it was their main precondition for peace. Like water on stone, over the weeks and months of 1943, indeed even into 1944, PWE began to wear down Himmler's resistance, and men such as Lockhart, Ingrams, and Bracken came to believe that their scheme to cause political turmoil in Germany would eventually succeed.

•••••

It was at this point, in mid- to late 1943, that a new personality was to enter into the British scheme. This was an aristocratic German named Adam von Trott zu Solz, who headed the Kreisau Circle: an anti-Hitler, though not necessarily anti-Nazi, faction in Germany that was determined to topple the Führer and make peace with the Allies. Trott was the son of a former Prussian minister of education, and the grandson of an American woman whose own grandfather had been John Jay, the first Chief Justice of the United States. After training at the eminent Kurt Hahn School at Schloss Salem, in 1931 he had gone on to study at Mansfield College, Oxford. This background gave him an internationalist outlook on the world, and by 1943, at the age of forty-one, he found himself a leading German diplomat, as well as the secret head of a society dedicated to the downfall of the Führer and an immediate end to the disastrous war into which he had led Germany. Trott had many influential supporters, ranging from Ernst Freiherr von Weiszäcker, who had been a State Secretary at the Foreign Ministry but had managed to get himself appointed Ambassador to the Vatican to escape serving under Ribbentrop, through to many leading German citizens and members of the Army. The Kreisau Circle even counted Albrecht Haushofer as a supporter; he had by now realised the disaster Germany was rapidly heading for and secretly thrown his support behind a faction prepared to seize power and make peace before it was too late.

In the summer of 1943 a British diplomat named Michael White submitted a report to London on this most interesting German aristocrat, who wanted to see an end to Hitler and the restoration of European peace:

Adam von Trott zu Solz may be destined to play an interesting part in the possible efforts to make a non-Nazi – or, perhaps, more accurately, a non-Hitlerian – peace offensive . . . He [is] imbibed [with] a certain degree of Anglophile sentiments, has [in the past] made a number of friends and contacts in Britain, and was indeed exceptionally popular largely because of a charm and sense of humour unusual in a German . . . Between the Munich Agreement [of 1938] and the invasion of Poland [in 1939] von Trott was several times in London where he was on one occasion taken to lunch with Mr. Chamberlain.

Having given a little background, White went on:

> The line of argument which von Trott . . . follows . . . is mildly anti-Nazi but of a strong German nationalist character. [He] deplored Munich and the subsequent partition of Czechoslovakia, but was at the time anti-Czech in sentiment . . . He urges tacit support of Britain and France for the overthrow of Hitler by the Army on the basis of the restoration of the former German colonies to the new regime . . .
>
> As I see him there is nothing of the intriguer about Adam von Trott, but there . . . [is], on the other hand, considerable ambition, and a certain confused political mysticism which has absorbed something of the stuff of which Nazis are made, and something of a vague Hegelianism which has induced in him a false sense of realism and a belief in power politics and his own part in them . . .
>
> His tendency to be 'starry-eyed' [has] led him not to the worship of the Führerprincip but to a deep veneration for German military and political traditions, and what he believes to be the innate integrity of the German soul.

This was a fascinating submission and it revealed much about the anti-Nazi resistance in Germany, but what most caught the attention of the Foreign Office and Ivone Kirkpatrick, who passed the details on to Robert Bruce Lockhart, was White's following comment:

> Trott's line to me was as follows: The Army did not want a general war; they were content with the success of the Polish campaign and would welcome an end to further hostilities.

[General] Falkenhausen [teacher of Erwin Rommel and officer commanding Belgium and northern France] and [General] Halder [Chief of the General Staff until sacked by Hitler in September 1942 following the setbacks in Russia] are anti-Nazi and particularly anti-Hitler. They would be prepared to take the initiative in due course [i.e. a coup d'état], restore the Rechtsstaat [democratic government] in Germany and make peace with Britain and France on the basis of the status quo.

Trott's attitude to the war in general has undergone some considerable change as a result of the German failure to defeat Russia . . . and the entry of the United States into the war.

White went on to outline Trott's concept of how peace could be achieved through a coup, and the peace terms – amounting to a peace plan – that he proposed to put forward:

. . . the general line is in essence: at some period an Army coup would substitute for the present regime a provisional government in Germany which could 'demand a new deal' [i.e. not the Casablanca demand for unconditional surrender] from the United Nations for decent Germans.

Once established, this government would take certain immediate measures which should serve as acts of good faith vis-à-vis the Allies. These measures would include:

1. The proclamation of the restoration of the Rechtsstaat.
2. The rescinding of anti-Jewish legislation.
3. The return of confiscated property to Jews and Gentiles alike.
4. The evacuation of all occupied territory in Western Europe.
(. . . Trott was unwilling to surrender any territory which would weaken the position of Germany against Russia).
5. A statement on the position which the new Germany sees for herself in a federated Europe which she would not seek to dominate.
6. A proposal that, in view of the chaos which would exist in Germany after the collapse of the Nazi regime . . . the German Army in a properly reduced form should be permitted to assist and co-operate with the forces of the United Nations in keeping order within the Reich.

Finally, White commented that:

> Trott [has] emphasized that there should be no let-up in the
> Allied attacks on Germany, for under this pressure the movement
> for peace would grow and gather strength . . .[21]

This was a dramatic development: here was a top-ranking German
heading a secret political clique prepared to launch a takeover bid in
Germany – a coup d'état – to topple Hitler and negotiate peace with the
Allies. Take into account that the Kreisau Circle was no mere rag-tag group
of disaffected Germans, but counted among its members leading men in
the fields of the Army, the diplomatic service, the civil service, the judiciary,
and the government, and it becomes clear that Trott's approach to the
British had to be treated very seriously indeed. If his group were to prove
capable of launching a coup to overthrow the Nazis, there was every possibility of stalling the war without further loss of life.

White's report is clearly marked in the accompanying civil servant
notes as having been read and considered by Mr Harrison, the Foreign
Office mandarin whose 1942 report on the possibility of causing instability in Germany through a coup attempt had been directed to Robert
Bruce Lockhart and the Political Warfare Executive. However, PWE
would no longer be able to keep this show as strictly its own affair. Soon
SOE was to be allowed access to the scheme, though it was to be kept
strictly away from the Himmler–Schellenberg–Krämer–Mallet affair
proceeding in Stockholm, whose objective was also to precipitate chaos in
Germany.

In the meantime, within just a few weeks of Trott's approach to the
British, his Kreisau Circle managed a telling demonstration of its intention
– if not, its ability – to remove Hitler from the equation of German politics. Trott was fortunate in counting as a member of his group a man
named Helmuth Stieff, a colonel and Chief of the Organisation Branch of
the Army High Command who served on Hitler's staff at his eastern field
headquarters at Rastenburg – known universally as the Wolfsschanze
(Wolf's Lair). Forty-two-year-old Stieff was a short man with a slight
hunchback, and he possessed a formidable enemy in the form of Himmler,
who called him the 'little poisoned dwarf'. Undeterred, and secure in his
Wehrmacht position on Hitler's headquarters staff, Stieff – under rather
optimistic instructions from Trott – made an attempt on the Führer's life
at Rastenburg in September 1943, when he planted a bomb near where he

knew Hitler daily exercised his dog Blonde. It is known that SOE was involved in the scheme, for it supplied the plastic explosives for Stieff's bomb – an indication of the speed with which it was able to move once it had heard of Trott's plan. However, Stieff panicked at the last moment and removed the bomb, fearing that it was not precisely enough placed. If it failed, he thought, that would only make any future attempt on Hitler all the harder. Now in a panic lest he be caught with the explosives (especially since they were of British make), he unfortunately dumped his bomb in one of the water towers at Hitler's Rastenburg headquarters – where he thought it would remain safe from discovery. Nothing could have been further from the truth. Within a few days the bomb exploded, destroying the water tank, and Hitler ordered an inquiry to discover what had happened. Stieff, Trott, and the Kreisau Circle realised that they would have to be very careful indeed, and very sure of success, before they made another attempt on the Führer's life.

In fact, Stieff's assassination bid was not the first time the Kreisau Circle had tried to kill the Führer. Well before contacting the British in the summer of 1943, Trott's group had made a similar attempt in March. At the time, Hitler had been on a visit to Army Group Centre headquarters at Smolensk. The Circle had at first toyed with having one of its members shoot him as he walked to Field Marshal von Kluge's mess, but the plan was abandoned; the Führer was so well protected by loyal men that the assassin would be bound to lose his life. In the end, the plotters determined upon a more intricate plan entailing the planting of a bomb on his aircraft (a Condor flown by his personal pilot, Hans Baur). After Hitler had concluded his visit to the forward command centre, a member of Trott's group, one Major-General Henning von Tresckow, handed a package – which appeared to contain two bottles of cognac – to Lieutenant-Colonel Brandt, a member of Hitler's entourage, requesting him to pass it on to Stieff when they arrived back at Rastenburg. Despite confidence that this second attempt to kill Hitler would succeed, the bomb failed to explode, and a horrified Stieff then found himself in receipt of the package from Brandt when Hitler and his men arrived back at the Wolf's Lair. It was another dud bomb that had somehow to be disposed of, and this time Tresckow had to fly specially all the way to Rastenburg to recover the deadly item.

Despite their good intentions, Trott and his Kreisau Circle had thus as yet managed neither to kill Hitler nor to launch their coup attempt. However, SOE was keen to support the group, and were not excessively discouraged by its failure. SOE, like PWE, wanted not only Hitler's death, but the political chaos in Germany that would result from a coup attempt – even one that failed. It was quick to realise that in the summer of 1943 the Kreisau Circle had not been in a position to launch such an ambitious operation, but SOE, like PWE, looked to the long term. Aware that it might be the late spring of 1944 before the Circle was sufficiently organised both to kill Hitler and carry out its coup d'état, SOE remained undeterred. British Intelligence knew very well that the new front (eventually to be launched as Operation Overlord – D-Day) was likely to occur in the late spring or early summer of 1944. This, then, would be the most auspicious time for launching chaos in Nazi Germany. It would give the Allies the advantage, enabling them to sweep largely unhindered deep into Continental Europe and swamp the disorganised German forces, faced with political and military turmoil at home.

•••••

One should not forget that, also at this time, PWE was secretly attempting to force the head of the SS to undertake the same task as the Kreisau Circle, and with the same objectives – political chaos in Nazi Germany, giving the Allies an overwhelming advantage that might with skill be used to cause the collapse of German resistance and a swift end to the war. The Mallet–Himmler negotiations were proceeding even as Trott's group, via Stieff, made its attempt on Hitler at Rastenburg in early September, an attempt that seemed likely to circumvent PWE's need to negotiate a deal with Himmler. However, Mallet was having major problems, and they had been emanating from a perhaps predictable source – Ewan Butler, the very man seconded from SOE to aid Mallet in his delicate negotiations with Kramer, Schellenberg, and Himmler.

As Mallet's nerves deteriorated under the strain of negotiating with the men of the SS, he was having increasing problems with the oft-drunk Butler. The British personnel at the Embassy in Stockholm found a nickname for Mallet; he became known as the 'angry rabbit' because of the habit he developed of stamping his feet furiously whenever anything began to go wrong – which with Butler's assistance was often. Still, PWE, via Mallet, worked on Himmler, gradually but surely wearing down his inbuilt resistance to turning against his benefactor. Yet still he prevaricated, twisted and turned, not keen despite his yearning for a post-war political career to be revealed as a traitor to Hitler, and quite possibly to have to kill him as the only sure means of allowing a smooth transition of power to himself. Had

Himmler known that he was negotiating not with the British government, but only with the Political Warfare Executive, he would surely have turned his back on the prospect of a deal with the British, and might have once again turned to the Americans. We may know with hindsight that there was never the slightest chance that the Americans would conclude a deal with the monster of the SS, but the British could not be sure of this at the time. There was a great deal of transatlantic mistrust during the war, particularly in 1943 and 1944 – and mainly, it has to be said, on the British side.

Himmler was proving to be an intelligent and quick-witted adversary, for the Reichsführer-SS was not content merely to woo Victor Mallet in his search for peace. He was intent on opening lines of communication to any leading Briton whom he perceived as capable of furthering the cause of an Anglo-German rapprochement. Accordingly, in the summer of 1943 the Foreign Office in London was sent two submissions that revealed that Himmler was not content to talk solely to Mallet in Stockholm, but was prepared to circumvent the inflexible nature of the Mallet talks by seeking to open alternative lines of communication to the British government. He was becoming impatient to make a deal and was not to be put off. It may also be taken that these approaches were intended to confirm to the British his intentions of (eventually) ousting Hitler, taking over himself, and making peace with the Allies.

The first indication that Himmler was preparing to take his desire for peace to more receptive ears came from the British Consul in Barcelona. Reporting that he had been approached by 'Mateu, the Alcalde of Barcelona, and a man of some influence', the Consul went on to reveal that Mateu 'told me last night that . . . he [had] received a visit from a German who gave his name as Dr Hansen and who he suspected of being an emissary of . . . Himmler.'[22] He continued:

> This Dr Hansen, after enquiring whether Mateu was on friendly terms with the [British] Ambassador [in Madrid – Sir Samuel Hoare] . . . then proceeded to discuss the war situation at length with the apparent intent of making use of Mateu as a stalking horse. According to Mateu, the general tenor of Hansen's language was to the effect that Germany could retire within her frontiers along the West and withstand a siege by the Allies for a long time; that at the moment Germany was only interested in one thing, the successful prosecution of the war in the East.

The Consul went on to disclose that Hansen had revealed 'that he, and those whom he represented in Germany, realised that the Allies would have nothing to do with Hitler, but what would their reaction be if certain forces in Germany were to undertake to liquidate Hitler and the party?'[23]

This submission is clearly marked in the civil servant notes as having been passed on to Mr Harrison, Frank Roberts, and William Strang for consideration. They did not miss the significance of Hansen's approach. Himmler, it appeared, despite the extremely protracted negotiations being conducted in Stockholm, was still keen on a separate deal with the British government, even if that meant abandoning the Mallet talks and establishing a new line of communication through the British Ambassador Extraordinary with Plenipotentiary Powers in Madrid, Sir Samuel Hoare.

This was not, however, Himmler's only attempt to circumvent Mallet, for the Foreign Office was soon in receipt of a second submission from the Iberian peninsula. Sent from Mr Hopkinson, attaché at the British Embassy in Lisbon, it revealed that Prince Max von Hohenlohe was back in town, and that he had much to disclose to his British counterpart. Hopkinson and Hohenlohe did not meet directly; a young Portuguese by the name of Nava de Tajo acted as intermediary. As Hopkinson reported, Hohenlohe had stated that:

> Germany could hold out for one and a half years more. Their only hope was to come to terms with America before the end of that time . . . they did not forget that Churchill was descended of Marlborough, who, once he had seen Louis XIV's power crippled, did not insist upon his destruction . . .[24]

Hopkinson continued:

> Prince Hohenlohe also said at one moment 'Germany and Russia must come to an understanding one day.' When Nava de Tajo suggested that such an understanding could only be achieved by Germany giving up all her territorial conquests in Russia, and that the Germans would cut Hitler's head off if such a surrender was the only result of so much sacrifice in the East, Hohenlohe replied [significantly] 'Well, Hitler is of no importance any more. The real ruler of Germany is Himmler.'[25]

Finally, he reported that, according to Hohenlohe:

> If Germany has to make [peace] overtures she will do it through Sweden. The Germans, and this primarily means Himmler, said Hohenlohe, mistrust both Franco and Salazar, and profoundly mistrust the Vatican.[26]

It was now – still trying to keep his options open – that Himmler, via Hohenlohe, made one last bid to contact the Americans. As Arthur Yencken, First Secretary at the Madrid Embassy under Hoare, notified his superior at the Foreign Office in London, he had learnt from the American military attaché, Colonel Hohental, of several such attempts by Hohenlohe. According to Yencken, Hohental:

> . . . said that Prince M. H[ohenlohe] made blatant and repeated efforts to make contact with him and other members of the U.S. Embassy, including the Ambassador, at the Alba ball in Seville.

Intriguingly, Yencken was to comment:

> This he failed to do, as, I may mention, he failed with me.

He concluded:

> Colonel Hohental added that Prince M. H[ohenlohe] tried the same game on members of the U.S. Embassy in Lisbon, again without success. He also seems to have tried the other Allied Missions in vain.

Yencken appended a report on Hohenlohe's line of approach, destined for the desk of Peter Loxley, who served under William Strang at the Foreign Office. Hohenlohe had imparted these points to a Portuguese banker by the name of Ricardo Espirito Santo, who, it was commented, was an 'Axis sympathiser'. It was this same Espirito Santo who had loaned his Lisbon home, Boca tel Toro, to the Duke of Windsor in the summer of 1940, when the former King Edward VIII had been forced by the British government to vacate with haste his cosy but temporary residence in Franco's Spain. It is also worthy of note that whilst residing in Espirito

Santo's home, Windsor had flirted with the Nazis, who had wanted him to assist them in making peace with Britain before the war got completely out of hand. And the top-ranking German who had been placed in charge of the operation to woo him was none other than the head of Amt VI of the SD, SS-Brigadeführer Walter Schellenberg.

As Yencken reported, the main tenets of Hohenlohe's view of the war situation and politics in Germany were:

1. Rift between German Army [Wehrmacht] and Police [Himmler's security service] is increasing.
2. No 'Bohemian' (referring to Hitler in answer to question whether Hitler now controlled situation) ever could have a following in Germany for any length of time. Hitler's attack on Russia is not his only mistake.
3. Although air bombardment in Germany is exacting heavy toll, the German people are steeled to resist it.
4. The bulk of war production industries has been moved to Eastern areas which means that German industrial potentials are not easily reached by mass air attack.
5. The German chief objective is to gain time. We count on dissension among the Allies and the USA disinclination to fight in Europe.

Finally, Yencken commented with interest that Hohenlohe had remarked:

6. I believe that the ousting of Hitler and a change of regime would greatly influence American public opinion to break off the war in Europe and concentrate on Japan. In this the Americans could expect aid from Germany, Germany would agree to allow the U.S. full sway in Africa.[27]

Despite this last attempt, late in the hour, to woo the Americans, nothing was to come of Hohenlohe's efforts. Having, it seems, finally become reconciled to the fact that there could be no opening of negotiations with them (and it is important to remember that he had made several concerted attempts to deal with the USA, via Schellenberg to Roosevelt's representative Abraham Hewitt, *and* via Hohenlohe to various American parties), Himmler, man of indecision and doubt, took the plunge in the autumn of 1943 and placed his peace proposals before the British. The details of his offer must have intrigued the men of PWE greatly. When Victor Mallet, on 26 October 1943, reported on his latest meeting with Schellenberg at the home of Marcus Wallenberg, he divulged the Reichsführer's peace terms as follows:

1. There must be an immediate cessation of the air war by the Allies.
2. The Allies must renounce their intent to invade western Europe and make clear their wish to prevent any further useless sacrifice of lives.
3. Germany will install a new provisional government, which will immediately evacuate all the occupied territories of north, west, and southern Europe [i.e. Norway, Holland, Belgium, France, and Italy (which had been occupied by Germany with the Italian declaration of war on her former Axis partner on 13 October)].
4. Germany is to be permitted a permanent defensible line in the east along her current strategic position.
5. Germany is to be permitted to retain Austria and the Sudetenland, but will restore sovereignty of Poland.
6. Russia is to be excluded from all negotiations with Britain and America. If peace is to be made with Russia, Germany will enter into separate negotiations with her at a suitable time.[28]

We know these terms must have been imparted personally to Mallet by Schellenberg because Mallet refers to the German emissary as 'W.S.'. Moreover, this was a pivotal moment in the negotiations, one too important to have been handled by Krämer, who may not have been party to the finer details of the 'Himmler Solution'. The details of the six-point plan reveal that Himmler must have spent a great deal of time working out his own 'wish-list' for peace; terms that he could 'sell' to the German people as an acceptable and honourable agreement with himself as the new head of state.

It may be wondered why Himmler's peace terms were not considered seriously by the British authorities; indeed, have been kept secret in Britain until comparatively recently. It may also be wondered why the men at PWE did not take this new development to Churchill and state that here was a prospect of returning peace to Europe without further devastating loss of life; especially when one bears in mind that 1944 and 1945 would turn out to be some of the most costly years, in terms of lives lost, of the entire war.

But then PWE, under the hardheaded leadership of Brendan Bracken, never intended to negotiate a truce with any German, Nazi or anti-Nazi – and certainly not with a man of Himmler's ilk, never mind how good the peace terms were. If Churchill had wanted peace, he could have had it in 1941 with the very pragmatic terms on offer from Hitler and Hess. The only objective of the British government, now as in 1941, was the complete and utter defeat of Germany.

On the German side, however, all this quasi-diplomatic negotiation was unfamiliar territory for a man who had started his political career by motor-cycling around the Bavarian countryside drumming up political awareness in the masses. Indeed, it was unfamiliar for Himmler even as head of Nazi Germany's state security service and the SS, for at no point in his daily routine did he come into contact with the diplomatic service or foreign affairs specialists. As such, the skills involved in negotiating a diplomatic deal with the Allies were entirely new to him. Many members of the SS were well-educated men – lawyers, diplomats, etc. – but it is nevertheless important to remember that no one in Germany, SS member or otherwise, could be permitted to know what was going on. Himmler was attempting to betray his Führer: until he was sure his position was secure, the only person who could be allowed to know of the plan was his own 'loyal Benjamin', Walter Schellenberg. Thus it must have been worked out by Himmler alone; there could have been no input from anyone else, except perhaps the occasional suggestion from Schellenberg. Himmler's desire for peace was surely the closest-kept secret in the Reich, for if one slip allowed Adolf Hitler to find out what was planned, he knew that it could cost him his head.

On 5 November 1943, a little over a week after Victor Mallet's report reached London, Brendan Bracken sent a memorandum to his close friend Lord Selborne, head of MEW and SOE. This memo makes it clear not only that PWE was involved in the negotiations taking place in Stockholm, but also that Bracken himself must have sanctioned 'Little H', as this most dangerous and sensitive operation had become known. (The code name given to it by this time is of some interest. As we have seen, the operation carried out by SO1 against Hitler in 1941 had been given the code name 'Messrs HHHH', which is presumed to stand for the names of the leading Germans involved: Hitler, Hess, and Karl and Albrecht Haushofer. During the latter years of the war, SOE considered an ambitious scheme to assassinate Hitler, which it code-named 'Operation Foxley'. The scheme was in the end abandoned, but not before a feasibility study was commissioned into the possible assassination of Himmler. This was given the code name 'Little Foxley'. There is clearly a correlation between the code names adopted by SOE for these plots and that given to the SO1/PWE scheme (the two organisations still shared many of their leading personnel). When PWE was put on the spot to come up with a cover name for the Himmler operation, it seems that the same logic was applied to its naming. Just as the scheme to deceive Hitler had been 'Operation Messrs HHHH', so the one to deceive Himmler became known as 'Operation Little H'.)

After a few sentences on mundane matters, Bracken swiftly let Selborne in on the developments in the Himmler operation:

> Further to my recent memo to you on this matter, I feel it pertinent to let you know of a sudden development in the matter of Little H. Victor M[allet] has in the last few days reported on a most interesting meeting with W.S[chellenberg] at the home of Wallenberg. At this meeting W.S. passed to Victor the draft of a six point peace plan from H.H[immler]. The points raised are of interest and reveal much to us about H.H[immler]'s inner thinking on peace, and in so doing reveals to us about how desperate the top men of the Nazi regime believe their military situation to be. Of course H.H.'s proposal is unrealistic, even if we had the slightest intention of making a deal, but nevertheless places us in a unique position to precipitate chaos in Germany at a moment of our choosing. I have passed Victor's report on the six points to Bruce [Lockhart] for his consideration, and I am sure he will contact you about this matter in due course.[29]

Both the content of Himmler's plan and Bracken's memorandum to Selborne reveal much about what was now going on. The memo also makes it clear that Victor Mallet, the Political Warfare Executive, and Brendan Bracken, were fully aware that they were in fact dealing with the infamous head of the SS and his loyal henchman.

For his part Himmler, a man inexperienced in the subtle art of diplomatic and geopolitical negotiations, had in the very writing of his peace plan made several critical mistakes that the British could use to their advantage. It is a golden rule of diplomacy never to let your opponent know what you most fear, for it can become a very effective weapon to be used against you. In their reference both to the Allies' halting of the air war and to their publicly announcing the abandonment of plans to invade western

Europe, points 1 and 2 of Himmler's peace offer made apparent what he feared most. It can be seen that he saw as the greatest threats to German survival the devastating consequence of unrelenting Allied bombing raids on the German cities, *and* the very real threat posed by an Allied invasion of mainland Europe.

Himmler realised that in the long run Germany's strategic position was untenable; therefore, like Hitler and Hess before him, he was making a tantalising offer to the Allies. Western Europe had suffered terribly in the German conquest of 1940 and the three years of occupation, yet the head of the SS was pragmatically offering to withdraw all German forces from the west, in exchange for a free hand in the east. It must have been very disconcerting to the men in London. They would immediately have realised that were this proposal to be placed before the Americans, the Americans might well, in their own pragmatic way, deem its terms acceptable in order to stop the appalling loss of life that the planned invasion of Continental Europe would cost.

The leading men of PWE must have felt a deep sense of satisfaction upon receipt of Mallet's secret submission to Britain. Their key objective, the precipitation of a coup d'état in Germany, was beginning to come to fruition. The first big hurdle had been to tempt Himmler with a promising opportunity for peace: he had now proposed to Mallet, whom he believed was directly representing the British government, an attractive six-point peace plan, thus revealing that he had swallowed the bait.

The next phase of PWE's Little H operation was to persuade Himmler to abandon his Führer and support a coup attempt in Germany. Much to its exasperation, this objective would turn out to be extremely difficult to attain. But attain it PWE did, complete with turmoil in Germany, even if Himmler had his own Machiavellian reasons for that support. As events turned out, PWE was inadvertently to cause devastating damage to post-war German politics through its covert operation. In the meantime, however, Mallet and PWE would continue to talk to the darker side of Nazism, unaware of what the appalling consequences of their actions would be.

NOTES

1. Doc. No. KV 2/99, National Archives, Kew, London.
2. Ibid.
3. Ibid.

4. Ibid.
5. Doc. No. FO 800/868, National Archives, Kew, London.
6. Ibid.
7. Doc. No. KV 2/99, National Archives, Kew, London.
8. Ibid.
9. Ibid.
10. Ibid.
11. Ibid.
12. Ibid.
13. Ibid.
14. Ibid.
15. Hugh Thomas, *SS-1* (Fourth Estate, 2001), p. 60.
16. Ibid., p. 61.
17. Ibid., p. 62.
18. Ibid., p. 64.
19. Ibid., p. 65.
20. Doc. No. FO 800/868, National Archives, Kew, London.
21. Doc. No. FO 371/34449, National Archives, Kew, London.
22. Ibid.
23. Ibid.
24. Ibid.
25. Ibid.
26. Ibid.
27. Ibid.
28. Doc. No. FO 800/898, National Archives, Kew, London.
29. Doc. No. HS 8/944, National Archives, Kew, London.

6
A PLOT TO KILL THE FÜHRER

It is important at this point to delve into the horrific world that was Himmler's dark side. Until now we have dealt only with his political personality. However, it is now necessary also to look at his work to, as he saw it, cleanse Europe of the dangers of Jewry.

As far back as 1920 Adolf Hitler had made it clear to his fanatical little band of followers that the Jews were to blame for Germany's defeat in the First World War. He even stated, 'If, at the beginning [of the First World War], someone had only subjected about 12 or 15,000 of these Hebrew enemies of the people to poison gas . . . then the sacrifice of millions at the front would not have been in vain.'[1] As we have seen, Himmler had been a devoted follower of Hitler almost from the very creation of the NSDAP. He had travelled Upper and Lower Bavaria on his motorcycle preaching the word of National Socialism, stirring up political awareness in the agricultural masses. He knew Nazi philosophy inside out, he understood Hitler's agenda against the Jews; indeed, he held the same beliefs dear to his heart.

Once the Nazis came to power in 1933, it could only be a matter of time before the Jews paid a heavy price for the Nazis' hatred of them. In the early days of the Third Reich, Hitler enacted a series of laws depriving Germany's Jewish citizens of their rights. First to be removed was the right to work for the state; then the right to own businesses; then had come the Nuremberg laws taking away the rights to property, healthcare, and soon life itself. It is, though, important to realise that even though the Nazis stripped Jewish citizens of all their rights – indeed, many ended up in concentration camps even in the 1930s – a strategy to murder as many Jews as possible did not materialise until well into the war.

The precise moment at which Hitler made up his mind that the Jews had to be physically destroyed cannot be determined from the available evidence, but there are some clues. The concentration camp at Auschwitz was set up in May 1940, while its first commandant, Rudolf Hoess, stated at his trial in 1946 that he personally received orders from Himmler in May 1941 to proceed with the gassing of Jews. Despite Himmler's order, however, a comprehensive structure for the murder of a race was not assembled until the Wannsee Conference, held on 20 January 1942.

This gathering, headed by the Reichsführer's most infamous protégé, Reinhard Heydrich, has long been recognised as the crucial moment when the Nazis crossed the boundary into a land of barbarism and horror almost too unspeakable to contemplate. A more subtle mechanism, however, was also at work. Until that day most of the Nazi government departments had been able to deny any knowledge of Hitler's plan to exterminate a race. What did the office of the Reich Chancellery, the Foreign Office, the Judiciary, know about concentration camps and murder? Almost nothing. It was territory into which they were careful not to stray. However, the extermination of the Jews was not a burden the SS intended to take on alone. Thus it was that in late January 1942, men such as the eminent Dr Stuckart, Minister of the Interior, Heinz Neumann of the Office of the Four Year Plan, Dr Roland Freisler, Minister of Justice, Martin Luther of the Foreign Office, and Ernst Kritzinger, Ministerial Director of the Reich Chancellery, found themselves at Heydrich's monstrous planning session. Heydrich's intention, and therefore Himmler's, was to make each man present – and hence all the organs of government, every politician and civil servant – an accomplice to the SS plan. In so doing the two men were protecting themselves against possible future repercussions if someone were to state that the SS must be held to account for the mass murder of the Jews. Cold and calculating as ever, Himmler well realised the political dangers to which his infamous course of action might lead. Thus the purpose of the conference was not only to orchestrate the most terrible plan in history, but also to make every leading German, from the Foreign Office to the Judiciary, an accessory to mass murder.

Preparations were made at succeeding conferences to carry out a mass movement of Europe's Jews to the concentration and extermination camps, and at the core of this activity lay Himmler's sinister realm of Gestapo, SD, and SS. The operation was strictly organised; the process was to be accelerated until there were no Jews left alive in occupied Europe. At the fulcrum of the extermination system lay Poland, complete with its camps at Auschwitz, Maidanek, Treblinka, Chelmno, Belzec, and Sobibor. Auschwitz was the most notorious of the extermination centres. At the height of its activity it could house more than 100,000 men and women, and could provide for the gassing and incineration of 12,000 persons a day. Ultimately Himmler's extermination policy would see the deaths of over six million people.

Since the end of the war, numerous historians, psychologists, and sociologists have examined the evidence for what was implemented by the SS between the Wannsee Conference of January 1942 and May 1945. Most have agreed that it was the furthest descent into utter barbarism in the entire course of civilisation. And at the centre of this web of organised murder sat Heinrich Himmler, aware of every intricate detail; indeed, it has been suggested that he knew considerably more about the Holocaust programme than Hitler, who was no doubt aware of its outline but was content to leave the management of the process in the capable hands of his Reichsführer-SS.

It is possible to conclude from what we know about Himmler that his personality fitted him to be an archetypal bureaucrat, a man whose life's work was laid out before him in the form of papers that needed signing, and that he was thus able to distance himself from the acts that so horrified the world in 1945. However, this is not so. Far from dealing with the murder of Europe's Jews only at a distance, Himmler embraced the very acts he ordered. He periodically toured the camps, knew every appalling, intricate detail of the Final Solution, knew the weekly and monthly statistics about how many Jews had been transported and killed, knew – even as he was in the throes of negotiating with the British via Mallet in Stockholm – that between the autumn of 1943 and the spring of 1944 the extermination of Jewish men, women, and children was being carried out with maximum efficiency.

It is pertinent here to disclose a short anecdotal tale from Martin Bormann's son. As the Second World War began, Himmler, apparently happily married to Marga, developed a relationship with one of his secretaries, Hedwig Potthast. The couple became extremely close, and Himmler fathered two children by her. It was an open secret that he housed this 'second family' in a villa in the countryside at Berchtesgaden. Hedwig and her children were soon accepted into the inner circle of the families of the Nazi leaders, who possessed homes there. It was at Berchtesgaden that Hedwig became known to the Bormann family, and soon they were on quite cordial terms. One day in early 1944, Martin Bormann junior (then aged fourteen), was approached by Hedwig in the street and invited to afternoon tea, together with his mother and younger sister. His mother accepted the invitation, and later that same day Bormann's wife and two children found themselves seated in Hedwig's comfortable Berchtesgaden home. Years later Martin junior was able to recall that Himmler's second

home on the Berghof stood 'in a wild sort of garden' and that Frau Potthast
gave the two children 'chocolate and cake'.[2] Whilst having tea with Frau
Bormann, Hedwig revealed to her guests that she had a very special collection of Himmler's, kept in his 'special lair' in an attic room. After tea she
led the way up the stairs into the attic, opened a door, and ushered her
guests into a light and airy room.

As Martin junior was to recall, Hedwig 'opened the door and we flocked
in. We didn't understand what the objects in that room were – until she
explained, quite scientifically . . . It was tables and chairs made of parts of
human bodies. There was a chair . . . the seat was a human pelvis, the legs
were human legs – on human feet. And then she picked up a copy of *Mein
Kampf* from a pile of them . . . she showed us the cover – made of human
skin, she said – and explained that the Dachau prisoners who produced it
used the . . . skin of the back to make it.' Everyone in the Bormann family
was horrified, and Martin junior's little sister, Eike, was terribly upset. Frau
Bormann hurried her children from the room, out of the house, and away
from Himmler's horrifying collection. The Bormanns never spoke to
Hedwig Potthast again.

It can thus be seen that Himmler was no mere petty bureaucrat, orchestrating the murder of millions whilst attempting to negotiate his own political future. Rather he was a ghoul of the first order, a man capable of
ordering the deaths of millions whilst at the same time so distanced from
reality that he was able to make a collection of the detritus; hideous
remnants of mass murder that no one in their right mind would want so
much as to see.

A process begun in the mid-1930s with the Nazis' T4 (Tiergarten 4)
programme, designed to murder most of the mental patients of the Reich,
had progressed during the Second World War to *Endlösung* – the murder
of the Jewish race in Europe. Yet, seemingly unaware that he had crossed
the boundaries of decent humanity, Himmler still believed without a qualm
of conscience that he could make a deal with the British to ensure himself
a post-war political career. What he was doing to the Jews did not enter
into the equation. However, such a mindset was not to last for ever; soon
he would begin to see a way of trading Jewish lives for concessions from
the western Allies. But by then it would be too late. Himmler would be
confirmed once and for all as the demon of the Reich, a man with whom
no one could possibly contemplate dealing.

•••••

By January 1944 it had become clear to nearly every German that the war was no longer winnable. Goebbels's propaganda machine still churned out claims that the conflict was undecided, and that it would yet be possible for Germany to turn the war in her favour. But the leading men of the Reich knew in their hearts that it would only be a matter of time before Nazi Germany was utterly defeated.

In the east the vast conquests of Russian territory were all gone, and by mid-January 1944 the Russians had pushed Germany's forces back to Poland. In the south the Americans and British had invaded Italy and now occupied half the country; the Italians had even surrendered to the Allies and changed sides. In the west the Germans were aware of a vast build-up of men and *matériel* in Britain, of the preparations being made for an invasion of France; yet, despite their installation of the complex 'Atlantic Wall' (extensive defensive fortifications that ran along the French coast from the Pas de Calais to the Bay of Biscay), no German knew where or indeed when the attack would come. Hitler and his generals pinned their hopes on repulsing the Allies on the beaches, but all knew that if the Allies managed to gain a foothold on the French coast, the military situation might quickly become desperate.

A few days before Christmas 1943 Himmler had met with Hitler to discuss the general war situation. He had tried to bring the Führer on side by declaring that if the German government were able to impress upon the British and Americans that Germany had no desire to challenge their positions as dominant world powers, then perhaps, even at this late hour, some form of agreement could be found. But his efforts washed over Hitler completely. His mind totally taken up with the desperate war being fought in the east, the Führer seemed no longer able to function objectively as a politician. Indeed, he declared with great seriousness that the war with Russia might last ten, twenty, or possibly even thirty years. 'And behind Russia stood the hordes of Asia whom the Bolsheviks were training and arming to descend on Europe and conquer the entire continent to the Atlantic.'[4] Hitler was adamant that Nazi Germany was the advance guard of Europe, and that if she should become exhausted by this titanic struggle, both Britain and America would eventually be forced to join her if they were not ultimately to be destroyed themselves.

This conversation must still have haunted Himmler in the early days of 1944. As he sat in the comfortable surroundings of his SS headquarters at Wewelsburg Castle in the Westphalian countryside, the Russian hordes were massing on the Russo-Polish frontier, preparing for a spring offensive that might see them sweep deep into Poland and perhaps into the German homeland as well. To him it must have been like watching the clock, counting the last minutes to midnight. His negotiations with the British therefore took on fresh urgency. He had delivered his six-point peace plan into the hands of Victor Mallet in Stockholm and yet the British still prevaricated. Krämer and Schellenberg had no good news to report.

It is known that at this time Himmler's patience with his men began to deteriorate, and whilst at Wewelsburg during January 1944 he endured stomach cramps that crippled him for hours at a time.[5] Despite all his power as head of the SS, he had always been prone to suffering with his nerves when he was troubled or things did not go as he planned. In his secret dealings with the British he had much to be anxious about. The British could not be persuaded into making concessions, and their sole demand was that he topple Hitler: an almost impossible undertaking for a man of Himmler's ilk.

In Stockholm, too, nerves were beginning to fray, and Victor Mallet also had much to be anxious about. On 24 January he reported to Robert Bruce Lockhart, the Political Intelligence Executive member of the Committee of Five at PWE:

> SECRET
> Dear Bruce,
> Developments here are progressing very slowly. Yesterday I had another meeting with W.S[chellenberg] at the home of M.W[allenberg]. It seems that H.H[immler] cannot be persuaded to act independently and launch his bid for power; he is just too cautious. S[chellenberg] does, however, believe that he would be prepared to act in concert with a third party's attempt. He further stated that H[immler] would be prepared to accept a third party coup attempt and step in at the last moment as the man of the hour, and seize power. This all seems highly Machiavellian to me, but it could, I am sure, be turned to our advantage. S[chellenberg] has departed for further instructions, but is keen to advance the negotiations now that a move to oust Hitler has in theory been agreed upon. I have agreed to meet him again on 17 February, so please advise me what our stance should be at this development.[6]

This letter gives the first hint of the thinking behind Himmler's negotiations in early 1944. Mallet and PWE had finally managed to wear down his reluctance to turn on his Führer. His peace plan of the previous autumn revealed that he was ready to make a deal with the British government, was indeed ready to 'install a new provisional government' in Germany.[7] He did not yet feel secure enough to turn against Hitler; if, however, someone else were to undertake the dirty business of treason, leaving it open for Himmler to step in at the eleventh hour and seize power, then that was a much more tenable position. It was a course of action his conscience would allow him to take: he would emerge from the business, his character untainted with the odium of treason, as the man who had been forced to take power to save Germany.

The men of PWE undoubtedly saw a logic to Himmler's plan, that he 'would be prepared to accept a third party coup attempt and step in at the last moment as the man of the hour, and seize power.'[8] It must be remembered that these Britons knew all about Adam von Trott, and his Kreisau Circle's plan to assassinate Hitler and launch a coup d'état. PWE did not really care whether the group succeeded, just so long as political chaos was precipitated in Germany, giving the Allies the upper hand at a key moment in the war. All the elements were now coming together whereby this objective might be realised. A few days after Lockhart received Mallet's letter, Brendan Bracken wrote a short missive to his old friend and co-conspirator Lord Selborne, who as Minister responsible for SOE was party to the scheme:

> I am sure that this latest development can be turned to our advantage. Now that Victor has managed to extricate from W.S[schellenberg] the fact that H.H[immler] is preparing to move against the Nazi leadership in his own interests, it can only be a matter of time (maybe just a few months) before we can see political chaos erupting in the Fatherland.[9]

Before that happened, however, things were once more to go awry for PWE, and the problem had a familiar name – Ewan Butler. Throughout the autumn and winter of 1943 Butler had been drinking to ever greater excess. Given that his mental health was none too stable, it seemed inevitable that his troubled relationship with the nervous Victor Mallet would soon reach a crisis. In the second week of February 1944, even whilst Bracken was writing to Selborne to discuss the progress of the Little H operation, Butler put in an official request for home leave; this at a time when his behaviour and alcoholism were causing increasing concern to all those he worked with at the British Embassy. Butler's loyal secretary, Janet Dow, even confided to Peter Falk's secretary, Bridget Pope, that she had tried in vain to contact Sir Richard Boord, Butler's superior officer, at SOE headquarters in London, only to discover that he, too, had become a patient at the Virginia Water Mental Hospital. The situation was serious and Butler was deteriorating every day. To his dismay Mallet refused his request for home leave at this most sensitive point in the Himmler negotiations; there was too much at stake for him to be allowed to depart Stockholm, leaving Mallet to handle the secret talks alone. However, Mallet failed to take into consideration Butler's mental state. He was unpredictable, and his presence in Sweden would soon become more of a hindrance than a help.

On the day Butler heard that his official request for home leave had been vetoed, his psychological state took a decided turn for the worse. He sought solace in a bottle of whisky, and eventually fetched up on Falk's doorstep in the middle of the night seeking advice. In a very drunken state, he blabbed all his troubles about his secret mission in Stockholm, and began to reveal to Falk his concerns at what was being negotiated. An astonished Falk sat and listened to Butler's outline of the Schellenberg negotiations: a deal cut with Himmler, the toppling of Hitler to precipitate political chaos in Germany, and a secret financial deal involving Marcus Wallenberg to protect German industrial interests. Butler left his biggest bombshell for last, revealing to Falk his impossible mission secretly to ensure the smooth exodus of top Nazis to neutral Sweden once the war ended, and the granting of immunity from prosecution for both Walter Schellenberg and Himmler.[10] He complained that his expressions of distaste for his mission had been completely ignored, and that his relationship with Mallet had deteriorated to one of mutual loathing.[11]

After hearing Butler out, a horrified Falk failed to persuade him to go home and sleep off his inebriated state. Butler was desperate, so Falk left him under the watchful eye of his wife whilst he dashed off across the sleeping city to consult with Peter Tennant. At first very sceptical of the whole tale, Tennant was astute enough to conclude that neither he nor Falk should become involved in the mess. It was obvious to him that Mallet must be operating under orders from London, otherwise SOE would not have sent Butler out to Sweden to help him. Tennant and Falk were still managing to purloin papers from Krämer's desk via agent 'Frau H12'; it was now clear to both men that these sensitive documents must have been sent from London for Mallet to use in his negotiations. Tennant could not discern from Butler's babblings the true purpose of Mallet's secret mission, but of one thing he was certain: that he and Falk should not reveal to Mallet that they had spent considerable SIS resources in Sweden watching his activities. It was apparent that Mallet had been operating under orders from London. Whatever mess he and Butler had stirred up, they, at least, should keep their hands clean.[12]

At the end of their discussion – it was now nearly 3.30 a.m. – Tennant told Falk that it was best that they did not become involved in the affair. Clearly Butler had not been reporting back to SOE, and the secrecy of his mission for Mallet explained a lot. Tennant and Falk had been extremely puzzled for months about why Butler's immediate superior in SOE, Roger Turnbull, had tolerated his often strange and extremely unprofessional behaviour; now they began to understand his secret mission as Mallet's assistant. Tennant's relationship with Mallet had already deteriorated to one of mutual animosity, due in no small part to Tennant's interference and surveillance of his ambassador's secret activity. It was time to back off before either he or Peter Falk inadvertently damaged Victor Mallet's secret undertaking – not that they understood his mission, but Tennant was sure his orders must have emanated from very high up indeed. At that time he had no inkling that Mallet was working for PWE but believed, owing to Butler's involvement, that he must have been working for the Foreign Office with SOE backing.[13]

Falk eventually left Tennant's apartment at 4.00 a.m., the two men having concluded that it was best to try to sober Butler up and send him home. Careful not to upset the still very drunken Butler, Falk managed to persuade him to go home at about 4.45 a.m. He departed much cheered, in the mistaken belief that Falk and Tennant would support him not only in his quest for leave, but also in seeking a permanent escape from Mallet's shady dealings. He well realised the depth of deceit involved in the Ambassador's negotiations with Himmler; it was a murky world of double bluff that he instinctively knew would accrue him no honour in the war against Germany. It could have no happy outcome for anyone involved, and it entailed considerable risk. The significance of Schellenberg's involvement in the kidnapping of British agents Stevens and Best at Venlo in 1939 would not have escaped Butler's attention: Himmler and Schellenberg were dangerous men to cross, especially since neutral Sweden was so close to Germany.

Fate, however, was not destined to favour Ewan Butler. He left Peter Falk's apartment in the early hours convinced that the SIS man would have a word with Victor Mallet, using his influence to get Butler posted home. Consequently, Butler arrived at the British Embassy late that morning, still drunk and in a state of high merriment, and under the mistaken belief that the Ambassador would give him a fair hearing about a posting back to London. He was seen by Embassy staff sauntering down the grand staircase to Mallet's office with an armful of quarto-sized SD reports (it should be realised that the trade in documents via Schellenberg, and between Krämer and Butler, was almost certainly a two-sided affair, and meant as an indication of good faith). Once Butler closed Mallet's door behind him, the staff at the Embassy were surprised and shocked to hear a mighty argument erupt between the Ambassador and his SOE appointed assistant. The argument lasted a brief ten minutes before Butler was ejected from Mallet's presence in a state of some distress. The Embassy staff were then subjected to the pitiful sight of a sobbing Butler retreating up the stairs, shedding SD quarto-sized papers in his wake as he sought the relative safety of his first-floor office and another bottle of whisky.

Within a few days, Peter Tennant was notified by his superior at SIS in London that any further attempt to obtain information from Butler was strictly forbidden. Falk was similarly reprimanded the following week by his London SIS boss Keith Liversidge, with whom he had enjoyed cordial relations up to that point. Tennant and Falk realised that they had stumbled into a secret game being played out at the very highest level, one in which they were being ordered not to play a part. The discovery of a hidden agenda behind their Ambassador's conduct transformed their understanding of the strange tensions at the Embassy, and they realised once and for all that the stakes were far higher than they had ever suspected.

Within a few short weeks Mallet dispensed with Butler's help. The unfortunate Butler found himself transferred with great haste to the intelligence staff of SOE headquarters in Cairo, far from the centre of intrigue in Stockholm and London, and the men conducting the Little H operation. He finished the war in this posting, left well alone to drown his sorrows in as much booze as he wished, just so long as he discussed with no one the purpose of his mission to Stockholm in 1943–44, and mentioned no details of the deal being struck between Victor Mallet and Heinrich Himmler.

•••••

The spring of 1944 saw momentous developments in the Second World War. The British and Americans continued their steady invasion of Italy, swallowing twenty valuable German divisions into the conflict. In the east the Russian front moved significantly westward; Soviet troops gained their first foothold back on Polish territory since 1941, also invading Germany's ally, Romania. June 1944 saw the greatest Allied successes thus far: on 4 June the United States Fifth Army occupied Rome, and a mere forty-eight hours later Allied forces launched the long-awaited second front and invaded France on the Normandy beaches. Operation Overlord – D-Day – had taken place, the greatest seaborne invasion in history. On the morning of 6 June a jubilant Winston Churchill stood before the House of Commons and declared:

> I have . . . to announce to the House that during the night and the early hours of this morning the first of the series of landings in force upon the European continent has taken place . . . An immense armada of upwards of 4,000 ships, together with several thousand smaller craft, crossed the Channel. Massed airborne landings have been successfully effected behind the enemy lines, and landings on the beaches are proceeding at various points at the present time . . . This vast operation is undoubtedly the most complicated and difficult that has ever taken place . . .[14]

In Germany the Nazi leadership's reaction to the invasion in Normandy was most curious. Instead of panic or dismay, Hitler oozed confidence that the Allies could at last be smashed under the weight and superiority of German forces. Indeed, Dr Goebbels recorded that Hitler seemed relieved, as if a great burden had fallen from his shoulders. What he had been expecting for months was now a reality. It had taken place, he said, exactly where he had predicted it.[15] No one dared to contradict the Führer. No one amongst his high command dared to comment that he had always predicted that the invasion would come at the Pas de Calais, and that no less than fifteen German divisions were hence incorrectly situated in the north of France to repulse the Allied invasion. Hitler was 'absolutely certain' that the Allied troops, for whose quality he had no high regard, would be repulsed. 'If we repel the invasion,' Goebbels noted, 'then the scene in the war will be completely transformed. The Führer reckons for certain with this. He had few worries that this couldn't succeed.' None of the Nazi leaders dreamed of contradicting Hitler. Göring thought the battle as good as won. And the Foreign Minister, Ribbentrop, was as always 'entirely on the Führer's side'.[16]

There were, however, two men in the Nazi hierarchy who felt that the successful landings by the Allies in Normandy were a disaster of the first magnitude. Himmler and Schellenberg were not at all certain that Hitler was correct in holding the Allied forces in low esteem. Whilst Hitler saw the potential for a showdown with the Allies in Normandy that would determine who gained the upper hand in the war, Himmler could see only the possibility of disaster. If the German forces did not quickly repulse the Allies in France and regain the lost coastal territory, then the Allies would have gained a foothold that they could use to pour in ever greater quantities of men and *matériel*.

The Allies, like Himmler, were quick to realise that overwhelming American might was turning the war against Germany. With the Allied conquests, Hitler would have no option other than to order Army reserves into the war in the west, reserves that were still desperately needed in the east to push the Russians out of Poland and back into Russia. Operation Overlord was doubly a disaster for Germany; not only had the Allies managed to invade France, but in order to hold them back, Germany was forced to transfer much-needed forces into the west to stem the Allied tide. The situation was destined to become unsustainable.

It was at this time – the beginning of June 1944 – that Himmler held a significant discussion with General Guderian about the need to replace staff officers who had spent too long behind a desk, losing touch with the daily need for action of the men at the front, and who as a result had become too slow in coming to decisions. Of primary concern was the post of Chief of Staff to the head of the Replacement Army, under General Friedrich Fromm (responsible for calling men to arms, he was currently charged with raising fifteen new divisions). Himmler asked Guderian who he thought might be the most suitable man to fill this post. Without a moment's hesitation, Guderian suggested the aristocratic thirty-seven-year-old Lieutenant Colonel Claus Schenk Graf von Stauffenberg, a war hero who had served with distinction in Poland, France, and North Africa. In April 1943, whilst serving in North Africa, he had been severely wounded, losing an eye, his right hand, and half of his left hand. He was currently Chief of Staff of the Army Ordnance Department in Berlin. Himmler liked the sound of this man and immediately agreed to his appointment – or so the Minister of Finance, Schwerin von Krosigk, would later recall in his memoirs.[17]

On such events do the great changes of history sometimes depend, for there was another side to Stauffenberg that it is hard to believe Himmler was unaware of.[18] Stauffenberg had wholeheartedly believed in Nazi

Germany's expansionist policies and had been a supporter of Hitler. But having had his life saved by Germany's most eminent physician, Dr Ferdinand Sauerbruch, he radically changed his opinion during his long convalescence. He now made no secret of his contempt for Hitler and Nazism. He had grown to resent any form of totalitarian dictatorship, especially National Socialism, and openly criticised Hitler as the 'Master of Vermin'.[19] It was a very dangerous stance, one that must surely have come to Himmler's attention: via the Gestapo and SD, he had his finger on the pulse of all dissident and anti-Nazi resistance in Germany.

During the eight months Stauffenberg had been serving at the huge Ministry of War on Bendlerstrasse – the Bendlerblock – his views had hardened, and he became convinced that Germany's only hope was to oust the Nazi regime and sue for peace with the Allies. It was during this period that he came (via his cousin, Peter Graf von Wartenburg) to the attention of the Kreisau Circle, headed by Helmuth James Graf von Moltke, legal advisor to the German High Command, and Adam von Trott, leading member of the Circle who had been in touch with the British authorities ever since 1942. The Circle had attempted several times since then to kill Hitler, but those attempts had failed; furthermore, it did not possess the infrastructure to seize power once the assassination of the Führer had taken place. That situation was to change radically with the recruitment of Stauffenberg. He possessed the drive and imagination to make such a plot succeed, not only in killing Hitler, but also in organising the anti-Nazi resistance once the deed had been done.

Key to seizing power on Hitler's death was the ability of the Kreisau Circle to isolate the top Nazis and prevent them from moving against the coup. The capable Stauffenberg soon came up with a plan. The Nazis had conceived the notion of a fallback position, code-named 'Operation Walküre', to be instigated in the case of civil unrest. In such an event, Army units based around Berlin would move to seize all communications centres and isolate the government sector in the heart of the city. Stauffenberg realised that such a plan could be used against the Nazis, so long as the leading men at the Bendlerstrasse headquarters, many of whom had joined him in the anti-Nazi resistance, controlled these army units. They could then launch Walküre on their own initiative and thus take charge of the capital, isolating the Nazi high command in the government sector long enough to accomplish their coup. The only ingredient that had eluded the Circle before June 1944 was reliable access to Hitler, who Stauffenberg realised had to be eliminated if any coup were to succeed.

It was at this moment that a chance to dispose of the Führer fell right into his hands. In his new position as Chief of Staff of the Replacement Army, it was necessary for Stauffenberg to attend briefings with Hitler at the Wolf's Lair in Rastenburg on an almost weekly basis. A man of action of the first order, regardless of his disabilities, Stauffenberg decided to take upon himself the responsibility for killing Hitler; he would assassinate the Führer just as soon as an opportunity presented itself. All that the leading men of the Bendlerstrasse and the Kreisau Circle could do now, in the latter weeks of June and the first weeks of July, was wait for Stauffenberg to perform the deed, initiating the coup attempt that would see the moderates of Germany seize power and sue for peace with the Allies.

However, this raises an intriguing question. Himmler had already made it known to the British that he would be amenable to a 'third party' coup attempt, and was prepared to step in at the last moment as the 'man of the hour, and seize power' himself.[20] That piece of tantalising news had been passed to Victor Mallet as far back as 24 January 1944. Since then Himmler had undoubtedly been waiting for the resistance to make their move, precipitating his move to take power and make his own bid for peace. As Mallet had commented in January, 'this all seems highly Machiavellian to me, but it could, I am sure, be turned to our advantage'.[21] Did Himmler, therefore, know in June that Stauffenberg was the new dynamo of the anti-Nazi resistance and was preparing for his coup attempt? Stauffenberg made no secret of his hatred of Hitler and the Nazis, and his outspokenness was a great danger to the Kreisau Circle.

It is equally hard to believe that General Guderian did not know of the plot. He had been approached by the Circle months before, but had declined to join; however, like many other generals in the Army, he is known to have despaired of Hitler's 'strategy of trying to hold every yard of ground in the east, and his true position can best be described as enigmatic; he would have welcomed a military take-over if it could be accomplished without civil war'.[22] Moreover, General Fromm, who naturally had a say in the appointment of his own Chief of Staff, was also party to the Kreisau conspiracy, having joined the Circle the previous year. Fromm was something of a waverer, described by one Kreisau member as a man who would act in support of the coup only when he saw that it had succeeded.[23] He was nevertheless complicit in the appointment of Stauffenberg, which from the beginning of July 1944 would give him access to Hitler.

The picture that presents itself is of three opaque characters – Himmler, Guderian and Fromm – all secretly aware (for very different reasons) of the need for Hitler's removal, equally aware of Stauffenberg's burning desire to accomplish it, and agreeing tacitly, without revealing their motives to each other, to give the young colonel his head.[24] Thus it was that Himmler personally signed the order granting Stauffenberg access to Hitler, and Stauffenberg took up his post on 1 July 1944. All he needed to do now was wait and see whether or not this would precipitate the long-awaited 'third party' coup attempt. As events were to turn out, he did not have very long to wait. When the catalyst of revolt did make his move, it would catch everyone except the Kreisau Circle by surprise.

On hearing that he had been promoted to Chief of Staff of the Replacement Army, and would thus be in a position to gain personal access to Hitler, Stauffenberg declared, 'Fate has offered us this opportunity, and I would not refuse it for anything in the world. It must be done because this man [Hitler] is evil personified.'[25] In his mind a plan crystallised for an assassination that would deprive the Nazi snake of its head in one fell swoop. The Kreisau Circle had been supplied by the British (i.e. by SOE) with the materials for a bomb. Thus Stauffenberg had at his disposal several pounds of plastic explosive and a chemical fuse (a metal tube containing a glass phial that, when crushed, released acid on to a trigger wire within the tube connected to a detonator). He would attend one of the Führer's briefings, at which he hoped Göring and Himmler would be present. He would then set off his bomb, killing all three men at the same time. It was an audacious plot, but already destined to fail in its perceived form, for a very good reason. Himmler, maybe aware of the broader aspects of the scheme, contrived never to be present at the Führer's briefings throughout July 1944, though it was noted that he had hardly ever missed such a meeting in the previous two years.

Stauffenberg did not have to wait long before he was in a position to make his attempt. Appointed as Chief of Staff on 1 July, he was summoned only ten days later to report to Hitler at the Führer's home, the Berghof, on 11 July. He attended that day's briefing armed with the bomb in his brief-case, but was too ambitious in his criteria for setting it off. Although Göring was present, Himmler did not make an appearance, and so Stauffenberg abandoned his mission and determined to wait for another day. Following the aborted attack, and after some debate with the Bendlerblock conspirators and Kreisau Circle, it was decided that he should give up his hope of killing Göring and Himmler at the same time. All that was necessary to launch the coup d'état was to kill Hitler; he was the main danger to any prospective insurrection.

The next opportunity to carry out his assignment came four days later, on 15 July. Hitler's latest briefing was to be held at the command head-quarters at Rastenburg, in East Prussia, a mere three-hour flight from Berlin. This time the men of the Bendlerblock and Kreisau Circle were much better prepared; they determined that it was necessary to coordinate Stauffenberg's attack on Hitler with the launch of Operation Walküre. The morning of 15 July 1944 dawned bright and warm. Indeed, the tempera-ture rose so high that day that Hitler was to be found taking refuge from the sultry heat of East Prussia deep in his command bunker, a huge air-conditioned concrete structure in the centre of the Wolf's Lair. His meet-ings were to be held near by in a large wooden hut and it was here that Stauffenberg planned to kill him. This time the conspirators were so certain of success that General Olbrecht, a leading member of the Kreisau Circle at the Bendlerblock, gave the order for Operation Walküre to take place at 11.00 a.m., some two hours before Stauffenberg's meeting with Hitler at 1.00 p.m. This would allow the Wehrmacht troops and the tanks of the nearby Panzer school time to move in to occupy the centre of the capital by early afternoon.

At 1.10 p.m. precisely, the conference at the Wolf's Lair began. Stauffenberg gave Hitler his report on the recruitment situation in Germany, then excused himself to make a telephone call to the Bendlerblock. He reported to Olbrecht that Hitler was present in the conference hut, and that he was going back to plant his briefcase bomb. However, when he returned he found the conference ending and Hitler already gone. Once more, his mission was aborted. It was another fifteen minutes before he could excuse himself again, by which time it was 1.45 p.m. and the troops in Berlin were already converging on the government sector. Olbrecht hurriedly gave the cancellation order. The juggernaut of men and tanks shuddered to a halt before dispersing quietly back to their barracks on the outskirts of the city. The excuse given to the commanders was that it had been a practice exercise; the men of the Bendlerblock knew there could be no more false starts. Some of the conspirators were discour-aged and shaken by the fiasco, but not Stauffenberg.

On the night of Sunday, 16 July, back in Berlin, Stauffenberg met with his fellow conspirators at his brother's home in Wannsee. There his cousin, the Kreisau's liaison officer to Erwin Rommel in France, gave a very encouraging report. Present, amongst others, were Yorck von Wartenburg, a leading light of the Kreisau Circle, Colonel Mertz von Quirnheim, Chief of Staff in the General Army office at Bendlerstrasse, and Adam von Trott from the Foreign Office. Stauffenberg's cousin reported on his recent trip to France and revealed that the overwhelming might of Allied forces in Normandy was certain to result in a breakout within the next few days. He further announced that he had met with Erwin Rommel, who realised the war was lost and was 'determined to support the conspiracy no matter what [his fellow commander] Marshal von Kluge did'.[26] Kluge's own position was that he would place himself at the disposal of the leaders of the coup d'état only if Hitler were removed from power. Beyond that he would not go, but it satisfied the putsch leaders.

Of more importance to the Kreisau members was the report that Rommel had received similar assurances of support from the two most senior Waffen-SS commanders in France, Oberstgruppenführer (general) Paul Hausser, in command of the Seventh Army, and an old stalwart of the Nazi Party, Sepp Dietrich, commanding the First SS-Panzerkorps.[27] 'That the commander of Hitler's original elite formation of guards, the SS-Leibstandarte, was apparently prepared to cooperate with the Reaktion in supporting a change of regime is remarkable testimony to the seriousness of the military situation as viewed from France. It is also inconceivable that Himmler was not [kept] fully informed.'[28]

On hearing of the death of Hitler, the Kreisau members were told, Rommel would order a ceasefire in France as a prelude to the opening of negotiations with the Allies by the new Kreisau Circle government in Berlin. Fate, however, was determined to deal the Kreisau plotters a bad hand. On that very weekend Rommel was badly injured when his car was strafed by an Allied plane. He was thus incapacitated, and after a spell in hospital, would go home to convalesce. He would play no further part in the Kreisau conspiracy, except to give it his support if and when Hitler was killed.

On the afternoon of 18 July, Stauffenberg received notification that his presence was again required at the Wolf's Lair for another conference with Hitler two days later. He was to give a briefing on the much-needed replacements to maintain the front in the east against the Russians, where the German centre was in peril of imminent collapse following recent defeats on both flanks. This time Stauffenberg was determined to succeed, and it was soon agreed with the Kreisau Circle that, to coincide with the murder of Hitler, orders were to be given to launch Walküre and isolate the government sector of Berlin. However, since there was the risk of a further mistake, the order from Bendlerstrasse would wait on word from Stauffenberg that Hitler was dead. On the following day, 19 July, Stauffenberg spent the whole day at the Bendlerstrasse headquarters preparing for the coup attempt; in the morning he made his last-minute preparations, double-checking the British explosives and detonator, and in the afternoon he took part in a series of meetings with his fellow Bendlerblock conspirators. Nothing could be left to chance, and it must have been plain to every man present that they were embarked upon a very hazardous exercise indeed. Success and the death of Hitler would result in their taking over Germany (they did not know about Himmler's plans to step in at the last moment and deftly usurp power); failure would almost certainly result in arrest by the Gestapo and an appointment with a firing squad at the hands of the SS. Their awareness of the extreme peril entailed in the act they were about to perform was set against the certainty that Germany otherwise faced defeat and complete destruction.

The word from their supporters amongst the high command in France had been that the Allies were about to break out any day soon. The more they gained the upper hand in the west, the less likely they were to be amenable to a negotiated armistice with a new German government. Most of the leading members of the Kreisau Circle were aware of a speech given by Churchill's deputy, Clement Attlee, on 6 July. He had stated (with obvious reference to a rival faction to the Nazis) that should any section of the German people wish to see a return to a government based on respect for international law and the rights of the individual, 'they must understand that no one will believe them until they have taken active steps to rid themselves of their present regime . . . The longer they continue to support and to tolerate their present rulers,' Attlee concluded, 'the heavier grows their own direct responsibility for the destruction that is being wrought throughout the world, and not least in their own country.'[29] For the Kreisau Circle, now was surely the time to act, before the tide of war made any possibility of negotiating an end to the conflict purely academic.

Thursday, 20 July 1944, again dawned bright and sunny, foretelling another hot and sultry summer's day. At 6.00 a.m. Stauffenberg was collected by a Bendlerblock staff car for the short journey to Rangsdorf airfield on the outskirts of the city. Here he met with his co-conspirators, General Helmut Stieff and his own ADC, Lieutenant von Haeften. After its three-hour flight to the east, the plane touched down at Rastenburg a little after 10.00 a.m. On their arrival the little group of conspirators broke up. Stieff and Haeften headed for the nearby OKH camp, whilst Stauffenberg travelled on into the Wolf's Lair for a late breakfast with a number of other officers, including the camp commandant.

After breakfast Stauffenberg was required to attend a low-echelon meeting on the situation regarding reinforcements for the eastern front. His ADC, Haeften, now rejoined him, just in time to be called into Field Marshal Keitel's office where the discussion was to take place. This continued until about 12.30 p.m., the time when Hitler's *Lagebesprechung* (situation conference) was due to begin; it should have started at 1.00 p.m. but had been brought forward half an hour because Mussolini was due to visit later that afternoon, and Hitler wanted the afternoon free to meet the ousted and much-diminished Italian dictator.

Before leaving Keitel's office to make his way to the Führer's conference, Stauffenberg asked Keitel's adjutant if there was somewhere he could freshen up and change his shirt. The adjutant showed him into his own nearby room and left Stauffenberg and Haeften alone. At this point the two men made an error in their assassination bid. They had actually brought with them two packets of British-made plastic explosive and two fuses (enough to destroy much of the building, never mind the fragile human form of Hitler). But Stauffenberg was in a hurry, and so he primed only one explosive charge with the chemical detonator, while Haeften placed the second, unprimed package of plastic explosive in his own briefcase.

Hitler's daily *Lagebesprechung* was again held in the large wooden hut – some forty feet by fifteen – hidden amongst the trees of the Wolf's Lair, near his own quarters and the massive concrete command bunker. The daily situation conferences were always well attended by the top ranks of the German Army. Today was no exception, though Stauffenberg noted with disappointment that neither Göring nor Himmler was present. It did not deter him, however; this time he was determined to succeed in killing Hitler. In the remains of his one hand he held his briefcase containing the bomb; he had primed the detonator and the acid was already eating through the activating wire. He must have known he had only minutes to plant the bomb and get away. His thoughts may also have dwelt upon the worrying fact that chemical detonators were notoriously unreliable: one fuse might explode in under ten minutes; an apparently identical one might not go off for nearly twenty. The heat of the day did not help, and it was known that chemical fuses tended to detonate more quickly in hot conditions.

On entering the conference room, Stauffenberg found Hitler sitting at the long map table, facing the open windows, his back to the internal partition wall, his hands fiddling with his glasses. He was the only man sitting down. Keitel moved to take up his usual position at Hitler's left shoulder. At the Führer's right, General Heusinger, chief of operations of the Army

High Command, was giving a melancholic account of the military situation in the east. Stauffenberg squeezed in to stand at Heusinger's right next to Colonel Brandt; it was as close to Hitler as he could get. He deftly placed his case on the floor on the inside of one of three solid wooden transverse plinths that supported the extremely large table. A moment or two later he murmured an excuse about having to make an urgent telephone call, and quickly left the building. He was joined outside by General Fellgiebel, chief of Army communications, who was also a dedicated member of the Kreisau Circle.

Back in the conference room, Heusinger's aide moved to take a closer look at the map table, and stubbed his foot on Stauffenberg's briefcase. It fell over. Leaning down, the aide picked it up and moved it to the *outside* of the wooden plinth. That trivial act changed the course of history. It was 12.41 p.m., and Hitler was leaning far over the table to check a detail on the map intently. Heusinger was saying, 'Unless at long last the army group is withdrawn from Peipus, a catastrophe –'[30] At that exact moment his words were obliterated by a deafening explosion. 'Flames shot up and a hail of glass splinters, timber and plaster rained down.'[31] A thick pall of smoke filled the room.

Over at the OKW Signals Office in Bunker 88, Stauffenberg and Fellgiebel stood outside waiting for the bomb to explode. They had been chatting in as unconcerned a manner as possible when they were joined by Haeften. The headquarters signals officer reported that Stauffenberg's car was ready to take him to the commandant's quarters for lunch. Just then came an explosion. 'What's happening?' exclaimed Fellgiebel. A nearby officer replied that an animal must have wandered into the minefield and set off a mine; it happened all the time.

The deed done, Stauffenberg bade farewell to Fellgiebel and with Haeften quickly boarded the staff car, ordering the driver to take them directly to Rastenburg airfield. The driver thought nothing of his change of orders and did as he was told, driving directly to the gate of the inner security cordon. The guards there had closed the gate on hearing the explosion and refused to open them for Stauffenberg. He hurried into the guardroom and demanded the telephone. He dialled, spoke to someone briefly, and without passing the receiver to the guard on duty stated simply, 'Lieutenant, I am allowed to pass.' The time was 12.45 p.m. Without question the lieutenant ordered the gate to be opened and Stauffenberg and Haeften passed through. Almost immediately a siren began to wail. Arriving some minutes later at the outer security gate, Stauffenberg could not this time bluff his way through so simply. Again he entered the guard-room and demanded access to a telephone. He made a call direct to the commandant's office and spoke with an adjutant with whom he had break-fasted earlier that morning, explaining that he had to be at the Rastenburg airstrip shortly to catch a flight back to Berlin. The adjutant, unaware of the attempt on Hitler's life, ordered the guard to let him pass.

It was 1.00 p.m. by the time Stauffenberg and Haeften arrived at the Rastenburg airfield and boarded their transport Heinkel 111. Within a few minutes they were in the air, a tense three-hour flight to Berlin ahead of them. The aircraft's radio did not possess the range to communicate with Berlin and the Bendlerblock conspirators. But, if everything was going as planned, Fellgiebel would have sent word to the Bendlerblock by now that Hitler was dead, and General Olbrecht would have ordered the launch of Operation Walküre, seizing the government sector of the city and its crucial communications facilities.

Unfortunately, everything was not proceeding as planned. There was one essential problem: unbelievably, Hitler had somehow survived the explosion, even though men mere feet away had been killed outright. The explanation lay in the fact that the bomb had been moved to the *outside* of the wooden plinth supporting the table; the main force of the explosion had thus been directed away from Hitler and the men to his left. He had suffered minor injuries – he had a perforated right eardrum, his trousers had been blown to tatters, he had injured his right arm, and his hair was singed – but they were not life threatening. Hitler's secretary, Traudl Junge, recalled many years later that in this state he presented an almost comical figure, 'his face blackened by the smoke and his hair standing on end like a brush'.[32]

'Well, my ladies,' he said to his secretaries when they rushed over to see him being tended by his personal physician, Dr Morell, 'once again every-thing turned out well for me. More proof that Fate has selected me for my mission. Otherwise I wouldn't be alive.'[33]

It was the worst of all situations as far as the Kreisau Circle was concerned. Hitler dead was the ideal; Hitler alive and aware how close to death he had been – and that men of his own high command had plotted his murder – was a terrible outcome.

In the air on his way back to Berlin, Stauffenberg must have been certain that the Führer had been killed. Had he not placed the bomb mere feet from Hitler himself? No, Hitler must be dead, and, even as he flew westward, General Olbrecht must by now be issuing the commands for

Operation Walküre to take place. It is known that Stauffenberg was by nature self-assured and confident. All he had to do now was sit back, relax, and wait for Berlin to fall into the hands of the Kreisau Circle. By the weekend they would rule Germany, and the war could be concluded by armistice within a fortnight. However, Stauffenberg was wrong.

Back at the Wolf's Lair, General Fellgiebel had been joined by a fellow conspirator, Colonel Sander, the headquarters signals officer. They had jointly ordered a complete shutdown of the headquarters communications centre, cutting all telephone and teleprinter links with the outside world. The Führer's headquarters was thus isolated, as required by the plans of the conspiracy to give the putsch the best chance of success.

This complete communications blackout was supposed to allow the conspirators in Berlin time to seize the capital, but they failed to act. Confusion and indecision was the order of the day at the Bendlerblock: uncertain whether Claus von Stauffenberg had succeeded in killing Hitler or not, the plotters were loath to activate Operation Walküre, since they were frightened of another complete fiasco such as had occurred with the false alarm on 15 July. No one, particularly General Fellgiebel whose responsibility it was, had contacted General Olbrecht back at the Bendlerstrasse. Thus everyone at the Bendlerblock nervously awaited Claus von Stauffenberg's return. Precious time passed as the conspirators waited for a call from General Fellgiebel at the Wolf's Lair, but none came.

What Himmler was doing at this time is most interesting. On hearing of the explosion at Hitler's conference – quite how he learnt of this is unknown, bearing in mind that all communications in or out of the Wolf's Lair had been cut – he immediately dashed from his own nearby field headquarters camp to see the Führer and offer him his congratulations on his lucky escape. They must have been bitter words indeed. He was surely aware of what had happened; but did he make his move to seize power himself? No, he did not, for the very good reason that Hitler was very much alive and the putschists had failed in their key objective. The meeting between Hitler and Himmler took place a little after 2.00 p.m., and Hitler gave his head of state security full authority to crush the rebellion, saying: 'Shoot anyone who resists, no matter who it is.'[34]

Still no one knew exactly what was happening, still Stauffenberg and Haeften flew on westward towards Berlin and the men waiting for instructions at the Bendlerblock; still General Olbrecht issued no order instructing the reserve units and Berlin garrison to seize the government sector of the city. The Bendlerblock conspirators were wasting precious hours, time that could have been used to good effect even if Hitler had survived.

It was not until 3.42 p.m. that Stauffenberg finally landed in Berlin. Whilst he was waiting for a car to take him into the city, Haeften telephoned the Bendlerblock to learn how the affair was proceeding. After a few moments he was connected with General Olbrecht, from whom he learnt to his great consternation that Operation Walküre had not yet been launched; the plotters had been waiting to hear whether or not Hitler was dead. Stauffenberg then took the telephone from Haeften, and assured Olbrecht that Hitler had indeed been killed. In fact, he lied, stating that he had seen the Führer carried from the building. This at last cajoled Olbrecht into action. The operation to isolate the government sector would be undertaken immediately, he assured Stauffenberg.

Whilst Stauffenberg commandeered a Luftwaffe car and driver at Tegel airfield (his own car and driver were waiting at Rangdorf airfield) to take him and Haeften to Bendlerstrasse, Olbrecht instructed General Kortzfleisch by telephone to mobilise the Spandau garrison and move into the centre of the city. Kortzfleisch, who was not party to the plot, did as he was ordered. Next Olbrecht telephoned General von Hase, the Berlin garrison commander, and ordered him to isolate the government sector. Hase, a member of the Kreisau plot, heard the order and understood the implications; Hitler must be dead and they were launching their bid for power. By 4.10 p.m. most of the troops in the city were on the march. General Olbrecht was now undertaking the tasks that he should have performed three hours earlier. Having issued the command to mobilise the Berlin garrisons, he went to see General Fromm and urged him, as the commander of the Replacement Army, to issue the Walküre alert to all remaining troops and Panzer units in the city and its environs. But Fromm hesitated as he had been doing for months, neither entirely in nor out of the conspiracy. Deciding that discretion was the better part of valour, he stated to Olbrecht that he would issue the order only if Hitler really were dead. He placed a call through to the Wolf's Lair (communications having been restored at 4.00 p.m.) and spoke to Field Marshal Keitel, who was with Hitler in the Führer's tea house.

'Everything is as usual here,' Keitel assured him. When Fromm responded that he had received a report that the Führer had been assassinated, Keitel became angry. 'That's all nonsense,' he insisted. He went on to state that Hitler was alive and well, and had been only slightly injured. Then a thought occurred to him: 'Where, by the way, is your chief of staff,

Colonel von Stauffenberg?'[35] Fromm responded that he did not know; he had not reported in yet. He backed away from outright confrontation. He ended his call to Keitel as quickly as he could, and then made it clear to Olbrecht that he was not going to support the putsch any longer. Olbrecht withdrew from his office, deciding that nothing could be done until Stauffenberg returned. He was the only man who held sufficient sway with Fromm to make him change his mind.

Everything now hinged on Stauffenberg, the catalytic force behind the Bendlerstrasse conspirators. It had been he who had seized the initiative by boldly announcing that he would kill Hitler himself; it had been he who had introduced the notion that the Walküre plan could be used to prise Germany free from the Nazis' iron grip of totalitarian rule; it had been he who had, through his cousin, contacted the high command in France and elicited their tacit support for the Kreisau coup attempt. Now every one of the conspirators at the Bendlerblock (and it should be remembered that 90 per cent of the men serving the high command at the Bendlerstrasse were not involved in the plot) waited for his return.

All the plotters had gravitated to General Olbrecht's spacious office to await him, when someone excitedly called out from the window that he had spotted the colonel crossing the courtyard. Moments later Stauffenberg burst into Olbrecht's office like a wave of energy, enthusing everyone there with a sense of purpose and destiny. He told all the men gathered what he had heard and seen – an explosion and a pall of smoke. 'As far as one can judge,' he stated, 'Hitler is dead.'[36] He informed them that they must act decisively without wasting another moment. Even if by some cruel miracle Hitler were still alive, they should do their utmost to overthrow the regime. General Ludwig Beck, one of the leaders of the conspiracy (he was to become Germany's head of state if the coup succeeded), agreed. The die seemed cast.

At the Wolf's Lair, Hitler was by this time entertaining Mussolini. The two men had walked to the wrecked conference room, where they surveyed the damage, and Hitler explained exactly what had happened. He showed Mussolini his tattered trousers and the back of his head where his hair was singed. Mussolini was horrified. How could such a thing have taken place at the Führer's headquarters? Far from being annoyed, Hitler was exhilarated: 'What happened here today is the climax!' he exclaimed.[37] He had miraculously survived such attempts on his life before, he revealed, and he told Mussolini that this was sure proof that destiny had a great mission for him; despite the setbacks, his will would prevail, and Germany would emerge victorious.

Mussolini brightened. 'Our position is bad,' he remarked, 'one might even say desperate, but what has happened here today gives me new courage.'[38] Hitler did not tell Mussolini that he had already ordered Himmler to crush the insurrection ruthlessly and without quarter. Yet – and it was by now late afternoon – Himmler had so far taken no action to prevent the insurrection from gaining the upper hand. He had not notified the Gestapo, he had not warned his SS commands around the country, especially those in Berlin, nor had he warned his RSHA security head-quarters on Prinz Albrechtstrasse in the centre of the city. It seems he was dragging his heels, waiting to see how the situation developed before moving either to put down the coup attempt, or to step in as the 'man of the hour' once the putschists had seized control.

It seems likely that during the afternoon of Thursday, 20 July 1944, Himmler spent hours pondering the complexities of the situation. In those crucial first hours of the uprising, he apparently held fire, waiting to see what was the Circle's true strength. How deep did the coup run? Was it restricted to a few men at the Bendlerblock, or was the majority of the Wehrmacht high command involved? Did he have the resources to take over with the SS units at his disposal? Would Germany be plunged into civil war if he opposed the putsch? And, most crucially, did Hitler still hold enough power to ride out the storm? Himmler was a deep thinker, a man used to holding his own counsel. He knew that the key criterion of the putschists' attempt to usurp power had been to kill Hitler at the outset. They had failed in this key objective. Hitler was still alive and was thus a rallying point for devoted Nazis. Under such circumstances the putschists would find it very difficult to seize power. That being the case, it would be hard for him to step in and take power himself. Was it still possible for the putschists to seize control of the country? Did he have enough nerve simply to wait and see? Was he sufficiently strong to overcome the odds and usurp power in the days ahead if the coup succeeded in toppling Hitler?

As the hours wore on, no indication reached him that a putsch was taking place. It was all very puzzling. The head of the nation's security service must have had at his disposal all the intelligence that would alert him if a putsch was underway, yet by 4.00 p.m. nothing seemed to be happening. All Himmler did on that Thursday afternoon was to summon a team of criminologists from Berlin to examine the bomb-damaged confer-ence room at the Wolf's Lair.

It had been established beyond much doubt that the bomber was Claus von Stauffenberg. In his haste to depart, he had abandoned his hat and gun belt at the conference-room entrance; he had, it was known, left the Wolf's Lair without permission and fled back to Berlin. The fact that the bomber was almost certainly the Chief of Staff of the Replacement Army was an ominous sign that the attempt to assassinate Hitler had emanated from the Wehrmacht high command. If that were so, how many men were involved, and did they possess sufficient forces to plunge the country into civil war? It must have been a tense time indeed, as the men at Rastenburg waited, for very different reasons, to see what would happen.

At the Führer's tea house, Hitler's earlier optimism faded away as an endless stream of telephone calls came in from generals wanting to know if the report of his death was true. He lapsed into a suspicious silence as Göring, Ribbentrop, and Keitel began to bicker, each blaming the others for the mistakes that had resulted in Germany's desperate strategic plight. He sat silently brooding, sucking brightly coloured pills supplied by Dr Morell. The argument expanded on the arrival of Admiral Dönitz, who was quick to accuse the Army of treason. Keitel was incensed. When Göring swung his support behind Dönitz, the dapper admiral turned on him angrily, citing the miserable performance of the Luftwaffe as the main cause of Germany's woes. The loss of air superiority over France and western Europe, he claimed, had given the Allies the upper hand. At this Ribbentrop joined in, supporting Dönitz. Furious, Göring threatened Ribbentrop with his marshal's baton, as if to strike him. 'Shut up, Ribbentrop, you champagne salesman!' he shouted. Ribbentrop was not cowed. 'I'm still Foreign Minister,' he retorted, 'and my name is *von* Ribbentrop!'

Still Hitler did not stir from his brooding, ignoring the argument raging about him until Göring made mention of the failed SA/Röhm 'putsch' ten years before. At this he flew into a rage, a sensitive nerve having been touched by one of the key men who had plotted the downfall of his once close friend. 'Traitors in the bosom of their own people deserve the most ignominious of deaths – and they shall have it!' he shouted. 'Exterminate them, yes, exterminate them!'[39] The men in the tea house lapsed into an embarrassed silence.

Back at the Bendlerblock in Berlin, Stauffenberg was rousing the supporters of the coup to action. First, he placed a call to General Karl von Stülpnagel, military governor of occupied France, at his headquarters in Paris. Stauffenberg described what he had seen, the explosion and a pall of smoke. 'As far as one can judge,' he told him, 'Hitler is dead.' Stülpnagel acted with much greater efficiency than the Bendlerblock conspirators; he immediately issued orders to cut all telephone and teleprinter links between

France and Germany, except for a single secure line via which he could keep in touch with what was happening in Berlin. He also issued orders for the immediate arrest of 1,200 Gestapo agents and SS officers in Paris.

Stauffenberg decided that the next move was to bring Fromm on side. He had to be persuaded to deliver the Walküre order to the remaining troops and Panzer units of the Home Army around Berlin. Stauffenberg insisted that Hitler had been killed, but Fromm countered that he had spoken with Keitel, who had told him that the Führer was in fact still alive. 'Field Marshal Keitel is lying as usual,' Stauffenberg retorted, and proceeded to lie himself. 'I saw Hitler being carried out dead.'

At this point Olbrecht intervened in the discussion. 'In view of this,' he declared, 'we have sent out the coded signal for internal unrest to the military district commanders.' Fromm leaped from his seat and furiously banged his fist on his desk. 'This is rank insubordination,' he shouted. 'What do you mean "we"?' He insisted that the Walküre alert be cancelled with immediate effect.

Stauffenberg made one last effort. 'No one in that room can be alive,' he insisted, but Fromm could not be swayed. 'Count von Stauffenberg,' he said pompously, 'the attempt has failed. You must shoot yourself at once.' Stauffenberg was not impressed and ignored the order. At this stage Olbrecht tried to intercede again, telling Fromm that the future of Germany was at stake; an effort to oust the Nazis and make peace with the Allies had to be attempted if the Fatherland were not to be obliterated in ignominious defeat.

'Olbrecht,' Fromm asked, 'does this mean that you, too, are taking part in this coup d'état?'

Olbrecht hesitated before answering, 'Yes, sir. But I am only on the fringe of the circle.'

Fromm stared around the room at the faces of Stauffenberg, Haeften, and Olbrecht, before responding, 'Then I formally put all three of you under arrest.'

'You can't arrest us,' Olbrecht informed him. 'You don't realise who's in power. It's we who are arresting you.' And with that Fromm was bustled into an adjoining room at the point of a gun, and locked in under arrest.

By 5.00 p.m. the conspirators controlled the huge Bendlerblock, with guards posted at all its entrances. Everyone now needed a pass signed by Stauffenberg if he wished to enter or leave.

Over at the Berlin garrison, General von Hase had problems. To him had fallen the task of isolating Wilhelmstrasse, where the government sector was situated. He had ordered the Guard Battalion to seal off the area; not a general or even a government minister was allowed to cross the barriers. On being given his instructions, the commander of the Guard Battalion, Major Otto Remer, a devoted National Socialist and former Hitler Youth Leader (he would try to resurrect the Nazi Party in the 1950s), at first expressed his surprise and suspicion of the orders. Hase needed the experienced Major Remer to follow his orders without question, and so he told him that Hitler was dead, adding that the Führer had been murdered by the SS. At this news Remer became all the more suspicious. 'Who is Hitler's successor?' he asked, expressing his feeling that the whole situation sounded 'fishy'. At this Hase – a man Remer knew was not a Nazi – told him to stop asking stupid questions and just follow his orders. Remer saluted smartly and left.

On leaving Hase's office, Remer sought out his close friend Lieutenant Hans Hagen, a fellow Guard Battalion officer and a fervent and loyal Nazi; so dedicated, indeed, that it fell to him to lecture the soldiers of the Guard Battalion on the virtues of National Socialism. The two men discussed the orders emanating from Hase, and Hagen was equally distrustful of their instructions. Something just did not feel right. Concurring that the situation looked suspiciously like a military putsch, they determined to establish conclusively what was going on. Was Hitler alive or dead, and what was the purpose of ordering Operation Walküre? Was there really a civil insurrection in the city that required troops to maintain order and protect the government sector? Soon Hagen was racing across the city in a motorcycle sidecar, his destination Dr Goebbels in the Ministry of Propaganda. Surely the highest-ranking Nazi Minister in Berlin would know the truth, would know whether the Führer was alive or dead. In the meantime Major Remer had no option other than to follow Hase's orders, but he adjured Lieutenant Hagen to hurry.

It was now shortly after 5.00 p.m. Hagen did not take long to reach the Ministry of Propaganda, where chaos seemed to rule. No one knew what was happening. Albert Speer (Hitler's architect and chief of the Todt organisation) had arrived to inform Goebbels that he had seen machine-gun-toting troops setting up a post at the Brandenburg Gate in the centre of the city, several hundred metres away. Soldiers of the Guard Battalion were establishing themselves outside the other ministries on Wilhelmstrasse. Lieutenant Hagen found a very nervous Goebbels on the telephone questioning party officials about what was taking place. The news was that troops from Potsdam and the provincial garrisons were marching on the city. This was alarming, but Goebbels – master of the spoken word – was much heartened by the news that the putschists had not had the wit to take over the radio station. This gave him an opportunity to talk to the people of the Reich and reassure them that Hitler was still very much alive and in control. It was a devastating oversight by the Bendlerblock conspirators, but they were military men who understood only military tactics and objectives. They were not versed in the consummate media skills required in controlling a nation.

Hagen told Goebbels about the orders Major Remer had received from General von Hase, and informed him of Hase's insistence that Hitler was dead. Goebbels immediately understood the implications: this was a military coup by certain officers of the Wehrmacht. Shaken, he told Hagen to return at once to Remer and summon him to the Propaganda Ministry for a meeting. If the two men were not back in half an hour, he would assume that Remer was either a traitor or was being held by force by the men attempting to wrest control of the state from the Nazi Party, and he would order the SS into the city to seize the headquarters of the Berlin garrison. Lieutenant Hagen departed in great haste to find Major Remer and summon him an urgent meeting with Goebbels.

Just as Hagen was leaving – at exactly 5.30 p.m. – Goebbels was called to the telephone. It was Hitler, who urged him to make an urgent broadcast to the nation assuring them that he was alive and well. The Führer, it seems, was by now aware of the precariousness of his position, knew that despite his orders to Himmler, an insurrection seemed to be gaining the upper hand in his capital. Goebbels immediately telephoned the text of a broadcast to the radio station, where it was intercepted by troops of the infantry school who had just occupied the premises. Despite their orders to maintain the normal daily schedule and prevent any government broadcasts, the captain of infantry in charge was so overawed at finding himself speaking to the Minister of Propaganda that he agreed to let the radio announcer make the broadcast.

In the meantime Major Remer was becoming increasingly troubled by his orders. He was sure that the whole situation smelled of treason, and that he had unwittingly been drawn into a putsch. Yet he was a career army officer, and until he heard otherwise he would continue to follow his orders from General von Hase. Since the departure of his close friend Hagen he had dispatched his men across the city, visiting their various positions to ensure that it was secure. Eventually he returned to the headquarters of the Berlin garrison to speak with Hase, and it was here at 6.40 p.m. that

Hagen eventually caught up with him. He informed Remer of his meeting with Dr Goebbels, and told him that Hitler was still alive. This is civil war, Remer thought, and he took Hagen upstairs to repeat to Hase the details of the meeting.[40] Hase pretended to be alarmed at the news, but told Remer it was his duty to go to the Ministry of Propaganda and arrest Goebbels. Remer was now positive that a putsch was taking place and that he was being deceived. As he left Hase's office he remarked to Hagen, 'Well, now I've got to gamble for my life.'[41] He rounded up twenty soldiers and set off for the Ministry of Propaganda in a truck.

It was 7.00 p.m. before he arrived, nearly an hour and a half after Hagen had met with Goebbels. He was immediately ushered into Goebbels's presence, and the Minister was very pleased to see him. Remer did not tell Goebbels that he had been sent to arrest him, but approached the meeting with an open mind, determined not to be an unwitting tool of the putschists. He told Goebbels that he would put himself at the disposal of the Party, but only after he had spoken to Hitler and was assured that he was still alive.

'As you wish, Major,' retorted Goebbels, who ordered that a call be put through to the Führer at Rastenburg. Within a few minutes the Propaganda Minister was talking to Hitler, telling him that he had with him an officer of the Guard Battalion who wished to speak to him. He passed the receiver over to Remer, who nervously heard the Führer ask, 'Are you on the line, Major Remer? What are you doing now?' It certainly sounded like Hitler, and Remer briefly gave him an account of his orders and his actions of the past few hours. Hitler listened intently before telling Remer that he was giving him complete authority to protect the state and the security of the government. 'Do whatever you think necessary. Every officer, regardless of rank, is now under your command.' Until now, such authority had been held only by Himmler, the head of state security. Remer was ordered to reinstate order immediately, 'If necessary by brutal armed force.' Hitler ended by promoting Remer to colonel, telling him that from then on, 'you are responsible only to me.'[42]

Remer set up a command centre at the Ministry of Propaganda, near to Goebbels. He put a telephone call through to General von Hase instantly, summoning him to report at once. 'Since when does a general come trotting to a little major?' Hase retorted indignantly. 'General, if you don't want to come, I will have you arrested,' replied Remer, and put the telephone down. Next he telephoned all the military units and garrisons in Berlin and its environs, telling the commanders that they were now under his sole command. No one dissented, and everyone fell into line. The blockade of the government sector was lifted, though the troops remained at their posts to protect the government offices.

Within half an hour a subdued General von Hase arrived at the Ministry of Propaganda, and was escorted to where Goebbels and Remer were waiting for him. No longer angry, he was instead so full of praise for Remer that it seemed for a moment that he was on the point of embracing his subordinate. He spoke briefly with Goebbels, asking whether it would be all right if he now left to find something to eat and telephone his wife. Goebbels, full of condescension, said he could do so. 'There go our revolutionaries,' he then remarked sarcastically to Remer. 'All they think about is eating, drinking, and calling up Mamma.'[43]

Even during the evening, Himmler did nothing. He left his field headquarters near the Wolf's Lair, bound for Berlin in his private aircraft, but up to this point he had taken no decisive action whatsoever. He had not ordered the Gestapo into action to arrest the Wehrmacht conspirators at the Bendlerstrasse, he had not placed his SS units around Berlin on alert, he had not authorised the RSHA to act in concert with Remer to destroy the insurrection. It seemed he was still waiting until it became clear who had the upper hand.

Meanwhile, over at the Bendlerblock, confusion still reigned. Telephone calls came in all evening from commanders who had received the Walküre alert; they wanted to speak to Fromm for confirmation of Hitler's death. Stauffenberg intercepted the calls, telling them that Fromm was otherwise engaged. He reaffirmed to the men that the Führer was dead, assuring them, if they were members of the conspiracy, that the insurrection would still succeed.

A little before 8.00 p.m. one of the leaders of the conspiracy, retired Field Marshal Erwin von Witzleben (formerly Commander-in-Chief of Army West), donned his full dress uniform and travelled to the Bendlerblock. As soon as he arrived he issued a communiqué to all Wehrmacht commands in the Reich, stating:

> The Führer, Adolf Hitler, is dead. An unscrupulous clique of non-combatant party leaders utilising this situation, has attempted to stab our fighting forces in the back and seize power for their own purpose.
>
> In this hour of extreme danger the Government of the Reich, to maintain law and order, has decreed a military state of emergency and placed me in supreme command of the German Armed Forces . . .[44]

It was an assertion that carried no weight whatsoever. The Bendlerblock conspirators did not hold a single government department. Their primary supporters were the high command in France. At a meeting held in Paris that evening, Field Marshal von Kluge, Commander-in-Chief of German forces in France, proposed an immediate armistice in the west and a cessation of V1 rocket attacks on London as a sign of good faith, if in return the Allies agreed to stop bombing Germany. Within half an hour of taking this stance, he received an urgent telegram from Keitel informing him that Hitler was alive and well, and that any orders from the traitorous Witzleben–Beck group at the Bendlerblock were to be ignored. Alarmed, Kluge ordered that a call be made to the Wolf's Lair to establish once and for all whether or not Hitler was still alive. After a fraught half-hour he managed to get through, only to learn that Hitler had indeed survived the bomb attempt. Dejected, he put the telephone down and remarked to his men, 'Well, the attempt on his life has failed.' That ended the affair for the Field Marshal. 'Gentlemen,' he said, 'leave me out of the question!' The Wehrmacht high command in France would play no further part in the conspiracy.

Back in Berlin, everything was still chaos and confusion at the Bendlerblock. Erwin von Witzleben, having been at Bendlerstrasse a brief hour, resigned from the conspiracy in disgust. Disregarding Stauffenberg's and Beck's pleas for him to remain, he marched out of the building, climbed into his car, and ordered his driver to take him straight home.

It was at this point that Himmler's SD were at last motivated into playing a part in putting down the insurrection. Otto Skorzeny, a colonel with Amt VI serving under Schellenberg, was boarding a train to Vienna at Anhalt station when he was stopped by a junior officer sent to catch him up. He told Skorzeny about the coup attempt mounted by members of the Wehrmacht high command, and instructed him to report to Schellenberg at the SD's Prinz Albrechtstrasse headquarters. Skorzeny was one of the adventurers of the Third Reich, a man with a reputation for reckless courage that made him Hitler's favourite commando. It had been Skorzeny, with his crack team, who in September 1943 had rescued Mussolini from the Gran Sasso d'Italia, high in the Abruzzi Apennines. Skorzeny rushed back to Prinz Albrechtstrasse to find Schellenberg seated behind his desk with his pistol in front of him, looking very pale. It is not clear whether he had received any orders from Himmler, but the involvement of the SD at this juncture, under the orders of Schellenberg, makes it likely that at last the Reichsführer had been galvanised into taking action. It was now after 8.00 p.m. and the putsch was beginning to unravel at the seams.

'The situation is obscure and dangerous,' Schellenberg said to Skorzeny. He motioned to his pistol: 'I'll defend myself here if they come this way!' Skorzeny laughed at the ridiculous picture presented by Schellenberg, and advised him to put his gun away before he had an accident and shot himself.

Under Schellenberg's orders, Skorzeny placed one of his crack sabotage units on alert in the outskirts of the city. He then left to ascertain the degree of insurrection in the capital; the government sector looked calm enough, and he departed to visit a Waffen-SS barracks at Lichterfeld. Again everything was quiet, and so he travelled on to the paratroop head-quarters at Wannsee. Here he found General Kurt Student in his dressing gown poring over paperwork, his wife seated with him sewing. Student refused to believe that an armed insurrection was taking place, until he received an urgent telephone call from Göring confirming that Skorzeny spoke the truth and there was indeed trouble in the city. He then mobilised his troops whilst Skorzeny rushed back to Schellenberg. No sooner had he arrived than Schellenberg received a call from General Jodl at the Wolf's Lair with Hitler. 'How many men have you?' Jodl asked him. One company, replied Skorzeny. 'Good,' retorted Jodl. 'Take them to the Bendlerstrasse and support Major Remer and his Guard Battalion, who have just been ordered to surround the building.' The time was 10.30 p.m.

At the Bendlerblock the situation was becoming ever more desperate. On mounting the insurrection, General Olbrecht had summoned a company of the Guard Battalion to surround the building and protect it. These troops had now suddenly all vanished, leaving the Bendlerblock completely vulnerable. Stauffenberg managed to find thirty-five men of the high command, whom he sent to the main entrance to defend the conspir-ators from any interference. It was, however, becoming increasingly clear that the coup was collapsing before their eyes. They had lost touch with the units in Berlin because the telephone lines had been interrupted at the exchange. Someone was making a concerted move to isolate the building. Worse yet, there was growing dissension inside from men of the high command who had nothing to do with the putsch and were demanding to know what was happening. Stauffenberg and his little band of supporters were increasingly beleaguered, isolated from the city and under scrutiny from their Bendlerblock colleagues. He ordered his supporters to man the six exits of the building and allow no one to enter or leave. With much reluctance, they obeyed their superior's orders.

At 10.50 p.m. a small group of armed men at the Bendlerblock – eight in all – secretly determined to stand by their oath to the Führer. They had come to the conclusion that Olbrecht and Stauffenberg were indeed mounting a military putsch, and were aggrieved that General Fromm was obviously being held against his will in an anteroom off Olbrecht's office. They well realised that when the putsch failed – as it was sure to do – they would be held to be as guilty as its instigators if they did not make a real effort to topple Olbrecht, Beck, and Stauffenberg. In short order the eight, armed with grenades and submachine guns, stormed Olbrecht's office. They caught all the plotters in the room by surprise, holding them at gunpoint until Fromm could be liberated.

'Well, gentlemen,' said Fromm, armed now with a pistol, 'I am now going to treat you as you treated me.' He ordered them all to lay down their weapons.

'You wouldn't demand that of me, your former commanding officer?' asked General Beck. 'I will draw the consequences from this unhappy situation myself.' And with that he picked up his pistol. Warned by Fromm to keep the pistol pointed at himself, he tried to diminish the tension in the room, saying, 'At a time like this I think of the old days . . .'

'We don't want to hear about that now,' Fromm interrupted, cutting him short. 'I ask you to stop talking and do something.'

Beck mumbled something to himself, pointed the gun at his head and fired. Unbelievably, he failed to kill himself, merely grazing the top of his head; he reeled back and slumped in a chair.

'Help the old gentleman,' an irritated Fromm told two junior officers. He turned to face the men in the room. 'Now, gentlemen,' he told them. 'If you have any letters to write, you may have a few minutes to do so.' With that he left the room, leaving them under guard. General Fromm was in a difficult position; he had himself been party to the conspiracy, and he must have known that once in the hands of the Gestapo all the men would talk. They would tell everything they knew, including the fact that he had initially supported the plan. As head of the Replacement Army, he was a leading man of the Wehrmacht high command, a key member of the putschists, even if he had backed away from decisive involvement at the last minute. That information must be kept from the security services at all costs if he were not to be condemned and shot, too. Anything he could do now to destroy the putsch would stand him in good stead when the time came to answer some very uncomfortable questions. Determined to act whilst he still had the chance, he returned to Olbrecht's office less than five minutes later to tell the leading putschists that a court-marshal 'in the name of the Führer' had pronounced a death sentence on them all. That sentence was to be carried out with immediate effect.

Beck, blood running down his head, asked for a weapon and permission to take his own life. Fromm nodded his agreement, and Beck was taken into the anteroom and once more given a pistol. As the door was being closed, he said in a small voice, 'If it doesn't work this time, please help me.' After a few moments there was the loud report of a shot. Fromm looked in to discover that Beck had failed yet again. 'Help the old gentleman,' he again told a junior officer, who refused. A sergeant took the lead; he went into the room and shot Beck through the neck. The general died instantly.

This task accomplished, and arrangements having been already made, the four leading putschists – General Olbrecht, Colonel von Stauffenberg, Lieutenant von Haeften, and Colonel Mertz von Quirnheim – were taken into the courtyard where the headlights of a lorry floodlit the back wall. They were lined up and executed. At the order to fire, Stauffenberg shouted, 'Long live sacred Germany!'[45] Even as the men fell to the ground, a teleprinter message was being dispatched to the Wolf's Lair: 'Attempted putsch by irresponsible generals crushed. All ringleaders shot . . .'

•••••

At the very moment that Fromm was executing the leaders of the putsch, Himmler arrived at the Ministry of Propaganda. 'Shoot anyone who resists,' Hitler had told him some hours before, 'no matter who it is.' Before going to see Goebbels, he had been to his headquarters on Prinz Albrechtstrasse, ordering the Gestapo to arrest and detain anyone suspected in any way of being a member of the resistance or of being complicit in the putsch. To Goebbels's assistant, Dr Werner Naumann, Himmler seemed indifferent to the crushing of the uprising, whereas Goebbels himself was exhilarated. From the way the Minister of Propaganda described the events of the day, one might be mistaken in believing that it was he who had single-handedly put down the rebellion. The placid Himmler nodded politely as he listened to Goebbels's account, without revealing that he had already unleashed the terror of a counterputsch and set up the machinery for a special investigation of the conspiracy.

Whereas Goebbels was satisfied in putting down the uprising itself – by midnight Remer and Skorzeny were in control of the Bendlerblock and General Fromm was under arrest (his last-minute gambit to kill the leading putschists and exonerate himself failed to protect him) – Himmler was more thorough in his destruction of the resistance. In the days and weeks ahead hundreds of men – the core of opposition to the Nazis in Germany – would be arrested, ranging from lowly civilian supporters to the generals of the Wehrmacht. General von Kluge in France committed suicide within a few weeks; General von Stülpnagel attempted suicide but failed and was brought before the Volksgericht for treason. The most eminent man to fall foul of Himmler's purge of the Wehrmacht high command would be none other than Field Marshal Erwin Rommel, who in October 1944 was compelled to commit suicide rather than face the ignominy of a court-martial and execution.

Himmler's rout of the Kreisau Circle and anti-Nazi resistance was merciless. Men and women alike found themselves submitted to the rigours of interrogation at the hands of the Gestapo, before a show trial in front of the dreaded Volksgericht. In almost every case the defendant was found guilty and executed. Even Field Marshal von Witzleben stood before the court; he was condemned to death and executed the same day. Himmler's purge of Nazi Germany was thorough and complete, and no one was safe. It was a terror that seemed to go on without end, and many in Germany lived in fear of the purge until the traumatic last days of the Reich. It is estimated that Himmler's investigation into the 20 July bomb plot resulted in the deaths of over 500 men and women, depriving Germany of many of its leading civil servants, economists, foreign affairs experts, politicians, and military men, all of whom would have made a significant contribution to the formation of a post-war German government.

In the event Himmler was the undoubted beneficiary of the failed attempt on Hitler's life. In addition to his multiple powers and incursions into every aspect of German existence, Hitler made him Chief of Army Armaments and Commander of the Replacement Army in place of the disgraced General Fromm (who would be tried and executed in March 1945).

His role in the plot, however, remains mysterious. On the afternoon of 20 July his masseur, Felix Kersten, visited his office to find him busily burning documents. For nearly two years he had been in touch with the British through Victor Mallet in Sweden. He had made it known to the British – meaning the Political Warfare Executive – that he was prepared to support a 'third party coup attempt' and step in at the last moment as 'the man of the hour'.[46] Along with Guderian and Fromm, he had given Stauffenberg (a man of fervent anti-Hitler beliefs) his head, to see what would result. After the coup attempt failed and Himmler eventually launched his counterputsch, he unerringly managed to arrest all the ringleaders within days. No lengthy investigation was necessary. His intelligence service, it would appear, had already infiltrated the faction, and he probably knew all about the scheme well before Stauffenberg made his attempt to kill Hitler. Should this be the case, then one can only view Himmler's destruction of the anti-Nazi resistance in the subsequent months with great cynicism. It was the calculated act of a man biding his time whilst the Reich fell into wrack and ruin, until the moment came for him to take the lead.

We know that this was Himmler's ultimate objective. He was aware by the spring of 1944 that Germany would eventually be defeated; he was also aware that all he needed to do until the end of the war was to sit tight and await its conclusion, whilst at the same time making clear his peaceful intentions to the Allies. The only trouble was that the PWE had no intention of letting him ride out the storm.

NOTES

1. Louis L. Snyder, *Encyclopaedia of the Third Reich* (Wordsworth Editions, 1998), p. 169.
2. Gitta Sereny, *Albert Speer: His Battle with the Truth* (Knopf, 1997), p. 309.
3. Ibid.
4. Karl Neuer interview, Telfs, Austria, 23 December 2003.
5. Ibid.
6. Doc. No. FO 800/868, National Archives, Kew, London.
7. Ibid.
8. Ibid.
9. Doc. No. HS 8/944, National Archives, Kew, London.
10. Hugh Thomas, *SS-1* (Fourth Estate, 2001), p. 68; Peter Allen, conversation with Peter Tennant, April 1968.
11. Peter Allen, conversation with Peter Tennant, April 1968.
12. Ibid.
13. Ibid.
14. Winston S. Churchill, *The Second World War* (Cassell, 1956), Vol. VI, p. 21.
15. Ian Kershaw, *Hitler, 1889–1936: Hubris (1st volume); Hitler, 1936–1945: Nemesis (2nd volume)*,(Penguin, 2000) p. 640.
16. Die Tagebücher von Joseph Goebbels. Teil II, Vol. 12, p. 418. quoted Kershaw, op. cit., p. 640.
17. Schwerin von Krosigk, *Es geschah in Deutschland* (Tübingen, 1952), p. 346.
18. Peter Padfield, *Himmler, Reichsführer-SS* (Cassell, 2001), p. 491.
19. Snyder, op. cit., p. 332.
20. Doc. No. FO 800/868, National Archives, Kew, London.
21. Ibid.
22. Padfield, op. cit., p. 491.
23. H. Kaiser's diary, 20 February, 1943. Imperial War Museum, AL 911.
24. Padfield, op. cit., p. 491.

25. Internet site: www.joric.com/Conspiracy/Cstauffenberg.htm.
26. John Toland, *Adolf Hitler* (Doubleday, 1976), p. 793.
27. H. Royce (ed.), *20 Juli 1944* (Berto-Verlag, 1952), p. 92.
28. Padfield, op. cit., p. 495.
29. A. Cave-Brown, *Bodyguard of Lies* (Star, 1977), pp. 740–41.
30. Toland, op. cit., p. 797.
31. Ibid.
32. Traudl Junge interview, Munich, 20 November 2001.
33. Ibid.
34. Cited Toland, op. cit., p. 811.
35. Ibid., p. 803.
36. Ibid.
37. Ibid., p. 801.
38. Ibid.
39. Ibid., p. 802.
40. Ibid., p. 805.
41. Cited Toland, op. cit., p. 805.
42. Ibid., p. 806.
43. Ibid.
44. Ibid., p. 807.
45. Cited Toland, op. cit., p. 809.
46. Doc. No. FO 800/868, National Archives, Kew, London.

7
OPERATION SUNRISE

In the first week of November 1944, British Intelligence submitted a report to the government (and primarily, therefore, for Churchill's eyes) on a top-secret SS-sponsored meeting that had taken place in Strasbourg the previous August. The gathering had been spied upon by an experienced member of the French Deuxième Bureau, who informed London of what he had discovered. It is evident from this report that despite the Nazi Party's best efforts to hide its intentions, by 1944 it was so effectively infiltrated by Allied Intelligence that nothing it decided to do would remain a secret for very long. It is also clear that many leading Nazis believed by August 1944 that the war was lost and that preparations were necessary for what would come next.

Modern Strasbourg is at the fulcrum of the European Union. Back in 1944, however, it was a city of dual personality. Ceded to France and at the centre of Alsace and Lorraine, it had become very French, with a heart and soul that had much in common with the other great cities of France. With the invasion of 1940, the Germans had determined to wrest Strasbourg back into the German fold. Despite vehement protests from Marshal Pétain's Vichy government, ever since 1941 the Germans had been organising mass deportations of French citizens back to France and transplanting large numbers of Germans from the Saar region.

At the heart of Strasbourg lay the cosmopolitan square of Place Kléber, complete with a statue of the French national hero General Jean-Baptist Kléber. Within the square stood the magnificent Hôtel de la Maison Rouge (the Red House), renamed the Grand Hotel Rotes Haus by the conquering Germans in 1940. Strasbourg had so far seemed to live a charmed and peaceful life in war-torn Europe. It had not been damaged during the German invasion, and had thus far escaped Allied bombing. That was until the night of 10 August 1944, the very evening of a high-level meeting of

German industrialists at the Hotel Rotes Haus. The bombing of central Strasbourg very late that night was no coincidence. The British authorities had learnt of the meeting, and were determined to cause as much disruption to it as possible. As luck would have it, the German industrialists met early in the evening, and so the British bombing of the Hotel Rotes Haus caused little inconvenience.

Prior to the bombing, however, the gathering had been brought to order in the Rotes Haus conference room by Dr Scheid, Obergruppenführer of the SS and a director of the Hece (Hermadorff and Schonburg) Company.[1] Present were Dr Kaspar, representative of Krupp; Dr Tolle, representing Rochling; Dr Sinceren, representing Messerschmitt; Drs Kopp, Vier, and Beerwanger of Rheinmetall; Captain Haberkorn and Dr Ruhe of Bussing; and Drs Ellenmayer and Kardos of Volkswagen. There were also three leading engineers named Drose, Yanchew, and Koppshen, representing various factories in Posen; Captain Dornbusch, head of the Industrial Inspection Section at Posen; Dr Meyer of the German Naval Ministry; and Dr Strossner of the Ministry of Armaments.[2]

The purpose of the meeting was soon made plain to all those present. Scheid began by informing them that

> From now on German industry must realise that the war cannot be won and that it must take steps in preparation for a post-war commercial campaign. Each industrialist must make contacts with foreign firms, but this must be done individually and without attracting any suspicion . . . the ground must be laid on the financial level for the borrowing [of] considerable sums from foreign countries after the war.

Such penetration of overseas economies had been most useful in the past. Scheid cited some examples, pointing out that:

> patents for stainless steel belonged to the Chemical Foundation, Inc., New York, and the Krupp Company of Germany jointly and that the U.S. Steel Corporation, Carnegie, Illinois, American Steel and Wire, and National Tube, etc. were thereby under an obligation to work with the Krupp concern. He also cited the Zeiss Company, the Leica Company, and the Hamburg-American Line as firms which had been especially effective in protecting German interests abroad, and gave their New York addresses to the industrialists at the meeting.[3]

The meeting lasted a little over an hour. Afterwards another was held, chaired this time by a certain Dr Bosse, a Nazi civil servant from the German Armaments Ministry. Scheid was again present, for this gathering, too, was sponsored by the SS. 'At this second meeting it was stated that the war was practically lost, but that it would continue until a guarantee of the unity of Germany could be obtained.' After making this statement Bosse informed the gathered industrialists, all confirmed Nazis, that 'they must also prepare themselves to finance the recovery of the Nazi Party, which would be forced to go underground as Maquis'[4] – political guerillas – until the moment for a recovery of power took place. As he went on to inform them:

> From now on the government would allocate large sums to these industrialists so that each could establish a secure post-war foundation in foreign countries. Existing financial reserves in foreign countries must be placed at the disposal of the [Nazi] Party so that a strong German Empire can be created after defeat.[5]

After enumerating this plan for the financial recovery of the Party so that it could once again seize power in a defeated Germany, Drs Bosse and Scheid explained a scheme to protect the Nazis' firm foothold in practical industry. Scheid instructed the industrialists that the Nazis

> immediately required that the large factories in Germany create small technical offices or research bureaus which would be absolutely independent and have no known connection with the factory. These bureaus will receive plans and drawings of new weapons as well as documents which they need to continue their research and which must not be allowed to fall into the hands of the enemy . . .

At this point Dr Bosse took over and informed everyone how this was to be done:

> these offices are to be established in large cities where they can be most successfully hidden as well as in little villages near sources of hydro-electric power, where they can pretend to be studying the development of water resources.

Scheid concluded the meeting with the following declaration:

> The existence of these is to be known only to a very few
> people in each industry and by chiefs of the Nazi Party. Each
> office will have a liaison agent with the Party. As soon as the Party
> becomes strong enough to re-establish its control over Germany
> the industrialists will be paid for their effort and cooperation by
> concessions and orders.[6]

Apart from confirming the extent to which Allied Intelligence had infiltrated the Nazi Party by 1944, this British Intelligence report makes two
things clear. It indicates the Nazis' intent to rise again to the political fore
in post-war Germany; and it makes plain that in the summer of 1944,
having already decided that the war was lost, they were busy putting in
place the means by which they might once again rise to power.

In the 1920s and 1930s the Nazis had been careful to woo Germany's
biggest industrialists. Once they took power they had been keen to infil-
trate successful industrial concerns, either by recruiting their top men
into the SS (many were already card-carrying Nazis) or by placing high-
ranking SS men on their boards. The Nazi Party – and, as we have seen,
Himmler, through his Freundeskreis-RFSS – had always maintained
close links with the major industries in Germany. It was a symbiotic relationship. The leading industrialists, those in charge of companies such as
Krupps and IG Farben, had played a key role in bringing the Nazi Party
to power in 1933. Since that time the Nazis had repaid them many
hundredfold in government contracts.

As Himmler's representatives, SS-Obergruppenfuhrer Scheid and Dr
Bose, were explaining to these leading industrialists, gathered together at
the Rotes Haus, the Nazi Party had now decided to strip the economic
wealth out of Germany before the Allies could acquire it in reparations,
as had happened at the end of the First World War. Himmler had
decided to remove this wealth – in effect the primary means of German
economic recovery in the post-war years – overseas as a means of
preserving the Nazi Party's, and thus his own, economic ability to regain
power after the war. It was proposed that the Party, and primarily the SS,
would pump money into such companies to be invested overseas, so as
to assist in safeguarding their assets in Germany from the Allies. In
return for this, the Nazis demanded that industry would finance the
recovery of the Nazi Party in a post-war Germany of the latter 1940s and

early 1950s. As reward, Scheid and Bose promised, the new Nazi Party that would be brought back to power after the end of the war would again favour these companies with lucrative contracts.

This would be a very dangerous development, one that the British government could not allow to take place, especially once it became evident that the SS was primarily behind the scheme. As the British Intelligence report made clear:

> These meetings [at the Rotes Haus] seem to indicate that the prohibition against the export of capital which was rigorously enforced until now has been completely withdrawn and replaced by a new Nazi policy whereby industrialists with government assistance will export as much of their capital as possible . . . The Nazi party now stands behind the industrialists and urges them to save themselves by getting funds outside Germany and at the same time to advance the [Nazi] Party's plans for its post-war operations. This freedom given to the industrialists further cements their relationship with the Party . . .[7]

The report concluded:

> This 'underground' which will keep the Nazi fire burning will be nourished and supported by the trustees of German heavy industry and the trustees of German economic and financial interests within and outside Germany. They are the true underground.[8]

This economic strategy confirms once again Himmler's awareness that the war was lost. However, it also reveals much more. He evidently believed that the same conditions would prevail again at the end of the current conflict as had pertained after the First World War; in other words, the Allies would demand massive reparations but would otherwise leave Germany to put her own political house in order. In 1919–20 this policy had allowed politicians in office during the First World War to retain their positions of authority when the Weimar Republic was established. The Nazis therefore believed – having only the end of the First World War and the 1919–20 situation as a comparison – that they, too, would be able to recover political power after the war. In Nazi logic this meant sowing the seeds of their economic recovery with Germany's industrial giants well before the final collapse came about.

Since the British were well aware of these secret Nazi plans, they were later able to take effective action against them. The Allied Control Commission that was established in occupied Germany after the war made great efforts to detail in full German industrialists' attempts to hide their assets. In any case, Germany was in such a state of total industrial and economic collapse at the end of the war that the endeavours of such companies as IG Farben and Krupps were completely wasted.

The Nazis – primarily the SS – also made efforts to secrete money in countries such as Switzerland and Argentina. These were largely successful, and many millions in foreign currency and gold bullion were never recovered.[9] It is known that much Nazi money found its way to Switzerland, Spain, and especially across the Atlantic to Argentina and Paraguay. It was therefore no coincidence that many Nazis fled to South America – particularly to Argentina and Paraguay – after the war; fled to where the money was. It is also now known that Eva Peron's 'Rainbow Tour' of Europe in mid-1947, two years after the end of the war, was a smokescreen to hide the fact that she was meeting with eminent former Nazis who had placed large sums of money in Argentina. She even met secretly with Otto Skorzeny, rescuer of Mussolini, in Madrid to discuss the exodus of Nazis to build new lives there. And one of those top-level Nazis was Adolf Eichmann, architect of the Holocaust, a man with the blood of six million people on his hands.[10]

But what the Nazis failed to foresee was that the Allies would declare the Nazi Party an illegal – criminal – organisation. Not only would Germany undergo extensive denazification, but the leaders of Nazism – at least those who were caught (it should be remembered that many less prominent party members fled abroad and were never captured) – would be banned from holding public office for the rest of their lives.

In mid-August of 1944 no one in Germany could have guessed accurately what would be the ultimate outcome of the war. It was certain only that it was lost, and the time had come to prepare for the future. However, Himmler's attempt to prepare the way for the post-war recovery of the Nazis was not his sole course of action in 1944. He began to see with sudden and startling clarity that if he was to save himself and ensure his much-desired post-war political future, he had to distance himself from the horrors of the Holocaust and appear a moderate amongst the evils of the Reich. As a result in the months ahead he would strive to make political deals not only with the Allies, but also with his avowed racial enemies as well.

•••••

The summer and autumn of 1944 brought a litany of disasters for Germany. Just five days after the Rotes Haus meeting in Strasbourg, Allied forces landed largely unopposed in the south of France. A week later there was a coup d'état in Romania and the country surrendered to the Russians; in one swift move Germany had lost both a valuable ally against the Soviet Union and an essential source of oil from Romania's Bukovina oilfields. Ten days later the Finns signed an armistice with the Russians and yet another ally fell away. As a result Russia was able to transfer much-needed troops from the conflict with Finland to the front against the Germans in Poland. On 12 September Allied forces in the west managed to invade their first tract of German territory near the Rhine, and within a few days yet another German ally, Bulgaria, signed an armistice with the Allies. It was a sign of the beginning of the end. Yet still Dr Goebbels's stream of hate and propaganda flowed, claiming that the war might yet be won with the new wonder weapons now coming off the production lines. In some degree this was true: Britain had in September been the first country in the world to be struck by a ballistic missile – the V2, which possessed tremendous destructive power. However, though ideal for hitting an enormous target like London, it was too inaccurate to do any real damage to the British war effort.

It was against this backdrop that Himmler renewed his efforts to make a peace deal with the Allies. Schellenberg and Krämer were still talking to Victor Mallet in Stockholm, but now a scheme began to form in the Reichsführer's mind to force the British to the negotiating table. It was a trait of the Nazi psyche to follow a carrot-and-stick approach to negotiations – seductive inducements in one hand, threat in the other. Himmler now began to see the threat as a way of establishing a second line of communication to the British.

In late October he secretly instructed his close friend SS-General Karl Wolff, German military governor of north Italy and plenipotentiary to Mussolini, to see if he could open a line to the Allies in Switzerland. It was of course to be an extremely covert action; Himmler greatly feared the possibility that the approach might become known to Bormann, Goebbels, or Ribbentrop, who would certainly inform Hitler. After mulling the notion over for a few days, Wolff took his police chief in northern Italy into his confidence. This was SS-Obergruppenführer Dr Wilhelm Harster, who informed Wolff that he knew just the man for so sensitive an undertaking. A close acquaintance of Harster, he was named Franco Marinotti, an Italian industrialist with major industrial and political contacts in Britain.

Thus Marinotti became Himmler's latest go-between with the Allies, and at a meeting held at Harster's villa on Lake Como on 24 October, the middle-aged Italian industrialist was drawn into the plot. The offer that Marinotti was to make to the British was somewhat basic when compared with Schellenberg's more delicate negotiations with Victor Mallet previously, but many things had changed now that Germany was most definitely losing the war, and held less in her hand with which to bargain. Essentially, Wolff's and Harster's bid to open negotiation was an undisguised mixture of Nazi blackmail and appeals to self-interest. Marinotti was instructed to inform the British that the western business community was in dire peril from the invading Russians; once they managed to encroach upon western Europe, they would turn it into a series of Communist states and then destroy western commercial interests. Wolff and Harster also issued a threat that Marinotti was to pass on to the Allies, which was that Hitler had decided upon a scorched-earth policy as his forces withdrew into Germany. The Führer had given orders that every industrial plant and factory was to be raised to the ground as his forces were driven back, leaving nothing with which to begin the enormous task of post-war recovery.

At this point Wolff and Harster offered their carrot. They told Franco Marinotti to inform the British that they could offer twenty-five divisions in Italy to maintain order in central Europe, preserving industry, preventing civil insurrection, and staving off Communist infiltration. This offer, they said, was made 'with the approval of the Reichsführer Himmler'. In return, all Himmler requested was that the Allies should end the bombing campaign against Germany, and guarantee the inviolability of the German Reich and its population (i.e. agree not to invade Germany), leading to a mutually agreeable armistice.[11]

Just under a week after his meeting with SS General Wolff and SS-Obergruppenführer Harster, Franco Marinotti crossed the border into Switzerland on 30 October. Once there, it took him a few days to obtain a meeting with the British Consul in Zurich. He finally gained an audience on 3 November, and spent a long time explaining in great detail the peace offer that had emanated from the Reichsführer-SS. Marinotti's primary concern was that the offer must remain absolutely top secret and must not be used for propaganda purposes; such a disclosure would be catastrophic, for Himmler was in a very delicate position. Hitler must not find out about the offer until agreement had been reached, by which time Himmler would possess sufficient power in the Reich to force it through.

The Consul forwarded the approach to London, but the almost instantaneous reply was that the British would not negotiate with Himmler. This stance may seem at odds with what we know to have been taking place in Stockholm, but it must be remembered that Marinotti's peace approach was made through the British Foreign Office, the head of which – Anthony Eden – had no intention of negotiating with a leading Nazi. In Stockholm, Schellenberg and Krämer, through Victor Mallet, were talking to the Political Warfare Executive, and Brendan Bracken still had every intention of using these negotiations to undermine the Nazi regime. The July plot to cause a coup d'état in Germany had failed, but there might even now be some advantage to be won from keeping the line of communication open between PWE and the head of the SS.

Hearing that his bid to open negotiations with the British had failed, Franco Marinotti was determined to make one more effort before he returned to Italy to report to General Wolff and Obergruppen-führer Harster. On 7 November, through the auspices of the Papal Nuncio in Berne, Marinotti met with President Roosevelt's head of intelligence in Switzerland, Allen Dulles. However, their meeting passed off with equal lack of success.[12]

Himmler's continuing failure to understand the loathing his name inspired amongst the western Allies was largely due to his National Socialist perspective on the world, undoubtedly intensified by the wishful thinking that he might become the saviour of his beloved Germany. He had long believed that much of the Allies' hatred of him was the result of propaganda whipped up by the Jews around Roosevelt and Churchill; once western financiers woke up to the terrible danger that Bolshevism posed to Europe, such a change of opinion would take place that the British and American press would soon be hailing him and the SS as the saviours of Europe.[13] However, his view lacked any comprehension of the Allies' attitudes as we know them to have been in the latter years of the war. They wanted to see Germany utterly defeated and her leaders put on trial for their crimes. But such an image of the future was far from clear to Himmler. Ever since his youth at the Royal Wilhelm Gymnasium as a podgy, shortsighted pupil, he had always been able to talk his way out of trouble, had possessed great skill at extricating himself from dire situations. He had harnessed this skill to become Propaganda Leader of Upper Bavaria; he had gone on to join, and then run, the SS, heading a body of loyal fanatics who had become the backbone of the Nazi Party. But that era of resolute anti-Semitism had outlived its usefulness. Himmler was now attempting to change his persona in an effort to appear a moderate within the Party. As for the odium and hatred surrounding his name, Felix Kersten tactfully broached the subject whilst treating him in late 1944. Himmler did not become angry, but considered the point for a few moments before replying that the west had accepted Stalin as an ally, and much worse could be said of him.[14]

Despite his credentials as the head of the SS and Gestapo, the monster behind the worst excesses of the Holocaust, Himmler well realised – now that Germany was about to lose the war – that the atrocities of the genocide that had been taking place in Germany and the occupied territories since January 1942 were unacceptable to the rest of the world. The actions of more than two years, justified with all the arrogance of the then victor, would be abhorrent to the rest of humanity. They had resulted in the murder – the extermination – of nearly six million men, women, and children.

The crime was too enormous to hide, but efforts were now made, on Himmler's orders, to cover up what had taken place. Accordingly, the mass murder ceased at many of the extermination camps in the east. Furthermore, he ordered that the gas chambers and crematoria at camps such as Auschwitz be demolished and the camp records of the deaths destroyed. A dastardly effort was instigated to burn the hundreds of thousands of pairs of shoes, items of clothing, huts full of hair. With the Russians closing in on the camps in Poland from the east in the late autumn of 1944, he issued orders for all able-bodied persons left in the camps to be force-marched to the southeast to build massive anti-tank fortifications near Vienna.

It was now, in tandem with his decision to 'discontinue with the Jew-exterminations'[15] that Himmler engaged upon a fresh initiative to engage the western allies in peaceable negotiations. The first of these bizarre exploits (bizarre in that they were totally unrealistic and reveal much about how desperate Himmler was) involved a young SS-Standartenführer (colonel) named Kurt Becher. He was dispatched to Turkey on Himmler's specific orders for a meeting with an agent of the US OSS. This time the deal being offered was the release to the Red Cross in Switzerland of several hundred thousand Jews – in return for a thousand American army trucks. The offer was treated with scepticism by the US State Department and rejected out of hand. The Allies would not consider any deal that propped up the German war machine by providing American vehicles.

Next Becher was sent to Switzerland for a meeting with some new contacts he had made whilst trying to make a deal for the American trucks.

In the course of this venture he had made the acquaintance of several leading members of an American-Jewish organisation. This time Himmler offered to spare the Jews of Hungary in return for foreign exchange payments – 50 Swiss francs for an ordinary Jew, 500 francs for 'prominent' Jewish persons. No such payments were ever made, but the negotiations lasted throughout the winter of 1944, and as a direct consequence Himmler ordered Adolf Eichmann to halt the shipment of Hungarian Jews to the extermination camps. Eichmann was a bureaucrat, albeit a murderous one, charged with the responsibility of feeding the Holocaust programme. He did not understand the political complexities of the situation; did not understand that Himmler was now using the lives of the remaining Jews as a bargaining tool, as he attempted to negotiate with the western Allies. According to Schellenberg, Himmler failed to realise that the release of Jews was an important aspect of Germany's foreign policy – in other words, the relations he was trying to foster with the west – and seemed concerned only with the effect it would have on Hitler and the Party.[16] Felix Kersten, too, believed that Himmler was terrified of Hitler's response were he to permit the wholesale release of Jews. Martin Bormann, he said, that malevolent force seated at Hitler's right shoulder, was ready to stab him in the back at the first opportunity.[17]

•••••

During the winter of 1944 Himmler's efforts to find an avenue for negotiation with the western Allies took a new turn. If we recall Operation Messrs HHHH, we will also recall the name of Hitler's confidential advisor on foreign affairs, the half-Jewish Albrecht Haushofer. Haushofer's importance in Nazi Germany had diminished somewhat after the flight of his patron, Rudolf Hess, to Scotland in May 1941. However, his expertise on Britain and the British political system was bound to keep him in the fore of German attempts to negotiate with the British. After the collapse of the German front in Russia during the winter of 1943, Haushofer had become increasingly disillusioned with Hitler and the Nazis. This had led him into dangerous territory; through his close friend Ulrich von Hassell, he became a member of the Kreisau Circle and was thus party to the plot to kill Hitler on 20 July 1944. On the collapse of the coup attempt, he had fled to his homeland of Bavaria, where he successfully evaded capture for many months, hoping that the Allies would eventually invade the region and he could come out of hiding. However, his luck could not last for ever, and he was captured by the SS on 7 December.

After the eminent prisoner had been identified, he was sent to the forbidding red-brick Moabit prison in Berlin. Moabit was run by the SS, and it was here that eminent prisoners were held, interrogated by the Gestapo, and often executed after swift National Socialist justice at the hands of the Volksgericht. If Haushofer quaked with fear at being sent to Moabit, in the short term he had little cause to worry. During December and early January of 1945 he was intensively interrogated by the Gestapo, who wanted to know the names of everyone with whom he had been in contact in the plot to kill the Führer. However, they were unusually careful with him. More eminent prisoners than Haushofer had endured a horrendous time in Moabit, especially those who had been party to the 20 July bomb plot, but it seemed that the SS had other plans for their unusual captive.

In mid-January 1945 the reason behind Haushofer's lenient treatment became apparent when he found himself contacted again by none other than Himmler himself. Himmler knew of the valuable advice Haushofer had given to Hitler in the latter 1930s and the early years of the war; he had himself consulted Haushofer in 1942 about the involvement of Foreign Minister Ribbentrop in peace negotiations with the Allies. He knew, too, that Haushofer had been consulted by his close friend, General Wolff, who had asked him in early 1944 for advice on how best to approach the Americans. At that time Haushofer had been adamant that any new approach to the Americans, or indeed the British, could not, indeed must not, involve either Ribbentrop or Hitler. He now gave the same advice to his new and dangerous patron. In a second meeting in the last days of January 1945, Haushofer again told Himmler that if he was serious about making peace with the western Allies – and it should be remembered that Haushofer was a German patriot who greatly feared a Russian invasion of his country – then he must not involve either Hitler or Ribbentrop. These men, he said, represented the antithesis of peace to the Allies. Over the past five years of war nothing had changed in the Allied mind, and they would absolutely not treat with anyone connected to Hitler or Ribbentrop. This was hardly news to Himmler, who had come to this conclusion for himself back in 1943. It did, however, convince him that he was correct in trying to seek a secret line to the Allies that did not involve Hitler. It was the only course of salvation left open for Germany, and for himself.

For the moment, as Himmler mulled over the notion of sending him as his emissary to the American Legation in Berne, Haushofer was protected in Moabit prison. But now a new man made his presence felt, and his arrival on the scene was to prove deadly for Haushofer. This was a fifty-year-old Swedish diplomat named Count Folke Bernadotte, cousin of King Gustav of Sweden, and vice-president of the Swedish Red Cross. With his appearance, Himmler gained a useful neutral intermediary he could use to contact the Allies; it also meant that he had no further use for Albrecht Haushofer, who would eventually be executed by the SS in the last days of the war.

In February 1945 new rumours of a possible negotiated peace began to appear in the newspapers of the neutral countries. These had largely been inspired by the efforts of Peter Kleist, a German Foreign Office diplomat who was Ribbentrop's expert on the east and the Soviet Union. On receiving orders from Hitler that no contact was to be made with the Russians, Kleist on his own initiative had opened a line of communication to the western Allies in Stockholm. This led, in mid-February 1945, to a meeting with Gilel Storch, an important representative of the World Jewish Congress. The two men met in secret at a Stockholm hotel, and Storch proposed that they should negotiate the release to Sweden of 4,300 Jews from various concentration camps. Kleist stated that it was impossible to solve the Jewish problem by this means. It could only be done politically. 'If the preservation of Jewry can be traded for the preservation of Europe,' he claimed, 'then we will have a genuine "deal" that's worth risking my life.'[18]

Storch immediately saw advantages in keeping this line of communication to the Nazi regime open. He suggested to Kleist that if they were to proceed, it would be worthwhile for him to meet with Ivor Olson, an American diplomat at the Stockholm Embassy who was the personal advisor to President Roosevelt for the War Refugee Committee of Northern and Western Europe. Storch, acting as intermediary, himself met with Olson. He reported back excitedly to Kleist that Olson had checked with Washington and that Roosevelt had expressed his willingness to bargain for the lives of 1,500,000 Jews in concentration camps by 'political' means.

On Kleist's return to Berlin he did not, as might be expected, take this new and very interesting development to his chief, Joachim von Ribbentrop. As a leading man in the Foreign Office, Kleist knew that Ribbentrop's star had well and truly set and that he was by this time a definite liability to German foreign policy. Instead, he met secretly with Ernst Kaltenbrunner, Himmler's head of the SD. The dangerous Kaltenbrunner immediately placed Kleist under house arrest for treating with the enemy against the direct orders of the Führer. However, in a typically underhand manner, he told Himmler about the Olson development to Himmler. It is not known precisely what now happened (i.e. it is doubtful that Himmler took Kaltenbrunner into his confidence with regard to his secret peace negotiations), except that a few days later Kaltenbrunner summoned Kleist to his Prinz Albrechtstrasse headquarters and informed him that Himmler was 'willing to take up this Swedish possibility'.[19] Under Himmler's orders, Kleist was to return to Sweden in a week or so to start negotiations and, as a token of good faith, he could take 2,000 Jews to freedom.

However, the machinations surrounding Himmler at this time were such that in only three days Kleist was summoned back to Kaltenbrunner's office and told that the matter had been dropped, and his services were no longer required. Himmler did not entirely trust Kaltenbrunner. Despite promoting him to become head of the SD, he knew that Kaltenbrunner was absolutely loyal to Hitler. As a result, Kaltenbrunner knew only what he told Kleist; he did not know that his arch-rival, Walter Schellenberg, had persuaded Himmler not to trust Kleist or share the possible peace breakthrough with the Foreign Office, and by implication with Ribbentrop. Instead, Schellenberg convinced a very indecisive Himmler to send his loyal friend and masseur Felix Kersten in Kleist's place, and to keep the entire matter secret until they managed a breakthrough.

As a first step Kersten travelled to Stockholm in the second week of February 1945, and began negotiations with the Swedish Minister of Foreign Affairs for the freedom of Scandinavian prisoners in concentration camps. The negotiations went very smoothly. It was soon agreed that Count Bernadotte should come to Berlin for a secret meeting with Himmler.

Bernadotte arrived in Berlin on 17 February. He was travelling to Germany ostensibly on behalf of a Red Cross team sent to negotiate the repatriation of Swedish-born women married to Germans, but who had lost their husbands during the war and now wished to return to neutral Sweden. However, his real purpose was to meet secretly with Himmler in order to negotiate the release of Scandinavian prisoners held in concentration camps,[20] whilst at the same time offering an olive branch should he wish to open a line of communication to the Allies, leading, perhaps, to an armistice. Within just a few days, on the evening of 19 February, he found himself being driven north from Berlin to an isolated sanatorium at Hohenlychen. This sanatorium was owned by Dr Gebhardt, another close friend of Himmler, and was conveniently close to his field headquarters at Birkenwald, in the countryside north of Berlin (Himmler's purpose-built headquarters in east Prussia having been overrun by the Russians). Bernadotte had approached the meeting with extreme caution, knowing from the Allied press that Himmler was regarded as the most dangerous man of the Third Reich. However, to his surprise he found him to be extremely affable and cultured. There was no sign of the dangerous and unpredictable man often portrayed in the press.

> He seemed strikingly and amazingly obliging. He displayed traces of humour with a hint of grimness, which he used to relieve the tension. Least of all was there anything diabolical in his appearance . . .[21]

Himmler had undoubtedly discussed the meeting with Walter Schellenberg before engaging in these peace negotiations, the first in which he had ever participated directly. Sitting down in private, Bernadotte began by explaining to him that much anger had been aroused in Sweden by the manner in which the SS had treated occupied Norway. It was known that the Gestapo and the SS had indulged in wholesale executions of resistance fighters in Norway and had seized many hostages in an attempt to control the country, and that large numbers of Scandinavians had been sent to concentration camps. To his relief Himmler did not become angry at these comments. Instead, he deftly sidestepped the subject, declaring to the Count that he was obviously misinformed and asking rather pointedly whether he had any concrete proposals.

Bernadotte most definitely did have an agenda. As his opening gambit he asked Himmler whether, as a sign of good faith, it would be possible to release all Norwegian and Danish prisoners (many of whom were resistance fighters) held in concentration camps into Swedish custody, where they would remain until the end of the war. At this request Himmler became very angry, revealing a side of his personality better kept hidden from the man he was hoping to use as a conduit for peace negotiations. Spouting a stream of vehement accusations against Sweden that made little sense to Bernadotte, he concluded by declaring angrily, 'If I were to agree to your proposals, the Swedish papers would announce with big headlines that the war criminal Himmler, in terror of punishment for his crimes, is trying to buy his freedom.'[22] He then changed the emphasis of his argument and said that he might just be able to do what Bernadotte proposed if, and only if, the Swedish government and the Allies gave a public assurance that all acts of sabotage and resistance in Norway were to stop.

'That's unthinkable,' replied Bernadotte. He then asked for several minor concessions, which Himmler, after some consideration, granted.

Following the meeting, which lasted two and a half hours, Himmler immediately summoned Schellenberg and charged him with ensuring German adherence to the terms agreed. These mainly concerned the repatriation to Sweden of Swedes who had been caught supporting the underground in Denmark and Norway, and were currently being held in camps in Germany; something he had agreed to despite the opposition to be expected from Kaltenbrunner and Ribbentrop. According to his memoirs, Schellenberg now urged Himmler to return to Berlin and open negotiations with the western Allies leading to a peace settlement. Since capitulation could not even be mentioned in the Führer's headquarters, he was probably advocating an SS putsch to remove the entire Führer circle before it was too late.[23]

Whatever the nature of what Schellenberg later described as a 'stormy conversation', which carried on late into the night of Sunday, 19 February, it seems likely that Himmler, who had formed a favourable impression of Bernadotte, was keen to keep open this conduit to the west. He may well have authorised Schellenberg to work out some concise peace terms – probably very similar to the six-point peace plan that Schellenberg had taken to Victor Mallet in the autumn of 1943 – which Bernadotte could pass on to General Eisenhower. According to Schellenberg's memoirs, this was what Himmler ordered him to do, but the next day, having had a qualm of conscience during the night, he revoked the order.[24] Schellenberg was merely to keep a line of communication open to Bernadotte, who was due to return to Sweden within a few days.

In the early weeks of 1945 Himmler had concentrated on attempting to open communications with the Allies – i.e. the Americans – through Sweden in the northwest. However, as the various fronts – north, east, south, and west – closed ever more tightly around an increasingly beleaguered Germany, Himmler now switched the direction of his peace-seeking endeavours, trying to contact the Americans in Switzerland. This time those endeavours mounted by Himmler and General Wolff would meet with a great deal more success.

•••••

On 22 March 1945, Himmler officially handed over command of Army Group Vistula – which was fighting vainly against the Russian advance in the east – to General Gotthard Heinrici. Himmler's own command of Army Group Vistula had been wholly unsuccessful. He had been revealed as a very poor field commander – hence the handover to Heinrici, who was now ordered to halt the Russian advance into Germany. A thousand years before, Germany had been hemmed in by the River Oder in the east and the Rhine in the west. Now Hitler's thousand-year Reich was limited in scope to these same borders, the Russians hemming Germany in on the Oder and the western Allies on the Rhine. With the war all but lost, handing over command was a futile gesture, but Heinrici accepted his charge from the Reichsführer SS without a single word of dissent.

Following the official handover, which took place at Himmler's temporary field headquarters at Birkenwald, Himmler sat with Heinrici and made a dramatic revelation. Heinrici's was a crucial job, Himmler told him: he must at all costs hold back the Russians until he, Himmler, could cut a deal with the western Allies. He confided to Heinrici that he was, independently of the Führer, already taking steps to negotiate a peace with the west. Once this was accomplished, he revealed, it would be possible for Germany to drive the Russians back to their homeland, saving Germany from invasion by the Soviets. It occurred to Heinrici that perhaps Himmler was testing his loyalty, sounding him out in case it became necessary for the SS to launch a putsch against Hitler and the Nazi Party (or so he recalled later).[25] But Himmler may have been emboldened to mention these secret peace negotiations to Heinrici because he at last felt close to success.

We have already several times come across SS-General Karl Wolff, one of Himmler's closest confidants. Wolff, whom Himmler called by his nickname, 'Wölffchen' (Little Wolf), was six years his junior and, at the age of thirty-nine, one of the youngest top commanders in the SS. Ultimately loyal to his patron, Wolff was currently the German military governor of north Italy, and a senior commander of the SS and Wehrmacht forces. Just a few weeks earlier, on 6 February, Himmler had met with his old friend Wölffchen in Berlin to discuss the progress of the war, and how they could negotiate an end to the conflict in the south. Indeed, his diary recorded the meetings for posterity: '13.45 SS-Obergruf. Wolff; Meal with Wolff, Oberg, Seyss-Inquart . . . 15.00 SS-Obergruf. Wolff.'[26]

The talks Himmler revealed to General Heinrici on 22 March had begun in mid-February 1945. As soon as he returned to northern Italy, Wolff sent a close confidant, Fascist businessman Luigi Parrilli, to Switzerland to begin peace negotiations with the Americans via a contact in the Swiss Intelligence Service. Luigi Parrilli had been successful in opening a line of communication directly to Allen Dulles, the US OSS station chief in Berne. Since 1942 Dulles had made a significant contribution to the intelligence war in central Europe, establishing many lines of communication to the anti-Nazi resistance in Germany. It was his latest contact, however, that would prove most important.

Using Parrilli as a go-between, Wolff communicated to Dulles that he, as military governor of northern Italy, recognised that the war was lost, and was prepared to conclude hostilities in this theatre by negotiated means. Furthermore, he confirmed that if a peace deal could be negotiated with SS and Wehrmacht forces in northern Italy, there would be no withdrawal into the Alps. It was one of the Allies' greatest fears that Germany would create an Alpine redoubt in order to continue the war through the summer of 1945, perhaps even until 1946. Such a redoubt, which it was believed would centre on Austria, would be a formidable stronghold, and taking it would cost many Allied lives. Thus Wolff's offer (he promised that he could carry the supreme German commander in the south, Field Marshal Albert Kesselring, with him into agreeing peace) was treated with great seriousness by the Americans.

Throughout the war the Swiss government had supposedly followed an even-handed policy towards the activities of the Allies and the Germans in their country. The Swiss Intelligence Service chief, Max Waibel, had been ordered by his government to liaise with the Allies, whilst another high-ranking officer had the task of liaising with the Germans. It was, however, often observed by Washington and London that this policy from time to time somewhat favoured one side or the other, depending on who seemed to be winning the war. By the early spring of 1945 it had become plain to the Swiss that the Allies were near to victory, so Swiss Intelligence swung behind the Allies, and especially behind Dulles, who had established cordial relations with Waibel.

Of particular concern to the Swiss government was that the battle for northern Italy should be concluded with minimal conflict; indeed, if they could facilitate a negotiated peace in this theatre, it would be greatly in their interests. The Swiss dreaded a long drawn-out conflict on its southern border. The country was already bursting at the seams with refugees from all over Europe, and it feared that the Italian port of Genoa, via which land-locked Switzerland received virtually all her supplies (foodstuffs, industrial materials, oil, and petrol), would be destroyed by the Allies as they fought to wrest control of the city from the Germans. As luck would have it, Allen

Dulles was in sympathy with the Swiss desire to achieve peace in northern Italy, and mindful of the danger that the retreating German forces might withdraw into a strongly defended Alpine redoubt.

This coming together of the Swiss and the Americans would see the success, for the first and only time in the war, of SS-inspired peace negotiations with the Allies. For in the background behind General Wolff lurked Himmler, though Wolff, aware of the Allies' insistence that they would never negotiate with any leading Nazi, was forced to deny that he was the inspiration behind this bid to make a separate peace. Even so, it was clear that Himmler was behind this latest peace bid. Dulles recognised that Wolff would not have dared to attempt such a bid without the Reichsführer's support. His suspicions were soon to be confirmed.

The first hint that the SS were preparing to negotiate a peace deal – in effect the complete surrender of all SS and Wehrmacht forces in Italy – had appeared in February when Waibel invited Dulles to dinner to meet with an important Italian named Parrilli. At first Dulles was very dubious of Parrilli's claim to be representing SS-General Wolff's interests. He did not believe that Wolff, having sworn complete loyalty to Hitler, as had every SS man, could be in the business of negotiating peace behind his Führer's back. However, as he was later to recall, 'We were wrong . . .':

> Only five days had passed since the meeting when I had an urgent call from Waibel. Parrilli had returned to Switzerland. Not only that; with him were two Waffen SS officers, Colonel Eugen Dollmann and Captain Guido Zimmer, from Milan. Waibel had quietly arranged for their admission to Switzerland and would find safe quarters for them in Lugano. Their presence in Switzerland could be kept a secret. They would have to return to Italy in a few days. The rest was up to us.[27]

Dulles was initially extremely cautious about this approach; he did not believe that the SS – the most dedicated Nazis of all – would be prepared to betray their Führer by secretly negotiating to surrender the southern front. Suspecting as he did that the Machiavellian hand of Himmler lay behind the approach, he had to tread very carefully indeed if he – representing American Intelligence in Switzerland – were not to hand a propaganda coup to the Nazis, who might exploit it for their own ends by revealing a split in the Allied high command. 'Could this approach really be taken seriously? Was it a trick? How could their [the Nazis'] sincerity be tested?'[28]

Whilst Dulles was considering this state of affairs, he had an inspired idea. It so happened that a few weeks earlier two leading Italian partisans, Feruccio Parri and Antonio Usmiani, had been captured by the Germans. The partisans had made a few abortive attempts to rescue their leaders, but their efforts had come to nothing. The two men were currently being held by the Gestapo inside the maximum-security jail in Verona, and Dulles had it on good authority that Parri had been tortured. He now had the idea that if the Germans were to release these men as a sign of good faith, this might indicate that Wolff was genuine in his bid for peace, and that this latest development was not, as it appeared to be, a Nazi trick.

Unwilling himself to be drawn into a trap, he therefore decided to send a member of his most experienced intelligence team, a young Jewish New Yorker named Paul Blum, to Lugano to meet with Dollmann and Zimmer. As a Jew, Dulles felt, Blum would not take what the Nazis declared at face value; he would drive an extremely hard bargain when dealing directly with two members of the SS. Before Blum left, Dulles held a long discussion with him. He later recalled that 'I told Paul that, if we were to continue the conversations with the German emissaries, we should have to have concrete evidence both of their seriousness and of their authority.' And he gave Blum a slip of paper with the names of the two partisans on it.

On meeting the two SS men in Lugano, Blum found them friendly and cordial. It never occurred to them that he was a Jew, and even if it had, he soon came to the conclusion that it would have had no effect at all upon their negotiations. They all shook hands and sat down to a detailed discussion about the course of the war, and what needed to be done to conclude the conflict as soon as possible without further useless loss of life. 'Almost immediately he [Dollmann] asked whether the Allies would be willing to treat with Heinrich Himmler if he supported a separate action for peace in northern Italy.' Blum, who knew the American government's position on this, immediately replied in English, 'Not a Chinaman's chance.'

Dollmann did not seem unduly surprised by this answer, and changed tack. He asked Blum what would happen if the negotiations were carried on in General Wolff's name alone, and stated that he had been ordered to reveal that Wolff was prepared to travel to Switzerland if it were possible for him to have a face-to-face meeting with Dulles. Blum had not been expecting this answer. In his private conversation with Dulles before his departure, it had been revealed to him that Dulles suspected Himmler was behind this SS bid for peace in Italy, and that under no circumstances were negotiations to be opened with him: the British would never stand for it.

Blum had therefore been sanctioned to state to the two SS men that Dulles would be prepared to negotiate the surrender of German forces in Italy only with Wolff. A secret meeting between Dulles and Wolff seemed the best way to further this American aim, and so Blum stated to Dollmann that such a meeting would be possible. But there had to be a sign of good faith from the Germans first. At this he produced the slip of paper that Dulles had given him with the names of Parri and Usmiani on it. As Dulles was later to record:

> I knew that in asking for his [Parri's] release I was asking for something that would be very difficult for Wolff to do, and in fact I was putting the stakes high . . . Yet if these men could be released, the seriousness of General Wolff's intentions would be demonstrated . . . Dollmann was shocked by the demand, but, after swallowing hard, agreed to do everything in his power to meet it. He said he would report back in a few days.[29]

When Blum returned to Berne, he held a confidential meeting with Dulles and reported in great detail on everything that had taken place. Dulles began to think that he had asked too much, but Blum was not of the same opinion. He had been very impressed with Dollmann's sense of purpose and believed that if anyone could open a line of peace negotiation, it was he. He also believed that Wolff was sincere in his intent to negotiate an end to the conflict in the southern theatre of the war, even if this intent did have the shadow of Himmler lurking in the background. It was therefore decided that the expedient thing to do was to ignore the possibility that Himmler was the unseen hand behind Wolff's endeavours – or orders.

A few days later, on 8 March, a German staff car drove up to the Swiss–Italian border at Chiasso. A captain of the SS stepped out, approached the checkpoint and gave a password to one of the Swiss border patrol guards. The guard immediately ran back to his hut to summon a member of Waibel's Intelligence Service, who was seated within. This man approached the German captain, who revealed his identity as Zimmer. A short discussion was held before Zimmer stated, 'I have two men here for you. Please take them to Mr Allen Dulles with the compliments of General Wolff.'[30] He returned to the car, opened the back door and summoned out two men in civilian clothes. They stepped out warily, expecting some Nazi ruse that might result in a bullet in the back; but no, Zimmer wished them a cordial goodbye, stepped into the car, and ordered his driver to drive away. Without a moment's hesitation, the dishevelled pair crossed the border into neutral Switzerland. Less than an hour later an extremely surprised Dulles was telephoned in Berne by Waibel and told that the two Italian partisan leaders, Feruccio Parri and Antonio Usmiani, had been released and were safely in Swiss hands. It seemed that the Germans could be trusted after all, and that Wolff's authority carried sufficient sway to secure the release of two key resistance leaders from Gestapo hands.

Two hours later the SS staff car arrived once more at the Chiasso frontier post.

This time four men, all clad in civilian clothes, alighted from the vehicle. After another exchange of passwords, Waibel's man watched the four cross the border. The first, Captain Zimmer, was closely followed by Colonel Dollmann; next came two men walking together – a high-ranking commanding officer and his personal adjutant. The adjutant was SS-Sturmbahnführer Wenner, who was accompanying a well-built, bronzed, blue-eyed man with a hawklike nose. This was Himmler's senior representative in Italy, commander-in-chief of SS forces, General Karl Wolff himself, come to talk peace and surrender with Allen Dulles on neutral soil.

That evening Dulles and Wolff met at Dulles's flat in Berne, and sat down together for a long conversation before a roaring log fire in the study. Dulles had already reported to Washington on this latest development in the struggle against Nazism, and the top-secret negotiations had been given a code name, 'Operation Sunrise'. Wolff at once immediately made it clear to Dulles that he believed all future resistance to overwhelming Allied might to be a futile act, but still the Germans had to defend the territory they held in northern Italy until they could agree terms. He promised to issue a declaration, signed by all principal army officers in Italy, setting forth the uselessness of the struggle and calling on the army to dissociate itself from Hitler. The declaration was to be reinforced by radio and leaflet action to convey the message to both soldiers and people.

In addition Wolff declared that just as he had released Parri and Usmiani to show his good intentions, he would now:

1. Discontinue active warfare against Italian partisans.
2. Release to Switzerland several hundred Jews interned at Bolzano.
3. Assume full responsibility for the safety of 350 American and British POWs at Mantua.

4. Facilitate the return to northern Italy of Italian officers in Germany who might be useful in keeping order during the post-hostility period.[31]

This last concession confirmed, to Dulles's discomfort, that Himmler's intellect undoubtedly lurked behind Wolff's declarations of peaceable intent. No such release of Italian prisoners could possibly take place without a direct order from the Reichsführer-SS himself. Dulles nevertheless decided not to make this conclusion too widely known for fear that the Germans' attempts to negotiate peace might thereby be undermined and perhaps even abandoned. No Allied government would openly concede that it had been secretly negotiating peace with the monster of the Third Reich, even if at one remove. Confidentially, however, Dulles had no such compunction – but only if his secret negotiations with General Wolff could end the fighting in Italy and prevent the formation of a strongly defended Alpine redoubt in Austria.

Following his secret discussion with Wolff, Dulles cabled the details to Allied Army Headquarters at Caserta, a few miles from Naples. There was an immediate response. Two high-ranking officers, one American (General Lemnitzer, Deputy Chief of Staff of the US Fifth Army) and one British (General Airey, Director of Military Intelligence, Allied Forces Italy) flew to Switzerland for a meeting with General Wolff. He had by this time left for northern Italy, but on being informed that the negotiations could proceed, he immediately returned to Switzerland on 19 March 1945. Both the British and American generals were at once impressed by his earnestness of purpose. They accordingly reported back to Allied Army Headquarters Caserta, London, and Washington that they believed a deal could be struck.

At this point a problem arose. Roosevelt and Churchill, concerned not to be accused of trying to make a separate peace with the Nazis, informed Moscow of the deal being negotiated with Wolff in Switzerland. Regardless of their openness, a paranoid Stalin immediately responded by sending a telegram accusing them of going behind his back and trying to sign a separate deal. Roosevelt in turn immediately sent a terse telegram to Stalin defending his position, attempting to appease the Soviet leader by stating that ultimately nothing would be done without Russian approval.

By this time the German supreme commander in Italy, Field Marshal Kesselring, had been ordered to take over as supreme commander in the west, relieving Field Marshal Runstedt who had been ordered back to

Berlin by Hitler for failing to stop the Allied advance. Kesselring was now replaced in Italy by General von Vietinghoff. However, Wolff was not unduly perturbed by this development. He told the Americans, 'Meine Herren, have a little patience and I will present you Italy on a silver salver.'[32]

Wolff's was not the only Himmler-inspired peace offensive to the Americans at this time, a small distraction having been provided by none other than Ernst Kaltenbrunner, the feared head of the SD. This approach proved most enlightening to the Americans. At the beginning of March, Kaltenbrunner made an approach through a Swiss intermediary to the American diplomatic mission in Zurich. The tenor of what he was offering revealed much about the Nazis' priorities in this last stage of the war. Kaltenbrunner promised that the Reich would not make a last-ditch stand in the Alps if the western Allies gave a guarantee that they would not let Austria be occupied by the Russians or divided into separate zones of occupation. Instead, he proposed – presumably with Himmler's backing, otherwise he would not have dared to make such an approach – that Austria's sovereignty be preserved and that the country should become an area excluded from war crimes trials, thus becoming a safe haven to which wanted Nazis could retire in relative safety.

Such a proposition never had the slightest chance of being favourably received by the Allies, despite their concern that the Nazis might withdraw into a hard core of fanatical resistance in the Alps. When Dulles had raised the question with Wolff during their talks on 19 March, the German took advantage, claiming that there was a great danger that the war would not end cleanly, but might drag on to an even more bloody end. He did, however, qualify his answer by stating that such a redoubt would be 'Madness!' He went on, 'It would only bring added suffering to the German people. Everything possible must be done to prevent such last-minute resistance.'[33]

Whether Wolff was playing a larger game in his bid for peace, hoping to negotiate a deal in the west as well – as had been Himmler's desire ever since 1943 – and thus splitting the Alliance, with the British and Americans on one side and the Russians on the other, is not known. It is known, however, that after his meeting with Dulles on 19 March, he travelled to Bad Nauheim on 23 March to meet Kesselring and try to bring him on side, and it is generally believed that Wolff was hoping thereby to expand his negotiations to encompass the whole of the western front.

His meeting with Kesselring over, Wolff travelled to Berlin for a brief meeting with his patron. After the war Wolff was to declare that Himmler had ordered him not to pursue his contact with the Americans, but rather to maintain a strong front in Italy and defend every last inch of territory. How much of this is truth, and how much an attempt to distance himself from the monster of the Holocaust, will never be known. The only hint we have is that Wolff had a series of meetings with Himmler throughout the winter of 1944 and the spring of 1945, during which time we know Himmler was doing his utmost to open negotiations with the Allies. We know Himmler had believed the war to be lost ever since 1943; we also know from his dealings with PWE via Victor Mallet that he wanted the war ended as soon as possible, thereby leaving him open to begin a new post-war political career. It therefore seems highly likely that he would have supported his friend's line of negotiation with the USA. It was in effect his last chance to have a foot in both British and American camps.

Everything appeared to be proceeding smoothly. Now, however, it seemed that a disastrous breakdown was about to occur. On 12 April, President Roosevelt died. His place was taken by Harry S. Truman who, as Vice-President, had had no idea that the OSS and Allied High Command had been in deep peace discussions with SS-General Wolff for many weeks. This was not unusual. Roosevelt had kept many of his secret operations very close to his chest; for example, Truman had no idea either that the USA was mere weeks away from perfecting the atom bomb. On 20 April there arrived on Allen Dulles's desk a top-secret telegram from Washington:

> JCS [Joint Chiefs of Staff] direct that OSS break off all contact with German emissaries at once. Dulles is therefore instructed to discontinue immediately all such contacts.
>
> CCS [Combined Chiefs of Staff] have approved message to [Field Marshal] Alexander [Commander-in-Chief, Allied forces in Italy] stating that it is clear to them that German Commander-in-Chief in Italy does not intend to surrender his forces at this time on acceptable terms. Accordingly, especially in view of complications which have arisen with the Russians, the U.S. and British governments have decided OSS should break off contacts.[34]

This development could not have come at a worse time for Dulles and his Sunrise peace negotiations. For, contrary to what Truman and the Joint Chiefs of Staff (JCS) believed, Wolff was sincere in his desire to end the conflict in Italy and was ready at any time to meet with the Allied High Command and surrender his forces. So sincere was he, in fact, that after his latest meeting with Dulles he had taken an OSS agent, a Free Czech Army radio operator, back with him to SS headquarters in Milan, charged with keeping a line of communication open to Dulles in Berne twenty-four hours a day. Moreover, Franz Hofer, the Nazi Gauleiter of the Tyrol and a close confederate of Wolff, had expressed his willingness to surrender the whole region and hand over his administration to the Allies without any further conflict.

Dulles was immediately alarmed and puzzled at receiving such a telegram from the JCS. Why had he been ordered to break off his negotiations at such a vital moment, before the battle for northern Italy was fought and whilst the prospect existed of saving so many lives? Could it be sabotage? A report had reached him that the German High Command in Milan had been approached by a mysterious officer in British Army uniform, who had urged the Germans to break off their negotiations with the Americans and instead begin direct talks with the British.[35] When Dulles made enquiries in Berne, approaching a contact at the British Consulate, the British behaved in a very furtive manner, denying any further assistance and refusing to discuss the matter.[36]

A few days later, on 23 April, Dulles received astounding news. On the telephone was Max Waibel. He revealed that General Wolff, his adjutant Major Wenner, and one of Vietinghoff's high staff officers, Colonel Viktor von Schweinitz, had arrived in Switzerland. 'They had come to surrender.' Furthermore, Wolff and Schweinitz were prepared to travel on, with Allied assistance, to Allied headquarters at Caserta to 'arrange for the capitulation of all German forces, Wehrmacht and SS, in North Italy. They proposed an immediate meeting with me [Dulles] in Lucerne to arrange the details of the trip to Allied headquarters.'[37] This immediately provided Dulles with a dilemma; here was Wolff come to surrender all German forces in northern Italy, effectively Hitler's southern front, and yet he was under the strictest orders from Washington not to negotiate with Wolff. It was a crazy situation. Dulles determined that the saving of countless Allied and German lives in the forthcoming battle for northern Italy was worth a tremendous risk, so he endeavoured to keep negotiations with Wolff going on his own. He would travel to Lucerne to negotiate (he could not meet Wolff personally for the moment, but would communicate through an intermediary), whilst at the same time trying to persuade both Truman and the Joint Chiefs of Staff that Wolff was sincere in his desire to secure peace.

After two days of fruitless communications in Lucerne through intermediaries, the Germans were becoming extremely worried; paranoid, in fact, that they had fallen for an Allied trap. Was General Wolff being detained in Switzerland to keep him away from the ferocious conflict in northern Italy? The Allies had already launched their push against the German lines and had won a desperate battle south of the River Po and around Bologna. Becoming suspicious, on 25 April Wolff left Lucerne and travelled back to his headquarters in Milan. He did, however, leave behind Major Wenner and Colonel Schweinitz to continue the negotiations and try by any means to cut a deal with the Allies that would see an end to the fighting.

A further two days later, under a constant barrage of urgent telegrams from Dulles, President Truman was eventually persuaded of the Germans' sincerity. Accordingly, on 27 April, he issued orders to Dulles and the Allied High Command at Caserta that they were to meet with the Germans and accept the surrender of all Axis forces – SS, Wehrmacht, and fascist Italian – in the southern theatre. It was too late for Wolff to travel back to Switzerland, but on 28 April Field Marshal Alexander's personal aircraft arrived at Annecy, just over the Swiss border in France. It picked up Major Wenner, Colonel Schweinitz, and Paul Blum, and flew them to Caserta where the Germans without any hesitation signed the papers of surrender for the whole theatre of war.

There would be no further bitter fighting in Italy; most important of all, through Dulles's endeavours and the efforts of General Wolff, there would be no German withdrawal into a strongly defended Alpine redoubt. An end to the war in the southern theatre of Europe had been brought about through peace negotiations conducted in secret by the SS. If the hand of Heinrich Himmler was suspected to be lurking in the background, everyone involved – Wolff, Dulles, and Allied High Command in Italy – chose to ignore that small but highly significant detail.

NOTES

1. Doc. No. BT 64/397, National Archives, Kew, London.
2. Ibid.
3. Ibid.
4. Ibid.
5. Ibid.
6. Ibid.
7. Ibid.
8. Ibid.

9. Uki Goni, *The Real Odessa – How Peron Brought the Nazi War Criminals to Argentina* (Granta Books, 2004).
10. Ibid.
11. Rechtsanwalt Greuter, 'Himmler contra Hitler', Die 7 Tage 1, No. 6 (17 December 1948), Wiener Library Press Archive.
12. Allen Dulles, *The Secret Surrender* (Weidenfeld & Nicolson, 1967), p. 43.
13. Felix Kersten, *The Kersten Memoirs 1940–1945* (Hutchinson, 1956), pp. 238–39.
14. Ibid., p. 239.
15. M. Broszat (ed.), *Kommandant in Auschwitz: Autobiographische Aufzeichnungen von Rudolf Hoess* (Deutsche Verlags Astalt, 1958), p. 164.
16. Walter Schellenberg, *Memoirs* (André Deutsch, 1956), p. 429.
17. Kersten, op. cit., pp. 204, 229.
18. Cited Toland, op. cit., p. 851.
19. Ibid.
20. R. Hewins, *Count Folke Bernadotte: His Life and Work* (Hutchinson, 1949), p. 109.
21. Ibid., p. 118.
22. Cited Toland, op. cit., p. 853.
23. Peter Padfield, *Himmler: Reichsführer-SS* (Cassell, 2001), p. 566.
24. Schellenberg, op. cit., p. 437.
25. C. Ryan, *The Last Battle* (New English Library, 1985), p. 71.
26. Himmler papers deposited by Manvell & Fraenkel in Wiener Library, London.
27. Leonard Mosley, *Dulles* (Dial Press/James Wade, 1978), p. 175.
28. Ibid.
29. Cited Mosley, op. cit., p. 177.
30. Ibid., p. 178.
31. Ibid., p. 179.
32. Joachim von Lang, *Der Adjutant Karl Wolff: Der Mann zwischen Hitler und Himmler* (Herbig, Munich, 1985), p. 269.
33. Dulles, op. cit., p. 116.
34. Cited Mosley, op. cit., p. 184.
35. Ibid., p. 185.
36. Peter Blum, discussion with Peter Allen, New York, 7 May 1962.
37. Cited Mosley, op. cit., p. 185.

8
ENDGAME

The latter half of April 1945 saw the last desperate struggles for survival of the Third Reich. Nazi Germany was steadily being split in two by the advancing Russians in the east, and the Americans and the British in the west. The territory controlled by Hitler now resembled an hourglass, which, at its narrowest central point between the two bulbs top and bottom, was now less than a hundred miles in breadth. It was clear that time was running out for Hitler and the rule of the Nazi Party. Once the Russians and western Allies met in the middle, it would spell the end of Hitler's thousand-year Reich. By mid-April, even whilst General Wolff was talking to Dulles in Switzerland, Berlin was being reduced to a pile of smoking ash and rubble as a real-life Götterdämmerung was played out in the once-smart suburbs of Germany's capital city between the last remnants of Hitler's formerly formidable armies and the Russians. The bulk of those armies were nothing more than memories now, and a significant number of the troops facing the Russians were just young boys and old men of the Volkssturm, the German Home Guard formed by Hitler at the end of September 1944 as a last-ditch force to defend their country. Against the well-trained and equipped Russians, they did not stand a chance; all that their valiant efforts and sacrifice would accomplish was to preserve Hitler's Reich by a few meagre days.

At 5.00 a.m. on 16 April 1945 the countryside to the east of Berlin erupted into a deafening cacophony as nearly 10,000 Russian artillery pieces and numerous rocket launchers bombarded the city. Central Berlin and its eastern suburbs burst into destructive explosions, sending a pall of dust and debris across the city as it was pummelled under the merciless force of Russian guns. The continuous roll of thunder, punctuated by the occasional loud blast as a shell landed near the Reich Chancellery, left no one in the Führerbunker in any doubt that this opening salvo heralded the bitter and brutal struggle that would be the battle for Berlin. Many have written since the war that Hitler had by now descended into his own make-believe world, ordering nonexistent battalions and divisions against the Russian onslaught. However, recent thinking reveals him as a man mentally shattered and suffering ill-health, as a result of both the assassination attempt on 20 July 1944 and the medical quackery practised on him by Dr Morell. Hitler was showing the first signs of Parkinson's disease: his hands shook, he walked with a stoop; he was mentally exhausted after nearly six years of war. Many eyewitnesses have attested that he looked closer to seventy than his true age of a mere fifty-five.

It became evident to many in the closer entourage of the Führer that just as the life was ebbing out of the Reich, so, too, was Hitler's own life drawing to a close. He had already made it clear to everyone that he did not intend to survive his Reich by a single minute. He had already rejected the pleas of close confederates and generals to quit Berlin and take the fight to the Nazi stronghold near Berchtesgaden. Spurning this suggestion, he declared to all, 'A captain also goes down with his ship!' The battle for Berlin would be the deciding factor in the life of the Reich, and if its destiny was such that the city fell to the Russian hordes – and a great many people east of Berlin had fled or committed suicide rather than fall into Russian hands – Hitler was adamant that he, too, would fall in the struggle.

Germany would go on once the war ended, however, and other leading men of the Reich determined that they would survive. One such was Heinrich Himmler. True to form, he tried to stand out publicly as a fanatical Nazi, ordering his forces to fight on with desperate fervour, dispatching units of the SS and Field Security Police to hunt down shirkers and deserters and hang them from the nearest tree or lamppost as a lesson to anyone who thought of running away before the onslaught of the Allied forces. At the same time, however, he was secretly wooing the Allies and making a bid to curry favour with the Jews; trying to ensure his own political future whilst ordering German troops to fight to the death to postpone the inevitable defeat.

This dichotomy of intent began to approach its zenith on Thursday, 19 April 1945, when he met two men whom he hoped would facilitate his final endeavours to reach an understanding with the west. The first of these was Count Bernadotte, who had come to Berlin ostensibly to negotiate the release of all Scandinavian prisoners still held in Germany. The other was someone infinitely more dangerous for Himmler if his secret meeting had become public knowledge. Norbert Masur, a representative of the World Jewish Congress, had taken his courage in both hands and flown from Sweden to the very heart of Nazi Germany, landing at Tempelhof airfield in Berlin with Himmler's masseur Felix Kersten. After a brief introductory meeting with Himmler in the middle of the night at an apartment in the centre of the city, they had then driven directly to Kersten's country villa at Hartzwalde to the north of Berlin. There, Masur was to await Himmler, who wanted to discuss Jewish affairs with him in greater depth.

On 20 April spearheads of Marshal Zhukov's Russian Second Guards Tank Army reached the northeastern outskirts of Berlin. To the south General Koniev's armoured units dashed towards Zossen to cut the city off from the southern flank. Only a broad corridor now connected Berlin with the northwest of Germany, and German forces were positioned around the north and west of Berlin to keep the capital from being cut off by the Russians. That day, 20 April, was also Hitler's birthday, and the old guard of Nazism gathered at the badly damaged Reich Chancellery to pay their respects. Standing in a reception room stripped of its carpets and opulent neoclassical furniture, Ribbentrop, Göring, Himmler, Goebbels, Speer, and other ministers came together for one final time in order to go through the ritual of congratulating Hitler on his fifty-sixth birthday. However, the Führer was a mere shell of his former self. Indeed, one eyewitness later asserted that 'he looked what I would call physically senile'. After the brief ceremony Hitler shuffled out to the bomb-cratered garden of the Chancellery to hand out medals to a valiant contingent of the Hitler Youth, who had been fighting the Russians on the outskirts of Berlin. A newsreel camera caught the moment for posterity; it was to be the last time Hitler would be filmed in public. After the brief ceremony he retreated to the labyrinth of the Führerbunker that was buried deep beneath the Reich Chancellery garden.

Heinrich Himmler, present throughout the birthday ceremony and Hitler's meeting with the young boys of the Hitler Youth, watched his Führer intently. It could be only a matter of days before the end of the Third Reich, and the continual background noise of the 'crump' of Russian shells from the eastern outskirts of the city emphasised the extremity of the situation.

That night Himmler, accompanied by Schellenberg, left Berlin for the last time, heading north to Kersten's villa at Hartzwalde. He would never again see the city or his Führer. However, there were other matters on his mind now. They arrived at Kersten's villa at 2.00 a.m., whereupon Himmler had a private discussion with Kersten in the darkened garden before going in to meet a representative of a race he had done his utmost to eradicate in the past three years. He was nevertheless determined to make a good impression on Masur. He greeted him cordially, whereafter all four men sat around a table and the discussion began.

At first, much as Kersten had feared, Himmler felt it necessary to try to justify himself and the deeds he had ordered since 1942. He began by making a long, rambling statement to Masur that in the 1930s he had tried his utmost to facilitate the emigration of all the Jews in Germany; however, the countries that had at first pretended to be hospitable to the Jews had quickly closed their borders and refused to take any more. He touched on Ribbentrop's scheme to make a Jewish homeland on the island of Madagascar, but this plan had proven fanciful and unworkable. With the coming of the war years, Germany had found itself taking over millions of Jews when the invasion of the east had taken place. He explained the crematoria in the extermination camps as having proven necessary to cope with the numerous victims of epidemic and disease. After rambling on for some time Himmler eventually subsided into silence. At this point both Kersten and Schellenberg impressed upon him the necessity of handing over to the Allies all the Jews still held in camps.

When Masur joined in the discussion, Himmler was quick to agree. He asserted that there would be no more killings, and that all the camps would be handed over intact. He also consented to the immediate release of all Jewish women held at Ravensbrück, provided that this be done secretly and kept out of the press. It would seem that Himmler, during his last meeting with Hitler, had received the Führer's permission to release all Polish women held in the camps, for an additional precaution was agreed: the women freed from Ravensbrück were to be described as 'Poles'.

The meeting with Masur ended at 5.00 a.m., and Kersten walked Himmler and Schellenberg out to their car. Before he got in, Himmler talked quietly with Kersten in the darkness, trying again to justify his actions of the past few years. He conceded that the war was lost, and admitted that he and his fellow Nazis had made terrible mistakes. They had wanted greatness and security for Germany. Did the ends justify the means? He was unsure. All that the world would remember, he asserted, was that the Nazis had left Germany in ruins. For himself, he had always wanted what was best, but so often he had had to work against his real convictions.

With that final remark, Himmler climbed into the car, held out his hand and shook Kersten's warmly, thanking him deeply for the years he had treated him with his skilled hands. 'My last thoughts are for my poor family,' was his parting comment as the car pulled away. The two men would never meet again.

Later that morning Kersten departed for Sweden with Masur by car, the Allies possessing such overwhelming air superiority by now that no German aircraft had a hope of getting through. On their arrival in Stockholm forty-eight hours later, Kersten and Masur went directly to the head of the Jewish delegation in Sweden. At first the man expressed doubt about Himmler's promises, but Kersten gave as strong an assurance as he could that the Reichsführer-SS would keep his word.

On leaving Kersten's home in the early hours of Saturday, 22 April, Schellenberg and Himmler travelled straight back to Himmler's field headquarters at Hohenlychen, where Count Bernadotte was waiting. Here a smorgasbord breakfast of great abundance had been laid out, regardless of the fact that the rest of Germany was starving. In the Reichsführer's circle the concept of rationing was non-existent. Bernadotte was unaccustomed to such lavish breakfasts, but Himmler ate with great relish. His night's activities had left him with an appetite, and he was in a state of high excitement now that it seemed he was finally making progress with his negotiations.

Over their meal Bernadotte again pressed Himmler over the release of all Scandinavian prisoners being held at Neuengamme camp. They also discussed the release of all 15,000 Jewish women from Ravensbrück; it was agreed that these would be taken to freedom by a Red Cross convoy of Swedish and Danish buses. Bernadotte found Himmler quite affable, but still the Reichsführer could not bring himself to open discussions about the capitulation of Germany. That subject was left to Schellenberg whilst he was driving Bernadotte back to the Swedish Embassy in Berlin. Schellenberg asked Bernadotte to travel with all haste to General Eisenhower and set up a meeting with Himmler. Bernadotte, ever the realist (indeed, he was probably in touch with the Allies already and aware of their attitude to negotiating with the Nazis), said this was impossible; the initiative had to come from Himmler. 'The Reichsführer no longer understands the realities of his own situation,' he declared. 'He should have taken Germany's affairs into his own hands after my first visit.'[1]

After dropping Bernadotte off at the Swedish Embassy in Berlin, Schellenberg returned to Himmler's temporary headquarters at Hohenlychen to find he had taken to his bed, a 'picture of misery' and saying he felt ill. Himmler's earlier optimism at his negotiations had failed him whilst Schellenberg had been in Berlin; he felt as though very little progress had been made. Schellenberg, however, realised that the end was coming, as the Russians drew their tactical net ever tighter around Berlin. He told Himmler there was very little more he could do under the present circumstances, and advised him to leave Hohenlychen before it was cut off by the Russians. Now was the time to withdraw to Ziethen Castle, whilst they were still able. Himmler agreed, and within the hour the two men, plus Himmler's personal entourage of secretaries and bodyguard unit, were on the road to the castle, safely far to the northwest of Berlin near the Danish border. It took them the better part of the day to reach Ziethen along roads gridlocked with refugees also fleeing the Russians. From here they could organise Himmler's final strategy of negotiating with the Allies. To do that, Schellenberg needed to keep in close contact with Bernadotte.

On their arrival at Ziethen, Himmler's courage returned to him and he dispatched Schellenberg to Lübeck, for he knew that Bernadotte had intended to travel there on his way home to Sweden. Schellenberg was instructed to tell the Count that Himmler was prepared to ask him officially and in his own name to take a message of surrender to Eisenhower.[2]

Struggling along roads teeming with refugees, Schellenberg eventually caught up with Bernadotte near the Danish border at Flensburg. Much against Bernadotte's better judgement, he found himself persuaded to meet with Himmler again that night at Lübeck. They met at the Swedish Consulate, but were forced to take refuge for several hours in the cellar after a particularly ferocious Allied bombing raid. Emerging a little after midnight, Himmler sat down with Bernadotte. On this occasion he was more certain of his ground, intent on making progress to end the war without further pointless loss of life. On the previous occasions when they had met, he asserted, Hitler had been very much still in charge. The situation had now changed. Hitler was in Berlin, resolved to end his life with its inhabitants in the besieged city rather than survive in ignominy. He was determined to die in the struggle to which he had devoted his existence, the fight against Bolshevism.[3]

In the present situation, Himmler went on to say, he had a free hand. Further resistance against the western Allies was futile, and would only cause Germany even more suffering and bloodshed. He was prepared to give way on the western front and allow the Anglo-American forces to advance eastward. Himmler asked Bernadotte to transmit this message to the Swedish government so they could convey it to General Eisenhower.[4] However, he confided to Bernadotte, 'To capitulate to the Russians is impossible for us Germans and particularly for me. We shall continue fighting them until the front of the western powers has replaced the

German front.'⁵ Bernadotte duly transmitted Himmler's peace offer to his government. Personally he was convinced that the west would not accept separate peace talks, especially with someone of the Reichsführer's ilk. Nevertheless, he was pleased that Himmler's desire for peace had provided a lever by which he might be manoeuvred into agreeing the inclusion of Norway and Denmark in any deal.

Predictably, Churchill and President Truman dismissed Himmler's offer out of hand and informed Stalin. There would be no peace until Germany surrendered unconditionally, as had been agreed at the Casablanca Conference of 1943. Whilst there were still factions within Germany determined to fight on against the Russians, even if others were inclined to sue for peace, there could be no cessation of hostilities. However, the secret Himmler had kept for so long was about to be revealed in spectacular fashion. In distant California, British Foreign Secretary Anthony Eden mentioned the peace offer to the British Director of Information Service, who in turn passed the news on to a colleague at Reuters. On 28 April, whilst the Russian forces were closing in on the Reich Chancellery, and as Adolf Hitler counted down the hours to his suicide (he had made up his mind to kill himself on 30 April, utterly convinced that the Russians would launch their final attack on 1 May; he greatly feared being captured and, in his words, to be 'paraded in a cage'), the world's press broke the news of Himmler's treachery.

It was nine in the evening before the sensational news of Himmler's secret attempts to make a separate peace deal with the west was received in the Führerbunker. It was picked up by a member of Dr Goebbels's staff, who immediately informed Martin Bormann. Long an enemy of Himmler, Bormann, after double-checking the source to ascertain the accuracy of the information, took great delight in running to his Führer with the shocking news. Those of Hitler's entourage who had previously seen him lose control of his temper were in for a spectacular show of volatile fireworks. Handed a copy of the radio broadcast, his shock was absolute, and his temper knew no bounds. He let out a cry of anguish and the eruption was as spectacular as it was dangerous. It was the ultimate betrayal. 'Der treue Heinrich', the longest serving of Hitler's paladins, head of Hitler's personal bodyguard, chief of the vanguard of the Nazi Party, the SS, and the state security service, had turned out to be a traitor.

Hitler stormed up and down the corridors of the Führerbunker, stopping everyone he met, waving the transcript of the Allied broadcast in their faces and screaming epithets against Himmler. Members of Hitler's entourage scattered in his path, avoiding confrontation with a man who was now capable of seeing treason at every turn. Finally, he ended his rampage through the bunker at a room in which the injured Ritter von Greim was lying (he had flown into Berlin with renowned woman pilot Hanna Reitsch to be appointed the new head of the Luftwaffe in Göring's place). Hitler ordered Greim to fly out of the besieged capital in a light-weight Storch reconnaissance plane that was secreted in the Tiergarten. First, he was to take over the Luftwaffe from Göring (who had incurred the Fuhrer's disfavour by trying to usurp his position as leader of the German Reich) and organise air attacks against the Russians, who were now less than a mile from the Reich Chancellery. Greim's second clear and concise order was that he was to organise Himmler's arrest. 'A traitor must never succeed me as Führer,' Hitler declared, his voice hoarse and shaking, his temper barely under control, and he informed Greim that he was stripping Himmler of every office of state.

In Plön, far to the northwest of Berlin near the Danish border, Himmler received on 29 April the first indication that his career was over. Greim arrived with Reitsch and immediately went to see Admiral Dönitz; they told the Admiral of Himmler's fall from grace and ordered his arrest. There was little Dönitz could do. Himmler was protected by a substantial entourage of high SS officers and a large section of his formidable escort battalion. These men were the elite of an elite fighting force, loyal and dedicated to their Reichsführer. Under such circumstances – with mayhem raging all about them, swamped with refugees and the homeless, his lines of communication nonexistent, hemmed into a small pocket to the northwest of Germany without reserves or *matériel* to call on – it was simply not possible for the Admiral to order the arrest of someone as powerful as Himmler, even if that order had emanated from Hitler himself.

•••••

In the early hours of Tuesday, 30 April 1945, Adolf Hitler placed the barrel of his gun in his mouth, pulled the trigger, and blew his brains out. Alongside him on the sofa in his private sitting room in the Führerbunker sat Eva Braun, whom he had married scant hours before; she had taken cyanide in a suicide pact with Hitler, following the love of her life into death. With his death the Third Reich effectively ceased to exist. He paid the ultimate price for his political and military failures of the past four years. With his suicide Hitler in effect cheated the world of bringing him to account for his numerous crimes against humanity and the intent to wage aggressive war of which he was undoubtedly guilty. In a grisly and Wagnerian act, his three loyal adjutants carried the bodies out of the Führerbunker into the Chancellery garden, laid them in a shell hole, and whilst Russian shells shrieked all about them wreaking havoc and destruction, poured petrol over the bodies and set them alight. Watched over from the shelter of the bunker entrance by Joseph Goebbels and Martin Bormann, the cremation obliterated every last trace of their Führer and his wife. It was clear to everyone present that as the roaring gasoline-fed flames consumed their leader, so, too, in fire had the Third Reich been brought to an end. The great experiment – Nazism – had failed and ended in unmitigated disaster: Germany now lay in smoking ruins, the country's industrial infrastructure had collapsed, the war in Europe had cost 55 million lives, and there were currently 30 million refugees wandering the continent without a home.

Following Hitler's death, Dönitz received the astonishing news on Wednesday, 1 May that he had been named as the Führer's successor. He was now leader of a nation that had been all but destroyed; it was a poor inheritance, but Dönitz, advised by Albert Speer, determined to end the war as soon as possible to prevent any further death and destruction. Meeting with Speer, Dönitz had asked the capable architect and government minister whether they should abandon using the swastika flag, as a sign that this was a new regime that was trying to distance itself from the worst excesses of Hitler's Reich. Speer responded that they could not now pretend to be something they were not; they owed everything to Hitler, however much they had disagreed with some of his policies. The swastika emblem was retained. On the subject of Himmler, however, Speer was adamant. Admiral Dönitz should not grant him any provisional government post whatsoever. He must be excluded from any official position within the new regime. Reluctantly Dönitz agreed, though he was doubtful that Himmler would give up his posts so easily. On the subject of the SS, Speer and Dönitz well realised that there was nothing they could do to take the organisation from Himmler. As long as he was excluded from the new provisional government, however, there was a chance of agreeing terms with the Allies for a surrender.

As it happened, Himmler, on meeting with Dönitz at Plön, faced the new situation with a startling degree of acceptance. Doubting whether Himmler would agree that there could be no position for him in the new provisional government, Dönitz had placed armed naval personnel around his headquarters to guard against possible trouble; he had even taken the precaution of placing a loaded pistol under the papers on his desk, the safety catch off. However, Himmler, shocked that Hitler had passed him over and had in his will appointed Dönitz as the new head of state, did not dissent. Cannily, Dönitz did not strip Himmler of his position as head of the SS. Perhaps he concluded that this would be a move too far, one that would prompt Himmler to order his men to seize power. Perhaps he realised that such a move might precipitate open fighting between his naval guard and Himmler's elite personal guard, and did not rate his own force highly against the Reichsfuhrer's excellently armed and trained men. After the war one of those men, Sturmbannführer Heinz Macher, described Himmler's honour guard as 'the most piratical, bravest and experienced warriors to be found in all Germany'.[6]

Thus Himmler was still an extremely dangerous adversary. Dönitz must have decided that it was best to leave the head of the SS alone: excluding him from the new regime was enough. Anyway, there was nothing left for him to do but organise the surrender. In such circumstances Himmler, too, had been rendered powerless.

Following his meeting with Dönitz, Himmler came out of the Plön naval headquarters and bumped into Hanna Reitsch. Germany's most famous woman pilot had been fanatically loyal to Hitler and immediately took the opportunity to berate Himmler for his betrayal of the Führer. At this most difficult time every member of the Nazi leadership was making new alliances, becoming – so to speak – new men. It was possible now to say things to powerful individuals such as Himmler and expect a reasonable answer. Fanatical Nazi that she was, Reitsch declared that Himmler's secret talks with the Allies through Count Bernadotte (no one knew of the Stockholm negotiations via Victor Mallet), had been acts of high treason.

'High treason?' replied Himmler. 'No. You'll see, history will evaluate it differently. Hitler wanted to continue the fight. He was mad with his pride and his honour. He wanted to shed more German blood when there was none left to flow. Hitler was insane. It should have been stopped long ago.'

'Hitler died bravely and honourably,' Reitsch retorted furiously, 'while you and Göring and the rest must now live branded as traitors and cowards.'

Considering Reitsch's response for a moment, Himmler's own was most interesting: 'I did what I could to save German blood and rescue what was left of our country.'[7] With that he turned on his heel and stalked away.

Despite not being given a post in Dönitz's new regime, Himmler was still a very important Nazi figure, and so, on 2 May, he and Schellenberg were invited to lunch with the Admiral at his Plön naval headquarters. Arriving at two in the afternoon, Himmler brought news that the Gauleiter of Hamburg had announced that he was determined to surrender his already shattered city to prevent any further loss of life. Also present at the lunch, Albert Speer offered to drive to Hamburg later that afternoon to persuade the Gauleiter to hang on a little longer. Dönitz agreed, but events were to overtake them. News was brought in to the lunch party that the British had broken out of a bridgehead across the River Elbe at Lauenburg and were currently racing north to the Baltic coast, in order to prevent the Russians from advancing across the Danish peninsula and in so doing reaching the North Sea. There were even now British tanks prowling the streets of Lübeck, a scant thirty miles away. Everyone, including Dönitz, immediately flew into a panic, and the Admiral ordered a tactical withdrawal of his ministers and minions to take place that night to Flensburg, on the Danish border and protected by the Kiel Canal. The canal would become the new defensive line and would be impassable to Allied tanks. His move was designed to buy a little more time until he could organise the surrender, his destination the Naval Cadet School, where he intended to set up the final seat of his new government.

That night saw a motley collection of vehicles in convoy set out north to Flensburg, Himmler driving his own heavily armoured Mercedes saloon, his SS men in trucks and cars running on potato schnapps, limousines carrying the Admiral and his staff, Speer at the wheel of a Volkswagen. The convoy reached Flensburg in the early hours of the morning before daybreak, safe from Allied air attack in the cover of darkness.

On 3 May Dönitz met with Generaladmiral Hans Georg von Friedenberg, and instructed him to take an offer of capitulation of German forces in the north to British Field Marshal Montgomery. It was a tactic designed to circumvent the west's refusal to accept a one-sided surrender whilst still buying time to rescue German troops and civilians trapped in the east. Later that night Friedenberg returned with the news that Montgomery was prepared to accept the surrender of all forces on his northern and western flank – Holland, Friesland, Schleswig-Holstein and Denmark – but not Army Group Vistula fighting the Russians on the north-eastern front. Calling a meeting on the morning of 4 May, Dönitz listened to Himmler's advice that Holland and Denmark should not simply be given up, but that the two countries, with occupied Norway, could be used as trump cards in negotiations. However, it was concluded that further resistance was futile. The German forces were growing weaker by the hour, the ammunition was running out, there was virtually no food with which to feed either the armed forces or the vast refugee population, and with every day that passed the threat of an uprising grew ever more likely. With these facts in mind, Dönitz chose to ignore Himmler's suggestion. He dispatched Friedenberg back to Montgomery with full authority to agree terms and sign a ceasefire. Negotiations on capitulation and surrender could be completed in the next forty-eight hours. Friedenberg duly set out from Flensburg, in the end signing a ceasefire agreement with the Allied Commander-in-Chief in the late evening of 4 May. Fighting finally stopped on the following morning.

Back in Flensburg an uneasy peace settled and the air raids ceased. On 7 May, at Reims, Generaladmiral von Friedenberg watched as General Alfred Jodl signed the paper agreeing the Germans' unconditional surrender. The cessation of all hostilities was to take effect on 8 May. The war that had cost so many lives had come to an end.

Despite the unconditional surrender of Germany to the Allies, it would be a mistake to think that the former great men of the Third Reich immediately gave themselves up. In Flensburg Admiral Dönitz and his provisional government remained at liberty, besieged by a multitude of Allied press who wanted the inside story of the end of Nazi Germany. The swastika flag continued to fly over Dönitz's headquarters for the moment, and the leading Nazis were daily spotted by the world's press, followed and photographed. Dönitz, Speer and Schwerin von Krosigk (Dönitz's Foreign Minister) gave interviews, and the rich panoply of the former Nazi hierarchy was on display for all to see. For the moment the Allied high command permitted this state of affairs to continue, though they apprehended every Nazi they could locate in their zones of occupation. Thus for two weeks much of Schleswig-Holstein, isolated from the rest of Germany by the British zone of occupation, was still under the control of Admiral Dönitz and his provisional government. But it was obviously not a situation that would last for long, and Nazis such as Albert Speer were busy during this time attempting to ingratiate themselves with the Allies. Heinrich Himmler, too, was still at liberty, and he was desperately trying to negotiate his future with anyone he could contact.

•••••

During that last week of the war Himmler had not yet been ready to consider himself a spent force, and he was still determined to play out his own political and diplomatic hand. On 4 May, four days before the uncon-ditional surrender came into effect, he dispatched Schellenberg to Sweden, accompanied by Bernadotte. His intent was to reopen his negoti-ations with the British and, more particularly, to open talks with the Swedish government, which it was hoped might be persuaded to provide sanctuary for wanted Nazis. This time he had very little up his sleeve with which to tempt the British, or indeed the Swedes. Thus, remarkably, Schellenberg travelled to Stockholm with six metal cases. These were stuffed full of German intelligence material on the Soviet Union (informa-tion on the Baltic states, broken Russian ciphers, etc.), along with formulae and blueprints of some of Germany's most significant wartime industrial developments; tempting bait to be used in a bid to further Himmler's standing with the British authorities. He now hoped in the main to buy concessions from the British that would give him immunity from war crimes prosecution. It is also worthy of note that Himmler promoted Schellenberg to the position of 'Sonderbevollmächtiger' – Plenipotentiary Extraordinary – empowered to negotiate on his behalf; as is the fact that the Swedes opened up the royal palace of Tullgarn on the Tosa archipelago near Stockholm for use as Schellenberg's private residence whilst he was in Sweden. The polished tiles of the entrance were buffed to a high gloss, and beech leaves were cleared from the steps leading down to the boat-house, from which Schellenberg daily travelled into Stockholm for his negotiations. He and his small entourage of two secretaries and a male assistant were treated to every luxury neutral Sweden could provide.

On 6 May Schellenberg arranged for Hans Thompson, the German Ambassador to Sweden, to fly to the Norwegian border courtesy of the Swedish Air Force, to meet with General Boehme to discuss the surrender of all German forces in Norway. However, Boehme did not appreciate Schellenberg's interference in diplomatic matters. He attempted to speak directly to Dönitz on the telephone to sort out the situation, only to discover that all the telephone lines from Norway to Germany had been cut. On the following day, 7 May, Schellenberg telephoned Dönitz's new Foreign Minister, Krosigk, to resolve the matter, only to learn that Dönitz was determined to capitulate and was surrendering Norway without any further discussions. Krosigk urged Schellenberg not to interfere any more in the matter for fear that he might endanger the peace negotiations that were already underway through Friedenberg. Schellenberg now withdrew completely from his diplomatic endeavours in Sweden, and instead focused all his attention on Victor Mallet at the British Embassy.

On the morning of 8 May 1945, the very same day that the war officially ended, Schellenberg decided to visit Mallet. Press photographers gathered outside the gates of the British Embassy were startled a little after 2.00 p.m. to see Count Folke Bernadotte's large open-topped car arrive with none other than the head of Amt VI of the SD, Himmler's very own representative in Sweden, SS-Brigadeführer Walter Schellenberg, sitting in the back. Of course he was not in uniform, but his arrival in Sweden a few days before had been a newsworthy item, and he was immediately recognised. The photographers captured for posterity the arrival of this high-ranking man of the SS, come to talk with the British Ambassador.

As a result of this startling and disturbing development, London sent fourteen secret telegrams to Mallet between 6 May and 14 May. All have remained classified and are not open to public scrutiny at the National Archives in Kew even today. Whatever was being discussed was, and is, evidently too sensitive for public disclosure. SIS officer Peter Tennant was convinced that Mallet had been deeply involved in secret financial negotiations between the Wallenberg brothers and the Germans, which also involved the Swedish royal family.[8] Since Ewan Butler's drunken breakdown in January 1944, Tennant and Peter Falk had both been painfully aware that Krämer, Schellenberg, Himmler, and the British government via Mallet had agreed some form of deal to grant Schellenberg and Himmler immunity from prosecution for war crimes. Now that the war had ended, it was evident that Schellenberg was meeting Mallet to see whether that deal still held.

Falk recalled how Schellenberg's visits affected those who saw him at the British Embassy: 'It was so incongruous. A modestly dressed man, dressed as if he was a country squire in tweeds, creating such a negative atmosphere. He seemed to carry it with him.' No one at the Embassy wanted to be seen to associate with him, and Mallet froze in horror when Schellenberg and Bernadotte arrived for their first meeting. It seemed that Schellenberg had no further use for Wallenberg now that the war was over, and was under the impression that he could now meet with Mallet publicly in the safe neutrality of Sweden. For his part Schellenberg believed that the agreement made through Ewan Butler guaranteed his existence in Sweden free from prosecution, and that a distinguished career in intelligence still lay before him. (As it happened, this logic operated successfully for an as yet unknown SS/SD officer named Reinhard Gehlen. A high-ranking intelligence officer, Gehlen was an expert on the Soviet Union. After a brief interval at the end of the war, he was recruited by the Americans and British to create West Germany's primary post-war organisation for intelligence gathering, the Bundesnachrichtendienst (BND), a German version of the CIA.[9]) Such was the future Schellenberg desired, but it was one he was not destined to enjoy. For so prominent a member of the SS there could be no such prospect. He had thrown in his lot with the Nazi hierarchy, and, most dangerous of all, it was known that he was Himmler's man. His status as Himmler's own 'Benjamin' had ensured his meteoric rise through the SD, but he was now to pay the price. Despite his sojourn in Sweden, the British were very keen indeed to get their hands on him.

Schellenberg's and Himmler's attempts to bargain well past the hour produced a very stern response from Churchill and his government. On 9 May Count Bernadotte received a terse letter directly from Victor Mallet ordering him to halt his visits to the British Embassy in Schellenberg's company. Later that same day Bernadotte received a second message from Mallet. It instructed him to tell Schellenberg that an RAF Dakota was awaiting him at Bromma airport, ready to fly him to London the next day. When Bernadotte's secretary rang the Embassy for an explanation she was told that Schellenberg was urgently wanted for questioning. Following this, Bernadotte himself contacted Mallet to discover what was happening, only to learn that the British no longer wanted discussions with Schellenberg; he was a former leading man of the SS/SD and as such a wanted war criminal. The following morning the Swedish papers – the Press having being primed by Jasper Leadbitter, the Press Attaché at the British Embassy – broke the story of how the Swedish government was sheltering a wanted war criminal. Bernadotte was furious, and refused to let Schellenberg leave, issuing a statement that he was too 'mentally and physically exhausted to travel'. Finally, it was becoming clear to Bernadotte and Schellenberg that they had misjudged the situation. The British were not inclined to honour any private deals or recognise Schellenberg's value as an intelligence source. In the face of British displeasure, the Swedish government could not be depended upon to offer Walter Schellenberg the security and status to which he and Bernadotte believed he was entitled. Interestingly, it was believed in some circles that the Swedes had offered Schellenberg immunity from prosecution should he choose to remain there.[10] They did, however, refuse permission for Himmler to enter their country – as did Denmark – the moment the war ended.

•••••

The 'Little H' protagonists at PWE had had very little to do with
Himmler ever since the 20 July bomb plot had failed to kill Hitler in the
summer of 1944. Nevertheless they had kept close tabs on Himmler's
activities since that time, even if the negotiable contact via Krämer to
Victor Mallet had not produced anything interesting as Germany's strategic
position had become increasing desperate, and the signs emerged that
Himmler would try one last gamble to save his neck. Nevertheless, the
information that an organ of British intelligence had been in touch with
Himmler during the war years was very dangerous; it had the potential to
cause a severe loss of face to the British authorities and could ruin political careers.

If the news that PWE/British intelligence had been secretly negotiating
with Himmler ever since early 1943 became public, then that would prove
very uncomfortable for the British government. It had the potential to sour
the Atlantic Alliance, and to undermine the War Crimes Trials that it was
planned to mount later that year. If Himmler were to take to the stand and
declare to the world that he was a moderate man who had wanted peace
and had been negotiating with the British since 1943, then who could say
what the outcome might be? At the very least it would undermine Britain's
moral high-ground at the War Crimes Trials yet to come; it would leave the
British government left to answer why, even as this leading Nazi was
offering a peace deal, Britain had not pursued this peaceable line that
could have save many lives. The Americans would also ask some very
uncomfortable questions, such as: 'If you had Himmler in your grasp since
1943, why did you keep that important fact secret? Why did you not use
this peace offer to end the war in 1943 or 1944? Why did you not use your
influence with Himmler to limit the scope of the SS's extermination of the
Jews?'

Britain – and this specifically means Churchill – had been the foremost
proponent of a policy of non-negotiation with men of the Nazi Party, or
indeed any German. At the very least it would reveal a dichotomy of intent
that would damage the British government's reputation; at worst it could
cause critical strains on the Atlantic Alliance, and that could prove very
dangerous indeed in this new post-war world where Stalin was not trusted
and a new 'cold' war was just about to come into existence.

Back in Flensburg, near the Danish border, Heinrich Himmler had
been lying low during the negotiations to end the war. He had maintained
a loose contact with Dönitz and the new regime at the Admiral's headquarters. He was seen by members of the Allied Press arriving for meetings

flanked by men of his personal staff. During the first few days of the peace he had lain very low at a large house near his temporary headquarters, comforted by the company of his lover, Hedwig Potthast, and his two young children.

Then, on 10 May, Himmler took a very surprising decision. He decided to move. His destination seemed to be the American zone of occupation in Bavaria. Why he took this decision is not known, but it is strongly suspected that he intended to travel to the south of Germany where he could make contact with the American OSS, who suspected he had secretly been behind the Wolff negotiations to end the war in Italy. Himmler had gambled and lost with the British; thus he did not trust the British, especially since they were now prevaricating in their negotiations with Walter Schellenberg. If Schellenberg had been able to telephone Dönitz's headquarters for guidance, which we know he did, then logic says that it was also very likely that he was in constant contact with Himmler. Himmler therefore knew that the British were now reneging on their deal with him and Schellenberg, denying that any deal for immunity had been agreed. Schellenberg also probably knew from Bernadotte that the Swedish government would not grant them sanctuary. Himmler therefore had little choice other than to now turn to the Americans in the hope of winning concessions that would grant him immunity from prosecution. It is also therefore extremely likely that Himmler decided to depart from Flensburg for the south of Germany where it would be possible for him to make direct contact with Allen Dulles, the top man of the OSS who had conducted the Wolff negotiations and had the President's ear. To a man like Himmler – not very worldly wise, and not having much understanding of the American infrastructure – this would have seemed like a logical course of action.

Thus on 10 May 1945, Heinrich Himmler departed from Flensburg in the company of his most trusted SS confederates. Dressed in a motley collection of civilian clothes, wearing a tatty blue raincoat, and sporting a piratical eye patch to further disguise his appearance, he headed south through refugee packed Schleswig-Holstein in the direction of the British zone of occupation, which he would have to pass through if he were to reach the American zone. The most notable members of Himmler's party were SS-Obergruppenführer Dr Karl Brandt, Hitler's former personal physician; SS-Obergruppen-führer Dr Karl Gebhardt, Himmler's personal friend and physician; SS-Obergruppenführer Otto Ohlendorf; SS-Sturmbannführer Josef Kiermaier, Himmler's personal aid and secretary, and Himmler's adjutants, SS-Obersturmbannführer Werner Grothmann and SS-Sturmbannführer Heinz Macher. In addition to these high-ranking men of Himmler's personal staff were two more officers of his escort battalion, and seven NCOs from his personal staff. All sixteen men crammed themselves in four cars and set off for the British zone of occupation in the south. These men, especially Himmler, realised their journey would be an arduous one, fraught with difficulty, their vehicles short of fuel, the roads, villages and towns crammed to overflowing with refugees who had sought sanctuary safe from the fighting. The war had ended mere days before, but still there were very high numbers of people who had only just heard that Germany had capitulated, people who had no homes to return to. Schleswig-Holstein was particularly crowded with refugees, and the whole infrastructure was creaking at the seams as it endeavoured to provide shelter and food to the homeless masses. Such a situation only served to make Himmler's travels all the more arduous. The roads were grid-locked, and there was no shelter to be found for love nor money.

Having left Flensburg on 10 May, it took Himmler's convoy of four vehicles two whole days to cover the sixty-mile journey to Marne in the southwest corner of the peninsular. Here, at the north bank of the Elbe estuary, Himmler and his entourage were forced to abandon their cars and proceed on foot. It was a situation they had not envisaged, and they were not certain how they could manage to get to the south of Germany. Surely, they discussed amongst themselves, they could not walk the whole way. Himmler was undaunted by this development and assured his men that if refugees could walk their way across the whole of Germany, then surely the well-trained and fit men of the SS could manage such a journey.[11] By 18 May Himmler and his party had got no further than the little town of Bremervörde on the River Oste, some twenty-five miles to the south-east of Marne; they had only averaged five miles a day, and their hopes of a forced march to the south of Germany had dwindled with every mile they tramped. Even the Reichsführer seemed to subside into sullen silence as he tramped alongside his men, most of whom towered over his diminutive frame. In his ill-fitting civilian clothes Himmler did not make for an impressive sight, whilst his men all wore their leather SS greatcoats with felt collars, even though they had removed all their insignia and SS collar flashes.

Himmler himself had taken the precaution of using someone else's identity card, that of a man named Heinrich Hitzinger, a sergeant of the Geheime Feldpolizei – the Secret Field Police – which had been affiliated to the SS. Indeed, Himmler's men had all been issued with Geheime

Feldpolizei papers, and their cover story was that they were all men suffering from ill health, travelling home under the supervision of Dr Gebhardt. It was a tale that would fool no one, and they had made the terrible error of using the GFP as a cover. The Allies were well aware that the Geheime Feldpolizei were affiliated to the SS, indeed they had been responsible for executing many deserters in the last days of the war, and as such the Allied standing orders were that any Geheime Feldpolizei men apprehended were to be held and interrogated. It was a mistake that would cost Himmler his life...

Here, at Bremervörde, Himmler and his party made a seemingly unaccountable decision. They could have forded the river Oste upstream of the town as countless other refugees had done, and indeed were doing at that time. Instead, Himmler and his party took the decision to cross the river by the town bridge, which was guarded by the British army at a very visible checkpoint. At this time the bridge was being used as an intelligence screening point by the 45 Security Section of the Intelligence Corp, and was guarded by men of the 51st Highland Division. To help them carry out checks on persons passing through their checkpoint, the men, Staff-Sergeant John Hogg and Sergeants Arthur Britton and Ken Baisbrown, had a directory of wanted SD, Gestapo, Nazi and SS personnel who were all regarded as war criminals. This directory, running to several hundred pages, had been compiled by CROWCASS, the Central Registry of War Criminals and Security Suspects.

After watching the checkpoint for a while, and trying to look as inconspicuous at possible, Himmler and his party retired to a farmhouse at 165 Waldstrasse to consider their next move. They remained here overnight, and came to the decision that they would stick to their original plan, masquerading as ailing policemen and would try to pass through the British checkpoint with their false GFP papers and demobilisation passes, which Himmler had had the foresight to obtain in Flensburg. The only problem was that their passes had all been stamped by the SD and that was considered a criminal organisation.

Late in the afternoon of 21 May Kiermaier and Gebhardt set off to reconnoitre the British Army checkpoint, with the intention of returning for the others if all seemed well. On the bridge they were stopped by Sergeant Baisbrown, who was immediately suspicious of the two men because of their furtive attitude, and because their papers bore the stamp of SD headquarters, although they had been carefully smudged to hide that important fact. Careful not to frighten the men off, the British assured the two Germans that all was well, and offered to send a lorry back for their party and bring them through the checkpoint. Gebhardt agreed, telling Baisbrown and Hogg his cover story of escorting ailing policemen home to Bavaria, and agreed to return to the farmhouse with the British soldiers to collect his party. To Gebhardt's surprise Himmler and his two adjutants, Grothmann and Macher, had gone, and the other SS men in the farmhouse did not know where they were. All the Germans were brought back to the bridge checkpoint, where their cover-story soon fell apart; some of the men denied they had been Geheime Feldpolizei, and all their papers were soon noted as being SD stamped on 1 May. It was an instant giveaway, and all twelve men were arrested and dispatched in a lorry under guard to the Allied internment camp at Westertimke, near Zeven, fifteen miles to the south. Here, further interrogation could take place to ascertain their true identities, and whether they were wanted war criminals.

The British, and Gebhardt in particular, were at a loss as to why the three top men of the party had vanished, and Gebhardt could not understand why Himmler had taken the decision to leave the farmhouse. Long after the war Heinz Macher was to reveal that once Gebhardt and Kiermaier had left to reconnoitre the checkpoint, Himmler at once had a very bad feeling about the whole matter, and had decided to leave the main party to see what was happening at the bridge. On spotting the lorry and an army escort heading back towards the farmhouse, Himmler immediately took fright and the three of them hid for twenty-four hours in a nearby barn to await developments.[12]

Finally, on the afternoon of 22 May, Himmler decided to make an attempt to cross the bridge, and so, accompanied by his two adjutants, they headed for the British checkpoint. The three men made for an incongruous and curious sight as they made for the bridge along the centre of Bremervörde high street. Two very impressive looking former SS men (both were over 6 feet tall), wearing their military leather greatcoats, accompanied by a smaller, furtive looking man in the middle, wearing an odd selection of civilian clothes and an old blue raincoat. The trio did not even reach the bridge before they were stopped by a British army patrol and escorted to a mill at the side of the bridge, which was acting as the guardroom. When they arrived at 5:00 p.m. they were met by Sergeant Britton, who telephoned Staff-Sergeant Hogg to report 'the three men have come in'.[13]

Baisbrown immediately went to the mill as soon as he heard that the last three men of Gebhardt's party had been captured. He found two very military looking characters standing looking nonchalantly about, and the third, a scruffy looking man with an eye-patch, squatting on his haunches on the floor. Asked for their papers, all three men produced their identity cards and discharge papers, but once again the smudge SD stamp on their papers gave them away. At the very least they were Geheime Feldpolizei, and as such wanted men; at worst they were men possessed of false papers, and were thus most likely wanted for something else. The British sergeants had no idea that they held in their custody none other than Reichsführer-SS Heinrich Himmler himself, one of the most wanted men of the Third Reich. Promptly arrested, the three men were confined under guard to the second floor of the mill, where they slept the night amongst the grain sacks. Himmler's liberty and freedom of action had ended.

The following morning, at 7:00 a.m. on Wednesday 23 May, the three men were placed under guard aboard a lorry that would take them the fifteen miles south to the civil interment camp at Westertimke. They stopped briefly at Zeven, where Sergeant Britton reported to Captain Excell of the 45th Field Security Station, who did not feel it worth his while to come out to see the prisoners. Instead he ordered Britton to proceed directly to the Westertimke 'Cage' – Camp 31 – where the prisoners would be registered.

The truck reached the Westertimke camp at about lunchtime, and Karl Kaufmann, former Gauleiter of Hamburg, who was standing with other prisoners behind the wire fence watching new prisoners arrive, noticed the lorry bringing in the latest batch of arrivals: 'Among those who got out was Himmler, minus his moustache and with a patch over one eye. This was, in my opinion, the time when he decided to give himself up.' Passed through the gates into the camp, Himmler and his two adjutants immediately proceeded behind some bushes, where they tidied themselves up – they had not had a wash or shave in twenty-four hours. It was at this time that Himmler removed his eye patch, and made the decision to give himself up. A few minutes later, according to Kaufmann, a great stir went through the camp as the news spread, and men came running out of their huts to view the spectacle. Extra guards were summoned from the guardhouse and posted on the gates. 'Soon the cause of the excitement was being passed over the grapevine in the camp. The British soldiers seemed overjoyed that Himmler was among their prisoners.'[14]

The officer commanding the Westertimke camp was Captain Thomas Selvester, and soon the cause of the stir in the camp was taken to his office.

When the trio entered his office, Selvester was immediately struck by the military bearing of the two large men in their greatcoats, one very slim, and the other thickset and strong looking. In between them stood their superior, a slight, diminutive and unimpressive looking man. Sensing something very unusual about the group, Selvester ordered his sergeant to take the two military-looking prisoners away under close custody and allow them no communication with anyone. Looking to their commander-in-chief for guidance, Himmler nodded to his two men with a slight smile; reassured, Macher and Grothmann allowed themselves to be taken outside.[15] As soon as the door closed behind him, the shabby little man rummaged inside his jacket breast pocket and produced a pair of glasses. He put them on and his identity was immediately apparent, and he said quietly, 'Heinrich Himmler.'[16]

Captain Selvester telephoned the headquarters of the British Second Army at Lüneberg, and informed the Intelligence staff there that he had apprehended none other than the Reichsführer-SS, Heinrich Himmler. The Intelligence staff at Lüneberg immediately dispatched a Major Rice to the Westertimke 'Cage' with a SHEAF index-card on Himmler to confirm his identity. This card held a detailed description of Himmler, two photographs, and a sample of his signature. In the meantime, until Major Rice arrived, Selvester was ordered to conduct a thorough search of the prisoner, paying particular attention to find out whether Himmler had any poison on him.

Following his conversation with British Army headquarters at Lüneberg, Captain Selvester summoned two sergeants to assist him, and ordered Himmler to strip. Himmler duly removed all his clothes, and a thorough search revealed a curious-looking brass case, similar to a cartridge case. It contained a small glass phial, which Selvester immediately recognised as a suicide capsule. Asked what the phial contained, Himmler lied, telling Selvester that it was medicine to cure stomach cramp. It was confiscated. Soon a second brass case came to light, though this one was empty. Selvester suspected Himmler had a phial of poison hidden on his body somewhere, and the prisoner was ordered to strip naked. He was then given a complete and extremely thorough body search; even his hair was combed, but no phial came to light. Puzzled, and worried in case Himmler had the poison phial hidden in his mouth, Selvester ordered some thick cheese sandwiches and tea for Himmler, who tucked in with relish. He was not careful in the manner he chewed the food, nor swallowed his tea, indeed he even chatted as he ate; the conclusion was that Himmler's mouth was empty, and he did not have a suicide phial upon him.

There have been many rumours since the war that concerned Himmler's death. One suggestion was that many of the leading Nazis had special phials of poison hidden in their mouths in a false tooth. This is completely erroneous. The phials of poison handed out in the war years to leading Nazis were not very sophisticated, and quite large – too large to be secreted in a false tooth, or indeed hidden in the mouth, which is something they were not designed to do. The Zyankali suicide phials were all manufactured at Sachsenhausen concentration camp. They measured 9mm in diameter, were 35mm long, and contained 8mg of hydrogen cyanide. Four thousand such phials were manufactured at the camp during the war years, 950 of which were ordered by Criminal Police Chief Artur Nebe for distribution to the leading men of the Reich. If Himmler had had such a phial of poison hidden in his mouth he certainly could not have chewed and eaten thick cheese sandwiches, nor even talked properly. A 35mm-long object in his mouth would have been evident to anyone watching him.

Later in the afternoon of 23 May, Major Rice arrived from Lüneberg, and the identity of the man claiming to be Heinrich Himmler was compared to the SHEAF index-card. Himmler provided a sample of his signature on a blank piece of paper (which he insisted be destroyed as soon as the comparison was made), and both Selvester and Rice came to the unanimous decision that the man standing before them was indeed the Reichsführer of the SS, Heinrich Himmler. At this time Himmler was provided with a British Army uniform, which he refused to put on, not wishing to be photographed in it. He did, however, agree to put on the regulation British Army pants, socks, and shirt, and wrapped himself in a blanket he had been provided with. Himmler then remained in Selvester's office under close guard until arrangements could be made to take him to British Army headquarters at Lüneberg.

At 8:00 p.m. Montgomery's chief of intelligence, Colonel Michael Murphy, arrived to escort Himmler to Lüneberg, where it was intended to interrogate him further. Himmler was escorted unceremoniously out to Murphy's car with his blanket wrapped around his waist to afford him some dignity. If Himmler had hoped for a little deference afforded to him due to his importance, he was to be bitterly disappointed by Murphy's attitude towards him. Murphy was bad-tempered and very brusque, using all sorts of epithets including 'Come on, you bastard!' and 'We'll teach you!'[17] Himmler could not speak English, but could have been in no doubt that Murphy was not going to treat him with any of the respect due his former importance in the Third Reich, and Murphy's abusive manner must have been unmistakable. Himmler must have wondered if it may not have been a better idea to remain in Flensburg with the other leading Nazis. Bundled into the back of Murphy's car, Himmler set off on his journey in the dark on a wet and windy evening. His destination was a private semi-detached red-roofed villa at Lüneberg, No. 33 Ülznerstrasse, which had been taken over by men of British Military Intelligence. Prior to his departure with his new prisoner, Murphy, described by some as 'a full young colonel, who was not much liked,' had telephoned ahead and ordered that a doctor be present to examine the prisoner as soon as he arrived. A British army doctor, Captain Clement Wells, was summoned, and ordered to wait with Colour Sergeant-Major Edwin Austin to receive a very important prisoner. At that time Captain Wells had no idea whom he was waiting to examine, and Austin teased him by making him guess who it was.

When Murphy's car arrived outside the villa, on a bitingly cold evening with a sharp east wind, Murphy was first to get out. The backdoor of the vehicle was opened, and a sergeant climbed out, dragging a dishevelled figure wrapped in a blanket behind him. The prisoner was firmly grasped by each arm by the sergeant and Austin, and frogmarched into the house without further ado.

The report made the following morning to the world's press has recorded for posterity the series of events that would now take place. Colonel Murphy is recorded as duly arriving with Himmler, who was immediately hustled into the house and taken into a front room, where he was ordered to strip naked and submit to a close examination by Captain Wells. It was at this time, the official report of the time declared, that Wells noticed something in Himmler's mouth. Before Wells could intervene, it was recorded that Himmler bit down on a phial of poison and expired within a few minutes. There was nothing Murphy and Wells could do to save the Reichsführer.

That is the official version of the events that night at No. 33 Ülznerstrasse. However, not everything was quite as it seemed.

On his arrival at his Ülznerstrasse headquarters, Colonel Murphy took himself off to use the toilet on the first floor, suffering from stomach problems, which had made him ill-tempered all day.[18] Himmler was taken into the bare front-room of the villa, where he was supposed to be examined by Captain Wells. Whether this examination was really done or not is not known. What is known, however, is that Himmler died at this time – within a few minutes of arriving at the Ülznerstrasse villa as a result of cyanide poisoning. Murphy was not present.

Nor has it ever been revealed that Brendan Bracken and his team of covert plotters at PWE – Leonard St Clair Ingrams, Richard Crossman, or Robert Bruce-Lockhart – had a vested interest in seeing to it that Heinrich Himmler did not live long enough to be interrogated by the Americans, or indeed to be left free to undermine the Nuremberg War Crimes Trials by stating openly in his evidence that he had been trying to negotiate a peace deal with the British government ever since early in 1943.

History has recorded that Heinrich Himmler died at 11:00 p.m. on Wednesday 23 May 1945. He ended up as an undignified heap upon the floor, clothes lying around him, half naked, with curious British Intelligence personnel peering in at the doorway to see what had occurred. Something curious had happened to prevent Himmler being interrogated by the Americans, or indeed questioned by Montgomery's chief of intelligence, Colonel Murphy, for that matter.

The following morning, 24 May 1945, Heinrich Himmler was posed on the floor of the front room at 33 Ülznerstrasse, dressed in his British Army issue shirt and socks, for the Allied Press to photograph. Colonel Murphy issued his statement that during a strip search of Himmler late the previous evening the former Reichsführer-SS had suddenly bitten down on a mysterious phial of cyanide concealed in his mouth and committed suicide. Everyone accepted the story – no one had any reason not to – and it has, over the last sixty years, been the version of the event that has been accepted as the truth.

There were men, however, for whom such an outcome was a relief; men such as the ruthless Brendan Bracken, Leonard St Clair Ingrams and Bruce-Lockhart, who knew that there was a very big secret indeed that had to be maintained. It would have been a disaster, had the truth leaked out that throughout much of the war Britain had been in covert talks with top men of the Nazi leadership. If the news had leaked out that none other than Heinrich Himmler had been negotiating with Britons – albeit with men of the Political Warfare Executive – who had secretly not wanted peace, but had used the talks as a means of causing political damage to the German leadership, then that could have resulted in major repercussions in this new post-war world where the Soviet Union was day by day being perceived more and more as the threat to European stability.

On the morning of Friday 25 May 1945, Sergeant Austin was ordered by Colonel Murphy to dispose of Himmler's body. He wrapped Himmler's corpse in a camouflage net, then baled him into a tightly wrapped parcel with Army telephone wire. With the assistance of two privates Austin placed Himmler's corpse in the back of a three-ton lorry, and then headed off alone across the wilds of Lüneberg Heath. At a suitably secluded spot Sergeant Austin dug a grave far from prying eyes and dropped the body into the hole. He filled in the hole, leaving no marker to indicate a grave. He then returned back to Ülznerstrasse and reported on his completed mission to Colonel Murphy. 'Nobody,' he declared, 'will ever know where he is buried.'[19]

Brendan Bracken and his men at the Political Warfare Executive had successfully concluded their mission against Heinrich Himmler. Himmler had, at the height of the war, at a time when Nazi Party power was at its zenith, secretly perceived that the good times could not last and realised that Germany would ultimately lose the war. He had on his own initiative, and with the help of Walter Schellenberg and Karl-Heinz Krämer, opened a secret line of communication to the British government via Victor Mallet in Sweden. He had hoped by this means to present himself to the British as a moderate and clear-thinking intelligent man in the hope that they would perceive him as politician material in post-war Germany. Himmler had also attempted to ensure the post-war recovery of German industry through his nefarious financial dealings with Marcus Wallenberg, and by his industrio-financial negotiations with the heads of German industry at the Hotel Maison Rouge in Strasbourg in the summer of 1944. However, all Himmler's plotting failed utterly. His bid to negotiate a peace accord with the British failed completely for the very good reason that Churchill and his loyal and ruthless stalwarts, such as Brendan Bracken, Leonard St Clair Ingrams and Robert Bruce Lockhart, had no intention of negotiating peace with any German. Their whole raison d'être was to precipitate political chaos – civil war, if possible – in Germany, and to accomplish that end they had supported the Kreisau Circle's bid to kill Hitler on 20 July 1944. If Himmler had turned against Hitler at this key moment, and swung his support behind the coup d'état, instead of hunting down the conspirators and executing them ruthlessly, then history may have formed a different perception of the black uniformed man who had been the Reichsführer-SS. Instead history has recorded Himmler as the monster of the SS, a key protagonist behind the Holocaust, and a man destined to spend eternity vilified and left to lie forgotten in an isolated and lonely grave on Lüneberg Heath.

NOTES

1. Walter Schellenberg, *Memoirs* (André Deutsch, 1956), p. 445.
2. Ibid., p. 448.
3. Ibid., p. 450.
4. R. Hewins, *Count Folke Bernadotte: His Life and Work* (Hutchinson, 1949), p. 139.
5. Ibid.
6. Cited in Peter Padfield, *Himmler: Reichsführer-SS* (Cassell, 2001), p. 600.
7. Hanna Reitsch, interrogation on 8 October 1945 by Captain Work titled 'The last days in Hitler's bunker', The National Archives, Washington DC.
8. Cited in Hugh Thomas, *SS-1* (Fourth Estate, 2001), p. 227.
9. Discussion with Peter Allen, former member of the Allied Control Commission and liaison officer to the BND, May 1992.
10. Josef Garlinski, *The Swiss Corridor* (Dent, 1981), p. 194.
11. Peter Allen interview of Heinz Macher in June 1963.
12. Ibid.
13. *After the Battle*, No. 14, p. 31.
14. R. Manvell & H. Fraenkel, *Heinrich Himmler* (Heinemann, 1965), p. 274.
15. Peter Allen interview of Heinz Macher in June 1963.
16. Manvell & Fraenkel, op. cit., p. 245.
17. Padfield, op. cit., p. 610.
18. Thomas, op. cit., p. 164.
19. W. Frischauer, *Himmler: The Evil Genius of the Third Reich* (Odhams, 1953), p. 258.

POSTSCRIPT

In November 2004 I was driving back across Germany from a conference I had attended in Erfurt with my German translator, Dr Olaf Rose. It was nearly two years since I had first met the very interesting Emil Klein at the Kunstlerhaus Hotel in Munich, and embarked on my quest to discover the true story of Heinrich Himmler's secret peace negotiations. I looked out of the car window at the Westphalian countryside at it passed by. It was late afternoon, and the light was just beginning to fade.

Suddenly Olaf spotted a roadside sign and exclaimed, 'Oh, Martin, look!' He swerved the car into the side of the road next to the sign. I peered out of the car window and looked up at the sign, which said 'Wewelsburg'. Wewelsburg had been Heinrich Himmler's castle deep in the Westphalian countryside. Olaf and I had been in the car all day, travelling back to Bochum in the Rhineland. It was 4.30 p.m. and we knew it would be dark in an hour or two. Regardless of this, a brief discussion determined our course of action: we would swing off the main road and take the country road deep through the forest in the direction of Wewelsburg. With luck it would be open, and we might have time to take a quick glance inside.

Three-towered Wewelsburg Castle was erected near Büren (in the district of Paderborn) between 1603 and 1609 on the site of a medieval castle. It had once served as a residence of the prince-bishops, independent sovereigns in their lands under the constitution of the Holy Roman Empire. At the end of the eighteenth century, the wars fought against revolutionary France brought about the gradual collapse of the Empire. By this time the religious principalities had already been abolished and transferred to secular rulers. As a result the renaissance castle, which was already falling into decay when the prince-bishoprics ceased to exist in 1802, passed into the hands of the Prussian state in 1815 following the Napoleonic Wars. The same year, its huge north tower was struck by lightning; all that remained standing were the outside walls, which were almost six feet thick. And so the castle lapsed into a state of severe dilapidation for over a hundred years, until late in the autumn of 1933 – the Nazis having been in power for less than a year – when Heinrich Himmler came across the ruins. The castle immediately struck him as the ideal seat of his new Order, the SS. Wewelsburg is situated in what remains of the Teutoburger forest where in AD 9 Hermann the Cherusker, having successfully united the Germanic tribes of Westphalia and Hesse, inflicted on the Romans one of the heaviest defeats they were ever to suffer. An entire Roman army was massacred. The historical associations were important to Himmler, and he immediately set about renovating Wewelsburg Castle.

Olaf Rose and I arrived at the castle in the rain on a late November afternoon. To our surprise, the staff at the entrance informed us that the castle would not shut until 6.00 p.m. that evening; that gave us nearly an hour to look about. It was a strange sensation to pass the 1930s sentry-box complete with lightning-strike SS rune carved into the stonework. We walked along the sweeping gravelled drive down to the main entrance, and into the inner courtyard. It started to rain heavily, so we ducked into the main exhibition room, where there was a model of the Wewelsburg development as Himmler had perceived it. To our astonishment, the model showed plans to expand the castle into a huge structure, an enormous complex of assembly halls, galleries, and connecting walls that would have covered most of the valley.

After looking around for a while, Olaf and I exited the main part of the castle and took a small footpath down the side. The destination of this path was the crypt deep beneath the north tower. In Himmler's mind the north tower was the centre of his world, the crypt beneath the epicentre of that world. In hushed tones Olaf and I entered the crypt and stood looking about in wonder. It had been renovated in the 1930s, and in a great circular room stood twelve empty alcoves and plinths. In Adolf Hitler's and Himmler's dreams of a thousand-year Reich, who could say what these alcoved plinths had been intended for. Looking high up into the vaulted ceiling, we had another surprise. Carved in deep relief into the ceiling rose was the emblem of Nazi Germany – a swastika. Of the many places I had visited in twenty years of visiting Germany, talking with people who had been prominent in the Nazi era, this was the first and only time I had the impression of being at the centre of Nazi Germany; here in the countryside of Westphalia was a lasting remnant of the Third Reich.

In a small display mounted on one wall were a few exhibition photo-graphs and text panels. These panels primarily showed victims of the Third Reich. Their striped concentration camp uniforms revealed to all their rele-vance to the story, a direct attempt to make every visitor to Wewelsburg remember the horrors of Nazism.

In my own mind, however, I believed the curators of this castle were mistaken in placing this display in Wewelsburg. Here, in the stone struc-ture of the castle itself, was the greatest warning to mankind of the dangers of National Socialism, of a man like Heinrich Himmler.

Thus Wewelsburg is an important place in the story of Nazi Germany. Himmler believed that this castle could become the centre of his SS world, one that would, once the disgusting and horrific murder of the Jews had been completed, become the focus of cultured Nazi Germany. It is worthy of note that Himmler did not necessarily believe that Nazism would continue to have the upper hand; in his world the SS would supersede the Nazi Party. Under his leadership, the Aryan supermen of the SS would inherit the Third Reich, making Germany a superpower in the post-war world. However, his make-believe world had slowly but inexorably shat-tered under the combined onslaught of Britain, Russia, and the United States. The only Germany that the Nazis left to the German people in 1945 was a world that was destroyed, shattered. In the end, Himmler's dreams came to nothing.

It was raining heavily as Olaf and I walked back to the car to continue our journey to Bochum. We did not talk much. Visits to such places as Wewelsburg seem to drain most people of conversation. Neither of us looked back at this last remnant of the Nazi dream. My thoughts as I walked, however, went back sixty years to that wet and windy evening in Lüneberg when Himmler found himself dragged from a car in just a shirt and socks, a blanket around his waist. Did he wonder whether it had all been worth while? Did he think of Wewelsburg? Did he think of the six million men, women, and children who had died in the Holocaust? Probably not; he was not that sort of a man. He was an opportunist, a narrow-minded, fanatical politician on the far-right of the Nazi Party, and as such he had become head of the SS, the most ruthless body of human automatons that the world had ever created.

Martin Allen
16 January 2005

ADDENDUM

With the launch of this book in May 2005, a great deal of controversy erupted in Britain over the inclusion of three mysterious documents, which I found in the National Archives, at Kew in London. I had been the first to discover these documents during my research in the autumn of 2003. I made a note of them and filed them away at the back of my mind for inclusion in the book when it neared completion.

These three documents were very important, for they revealed certain doubts that Heinrich Himmler died by his own hand on the night of 23 May 1945.

The trail of evidence that something strange might possibly have occurred concerning the death of Himmler began with a British interdepartmental memorandum sent by John Wheeler-Bennett of the Foreign Office to Robert Bruce-Lockhart of PWE on 10 May 1945. In his memo to Lockhart, Wheeler-Bennett stated:

> We cannot allow Himmler to take to the stand in any prospective prosecution, or indeed allow him to be interrogated by the Americans. Steps will therefore have to be taken to eliminate him as soon as he falls into our hands.
>
> Please give the matter some thought, as if we are to take action, we will have to expedite such an act with some haste.

This document was found in the National Archives under document number FO 800/868 in the autumn of 2003.

Everything went quiet on the British side of the communications for the next two weeks. There is no indication that anything untoward was afoot, and there is no sign that Britons of the Intelligence Service were planning to assassinate leading Germans. There is, however, other evidence in the British archives under code-name 'Operation Little Foxley,' in which the British drew up plans to assassinate top Germans as soon as they fell into British hands; amongst those destined to die were Dr Goebbels, Otto Skorzeny and Otto Remer. It is therefore quite likely that there were also other lists of top Germans the British authorities wanted to die. As has already been covered in the previous pages of this book, it is known precisely how Himmler fell into British hands, and that he was taken to Luneberg under close guard for interrogation. The conventional history surrounding Himmler's death is also known. However, discovered in the National Archives at Kew was a curious telegram dated 24 May 1945, the time it was sent is recorded as 2.50 a.m., some four hours after Himmler's death. It stated:

> We successfully intercepted HH last night at Luneberg before he could be interrogated. As instructed, action was taken to silence him permanently. I issued orders that my presence at Luneberg is not to be recorded in any fashion and we may conclude that the HH problem is ended.

This document was found at the National Archives under document number FO 800/868 in the autumn of 2003.

The evidence would seem to indicate that the men of the British Foreign Office and the Political Warfare Executive fulfilled their intention of silencing Himmler before he could be interrogated; indeed it seemed of some importance to prevent him talking to the Americans. That something strange happened to Himmler the night he died is not just reliant on these few documents. The Company Record Book of the Second Army Headquarters at Luneburg has been tampered with. The very page dealing with events the night Himmler died has been removed, and replaced some time later with a newly typed-up page. There are other things too that just do not tally in the records concerning Himmler's death, and no one has ever been able to give a satisfactory explanation for them.

Perhaps a hint about what took place on the night Himmler died is explained by the third contentious document found by me in the autumn of 2003. This is a letter from Brendan Bracken (Minister for PWE) to Lord Selborne (Minister for SOE), written a few days after Himmler's death. In his letter Bracken declared:

> Further to the good news of the death of Little H [PWE code-name for Himmler], I feel it is imperative that we maintain a complete news blackout on the exact circumstances of this most

evil man's demise. I am sure that if it were to become public knowledge that we had a hand in this man's demise, it would have devastating repercussions for this country's standing. I am also sure that this incident would complicate our relationship with our American brethren; under no circumstances must they discover that we eradicated 'Little H', particularly so since we know they were so keen to interrogate him themselves.

This document was found at the National Archives under document number HS 8/944 in the autumn of 2003.

Following the publication in Britain of *Himmler's Secret War* a great furore erupted over the revelation that British agents may have been complicitous in the death of Heinrich Himmler. Certain key files were withdrawn from public access at the National Archives. It was at this time that the three documents I discovered were subjected to forensic examination and, after much consideration, deemed to be inauthentic.

As the author responsible for the writing of this book, I have to say that when I first examined the documents in the autumn of 2003, there was nothing about them to indicate that they were anything but genuine letters and memoranda. There seemed to be no purpose in 'seeding' the British National Archive with inauthentic documents. Given the evidence, I have to say that I accept that certain documents now held by the National Archives and proclaimed as fake are likely to be inauthentic. However, the situation of inauthentic documents is a complex one, for when does an authentic document become an inauthentic one? It seems to me that there are three criteria here. Firstly, an inadequate copy of an original document (crafted in a time before photocopying), that although not an original document, is nonetheless a contemporary copy of an original document. There then exists an original authentic document, which has been altered at a later date to add or subtract a phrase or a few words. And of course, there is the last type of inauthentic document, which is an outright false document created with the objective of altering the historical record. However, what is the purpose of this sort of documentation lying in the Archive until an unwitting historian comes across it? Not only this, it may have lain there for years before its discovery.

However, the very manner in which the National Archive handled this matter is strange. These documents were proclaimed as 'fake' by a British journalist who would seem to have had no experience of wartime British Intelligence or PWE. Indeed, he is not even on the literary desk of the paper. Yet he alone went to the National Archives, demanded several files, and unerringly targeted exactly onto four documents (previously examined by several eminent historians including myself) questioned their authenticity. Regardless of this unusual situation, the National Archive immediately arranged for four files to be submitted to examination on the say so of a journalist. Indeed, the files were unhesitatingly handed over to an outside agency for forensic examination, despite the fact that the National Archive has access to their own most eminent experts in the field of documentary evidence. I believe this situation is totally unprecedented in the history of Britain's foremost archive.

Has the National Archive been corrupted? Have documents dangerous to the perceived British history of the period been 'seeded' into the Archive to alter our perception of history? Or, and it is a big 'or', have 'real' documents been replaced by inauthentic ones to cover up certain British wartime activities? These documents, seen by me in 2003 and viewed by too many persons engaged in research, could not simply have been taken out of the Archive. The only seemingly possible way to protect the reputation of PWE would be to 'seed' the archive with reproduced and, it has to be said, badly created forgeries to cast doubt on the evidence.

It has to be said that the National Archive is likely to have major problems that are going to come to fruition in the near future. At the end of the war, the files on the many secret operations and shady facts about Britain's conduct during that time were sealed under the sixty-year rule; indeed several are sealed away from public scrutiny for seventy-five years. The time is fast approaching when these documents will have to be released to public scrutiny. No one knows what will happen then. Will the British authorities reseal the files until some date later in the century when they will have lost their impact with the passing of time? Or, and it is a big 'or', will an effort be made to undermine their impact by 'seeding' the archive with inauthentic documents to defuse the impact of these new revelations?

However, back to the ongoing situation with regard to the Himmler papers. If the Archive has been corrupted with inauthentic documents to undermine the Himmler revelations, I, as the historian and author of this book, have no guarantee that the documents now proclaimed as 'fake' by the National Archive are the same documents I viewed in the autumn of 2003. Have the documents I discovered been replaced by fakes to destroy my credibility as an investigative historian, or to shatter the credibility of my book on Himmler so that British secrets kept for sixty years might be kept secret for a while longer, until such time as the truth would no longer be of importance? Clearly, there are still many questions that remain unanswered.

BIBLIOGRAPHY

Allen, Martin: *Hidden Agenda*, Macmillan, 2000
— *The Hitler/Hess Deception*, HarperCollins, 2003
Allen, Peter: *The Crown and the Swastika*, Robert Hale, 1983
Aronson, S.: *Reinhard Heydrich und die Fruhgeschichte von Gestapo und SD*, Deutsche
    Verlag, 1971
Below, Nicolaus von: *Als Hitlers Adjutant*, Mainz, 1980
Bloch, Michael: *Ribbentrop*, Abacus, 2003
Bolmus, Reinhard: *Das Amt Rosenberg und seine Gegner*, Deutsche Verlags Anstalt,
    1970
Brissaud, André: *Histoire du Secret Service Nazi*, Plon, 1972
Broszat, M. (ed.): *Kommandant in Auschwitz: Autobiographische Aufzeichnungen von
    Rudolf Hoess*, Deutsche Verlags Astalt, 1958
Bullock, Alan: *Hitler: A Study in Tyranny*, Odhams, 1952
Calvocoressi, P., and Wint, G.: *Total War*, Penguin, 1972
Camp 020, MI5 and the Nazi Spies, Public Records Office, 2000
Cave-Brown, A.: *Bodyguard of Lies*, Star, 1977
Charmley, John: *Duff Cooper: The Authorised Biography*, Weidenfeld & Nicolson, 1986
Chisholm, A., and Davie, M.: *Beaverbrook*, Hutchinson, 1992
Churchill, W.S.: *The Second World War, vols. I–V*, Cassell, 1948–52
Clark, Alan: *Barbarossa: The Russian–German Conflict 1941–45*, Macmillan, 1985
Colville, John: *The Fringes of Power*, Hodder & Stoughton, 1985
Convers-Nesbit, Roy: *Failed to Return*, Patrick Stephens Ltd, 1988
Costello, John: *Ten Days that Saved the West*, Bantam, 1991
Cruickshank, Charles: *SOE in the Far East*, Oxford University Press, 1983
Day, D.: *Menzies and Churchill at War*, Angus & Robertson, 1986
Delmas, Sefton: *Black Boomerang*, London, 1962
Dilkes, D. (ed.): *The Diaries of Sir Alexander Cadogan, O.M., 1938–45*, Cassell, 1971
Documents on British Foreign Policy, Series 4, Vol. I, HMSO, 1949
Documents on German Foreign Policy, Series D, Vols. IX–XII, HMSO, 1961
Dornberger, Walter: *V2 – Der Schuss ins Weltall*, Bechtle Verlag, 1952
Douglas-Hamilton, J.: *The Truth about Rudolf Hess*, Mainstream, 1988
Dulles, Allen, *The Secret Surrender*, Weidenfeld & Nicolson, 1967

Eade, Charles (ed.): *Churchill, by his Contemporaries*, Hutchinson, 1953
Farago, Ladislas: *The Game of Foxes*, London, 1956
Frank, Dr Hans: *Im Angesicht des Galgens*, Neuhaus b. Schliersee, 1955
Frischauer, W.: *Himmler: The Evil Genius of the Third Reich*, Odhams, 1953
Garlinski, Josef: *The Swiss Corridor*, Dent, 1981
Garnett, David: *The Secret History of PWE*, St Ermin's Press, 2002
German Library of Information: *The War in Maps*, 1955
Gilbert, G.M.: *Nuremberg Diary*, New York, 1948
Gilbert, Martin: *Winston Churchill: The Wilderness Years*, Macmillan, 1981
— *Churchill: A Life*, Heinemann, 1991
Gisevius, H.-B.: *To the Bitter End*, Houghton Mifflin, 1947
Goni, Uki: *The Real Odessa – How Peron Brought the Nazi War Criminals to Argentina*, Granta Books, 2004
Gossweiller, K.: *Die Röhm Affäre*, Rugenstein, 1983
Hanfstaengl, Ernst: *15 Jahre mit Hitler*, Piper, 1980
Hansard, Vol. 371
Hassell, U. von: *Vom andern Deutschland*, Atlantis, Zurich, 1946
Haushofer, Albrecht: *Allgemeine politisches Geographia und Geopolitik*, Vowinckel Verlag, 1931
Haushofer, Karl: *Dai Nihon*, Berlin, 1913
Hess, Ilse: *Gefangener des Friedens*, Druffel Verlag, 1955
Hess, Wolf Rüdiger: *My Father Rudolf Hess*, W.H. Allen, 1986
— *Rudolf Hess: Briefe 1908–1933*, Langen Muller, 1987
Hewins, R.: *Count Folke Bernadotte: His Life and Work*, Hutchinson, 1949
Hill, Leonidas (ed.): *Die Weizsäcker Papiere*, Vol. II, Ulstein Verlag, 1974
Hinsley, F.H., et al.: *British Intelligence in the Second World War*, Vols. I–IV, HMSO, 1979
Hitler, Adolf: *My New Order*, Angus & Robertson, 1942
Hoare, Sir Samuel: *The Fourth Seal*, Heinemann, 1930
Hoch, Anton: *Das Attentat auf Hitler in Munchen Bürgerbraukeller 1939*, Vierteljahrsheft, 1969
Hoettl. W.: *The Secret Front*, Praeger, New York, 1954
Hoffman, Heinrich: *Hitler was my Friend*, London, 1955
Howe, E.: *The Black Game*, Michael Joseph, 1982
The International Military Tribunal: Trial of German Major War Criminals, HMSO, 1946–51
Irving, David: *Churchill's War*, Hutchinson, 1987
— *Goebbels*, Focal Point Publications, 1996
Kershaw, Ian: *Hitler: Hubris 1889–1936*, Penguin, 1998
— *Hitler: Nemesis, 1936–1945*, Penguin, 2000
Kersten, Felix: *The Kersten Memoirs 1940–1945*, Hutchinson, 1956
Kessler, Leo: *Betrayal at Venlo*, Leo Cooper, 1991
Kirkpatrick, Ivone: *The Inner Circle: Memoirs of Ivone Kirkpatrick*, Macmillan, 1959
Krosigk, Schwerin von: *Es geschah in Deutschland*, Tübingen, 1952

Lang, Joachim von: *Der Adjutant Karl Wolff: Der Mann zwischen Hitler und Himmler*, Druffel Verlag, 1985

Laqueur, W.: *The Terrible Secret*, Weidenfeld & Nicolson, 1980

Leasor, James: *Rudolf Hess: The Uninvited Envoy*, London, 1962

Liddell Hart, B.H.: *History of the Second World War*, Cassell, 1970

— *The Other Side of the Hill*, Cassell, 1948

Loewenheim, F., Langley, H. and Jonas, M. (eds): *Roosevelt and Churchill: Their Secret Wartime Correspondence*, Barrie & Jenkins, 1975

Ludecke, Kurt: *I Knew Hitler*, Jarrolds, 1938

Mackinder, H.J.: *The Geographical Pivot of History*, London, 1904

Manvell, R. and Fraenkel, H.: *Heinrich Himmler*, Heinemann, 1965

Masterman, J.C.: *The Double Cross System*, Yale University Press, 1972

Mayor, Andreas (ed.): *Ciano's Diary 1937–1938*, Methuen, 1952

McKale, Donald M.: *Kurt Prüfer*, Kent, Ohio, 1987

Moran, Lord: *Winston Churchill: The Struggle for Survival*, Sphere, 1968

Mosley, Leonard: *Dulles*, Dial Press/James Wade, 1978

Muggeridge, Malcolm (ed.): *Ciano's Diary 1939–1943*, Heinemann, 1947

Newton, S.: *Profits of Peace*, Clarendon Press, 1996

Nicolson, N. (ed.): *Harold Nicolson: Diaries and Letters 1939–45*, Collins, 1967

Noakes, J. and Pridlam, G.: *Documents on Nazism*, Jonathan Cape, 1974

N-S Jahrbuch, editions 1938–40

Overy, Richard: *Why the Allies Won*, Jonathan Cape, 1995

Padfield, Peter: *Hess: The Fuhrer's Disciple*, Cassell, 2001

— *Himmler: Reichsfuhrer-SS*, Cassell, 2001

Payne-Best, S.: *The Venlo Incident*, Hutchinson, 1950

Picknett, Prince, Prior and Brydon: *Double Standards*, Little, Brown, 2001

Poole, J. and S.: *Who Financed Hitler?*, Macdonald & Jane's, 1978

Reed, Douglas.: *The Burning of the Reichstag*, Covici-Friede Inc., 1978

Ritter, G.: *The German Resistance*, George Allen & Unwin, 1958

Roberts, Andrew: *The Holy Fox*, Weidenfeld & Nicolson, 1991

Royce, H.: *20 Juli 1944*, Berto-Verlag, 1952

Ryan, C.: *The Last Battle*, New English Library, 1985

Schellenberg, Walter: *Memoirs*, André Deutsch, 1956

Scholder, Klaus: *Die Mittwochs-Gesellschafts. Protokolle aus dem geistigen Deutschland 1932–44*, Berlin, 1982

Schuschnigg, K.: *Im Kampf gegen Hitler*, Molden, Vienna, 1969

Schweitzer, A.: *Big Business in the Third Reich*, Eyre & Spottiswoode, 1964

Sereny, Gita: *Albert Speer: His Battle with the Truth*, Knopf, 1997

Shirer, William: *The Nightmare Years*, Little, Brown (Boston), 1964

— *The Rise and Fall of the Third Reich*, Pan, 1964

Smith, B.F.: *Heinrich Himmler: A Nazi in the Making, 1900–1926*, Hoover Institute Press, 1971

Snyder, Louis L.: *Encyclopedia of the Third Reich*, Wordsworth Editions, 1998

Speer, Albert: *Inside the Third Reich*, Weidenfeld & Nicolson, 1970

— *Spandauer Tagebücher*, Ullstein Verlag, 1975

Stafford, David: *Roosevelt and Churchill*, Abacus, 1999

Strasser, Otto: *Mein Kampf: Enie politische Autobiographie*, H. Heine, 1969

Taylor, F. (ed.): *The Goebbels Diaries*, Hamish Hamilton, 1982

Thomas, Hugh: *SS-1*, Fourth Estate, 2001

Thyssen, F.: *I Paid Hitler*, Hodder & Stoughton, 1941

Toland, John: *Adolf Hitler*, Doubleday, 1976

Trevor-Roper, H.R.: *The Last Days of Hitler*, Macmillan, New York, 1947

— (ed.): *Hitler's Table Talk*, Weidenfeld & Nicolson, 1953

Vansittart, Lord: *The Mist Procession: The Autobiography of Lord Vansittart*, Hutchinson, 1958

Völkischer Beobachter, editions from 1937 to 1941

Warlimont, W.: *Inside Hitler's Headquarters*, Weidenfeld & Nicolson, 1964

West, Nigel: *Secret War: The Story of SOE*, Hodder & Stoughton, 1992

Whiting, Audrey: *The Kents*, London, 1985

Winterbotham, F.W.: *Secret and Personal*, William Kimber, 1969

— *The Nazi Connection*, Weidenfeld & Nicolson, 1978

Wulf, Josef: *Die SS*, Bonn, 1956

Young, K. (ed.): *The Diaries of Sir Robert Bruce Lockhart*, Vol. II, Macmillan, 1980

Zeitschrift für Geopolitik, editions from 1934 to 1940, Vowinckel Verlag, Heidelberg

INDEX